Lecture Notes in Computer Science 9800

Commenced Publication in 1973
Founding and Former Series Editors:
Gerhard Goos, Juris Hartmanis, and Jan van Leeuwen

Editorial Board

Shigeru Chiba · Mario Südholt
Patrick Eugster · Lukasz Ziarek
Gary T. Leavens (Eds.)

Transactions on Modularity and Composition I

 Springer

Editors-in-Chief

Shigeru Chiba
The University of Tokyo
Tokyo
Japan

Mario Südholt
École des Mines de Nantes
Nantes
France

Guest Editors

Patrick Eugster
Purdue University
West Lafayette, IN
USA

Gary T. Leavens
University of Central Florida
Orlando, FL
USA

Lukasz Ziarek
SUNY at Buffalo
Buffalo, NY
USA

ISSN 0302-9743   ISSN 1611-3349 (electronic)
Lecture Notes in Computer Science
ISSN 2509-761X   ISSN 2509-7628 (electronic)
Transactions on Modularity and Composition
ISBN 978-3-319-46968-3   ISBN 978-3-319-46969-0 (eBook)
DOI 10.1007/978-3-319-46969-0

Library of Congress Control Number: 2016952535

Printed on acid-free paper

This Springer imprint is published by Springer Nature
The registered company is Springer International Publishing AG Switzerland

Editorial

Welcome to the first volume of the Transactions on Modularity and Composition. This journal is the successor of the Transactions on Aspect-Oriented Software Development, which consisted of twelve volumes. The Transactions on Modularity and Composition covers not only aspect-oriented software development but a broader range of topics related to software modularity and composition. It reports research results on how to understand abstraction boundaries of software and also how to combine abstract modules for rapid, maintainable, and/or reliable software development.

This first volume has two special sections. The first special section is "Aspects, Events, and Modularity" guest edited by Patrick Eugster, Mario Südholt, and Lukasz Ziarek. Event-handling systems have been independently studied but it is also known that this paradigm is strongly related to aspects and both are motivated by software modularity. This special section collects three papers tackling this issue. The second special section constitutes a collection of the papers selected from the Modularity 2015 conference. These papers are journal versions of the selected papers from the conference. Their original versions are available from ACM digital library. This section was guest edited by Gary T. Leavens, Research Results Program Chair of the conference.

We thank the guest editors for soliciting submissions, running review processes, and collecting final versions within such a short period. We are pleased to publish these special issues in a timely fashion. We also thank the editorial board members for their continued guidance and input on the policies of the journal, the reviewers for volunteering a significant amount of time despite their busy schedules, and the authors who submitted papers to the journal.

May 2016

Shigeru Chiba
Mario Südholt
Editors-in-Chief

Guest Editors' Foreword

Special Section on Aspects, Events, and Modularity

There exist a number of synergies between paradigms such as implicit invocations, aspects, first-class events, asynchronous methods, as well as design and architectural patterns such as subject/observer and publish/subscribe respectively. Many of these abstractions have been used directly or indirectly to devise software systems in an event-oriented manner. The different paradigms have emerged from different communities, and with slightly different motivations. Concurrency and distribution are common driving forces for event-oriented design. Another motivation is software modularity. In fact, the decoupling of runtime components, which is paramount to concurrent or distributed systems, may also translate to a separation between the software modules used to define these individual components. With the ever increasing pervasiveness of reactive, concurrent, and distributed systems, the goal of this special issue is to publish novel work in the context of event-oriented software design and implementation related to any of the above paradigms. Of particular interest is work which bridges the gap between the different paradigms and motivations, and helps to clarify the relations between them. In this special section we present three papers covering topics on context-oriented software development, specifications for even-based systems, and development of modular software.

May 2016

Patrick Eugster
Mario Südholt
Lukasz Ziarek

Guest Editor's Foreword

Special Section of Selected Papers from *Modularity 2015*

This special section contains selected papers presented at *Modularity 2015*, the fourth annual conference on modularity. I had the honor to chair the conference's "research results" Program Committee and thus to edit this special issue. The papers in this special issue were selected based on input from the conference Program Committee. Authors of these selected papers were invited to submit a revised and extended version of their work. Each revised paper was refereed by three experts, including members of the original Program Committee when possible. As is usual, papers were revised if necessary.

The papers in this section thus represent several interesting points in current research on modularity. The topics covered include: software unbundling, layer activation in context-oriented programming, modular reasoning in event-based languages that allow subtyping for events, and dynamic dispatch for method contracts using abstract predicates.

Many thanks to the authors and referees for their work on this special section. Enjoy the papers!

May 2016

Gary T. Leavens

Editorial Board

Contents

Aspects, Events, and Modularity

Context-Oriented Software Development with Generalized Layer Activation Mechanism

Tetsuo Kamina[1($\boxtimes$)], Tomoyuki Aotani[2], Hidehiko Masuhara[2],
and Tetsuo Tamai[3]

[1] Ritsumeikan University, 1-1-1 Noji-higashi, Kusatsu, Shiga 525-8577, Japan
kamina@acm.org
[2] Tokyo Institute of Technology, 2-12-1 Ohokayama, Meguro, Tokyo 152-8550, Japan
aotani@is.titech.ac.jp, masuhara@acm.org
[3] Hosei University, 3-7-2 Kajino-cho, Koganei, Tokyo 184-8584, Japan
tamai@acm.org

Abstract. Linguistic constructs such as if statements, dynamic dispatches, dynamic deployments, and layers in context-oriented programming (COP) are used to implement context-dependent behavior. Use of such constructs significantly affects the modularity of the obtained implementation. While there are a number of cases where COP improves modularity related to variations of context-dependent behavior and controls of dynamic behavior changes, it is unclear when COP should be used in general.

This paper presents a study of our software development methodology, context-oriented software engineering (COSE), which is a use-case-driven software development methodology that guides us to specification of context-dependent requirements and design. We develop a systematic method to determine an appropriate linguistic mechanism to implement context-dependent behavior and dynamic changes in behavior during modeling and design, leading to the mechanized mapping from requirements and design artifacts formed by COSE to the COP implementation, which is demonstrated in our COP language ServalCJ through three case studies. We then identify the key linguistic constructs that make COSE effective by examining existing COP languages.

1 Introduction

Context awareness is a major concern in many application areas. Hirschfeld et al. define *context* as "(a piece of) information which is computationally accessible" [26]. However, this definition is too general to identify contexts; therefore, criteria for identification of contexts are necessary. For example, one important factor of context-awareness is a system's capability to behave appropriately with

---

This paper is an extended version of our previous papers [31,33]. In this paper, we refine principles and provide a more detailed description of our methodology. It also contains a case study not included in previous work.

© Springer International Publishing Switzerland 2016
S. Chiba et al. (Eds.): ToMC I, LNCS 9800, pp. 3–40, 2016.
DOI: 10.1007/978-3-319-46969-0_1

respect to surrounding contexts. Thus, a context is identified by observing behavioral changes in the application. An example of a context-aware application is a ubiquitous computing application that behaves differently in different situations, such as different geographical locations, indoor or outdoor environments, or weathers. In this case, some specific states or situations are contexts. An adaptive user interface is also context aware as it provides different GUI components (behavior) depending on the current user task (context).

There are a number of constructs to implement context-dependent behavior, such as conditional branches using if statements, method dispatch in object-oriented programming (e.g., state design pattern), and dynamic deployment of aspects in aspect-oriented programming (AOP). Context-oriented programming (COP) [26] provides another mechanism to implement context-dependent behavior. This mechanism is often called a *layer*, which is a program unit comprising implementations of behavior that are executable only when some conditions hold.[1] In particular, COP provides disciplined activation mechanisms to ensure some consistency in dynamic changes in context-dependent behavior, such as scoping [7], model checking [29], dynamic checking of required interactions and constraints between different contexts [21], and a generalized layer activation mechanism [32]. Use of such constructs significantly affects the modularity of the obtained implementation, and research into COP shows a number of cases where COP can modularize variations of context-dependent behavior that are difficult to modularize using other approaches.

However, it is unclear when COP should be used in general. In particular, there are no systematic methodologies to determine a method to implement context-dependent behavior and the associated dynamic changes, which significantly affect software modularity and should be determined during modeling and design. Furthermore, there are no systematic methods to determine an appropriate activation mechanism to implement dynamic changes in behavior. A number of COP mechanisms have been proposed to date [7,9,17,21–23,25,26,29,47,51]. An appropriate mechanism must be selected from among them to implement a design artifact.

This paper presents a study of our software development methodology, context-oriented software engineering (COSE), that organizes the specifications of contexts and the dependent variations of behavior.[2] An overview of the COP development process, even if it is not in depth, can lead to further research on each stage of the development process. In particular, we answer the following research questions (RQs) based on this methodology.

---

[1] Some COP languages do not provide a linguistic construct to pack such implementations as a single unit. However, this is not a significant difference. In the remainder of this paper, we refer to a set of functions (methods) annotated with the same "conditions" for dispatch as a layer irrespective of whether they are packed into a single unit.

[2] This approach is based on Jacobson's object-oriented software engineering (OOSE) [27]. We refer to our approach as "COSE" to make its connection to OOSE clear.

RQ1. How should contexts and behavior depending on the contexts be elicited from the requirements?

RQ2. When should we apply COP rather than other development methods?

RQ3. How do COP mechanisms support predictable control of changes in context-dependent behavior?

We answer **RQ1** and **RQ2** by providing a systematic way to identify contexts and determine an implementation method for context-dependent behavior during modeling and design. This systematic approach is based on several principles, which are validated through three case studies. To answer **RQ3**, we provide a mechanized modular mapping from a specification developed by COSE to an implementation in the ServalCJ COP language[3]. ServalCJ provides a generalized layer activation mechanism that supports all existing COP mechanisms.

Methodology. Based on the use-case-driven approach [27], COSE represents the requirements for a context-aware application using contexts and context-dependent use cases. A context is represented in terms of Boolean variables that determine whether the system is in that context[4]. A context-dependent use case is a specialization of another use case that is applicable only under specific contexts. From these requirements, COSE derives a design model that can be translated into a modular implementation. This design method classifies variations of context-dependent behavior into those implemented by appropriate mechanisms, such as layers in COP and other traditional mechanisms, such as class hierarchies and `if` statements. This classification drives mechanized mapping from requirements to implementation. We selected ServalCJ as the implementation language because it provides a generalized layer activation mechanism, which, to the best of our knowledge, supports all existing COP mechanisms. This mapping ensures that each specification in the requirements is not scattered over multiple modules in the implementation, and each module is not entangled with multiple requirements.

Case Studies. We conducted three case studies of different context-aware applications to demonstrate the effectiveness of our approach. The first is a conference guide system, which serves as a guide for an academic conference, including management of an attendee's personal schedule, navigation help inside the venue and around the conference site, and a social networking service function, such as a Twitter client. The second is CJEdit, a program editor that provides different functionalities relative to cursor position. This example, which was first introduced by Appeltauer et al. [8], is a well-known COP application. The third is

---

[3] https://github.com/ServalCJ/pl.

[4] Keays also proposed COP [35], where a context is a named identifier (e.g., location) that identifies the type of *open terms* (holes in the code skeleton) that are filled at runtime with pieces of code corresponding to a specific context value (e.g., location in "Tokyo"). This paper is based on Hirschfeld's COP [26] where a context is represented as a *layer* that dynamically takes two states, i.e., active and inactive, and thus can be represented as a Boolean variable.

a maze-solving robot simulator that provides a number of variations of context-dependent behavior, such as adaptive user interfaces and adaptive robot behavior. In these case studies, we successfully organized context-related specifications by applying COSE and directly mapped these specifications to their implementations in ServalCJ.

To examine existing language features and discuss the features that make the COSE methodology effective, we analyze linguistic constructs from several existing implementation techniques (including non-COP techniques). A notable finding is that, while most existing COP languages directly specify the execution point when the corresponding context becomes active, in the case studies there are a number of situations where the use of the implicit layer activation mechanism that indirectly specifies layer activation using conditional expressions would be preferred. Although currently the implicit layer activation mechanism may not function effectively, it can be an effective tool to independently implement the dynamic changes of behavior specified in the requirements.

Research Roadmap. Although the case studies indicate that our approach is promising, we also identify a number of interesting open issues, which comprise our future research roadmap. First, to address scattered context-dependent behavior in requirements of the system-to-be written in inconsistent formats, we plan to develop a systematic method to identify contexts. Second, our approach is based on use cases; however, it is also desirable to explore how similar approaches can be applied when use cases are not appropriate to analyze requirements. Third, we have identified issues in the evaluation of our methodology. Fourth, since there is a performance issue in the implicit layer activation, we plan to investigate the optimization of implicit activation. Furthermore, analyzing when event-based activation (i.e., the way in which the execution points where context activation occurs are explicitly represented) is expected to be useful and desirable. Finally, since the case studies used in this paper are stand-alone and conducted using a single language, it is also desirable to study how the approach can be applied to more sophisticated environments, e.g., distributed, multi-language environments.

Organization. The remainder of this paper is organized as follows. In Sect. 2, we identify the difficulties in the development of context-aware applications and discuss the limitations of existing approaches. In Sect. 3, we elaborate the research questions and list the principles that will be validated through the case studies. In Sect. 4, we illustrate the systematic organization of context-dependent requirements and their classification into those implemented by appropriate linguistic mechanisms. In Sect. 5, we provide mechanized mapping from the artifacts obtained by COSE to modular implementation in existing COP mechanisms. In Sects. 6 and 7, we show other case studies and provide an informal evaluation of COSE using these case studies, respectively. Finally, Sect. 8 concludes the paper and presents our future research roadmap.

Differences from Previous Work. This paper is an extended version of our previous papers [31, 33]. In addition to the identification of context-dependent behavior whose activation should be controlled by COP mechanisms, this paper addresses the following issues:

Identification of the subject of a particular layer activation. While our
  previous papers implicitly considered that layer activation globally affects the
  whole application, this paper identifies other cases wherein layer activation
  affects a particular object or control-flow.
Selection of different layer activation mechanisms. This paper discusses
  the selection criteria for different layer activation mechanisms, which was not
  discussed in our previous papers. Existing layer activation mechanisms differ
  in scope and duration, and we should select the most suitable mechanism.

These issues are discussed using the maze-solving robot simulator case study, which also considers the case where a context-dependent use case appears in the top-level, thereby leading to refinement of principles.

2 Motivation

We explain the motivation to develop a new context-oriented software development methodology by introducing an example of a context-aware application and explaining the difficulties in the development of context-aware applications and the limitations of existing approaches.

2.1 Context-Aware Application Example: Conference Guide System

The conference guide system serves as a guide for an academic conference. This system, which provides the conference program, schedule management, and navigation help inside the venue and around the conference site, is implemented on an Android smartphone. The guide system also has a Twitter that attendees can use to comment on talks presented at the conference. This system has several context-related behavioral variations.

– The conference program is provided online. The user can view the online
  program on an Android smartphone. The program is downloaded and cached
  in a local database in case the online version becomes unavailable. In the
  program, the user can select the sessions they will attend. The selected sessions
  are listed in the personal schedule. If sessions have not been selected, the listing
  cannot be accessed.
– The system provides a map function. When the user is within the conference
  venue, the map provides a floor plan of the venue. When the user is outside the
  venue, a map of the area around the conference site is provided. This area is
  updated when the user's position changes. Positioning is based on GPS or the
  Wi-Fi connection. If the system cannot determine whether the use is outdoors
  or indoors, it provides a static map of the area around the conference site.

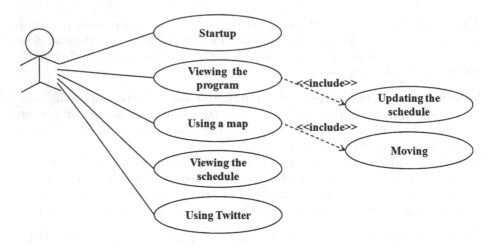

Fig. 1. Use case diagram for the conference guide system

– The system provides a Twitter client, which is available only when the Internet is available.

A use case diagram for the conference guide system is shown in Fig. 1. In addition to the initial "Startup" use case, there are four use cases that involve user interactions. "Viewing the program" includes "Updating the schedule," i.e., the user selects sessions to attend, and "Using a map" includes "Moving," i.e., the user moves, and the new position is detected by the positioning system.

2.2   Difficulties

Even though this is a simple example, a number of difficulties in the development of context-aware applications can be identified. Before discussing these difficulties, we note that the definition of a context tends to be too general for identifying context-dependent behavior. Therefore, we first summarize three viewpoints that should be considered when identifying contexts.

Requirements Variability. A context-aware application changes behavior with respect to the currently executing context, i.e., there are a number of variations of behavior depending on the context. Thus, we need to identify contexts and the related requirements variability. For example, in the conference guide system, contexts such as outdoors, availability of the list of selected sessions, and availability of the Internet can be identified. However, identification of contexts is not trivial. After the identification of the outdoor context, it is unclear whether we should also identify the indoor context, or represent it by means of the outdoor context (i.e., !outdoors).

Different Levels of Abstraction. Contexts have different abstraction levels, and contexts at the abstract level consist of multiple concrete contexts. For example, the availability of positioning systems depends on hardware specifications, such as the availability of GPS and/or wireless LAN functions. Thus, we must define contexts precisely in terms of the target machine. This multiple dependency leads to difficulty in defining precisely when the variation of behavior switches at runtime because there may be a number of state changes in the target machine that trigger a context change. Furthermore, some executing hardware states may barrier or guard the change of abstract contexts.

Multiple Dependencies among Contexts and Behavior. We must also analyze dependencies between contexts and variations of behavior carefully because some variations depend on multiple contexts. For example, in the conference guide system, if we identify outdoor and indoor situations as different contexts, the display of a static map is dependent on such contexts because this behavior is executable only when the system cannot determine whether the user is outdoors or indoors. Generally, multiple dependency depends on how we identify contexts, and multiple contexts may barrier or guard the execution of context-dependent behavior. This dependency becomes more complicated when we consider different levels of context abstraction.

We assume that contexts are identified based on these viewpoints. In our methodology, we address the following difficulties in the development of context-aware systems.

Proper Design and Implementation. We must select an appropriate method of design and implementation. In particular, a number of context-dependent requirements are volatile and crosscut multiple use cases. Therefore, such requirements require modular implementations to hide details that are likely to change [41].

Requirements Volatility in Context Specification. Technologies for sensing context changes are very complex. Such technologies evolve continually, which indicates that requirements specifications for context sensing are subject to change. For example, it seems initially appropriate to define the outdoor/indoor contexts based on the status of the GPS receiver. However, in future, this definition may need to be based on the status of air pressure sensors or other technologies, such as an RFID receiver, that are not currently implemented in smartphones.

Crosscutting of Contexts in Multiple Use Cases. In context-aware applications, a number of contexts are scattered over multiple use cases. For example, in the conference guide system, the conference program is downloaded through the Internet (to let the user access an up-to-date program) only when the Internet is available. Similarly, the availability of the Twitter client depends on the availability of the Internet. Thus, the context "the Internet is available" crosscuts two use cases, "Viewing the program" and "Using Twitter." A systematic way to determine such a situation and select the appropriate implementation mechanism for this specification is necessary.

Managing Dynamic Changes. Predictable control of contexts and behavioral changes is required, and this is a challenge for the following reasons.

Crosscutting of Behavior Changes. One of the most important properties of context-aware applications is that they change behavior at runtime. Thus, we need to identify when a behavior variation switches to another variation. However, as discussed above, a behavior variation may depend on multiple (abstract) contexts, and each context may depend on a number of concrete contexts. Furthermore, changes of such concrete contexts are scattered over the execution of the application. Since context specifications are subject to change, it is desirable to encapsulate them.

Interferences Between Behaviors. A situation wherein dynamically activated behaviors can interfere with other behaviors may occur. Such interference may result in unpredictable behavior and should be avoided. Determining whether such interference exists is also a challenge in the development of context-aware systems.

Translation to Modular Implementation. We must carefully trace which requirements are implemented by which modules. It is also desirable that a module in the implementation only serves a single requirement and is not entangled by several requirements. Thus, to support modularity, it is desirable that there be injective mapping from the specification to the implementation.

2.3   Problems in Existing Approaches

Although there have been intensive research efforts to improve each stage of development of context-aware applications, few attempts have been made to develop a methodology to organize the whole development process.

A number of COP languages have been developed. A family of COP languages provides a linguistic construct called a layer to pack related context-dependent behavior into a single module [7,9,17,25]. Other COP languages emphasize representing the dependency between contexts [21,22] and do not provide "layers," though, in this paper, this difference is not significant, and we refer to a set of functions (methods) annotated with the same "contexts" as a layer, irrespective of whether they are packed into a single module.

Compared to research into programming languages, little research effort has been devoted to systematizing the design of context-oriented programs. For example, the process of discovering layers from requirements is unclear. Determining when the use of layers is preferable to the use of existing object-oriented mechanisms and `if` statements in order to implement context-dependent behavior also remains unclear. Cardozo et al. proposed the feature clouds programming model [14], which equates layers (i.e., "behavioral adaptations") to features in feature-oriented software development (FOSD) [4]. Although this model clarifies correspondence between features and COP and advances the feature model by introducing dynamic adaptation of features by means of COP mechanisms, it does not clarify the process of discovering contexts and layers. Context petri nets (CoPNs) [13] were proposed to formalize the semantics of COP, in particular the semantics of multiple context activations in Subjective-C [21]. A tool based on CoPNs was developed to analyze consistency in the activation of contexts. However, this tool does not target the discovery of contexts and layers.

There are a number of software development methodologies. Object-oriented methodologies are useful for discovering objects and classes through requirements analysis. Aspect-oriented software development (AOSD) methodologies [28,43] are useful for determining and modularizing crosscutting concerns. FOSD [4] maps feature diagrams [34] to implementation. Feature diagrams, which are obtained by analyzing the software to be developed, are useful for analyzing dependencies among the features from which the software is constructed. Even though these methodologies provide a good starting point to consider how to develop context-aware applications, they do not focus on solutions for the aforementioned difficulties. We must extend existing methodologies to identify contexts and dependent behavior systematically to provide predictable control of changes in context-dependent behavior.

Recently, a number of approaches to discover, analyze, and implement contexts and variations of dependent behavior have been investigated. A number of requirements engineering methods [3,19,38,39,45,46,49] primarily focus on the discovery and analysis of (abstract) contexts and the variations of behavior that depend on them. These requirements engineering methods do not provide systematic ways to select implementation mechanisms for context-dependent behavior. Henrichsen and Indulska proposed a software engineering framework for pervasive computing [24]. However, they did not provide systematic ways to manage volatile requirements for concrete levels of context and implement them modularly. Specifically, they did not identify a set of variations that comprises a single module. Frameworks and libraries for context-aware applications provide context-aware software components and thus enhance reusability, which addresses some of the difficulties mentioned above [1,12,15,44]. However, such frameworks and libraries are domain specific, and few general solutions for context-aware applications are provided.

3   Research Questions and Principles

To organize the software development methodology for context-aware applications, we provide three research questions. To answer these questions, we also list three principles and validate them through case studies.

3.1   Research Questions

We answer the following research questions.

RQ1. How should contexts and behavior depending on the contexts be elicited from the requirements?

This research question, which has been partially answered by existing approaches, is the most fundamental. To implement context-dependent behavior, we must first determine what the contexts are. However, this identification of contexts should be organized as input for a decision about the design of modules made in the subsequent development stage. The existing requirements engineering methods explained above do not have such a concern, and we provide the answer for **RQ1** from this perspective.

RQ2. When should we apply COP rather than other development methods?

There are a number of linguistic constructs to implement context-dependent behavior, and we must select the appropriate construct to realize better modularity. In particular, existing work into COP has not provided an answer for when we should use COP.

RQ3. How do COP mechanisms support predictable control of changes in context-dependent behavior?

A number of COP mechanisms, in particular *layer activation mechanisms*, have been proposed, and they support predictable control of behavioral changes with respect to context changes by, e.g., preventing us from simultaneously activating conflicting layers. Each mechanism has its own advantages and disadvantages, and there are no methods to select the most appropriate mechanism.

3.2   Principles

As the first step to provide the answers for these research questions, we identify the following principles to identify contexts and context-dependent behavior. We then developed the context-oriented software development methodology, COSE, which is explained in the following sections.

Principle 1. *Factors that exist outside a particular unit of computation and dynamically change the behavior of that unit are candidates for contexts.*

A context is a factor that changes the behavior of something on which we focus. Thus, to identify contexts, it is good to begin by looking for factors that change the behavior of such a "something," which is also identifiable under the specific computation model (e.g., an object in OO programming languages or a function in functional programming languages).

Note that this principle is revised from a previous description [33] by considering the *unit of computation* that is affected by the contexts. This consideration leads to proper selection of layer activation mechanisms in the implementation (e.g., selecting global activation rather than per-instance activation). Further discussion is provided in Sect. 4.

Principle 2. *Each factor that dynamically changes the system's behavior is represented as a variable, and an activation condition for a context that determines whether the system is in that context is a logical formula comprising those variables.*

In many cases, a factor that changes system behavior has only two states. For example, whether a user is outdoors has only two states, yes or no. The availability of a network also has two states, available or unavailable. Battery level can also have two states, low or high. Each of these factors can be represented as a Boolean variable.

Sometimes, such a factor is composite, which implies that a context can be represented as a logical formula comprising a set of factors that can be represented as a Boolean variable. This principle fits well with existing COP languages wherein a context consists of subcontexts, such as in Subjective-C [21], or a layer activation is triggered by a composition of other layer activations [16,30].

In some cases, such factors may have more than two states. For example, a location may take a number of values such as "Tokyo," "Lugano," etc. In such cases, we consider each value as a context. For example, we consider the context "whether the user is in Tokyo." This may result in quite a large number of contexts (e.g., we may list thousands of cities), and it is difficult to prepare such a listing. Generally, COP requires pre-listing of behavior variations, and a large number of contexts are unlikely to be modularized using COP but can be implemented using other techniques, such as abstraction over parameters.

In some COP languages like Subjective-C, a context is not a Boolean but has an actual activation count. The above principle does not rule out such languages. A context is identified in terms of an activation condition that is a trigger for the context-dependent behavior. This activation condition should be Boolean even when a context has an actual activation count.

Principle 3. *If multiple variations of context-dependent behavior share the same context and variations are not specializations[5] of the same behavior, they should be implemented using a layer.*

This principle explains the situation wherein the same context is scattered over a number of behavioral variations in the system. A layer in COP can modularize such crosscutting behavior. In contrast, if the context affects only a single behavior variation or such variations are a specialization of the same behavior, we may also consider other implementation mechanisms, such as `if` statements and method dispatching in object-oriented programming.

4   Context-Dependent Requirements and Design

We propose COSE, a use-case-based methodology for context-oriented software engineering. It represents the requirements for a context-aware application using contexts and context-dependent use cases. A context is represented

---

[5] By "specialization," we mean a specialization relationship that appears in class and use case hierarchies, i.e., a specialization consists of more details than its parent.

as a Boolean formula that represents whether the system is in that context. A context-dependent use case is a specialization of another use case applicable only in some specific contexts.

Based on this requirements model, COSE further derives a design model that can be translated into a modular implementation (Sect. 5). COSE is based on the use-case-driven approach. It provides a systematic mapping from context-dependent use cases to modules provided by existing COP languages, i.e., *layers*, just as the AOSD method proposed by Jacobson where each use case is implemented using an aspect [28]. Our design method classifies context-dependent behavior variations into those implemented by appropriate implementation mechanisms, such as layers in COP, and those implemented by other traditional mechanisms, such as class hierarchies and `if` statements. We identify the following design constituents.

1. Groups of context-dependent use cases, each of which share the same contexts. Context-dependent use cases in the same group simultaneously become applicable when the contexts hold. To modularize dynamic behavioral changes, they should be modularized into a layer in COP languages.
2. Classes participating in use cases by applying the standard use-case-driven approach.
3. Detailed specification of contexts based on the identified classes and frameworks on which the system depends.

In the following sections, we overview each step of COSE using the conference guide system example introduced in Sect. 2.

4.1   Identifying Contexts and Context-Dependent Use Cases

The first step of COSE is to identify contexts and context-dependent use cases. We extend the original use-case-driven method [27] with context-dependent use cases that are applicable only in specific contexts. By observing use cases, we can see that a number of behavior variations of some units of the system exist with respect to some outside conditions, which are subject to change at runtime. As mentioned in Principle 1, such conditions are candidates for the variables that determine the current context. For example, in the conference guide system, we identify the use case "Startup" where the user starts the system. This use case includes the behavior of the whole application initializing several parts of the system, and has two sub-use-cases, i.e., "Startup scheduler" (prepares the menu for the user's schedule) and "Startup Twitter" (prepares the menu for the Twitter client). All these sub-use-cases are applicable only when some conditions hold, such as the availability of the user's schedule and availability of the Internet. We can identify these conditions as candidates for contexts that change the behavior of the application. In the remainder of this paper, we refer to a context that changes the behavior of the entire application as a *global context*.

Another example is the "Using a map" use case, which is specialized to three use cases: "Using a city map," "Using the floor plan," and "Using a static map."

Table 1. Listing of variables: the first stage

subject	name	description
global	hasSchedule	the user has registered at least one session or not
	hasNetwork	the Internet is available or not
	outdoors	the situation is outdoors or not
	hasPositioning	the positioning systems are available or not
	batteryLow	the battery level is low or not

Table 2. Refined listing of variables

subject	name	description
global	hasSchedule	the user has registered at least one session or not
	hasNetwork	the Internet is available or not
	outdoors	the situation is outdoors or not
	indoors	the situation is indoors or not
	batteryLow	the battery level is low or not

These are applicable when the user is outdoors, when the user is indoors, and when the system cannot determine the user's location, respectively. Again, these specializations affect the whole application; thus, these user's situations are also candidates for global contexts.

Generally, a context in our model is defined in terms of a set of Boolean variables that represents the condition of the subject of the behavior. We list the candidates for variables in the conference guide system in Table 1. In this table, we represent the subject (the whole application) as global. Note that this is the very early stage of listing candidates for variables that are directly observable from the behavior of the system-to-be, and we introduce one important criterion used to refine this listing.

Each variable should not depend on other variables because such dependencies imply that a variable can be represented in terms of others.

A context should consist of a set of orthogonal variables; if they are not orthogonal, they should be exclusive. This criterion is required to keep the conditions constructed by these variables simple and ensure the completeness of contexts. Intuitively, being orthogonal means that every combination of values is possible. For example, in Table 1, hasSchedule, hasNetwork, outdoors, and batteryLow are orthogonal. However, outdoors and hasPositioning are not orthogonal because the combination outdoors && !hasPositioning is impossible (we assume that the conference guide system determines the outdoors situation using positioning systems). If it is not possible to represent such variables using just one single Boolean variable, then we should reformulate them as exclusive variables, which help analyze dependencies between layers. Thus, the variables outdoors

Table 3. Use cases for the conference guide system

name	activation condition
Startup	
Startup scheduler	hasSchedule
Startup Twitter	hasNetwork
Viewing the program	
Viewing the online program	hasNetwork
Updating the schedule	
Using a map	
Using a city map	outdoors
Using the floor plan	indoors
Using a static map	!outdoors && !indoors
Moving	
Moving when outdoors	outdoors
Viewing the schedule	hasSchedule
Using Twitter	hasNetwork
Updating timeline frequently	!batteryLow
Updating timeline infrequently	batteryLow

and hasPositioning are divided into three exclusive variables representing outdoors, indoors, and no positioning is available, and the final one is exactly the case where the system cannot determine whether it is outdoors or indoors. The refined listing of variables is shown in Table 2.

Note that, as discussed in Sect. 2, requirements for context changes are often volatile. Thus, at this stage, it is preferable to keep contexts abstract to be prepared for future requirements changes.

A context-dependent use case is annotated with a logical formula that consists of the set of variables identified above. We call this formula an *activation condition* for that use case. Context-dependent use cases for the conference guide system are summarized in Table 3. The names of use cases are listed in the left column, and activation conditions that represent when the use case is applicable are listed in the right column. A name with an indent represents that this use case is a specialization of the use case listed in the above row in italics. A use case with an empty condition is context independent.

4.2   Grouping Context-Dependent Use Cases

A situation where multiple use cases are applicable in the same context implies that the context-dependent behavior is scattered over those use cases. To modularize dynamic behavioral changes, these context-dependent use cases should be grouped into a single module that is enabled (activated) when the condition

Table 4. Groups of context-dependent use cases

activation condition	use case
hasSchedule	Startup scheduler
	Viewing the scheduler
hasNetwork	Startup Twitter
	Viewing the online program
	Using Twitter
outdoors	Using a city map
	Moving when outdoors
indoors	Using the floor plan
!outdoors && !indoors	Using a static map
hasNetwork && !batteryLow	Updating timeline frequently
hasNetwork && batteryLow	Updating timeline infrequently

holds and disabled (deactivated) when the condition does not hold. This is the situation Principle 3 explains, which is rephrased in terms of the use case driven method as follows. *If multiple context-dependent use cases that are not specializations of the same use case share the same context, their behavior should be implemented by using a layer.*

Table 4 lists the groups of context-dependent use cases. We can see that three contexts, i.e., hasSchedule, hasNetwork, and outdoors, are assigned to multiple context-dependent use cases. Thus, these use cases are grouped into a layer. We rename such contexts by capitalizing the first character (e.g., HasSchedule, HasNetwork, and Outdoors), following naming traditions for layers in COP languages.

We must also consider how to treat the remaining context-dependent use cases. Even though they do not share the condition with other use cases, some still have a relationship with other layers in that a subterm of their condition is the condition that activates the layer. For example, the condition for "Using a static map" includes the subterm outdoors, which is the condition that activates the layer Outdoors. To control dynamic behavior changes uniformly, activation of "Using a static map" should be managed in the same way as Outdoors. Thus, we also identify the context-dependent use case "Using a static map" as a layer, i.e., StaticMap. Similarly, we identify the context-dependent use case "Using the floor plan" as a layer, i.e., Indoors.

So far, we have identified at least five layers. We do not identify other use cases, e.g., "Updating timeline frequently" and "Updating timeline infrequently," as context-dependent. They are conceptually the same as alternative use cases, and the behavior variations should be so local that each of them can be implemented within a single class. Thus, they can be implemented by traditional OO mechanisms, such as inheritance and if statements.

Table 5. Classes for each layer

layer	classes	position
HasSchedule	MainActivity, Schedule	class-in-layer
HasNetwork	MainActivity, Program, Twitter	class-in-layer
Outdoors	Map	layer-in-class
Indoors	Map	layer-in-class
StaticMap	Map	layer-in-class

4.3 Designing Classes

Each layer in COP consists of (partial) definitions of classes. By extending the original use-case-driven approach in a straightforward manner, we can identify classes and methods that participate in each layer.

First, from use case scenarios, we identify the names of classes. Since this is a straightforward adaptation of the original use-case-driven approach, we do not describe the details but briefly illustrate the result. Since the conference guide system is an Android application, each view of the application should be implemented as a subclass of the `android.app.Activity` class from the Android SDK framework[6]. The use case *"Startup"* identifies the `MainActivity` class, which will implement the main view of the application. Similarly, in the use cases *"Viewing the program," "Using a map," "Viewing the schedule,"* and *"Using Twitter,"* we identify an `Activity` class for each, i.e., `Program`, `Map`, `Schedule`, and `Twitter`, respectively. There are some other helper classes; however, only the `Activity` classes participate in the context-dependent behavior.

Table 5 summarizes this assignment of classes for each layer. While the layers `HasSchedule` and `HasNetwork` consist of multiple classes, other layers consist of just the `Map` class. This table also shows the preferred ways to allocate layers. There are two alternative ways to allocate layers, i.e., the class-in-layer style allocates the (partial) classes that implement the context-dependent behavior in the layer, and the layer-in-class style allocates the layer within the class. When a layer is scattered over several classes, the class-in-layer style is preferable. When a class is scattered over several layers, the layer-in-class style is better. Note that some COP languages support only one style [6]. In this case, we must conform to the style provided by the implementing language.

4.4 Designing Detailed Specification of Contexts

After designing classes, we can determine a more concrete representation of the contexts. While it is desirable to keep contexts abstract to allow changes in the details, we must also derive information about how they should be implemented. In particular, there are a number of layer activation mechanisms, and we must select an appropriate mechanism. Furthermore, as explained later, specifications

---

[6] http://developer.android.com/sdk/.

for some contexts are complex; thus, we must identify more granular contexts that comprise the specified context.

Section 4.1 defines that the context hasSchedule holds when the user has selected at least one session to attend from the conference program. In terms of the Android SDK framework, this is represented as "a query on the SQLite instance returns at least one result." Thus, we define when the layer HasSchedule becomes active as follows, which is read as "the getCount method on the result of a query on an SQLite instance (i.e., db) returns an integer value that is greater than 0."

```
HasSchedule(SQLite db) :: db.query(..).getCount() > 0
```

Similarly, by inspecting Android SDK framework specifications, we can define when the layer HasNetwork becomes active as "the result of the call of the getDetailedState method on the result of the call of getActiveNetworkInfo on a ConnectivityManager instance (i.e., cm) is equal to the result of the access to the static field NetworkInfo.DetailedState.CONNECTED."

```
HasNetwork(ConnectivityManager cm) ::
  cm.getActiveNetworkInfo().getDetailedState() ==
  NetworkInfo.DetailedState.CONNECTED
```

The cases for the outdoors and indoors contexts are more complex. They are affected by multiple states of the running machine. First, to determine whether the user is outdoors, the GPS device should be available. Second, the conference guide system determines whether the user is in the conference venue using the SSID of the connecting wireless LAN, which means that the wireless LAN connection should be available. Thus, activation of the Outdoors and Indoors layers is determined in terms of more fine-grained contexts.

```
Outdoors :: !WifiAvailable && GPSAvailable
Indoors :: WifiAvailable
```

In other words, Outdoors and Indoors are composite layers [30].

The context WifiAvailable is defined as follows assuming that isWifiConnected is an application method that returns true when the wireless LAN is connected and its SSID is some pre-defined value.

```
WifiAvailable :: Config.isWifiConnected()==true
```

The context GPSAvailable is defined as follows using the isProviderEnabled method provided by the framework.

```
GPSAvailable :: LocationManager.isProviderEnabled(
  LocationManager.GPS_PROVIDER) == true
```

All these concrete representations of contexts reveal that they are conditionals and can be implemented directly using a layer activation mechanism triggered by conditionals.[7] In Sect. 6.1, we show cases where other activation mechanisms are selected.

---

[7] For COP languages that do not provide layer activation by conditionals, we must provide a workaround to implement such conditionals.

5   Mapping to Implementation

This section demonstrates how the design artifacts developed by COSE are systematically translated into a program with existing COP mechanisms. Generally, a layer identified in the previous section is implemented using a corresponding mechanism provided by the COP language chosen as an implementation language, such as a layer in ContextJ, a set of methods that share the same context in Subjective-C, or a context trait [23]. The detailed specification of contexts is then mapped to the corresponding layer activation mechanisms provided by that language.

In this paper, we choose ServalCJ [32] (a successor of EventCJ [29]) as the implementation language because it provides a generalized layer activation mechanism that supports most existing COP mechanisms. A context in ServalCJ is defined as a term of temporal logic with a call stack, which can represent most existing layer activation mechanisms. For example, it can specify two events, one of which activates the corresponding context and the other which deactivates that context (as in EventCJ's event-based layer transition). ServalCJ can also specify a control flow under which the corresponding context is active (as in JCop [9]). ServalCJ can select the target where such context specifications are applied, and that target can be a set of objects (*per-instance* activation) or the whole application (*global* activation). Furthermore, ServalCJ supports *implicit activation*, where activation of a context is indirectly specified using a conditional expression. As shown in the following sections, our methodology clarifies that this mechanism is notably useful for modular implementation.

A ServalCJ program comprises a set of classes, layers, and *context groups* where dynamic layer activation and the target for this activation are specified. The layers and classes identified in Sects. 4.2 and 4.3 are implemented directly in layers and classes in ServalCJ, and the context specifications in Sect. 4.4 are implemented directly in context groups in ServalCJ. We explain the details in the following sections.

5.1   Implementing Layers

As in other COP languages, layers and partial methods comprise the mechanism for modularization of context-dependent behavior in ServalCJ.

Figure 2 shows an example of layers and partial methods in ServalCJ for the main view of the conference guide system. The `MainActivity` class extends the `Activity` class provided by the Android SDK framework and overrides the `onResume` method, which is called from the framework when this view resumes the execution. This method displays the main menu of the conference guide system as buttons for viewing the conference program and using the map. `MainActivity` also declares two layers, i.e., `HasSchedule` and `HasNetwork`. These layers define the context-dependent behavior of `MainActivity`[8].

---

[8] Although Table 5 shows that it is preferable to implement these layers in the class-in-layer style, in Fig. 2, they are implemented in the layer-in-class style because ServalCJ currently only supports this style.

```
1  class MainActivity extends Activity implements View.OnClickListener {
2    private GridLayout layout;

4    @Override
5    protected void onResume() {
6      super.onResume();
7      layout = new GridLayout(this);
8      layout.addView(makeMenu("program", "Program"));
9      layout.addView(makeMenu("map", "Map"));
10   }

12   private Button makeMenu(String tag, String label) {
13     ..
14   }

16   layer HasSchedule {
17     after protected void onResume() {
18       layout.addView(makeMenu("schedule", "Schedule"));
19     }
20   }
21   layer HasNetwork {
22     after protected void onResume() {
23       layout.addView(makeMenu("twitter", "Twitter"));
24     }
25   }
26 }
```

Fig. 2. Layers and partial methods in ServalCJ

Has- Schedule defines the behavior when there is at least one session that the user would like to attend, and HasNetwork defines the behavior when the Internet is available. These layers extend the original behavior of onResume by declaring *after* partial methods, which are executed just after the execution of the original method when the respective layer is active[9]. For example, when HasSchedule is active, onResume also displays the menu button to check the user's schedule.

5.2   Implementing Layer Activation

In COP languages, layers can be activated and deactivated dynamically, and ServalCJ provides declarative ways to perform such layer operations. These declarations are obtained directly from the design of detailed contexts (Sect. 4.4).

First, detailed context definitions are grouped based on the variables and contexts to which these definitions refer. We refer to such group as a *context*

---

[9] There are also *before* and *around* partial methods that execute before the original method and instead of the original method, respectively, when the respective layer is active.

```
1  global contextgroup Network(ConnectivityManager cm)
2      perthis(this(ConnectivityManager)) {
3    activate HasNetwork if(
4      cm.getActiveNetworkInfo().getDetailedState()
5        ==NetworkInfo.DetailedState.CONNECTED);
6  }
```

Fig. 3. Context group responsible for activation of HasNetwork

```
1  global contextgroup Schedule(MainActivity main)
2      perthis(this(MainActivity)) {
3    activate HasSchedule if(main.scheduleCounter > 0);
4  }
```

Fig. 4. Context group responsible for activation of HasSchedule

group. For example, HasNetwork refers to an instance of ConnectivityManager (and this is the only context that refers to that instance); thus, this context definition makes up one context group.

Figure 3 shows a context group that is responsible for activating HasNetwork. The first line specifies the name of the context group, i.e., Network, followed by a specification of how this context group is instantiated. Since the context HasNetwork is identified as global (Sect. 4), this context group is declared as global, as specified by the modifier global. In line 2, the perthis clause specifies that the instance of Network is associated with an instance of ConnectivityManager (as specified using the this pointcut), which can be referenced through the variable cm.

Line 3 declares when the layer HasNetwork is active using an *activate declaration*. A when clause specifies the condition when the layer is active. There are a number of ways to specify this condition, e.g., specify the join points where that context becomes active and inactive, specify the control flow under which that context is active, and specify the condition when that context is active. In Fig. 3, we use the if expression to specify the condition. With the if expression, we can use any Boolean-type Java expression. In this case, we simply copy the expression from the definition in Sect. 4.4.

We can declare a context group for HasSchedule in a similar way. One subtle issue is that the definition of HasSchedule contains an expression that requires local database access. If the developer has performance concerns, this definition is not preferred because this condition is tested at every call of the layered method (i.e., a method that consists of a set of partial methods) in ServalCJ. In our case, the definition of HasSchedule is refined to access the counter variable that is introduced to MainActivity and updated when the local database is updated as follows.

```
HasSchedule(MainActivity main) :: main.scheduleCounter > 0
```

The definition of the context group for HasSchedule is shown in Fig. 4.

```
1  global contextgroup Situation {
2    context WifiAvailable is if(Config.isWifiConnected()==true);
3    context GPSAvailable is if(LocationManager.isProviderEnabled(
4      LocationManager.GPS_PROVIDER)==true);
5    activate Outdoors when !WifiAvailable && when GPSAvailable;
6    activate Indoors when WifiAvaileble;
7    activate StaticMap when !Outdoors && when !Indoors;
```

Fig. 5. Context group responsible for activation of Outdoors, Indoors, and StaticMap

The remaining layers are Outdoors, Indoors, and StaticMap. Since they
share the same set of context references, they are grouped into one context
group, which is shown in Fig. 5. Since this context group does not refer to any
instance variables, it specifies no **perthis** and **pertarget** clauses. This context
group is a *singleton*, i.e., it is created when execution initializes and remains
until the application terminates.

Lines 2 and 3 define the *named contexts* WifiAvailable and GPSAvailable,
which make it possible to refer to the activation conditions from several activate
declarations that are used to specify when Outdoors and Indoors are active.
The conditions declared by these named contexts are directly obtained from the
definitions given in Sect. 4.4. Activate declarations for Outdoors, Indoors, and
StaticMap are also obtained from the definitions given in Sect. 4.4. Note that
we can use the logical operators ||, &&, and ! to compose propositions in the
when clauses.

6   Other Case Studies

This section demonstrates two other case studies using COSE. The first is conducted to investigate the applicability of COSE to an existing, well-known COP
application. The second study shows more interesting cases, which are not discussed in our previous paper [33], where different activation mechanisms with
respect to the scope and duration are applied. Among these mechanisms, we
should select the most suitable mechanism.

The first case study develops the CJEdit program editor that is first implemented by Appeltauer et al. [8]. Since the original implementation of CJEdit
exists, we do not perform this case study from scratch. Instead, we use the original implementation as a prototype for this case study. This case study shows
that COSE is applicable to the development of a well-known COP application.
Details of this case study are found in our previous paper [33].

The second case study develops a maze-solving robot simulator [32] wherein
a context can be per-instance, per-control-flow, and global and the events triggering the context changes are explicit. The second case study also shows the situation where a context-dependent use case is *not* a specialization of another use
case. Principle 3 assumes that there is a *default* use case for context-dependent

use cases; however this assumption does not hold in this case study. The following principle compensates for such a situation.

Principle 4. *If a top-level use case is also context-dependent, it should be implemented using a layer.*

Generally, multiple objects can participate in a use case and, as Jacobson suggests [28], behavior in such a use case crosscuts multiple objects and thus should be implemented using a layer.

6.1 Maze-Solving Robot Simulator

This application simulates how a line-tracing robot solves a maze[10]. The robot solves a maze comprising black lines on a sheet of white paper. After solving the maze, the robot runs the optimized path from the starting point to the goal. The maze-solving phase comprises the following behavior.

- Performing line tracing until the robot reaches an intersection, a corner, or a dead-end (we refer to these as *intersections* for simplicity).
- Detecting intersections using reflectance sensors attached to the robot.
- Making a turn at each intersection according to the implemented algorithm, e.g., left-hand rule, right-hand rule, and Trémaux's algorithm[11]. In this example, we set the left-hand rule as default behavior.
- Remembering the sequence of behavior at each intersection (and possibly all visited intersections) and calculating the optimized path from the starting point to the current intersection by eliminating dead-ends.

The robot can also display some debugging information, such as currently visited paths, on the small display attached to the robot.

The simulator emulates the behavior of the maze-solving robot. In this simulator, the maze is modeled as a graph where each node represents an intersection that provides coordinates to represent its position. An instance of the robot emulates maze-solving on this model, e.g., line-tracing is simplified by updating the current position of the robot according to the destination of the selected edge, which models the segment. Here, a segment is a part of a path from one intersection to another.

For the user, this simulator provides a number of functionalities: editing a maze, simulating how the robot solves the maze, and simulating how the robot follows the optimized path after solving the maze. These functionalities are exclusive, i.e., when we are editing a maze, we cannot run any simulations for solving the maze and running the optimized path, and so on. These functionalities are switched when the user finishes editing the maze (or loads the pre-edited maze) and when the robot finishes solving the maze. The simulator provides GUI tools,

---

[10] This simulator is inspired by a real maze-solving robot (Pololu 3pi Robot: http://www.pololu.com/product/975) and the behavior of the simulator is modeled by following the sample program provided by the 3pi Robot distribution.

[11] Only Trémaux's algorithm can solve the maze with loops.

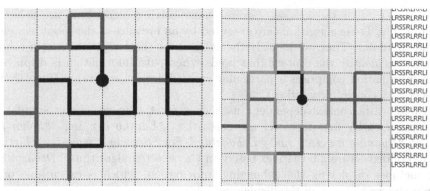

(a) Simulator solving a maze. The red lines represent the traced path.

(b) Simulator in the debug mode. The green lines overwrite the red lines and represent the optimized path. The textbox displays the text-based notation of the optimized path.

Fig. 6. The maze-solving simulator. The lines indicate paths within the maze. The start is the lowermost dead end. The black circle represents the goal.

such as a menu bar and menu buttons that are automatically switched when the functionalities are switched. During maze-solving, the visited intersections and segments are colored to visualize the traced path (Fig. 6(a)). Furthermore, while the robot is solving the maze, the user can select the debug mode. In debug mode, the color of intersections and segments in the currently calculated optimized path are changed and text based notation of the optimized path is displayed (Fig. 6(b)).

From this description of the behavior, we first derive the variables that determine the current context (Table 6). Unlike the previous examples, in this case we identify three types of subjects. From the perspective of the user, this simulator provides different functionalities with respect to the current user task. These functionalities are identified as global because the user is not aware of a

Table 6. Maze-solving simulator variables

subject	name	description
global	editingMaze	The user is editing a maze
	solvingMaze	The user is simulating maze-solving
	runningMaze	The user is simulating running the solved maze
	debugging	Showing the debugging information
robot	rightHand	Solving maze using the right-hand rule
	tremaux	Solving maze using the Trémaux algorithm
cflow	displaying	Displaying the path information

particular part of the system. Several maze-solving algorithms are selected dynamically. These algorithms are executed by an instance of the robot modeled in the simulator. Thus, we identify the subject for these algorithms as a robot. Finally, we identify the context that holds when path information is displayed. Path information comprises a particular control flow; therefore, we identify its subject as a control flow (cflow).

Table 7 lists context-dependent use cases for the maze-solving simulator. First, we identify four top-level use cases, i.e., *"Editing a maze," "Solving a maze," "Running a maze,"* and *"Debugging."* For *"Solving a maze,"* we further derive context-aware alternatives based on the selected algorithm. *"Debugging"* also includes displaying the debugging information, which is executable only within the control flow of the displaying behavior.

As suggested by Principle 4, we first identify the top-level use cases as layers, i.e., `EditingMaze`, `SolvingMaze`, `RunningMaze`, and `Debugging`. "Displaying debug info." is a use case included by "Debugging," but it is not a specialization of other use cases; therefore, we identify it as a layer, i.e., `UnderDebugging`. By following COSE, the remaining two use cases are not identified as layers here. However, in a later step we actually come to consider that they are layers.

Next, we identify the names of classes from the use case scenarios. Table 8 lists the important classes for implementing context-dependent behavior. The class `Robot` models the behavior of the virtual robot, and the class `View` provides the view for the user. Many of the layers crosscut both classes. The layer

Table 7. Use cases for maze-solving simulator

name	activation condition
Editing a maze	editingMaze
Solving a maze	solvingMaze
Solving with right-hand rule	rightHand
Solving with Trémaux	tremaux
Running a maze	runningMaze
Debugging	debugging
Displaying debug info.	debugging &&displaying

Table 8. Classes for each layer of maze-solving simulator

layer	classes
`EditingMaze`	`View`
`SolvingMaze`	`Robot, View`
`RunningMaze`	`Robot, View`
`Debugging`	`Robot, View`
`UnderDebugging`	`Segment, Intersection`

`UnderDebugging` changes the color of segments and intersections accessed from the path-printing methods.

While identifying classes, we noticed that two context-dependent use cases, "Solving with right-hand rule" and "Solving with Trémaux," which were not identified as layers, also crosscut multiple classes. The selected algorithm changes not only the behavior of the virtual robot instance but also the enabling configuration for the menu items in GUI components. Thus, we can identify two other layers, i.e., `RightHandRule` and `Tremaux`, that cut across two classes, i.e., `Robot` and `View`. This observation reveals that a context-dependent use case that does not share contexts with other use cases can crosscut multiple classes, and could be a layer. To determine whether such a use case should be identified as a layer, we must assess the use case scenario carefully to determine whether the context-dependent use case includes multiple objects, or to postpone the decision until we design the classes.

After designing the classes, we define the detailed specifications of the contexts. In the previous examples, we provide the specification of each context as a `boolean` type method call implemented using an `if` expression in ServalCJ. In this case study, we follow a different approach. There are apparent state changes in the simulator user interface. First, the interface provides the maze editor to the user. Then, it provides the menus and tools to solve the maze. During maze solving, the user can switch to the debugging mode. After solving the maze, the user interface provides menus and tools to run the optimized path. Each state corresponds to each global context in Table 6, and, by observing use case scenarios, we explicitly identify events by following the method described in [31]. The contexts and events are summarized in Fig. 7.

Using events, we specify each global context (Table 6) as follows.

```
EditingMaze:: after startEditor until startSolver.
SolvingMaze:: after startSolver until solved.
RunningMaze:: after solved.
Debugging:: after startDebug until endDebug.
```

Each condition is read as a term in temporal logic that holds after the specified event (e.g., `startEditor`) after another specified event (e.g., `startSolver`). ServalCJ provides *active until expressions* that correspond to such temporal logic terms (Fig. 8).

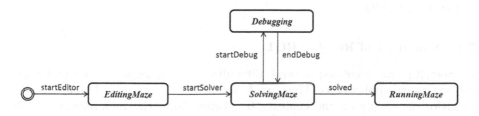

Fig. 7. Context transitions and events in the maze-solving simulator

```
1  global contextgroup MazeUI() {
2    activate EditingMaze from startEditor to startSolver;
3    activate SolvingMaze from startSolver to solved;
4    activate RunningMaze from solved to never;
5    activate Debugging from startDebug to endDebug;
6    context Displaying is in cflow(call(void Simulator.printPath()));
7    activate UnderDebugging when Debugging && when Printing;
8  }
```

Fig. 8. Context group for UI in the maze-solving simulator

How to determine whether we should use explicit or implicit events will be addressed in future work. One possible criterion is performance. Implicit events impose additional overhead on the application (because each conditional in `if` is evaluated before each call of a partial method); therefore, if events are explicit in the specification, we should consider using explicit events. Another criterion is modularity. Explicit events easily raise the scattering problem or the fragile pointcut problem [37], and implicit events are the solutions to these problems. For the global contexts of the maze-solving simulator, we apply explicit events because events are apparent in the specification, and the specification is unlikely to change.

The context "displaying" in Table 6 is identified as cflow, which means that the subject of this context is a particular control flow. For this purpose, ServalCJ provides the `cflow` construct that declares that the specified context holds under the specified control flow. In Fig. 8, this context is declared to be active under the `printPath` call control flow on an instance of `Simulator` (line 6).

The contexts "rightHand" and "tremaux" are specified as a `boolean` type method call, similar to the cases in the conference guide system and CJEdit.

```
activate RightHandRule if(sim.isRightHandRule());
activate Tremaux if(sim.isTremaux());
```

7   Discussion on Modularity

The case studies demonstrate our COSE methodology and effectively answer the research questions described in Sect. 3. In this section, we summarize and validate our results.

7.1   Summary of Results: RQ1

In Sect. 2.2, we identified several difficulties encountered when developing context-aware applications. Thus, we formed RQ1, "How should contexts and behavior depending on the contexts be elicited from the requirements?." To answer RQ1, we suggested Principles 1 and 2 and analyzed their validity through case studies. The results of the case studies are summarized as follows.

Identification of Contexts and Requirements Variability. As illustrated in Sect. 4.1, COSE systematically identifies contexts by observing the behavior of the system-to-be, such as use cases and prototypes. Furthermore, we clarify a criterion that should hold for each context, i.e., a context should not be a subcase of other contexts. Requirements variability based on contexts is also represented by context-dependent use cases.

Different Levels of Abstraction. As discussed in Sects. 4.1 and 4.4, COSE provides a concretization process for contexts. A context may be composed of other contexts that are less abstract than the composed context. Each level of abstraction of contexts in the specification is also directly represented by the implementation language using composite layers.

Multiple Dependencies Between Contexts and Behavior. As discussed above, given composite layers, layer activation can be triggered by complex activation conditions.

Requirements Volatility in Context Specification. Each context-dependent use case is represented in terms of abstract contexts; therefore, it is robust against changes in detailed specifications of concrete contexts. For example, in the conference guide system, the specification of the outdoor context may change according to the evolution of sensor technologies. Context-dependent use cases that depend on the outdoor context will not be affected by such changes because the detailed specification of the outdoor context is abstracted from the context-dependent use cases. We may also separately perform such changes because the definitions of contexts are encapsulated in context groups in ServalCJ.

Crosscutting of Contexts in Multiple Use Cases. COSE groups a number of behavior variations that are executable under the same contexts and scattered across multiple use cases into a single layer. As discussed in Sect. 4.2, COSE also provides a guideline to determine when to use COP.

Crosscutting of Behavior Changes. Dynamic changes of contexts and dependent behavior scattered across the whole execution of the program are separated as specifications of contexts and implemented directly using context groups. Specifically, definitions of such changes are specified declaratively and completely separated from the base program.

Interferences Between Behaviors. The case studies show that there are dependencies between layers (e.g., outdoors and indoors are exclusive variations of behavior), and COSE clarifies such dependencies due to the orthogonality and exclusiveness of the variables used in the context conditions. These conditions are straightforwardly implemented using composite layers in ServalCJ, and the dependencies are ensured by the implementation language.

Modular Translation to the Implementation. The layers and classes identified in Sects. 4.2 and 4.3 are implemented directly in layers and classes in ServalCJ. Context specifications (Sect. 4.4) are directly implemented in context groups in ServalCJ. Each requirement in the specification is not scattered across multiple modules in the implementation, and each module is not entangled with multiple requirements.

In summary, the case studies reveal that the factors that change system behavior are "candidates" for contexts, and each context can be represented as a Boolean variable. A criterion to identify contexts can be derived from this representation of contexts, i.e., each context at the abstract level should not depend on other contexts. A context and other contexts should be orthogonal or, if they are not orthogonal, they should be exclusive. This criterion enhances the exhaustiveness of contexts and makes it easy to discuss the equivalence between contexts.

7.2 Summary of Results: RQ2

The answer to RQ2, "When should we apply COP rather than other development methods?," is represented by Principles 3 and 4, and to validate that, we must further discuss the validity of the decision made in the case studies because there are other alternatives to implement such variations.

We can validate it using Tables 4 and 5. First, the layers `HasSchedule` and `HasNetwork` crosscut multiple classes; thus, the same concern may scatter over those classes if we naively implement them using `if` statements. Applying design patterns may also produce this scattering problem. Extracting such scattered code as a common superclass requires an additional class hierarchy, which may be orthogonal to the existing hierarchies. Applying multiple inheritance, mixins [11], and traits [48] makes it difficult to look at all classes that are composed of the same context-dependent behavior. In contrast, layers in COP provide a good solution to encapsulate such concerns. More importantly, techniques other than COP make it difficult to separate behavior changes from the base program, which is possible in (some variants of) COP languages.

In contrast, the `Outdoors`, `Indoors` and `StaticMap` layers in Table 5 exist in only the `Map` class; thus, they do not appear to contribute to the separation of crosscutting concerns. However, from Table 4, we observe that `Outdoors` consists of two use cases implemented by different methods. Therefore, using `if` statements would result in scattering of the same conditions over those methods. We can avoid this scattering by, for example, allowing the `Map` object to have a state of the current situation and by defining behavioral variations for each state using the state design pattern. The problem with applying design patterns is the scattering and tangling of behavioral changes. The state changes of the `Map` object are triggered by external environment changes, which are observed by the framework. We must embed state changes of the `Map` object by implementing appropriate event handlers of possibly multiple modules (e.g., the Wifi and GPS related classes). Thus, it is difficult to localize the overall state changes in the Map object. By applying COSE with appropriate COP languages, we can separate such context changes into a single module.

Similar discussion holds in the case study of CJEdit. However, in the maze-solving robot simulator example, the case wherein the context-dependent use cases whose contexts are not shared with other use cases are also identified as layers. This indicates that, while the principles hold, there are cases where we should postpone the decision to implement variations of context-dependent behavior using layers until we are designing classes.

7.3 Summary of Results: RQ3

The implementation in ServalCJ discussed in Sect. 5 implies that the implementation is *directly obtained* from the requirements in our approach. There are injective mappings from layers and contexts discovered in the requirements to those in the implementation language. Thus, this mapping promotes separation of concerns in that requirements are not scattered across several modules in the implementation, and each module is not entangled with a number of requirements.

The implementations in the case studies rely on the specific linguistic constructs provided by ServalCJ. To answer RQ3 "How do COP mechanisms support predictable control of changes in context-dependent behavior?," we identify the properties that the implementation languages should have to make COSE effective, and we compare ServalCJ with other languages and implementation techniques, such as ContextJ [7], EventCJ [29,30], and a pseudo AOP language with a dynamic layer activation mechanism (similar to the one discussed in Sect. 2 of [29]), with respect to those properties. Table 9 summarizes the comparison. The leftmost column shows the numbers and titles of the following sections.

We do not argue that programming languages that do not support the features listed below are not useful in COSE. In such languages, we can still apply useful workarounds to implement specifications organized by COSE, which would not be a poor choice in some circumstances, such as the availability of

Table 9. Comparison with other activation mechanisms

	ContextJ	AOP+COP	EventCJ	ServalCJ
Separation of context-dependent behavior[a]	a	a	a	a
Separation of context changes	n/a	a	a	a
Expressing relations between layers and contexts	n/a	n/a	a	a
Implicit activation	n/a	n/a	n/a	a

[a] ServalCJ (and EventCJ) only supports the layer-in-class style. Thus, the same layer may be scattered across multiple classes. In fact, such layers exist in both case studies. This scattering can be addressed by supporting the class-in-layer style in the syntax.

libraries and a development environment, and programmer preference. Nevertheless, Table 9 indicates that recent progress in COP languages effectively supports COSE, which will be good input for future language design.

Separation of Context-Dependent Behavior. First, in COSE, the implementing language should separate context-dependent behavior that is dynamically enabled and disabled from the base program. The layers of COP languages provide an effective way to achieve this. Each partial method implements the context-specific behavior of the base method, and a layer packs all partial methods executable under the same context into a single module. Besides COP, other programming paradigms, such as AOP and feature-oriented programming (FOP) [42], also provide such modularization mechanisms; however, for these paradigms, we require an additional mechanism for dynamic composition of modules. For example, dynamic aspect deployment [10] may be applied for this purpose.

Separation of Context Changes. We can also see that, in COSE, specifications and implementations of dynamic changes of contexts and dependent behavior are also separated from other specifications and modules, respectively. From an implementation perspective, such dynamic changes can be easily scattered over the whole application execution. Such scattering behavior can be avoided using the pointcut-advice mechanism in AspectJ [36] (provided that it is also equipped with some imperial layer activation mechanism) or other COP languages with AOP features, such as EventCJ and JCop [9].

In some COP languages, layer activation is controlled in a *per-thread* manner whereby the generation of the event activating the layer and layer activation occur synchronously. In such languages, it is difficult to separate dynamic behavior changes. For example, in ContextJ, layer activation is expressed using with-blocks, which ensures that layers are active only within the explicitly specified dynamic scope.

```
with (activeLayers) { onResume(); }
```

However, context changes are triggered by external events that asynchronously occur with the dynamic behavior change. For example, in this case, we must remember the active layer within the body of the event handler that handles the change of contexts to activate context-dependent behavior that does not appear in the scope of the event handler:

```
void someEventHandler(Event e) {
   activeLayers.add(Outdoors);
}
```

In this case, the scattering problem is readily encountered, and the base program is entangled with the concerns about dynamic changes of behavior.

Expressing Relations Between Layers and Contexts. From COSE, we also see that a behavior variation may depend on multiple contexts. For example, from Table 4, we see that the use case "Using a static map," which is implemented in the layer `StaticMap`, depends on both the outdoors and indoors contexts, one of which, i.e., outdoors, is further decomposed into two contexts, i.e., `WifiAvailable` and `GPSAvailable`. To separate context-dependent behavior from the detailed specification of contexts, such an abstraction mechanism is necessary. From an implementation perspective, composite layers [30], which are supported by EventCJ and ServalCJ, are useful for this purpose.

Implicit Activation. In most existing COP languages, we must specify the join point where the context change occurs explicitly. In COP languages with AOP features, we perform such specification using the pointcut sublanguage. In COP languages with `with`-blocks, we explicitly inject the layer activation block into the base program. However, from the case studies, we have learned that a more declarative way to specify the condition that activates the corresponding context is used heavily in the context specification, which is directly implemented using the implicit layer activation mechanism provided by ServalCJ (i.e., the `if` condition that specifies the condition when the corresponding context is active). This indicates that, even though it currently suffers performance problems, the implicit layer activation mechanism can be a strong tool to implement dynamic behavior changes modularly from the specification.

It is also possible to translate implicit layer activation manually into an explicit activation by identifying the join points where the condition is changed. However, with multiple join points, we must list all of them, which is an error-prone task. Furthermore, explicitly specifying join points using a pointcut often raises the fragile pointcut problem [37].

7.4 Open Issues

Our preliminary case studies on COSE raise the following open issues that should be explored.

First, all case studies in this paper are simple. Although these case studies demonstrate the effectiveness of COSE, they do not guarantee success in more complex cases. In large systems, we may have a large number of dynamic behavior changes, some of which would be context dependent. Eliciting contexts from such systems may be time consuming. Furthermore, in all case studies, the target system is standalone and implemented using a single programming language. We should not assume that the results of the case studies imply that we can easily apply COSE to distributed systems implemented using multiple programming languages.

Second, COSE represents variations of context-dependent behavior using use cases. There may be some cases in which we prefer to use methods other than use cases, such as feature diagrams and goal models. The results in this paper do not guarantee that we can apply similar context-oriented extensions to such methods.

Third, the case studies do not convey compelling results regarding the costs and benefits of COSE. The results ensure modularity of the products. However, they do not reveal how such modularity affects the real software production process and the quality of its products. We believe that COSE would have a significant impact on software development, in particular on software maintenance, because it provides comprehensive abstractions, clarifies complex relations between contexts and behavior, and provides good modularity. However, this should be validated through a number of control experiments. Furthermore, the principles explained in Sect. 3.2 should be validated through a number of demonstration experiments and industrial software development.

Finally, as mentioned above, there are open performance issues with implicit activation, which is heavily used in the case studies. The performance problem is not significant in the case studies; however, this assumption will not always hold in larger applications. In some cases, we may optimize implicit activation, but such optimization may not be feasible in other cases. The case studies do not provide a concrete criterion for when implicit activation is preferable (because, e.g., it enhances modularity) or when other mechanisms, such as event-based activation, should be used (e.g. due to the performance considerations).

8   Future Research Roadmap

In this paper, we have presented COSE and proposed that it can be employed for the effective development of context-aware applications. Specifications systematized by COSE effectively represent different levels of abstraction of contexts, which makes the system robust with respect to changes in the detailed definitions of contexts. Context-dependent use cases are used to discover a layer, i.e., a modularization unit in COP, from the specifications. The injective mapping from specifications to implementations ensures that each specification in the requirements is not scattered across multiple modules in the implementation, and each module is not entangled with multiple requirements. The comparison among several implementation techniques shown in Sect. 7.3 reveals the key linguistic constructs that make COSE effective and indicates important research directions for context-oriented software development.

This paper has presented preliminary studies on COSE. Although these studies reveal that our approach is promising, there are a number of open issues. In this section, we discuss our future research roadmap.

8.1   Systematizing Context Identification

The applications mentioned in the case studies are simple, and the number of identified contexts is not large. In large systems, the number of "candidates for contexts" will be very large. Furthermore, the system-to-be will be described using natural languages including diagrams in inconsistent syntax. In some cases, such descriptions will be scattered over various resources, such as text documents, spreadsheets, and emails. This unstructured piling up of descriptions can easily results in a situation whereby conceptually equal contexts are described in different words and notations.

In Sect. 4, we listed the factors that change the system behavior as candidates for contexts. This is the most fundamental property of contexts. To identify contexts systematically and deal with a large number of candidates for contexts, more precise criteria to find candidates for contexts are required. For example, for a factor that changes the system behavior to be identified as a context in COP, it should affect the behavior of a number of objects in the system. Moreover, all contexts in the case studies are external with respect to the affected entities.

From this perspective, we plan to develop a systematic context elicitation process that is applicable in the early stages of requirements elicitation. Some work in requirements engineering, such as context-dependent domain analysis [19], will be a good starting point.

8.2 Requirements Based on Other Methods

Using use cases is a very effective way to identify the functional requirements of the system-to-be. Use cases do not require special languages to describe them; thus, people from various backgrounds can understand them easily. Nevertheless, they effectively describe system behavior. Furthermore, they prevent hasty design; design methods based on use cases have been well studied.

However, using use cases is not a panacea. For example, they are not suitable for representing non-functional requirements, which are better specified declaratively elsewhere, or for describing the requirements specifications of platforms, such as operating systems and frameworks. There are also a number of methods for analyzing requirements that are not based on use cases. It is natural to ask whether it is possible to apply methods similar to that described in this paper to other requirements analysis methods.

Goal-oriented methods for requirements engineering [18,40] are complementary approaches suitable for eliciting requirements variability and constraints. Non-functional requirements are derived from their *soft goals*. Their variability and constraints may depend on executing contexts. Although a goal-based approach for contextualization has been proposed previously [3], further research should be conducted to explore, for example, approaches to align goal-based approaches and use-case-driven approaches.

Feature modeling presents a compact representation of all products of a software product line. Feature models are represented by means of feature diagrams [34]. Features provide requirements for architectures (including non-functional requirements) and reusable functions. At the programming language level, layers in COP resemble features in FOP [5,50]. This similarity indicates that we may develop a context-oriented extension of FOSD [4]. For example, some existing work in this field [14] would be a good starting point.

Application of the context-oriented software development described in this paper to these major requirements engineering methods is a future challenge.

8.3 Evaluation

To ensure that our methodology is effective, it is necessary to perform further evaluation. For example, we must evaluate the costs and benefits of our methodology, and the validity of the decision to use layers to implement context-dependent behavior rather than other mechanisms through controlled experiments that compare our methodology with other software development methods. It is difficult to conduct controlled experiments, and derivation of quantitative evaluations would be a length process. Meanwhile, we think that it is important to conduct a number of demonstration experiments to collect experience by applying our approach. In particular, we believe that the application of our methodology to industrial software development is particularly important.

Since one purpose of our study has been to enhance modularity, an evaluation will be performed from this perspective. For example, an experimental study of how our approach makes it easy to deal with volatile requirements regarding contexts and analysis of the effects of requirement changes should be performed.

8.4 Implicit Activation

In two of the three case studies, all contexts are implemented by means of layer activation triggered by conditionals (i.e., if expressions in ServalCJ). As mentioned above, this implies the importance of implicit layer activation. However, there is a performance problem with implicit layer activation. A naive implementation strategy is to evaluate the condition that specifies when the corresponding context is active at every call of the layered methods, and when that condition holds and the corresponding context is not active, then that context is activated. This strategy will not produce a serious problem if the number of layered method calls is not so high. However, in the case where calls of layered methods frequently and repeatedly occur (e.g., where calls of layered methods are included within a loop statement), this strategy may result in serious performance problems.

Thus, developing an optimization mechanism for implicit layer activation so that the evaluation of the context condition occurs only when necessary is an important research topic. There are several approaches for this purpose.

One approach is to develop an ad hoc method that optimizes parts of the program where calls of layered methods may occur frequently, such as loop statements. For example, if we can determine that the context condition will never change during the execution of the loop, we can rewrite the loop so that the context condition is evaluated just once at the entrance of that loop.

For a more effective approach, we may explore a method to statically analyze when the value of the context condition changes. For example, assuming that c is a condition for the context C, if we can derive a pair of predicates (p, q) for which it can easily be checked that $(p \wedge p \implies c) \wedge (q \wedge q \implies \neg c)$, then we can insert evaluations of c where the values for p or q change. We are currently considering an application of predicate abstraction for model checking for this purpose.

Although it is desirable to limit changes of a given context condition in a small amount of code, it is generally possible that the change of context condition can occur anywhere in the program execution, which requires a whole program analysis. To make the whole program analysis lightweight and feasible in the case when the whole code is not available for analysis, it is also necessary to study the application of whole program analysis without the whole program [2] for COP programs.

The emphasis on implicit activation does not mean that event-based activation of contexts is not necessary. First, event-based activation should be used where layered methods are frequently called and optimization of implicit layer activation is difficult for some reason. There are also cases where the specification of a context is defined in terms of events (even though this did not occur in our case studies). For example, there may be a specification of stateless objects whose contexts are changed by clicking buttons. In this case, it is better to implement context activation in an event-based manner than to introduce a state for each object to manage context activation using the implicit activation mechanism. There are also cases where context changes can be observed from both conditions and events.

The problem is that there are no clear guidelines for when to use implicit layer activation and when to use the event-based mechanism. To create such guidelines, we must study this problem from both programming language and programming practice perspectives. From the programming language perspective, as mentioned above, it is necessary to determine the feasibility of efficient implementation of implicit activation. Meanwhile, formalization of implicit activation is also desirable to precisely study the semantics of implicit activation. We think that implicit activation (of layers) is a special case of functional reactive programming (FRP) [20] in that the change of the condition (value) reactively changes the result of the activation (computation). FRP is considered a special case of implicit activation (of behavior) by viewing it as a way to propagate values in a constraint graph of variables and expressions. It is possible that both have some shared foundations in continuous constraint solving. Understanding implicit activation in terms of FRP may further clarify the semantics of implicit activation.

From the programming practice perspective, through a number of other case studies, we plan to discover common *patterns* in context activation, which will serve as guidelines.

8.5   Distributed, Multi-language Environment

Both case studies in this paper are standalone applications written in a single programming language. However, in real products, systems are implemented using multiple programming languages and sometimes comprise a number of components and services over networks. There are two problems with applying our methodology to such systems.

First, to the best of our knowledge, ServalCJ is the only language that has all the desirable properties shown in Sect. 7.3. We must explore how to realize the mechanism supported by ServalCJ in a wide range of programming languages including those suitable for high performance computing such as C and C++, and scripting languages such as JavaScript.

Second, little COP research has been devoted to sharing the same context among multiple application processes. Sharing a context among processes over a network is possible in programming languages that support network-transparent communications between processes such as ContextErlang [47]. Further research is required to support network-transparent contexts in other programming models and develop a mechanism to share contexts among multiple programming languages, which may communicate with each other over the network.

Based on these technical elements, we will study the applicability of COSE to more realistic and sophisticated software development situations.

References

1. Abowd, G.D., Atkeson, C.G., Hong, J., Long, S., Kooper, R., Pinkerton, M.: Cyberguide: a mobile context-aware tour guide. Wireless Netw. **3**(5), 421–433 (1997)
2. Ali, K., Lhoták, O.: AVERROES: whole-program analysis without the whole program. In: Castagna, G. (ed.) ECOOP 2013. LNCS, vol. 7920, pp. 378–400. Springer, Heidelberg (2013). doi:10.1007/978-3-642-39038-8_16
3. Ali, R., Dalpiaz, F., Giorgini, P.: Goal-based self-contextualization. In: CAiSE 2009, pp. 37–43 (2009)
4. Apel, S., Kästner, C.: On overview of feature-oriented software development. J. Object Technol. **8**(5), 49–84 (2009)
5. Apel, S., Leich, T., Rosenmüller, M., Saake, G.: Feature C++: on the symbiosis of feature-oriented and aspect-oriented programming. In: GPCE 2005, pp. 125–140 (2005)
6. Appeltauer, M., Hirschfeld, R., Haupt, M., Lincke, J., Perscheid, M.: A comparison of context-oriented programming languages. In: COP 2009, pp. 1–6 (2009)
7. Appeltauer, M., Hirschfeld, R., Haupt, M., Masuhara, H.: ContextJ: context-oriented programming with Java. Comput. Softw. **28**(1), 272–292 (2011)
8. Appeltauer, M., Hirschfeld, R., Masuhara, H.: Improving the development of context-dependent Java application with ContextJ. In: COP 2009 (2009)
9. Appeltauer, M., Hirschfeld, R., Masuhara, H., Haupt, M., Kawauchi, K.: Event-specific software composition in context-oriented programming. In: Baudry, B., Wohlstadter, E. (eds.) SC 2010. LNCS, vol. 6144, pp. 50–65. Springer, Heidelberg (2010). doi:10.1007/978-3-642-14046-4_4
10. Aracic, I., Gasiunas, V., Mezini, M., Ostermann, K.: An overview of CaesarJ. In: Rashid, A., Aksit, M. (eds.) Transactions on Aspect-Oriented Software Development I. LNCS, vol. 3880, pp. 135–173. Springer, Heidelberg (2006). doi:10.1007/11687061_5
11. Bracha, G., Cook, W.: Mixin-based inheritance. In: OOPSLA 1990, pp. 303–311 (1990)
12. Cappiello, C., Comuzzi, M., Mussi, E., Pernici, B.: Context management for adaptive information systems. Electron. Notes Theoret. Comput. Sci. **146**, 69–84 (2006)
13. Cardozo, N., González, S., Mens, K., Van Der Straeten, R., Vallejos, J., D'Hondt, T.: Semantics for consistent activation in context oriented systems. Inf. Softw. Technol. **58**, 71–94 (2015)

14. Cardozo, N., De Meuter, W., Mens, K., González, S.: Features on demand. In: VaMoS 2014 (2014)
15. Ceri, S., Daniel, F., Facca, F.M., Matera, M.: Model driven engineering of active context-awareness. World Wide Web **10**, 387–413 (2007)
16. Costanza, P., D'Hondt, T.: Feature description for context-oriented programming. In: DSPL 2008 (2008)
17. Costanza, P., Hirschfeld, R.: Language constructs for context-oriented programming - an overview of ContextL. In: Dynamic Language Symposium (DLS 2005), pp. 1–10 (2005)
18. Dardenne, A., van Lamsweerde, A., Fickas, S.: Goal-directed requirements acquisition. Sci. Comput. Program. **20**, 3–50 (1993)
19. Desmet, B., Vallejos, J., Costanza, P., De Meuter, W., D'Hondt, T.: Context-Oriented Domain Analysis. In: Kokinov, B., Richardson, D.C., Roth-Berghofer, T.R., Vieu, L. (eds.) CONTEXT 2007. LNCS (LNAI), vol. 4635, pp. 178–191. Springer, Heidelberg (2007). doi:10.1007/978-3-540-74255-5_14
20. Elliott, C., Hudak, P.: Functional reactive animation. In: ICFP 1997, pp. 263–273 (1997)
21. González, S., Cardozo, N., Mens, K., Cádiz, A., Libbrecht, J.-C., Goffaux, J.: Subjective-C: bringing context to mobile platform programming. In: Malloy, B., Staab, S., Brand, M. (eds.) SLE 2010. LNCS, vol. 6563, pp. 246–265. Springer, Heidelberg (2011). doi:10.1007/978-3-642-19440-5_15
22. González, S., Mens, K., Cádiz, A.: Context-oriented programming with the ambient object systems. J. Univ. Comput. Sci. **14**(20), 3307–3332 (2008)
23. González, S., Mens, K., Colācious, M., Cazzola, W.: Context traits: dynamic behaviour adaptation through run-time trait recomposition. In: AOSD 2013, pp. 209–220 (2013)
24. Henrichsen, K., Indulska, J.: A software engineering framework for context-aware pervasive computing. In: PERCOM 2004 (2004)
25. Hirschfeld, R., Costanza, P., Haupt, M.: An introduction to context-oriented programming with ContextS. In: Lämmel, R., Visser, J., Saraiva, J. (eds.) GTTSE 2007. LNCS, vol. 5235, pp. 396–407. Springer, Heidelberg (2008). doi:10.1007/978-3-540-88643-3_9
26. Hirschfeld, R., Costanza, P., Nierstrasz, O.: Context-oriented programming. J. Object Technol. **7**(3), 125–151 (2008)
27. Jacobson, I., Christerson, M., Jonsson, P., Övergaard, G.: Object-Oriented Software Engineering: A Use Case Driven Approach. Pearson Education, New Delhi (1992)
28. Jacobson, I., Ng, P.-W.: Aspect-Oriented Software Development with Use Cases. Pearson Education, New Delhi (2005)
29. Kamina, T., Aotani, T., Masuhara, H.: EventCJ: a context-oriented programming language with declarative event-based context transition. In: AOSD 2011, pp. 253–264 (2011)
30. Kamina, T., Aotani, T., Masuhara, H.: Introducing composite layers in EventCJ. IPSJ Trans. Program. **6**(1), 1–8 (2013)
31. Kamina, T., Aotani, T., Masuhara, H.: Mapping context-dependent requirements to event-based context-oriented programs for modularity. In: Workshop on Reactivity Events and Modularity (REM 2013) (2013)
32. Kamina, T., Aotani, T., Masuhara, H.: Generalized layer activation mechanism through contexts and subscribers. In: MODULARITY 2015, pp. 14–28 (2015)
33. Kamina, T., Aotani, T., Masuhara, H., Tamai, T.: Context-oriented software engineering: a modularity vision. In MODULARITY 2014, pp. 85–98 (2014)

34. Kang, K.C., Cohen, S.G., Hess, J.A., Novak, W.E., Spencer Peterson, A.: Feature-oriented domain analysis (FODA) feasibility study. Technical report CMU/SEI-90-TR-21, Software Engineering Institute, Carnegie Mellon University (1990)

35. Keays, R., Rakotonirainy, A.: Context-oriented programming. In: MobiDE 2003, pp. 9–16 (2003)

36. Kiczales, G., Hilsdale, E., Hugunin, J., Kersten, M., Palm, J., Griswold, W.G.: An overview of AspectJ. In: Knudsen, J.L. (ed.) ECOOP 2001. LNCS, vol. 2072, pp. 327–354. Springer, Heidelberg (2001). doi:10.1007/3-540-45337-7_18

37. Koppen, C., Störzer, M.: PCDiff: attacking the fragile pointcut problem. In: European Interactive Workshop on Aspects in Software (2004)

38. Lapouchnian, A., Mylopoulos, J.: Modeling domain variability in requirements engineering with contexts. In: Laender, A.H.F., Castano, S., Dayal, U., Casati, F., Oliveira, J.P.M. (eds.) ER 2009. LNCS, vol. 5829, pp. 115–130. Springer, Heidelberg (2009). doi:10.1007/978-3-642-04840-1_11

39. Liaskos, S., Lapouchnian, A., Yu, Y., Yu, E., Mylopoulos, J.: On goal-based variability acquisition and analysis. In: RE 2006, pp. 79–88 (2006)

40. Liu, L., Yu, E.: Designing information systems in social context: a goal and scenario modelling approach. Information Systems 29(2), 187–203 (2004)

41. Parnas, D.L.: On the criteria to be used in decomposing systems into modules. Commun. ACM 15(12), 1053–1058 (1972)

42. Prehofer, C.: Feature-oriented programming: a fresh look at objects. In: Akşit, M., Matsuoka, S. (eds.) ECOOP 1997. LNCS, vol. 1241, pp. 419–443. Springer, Heidelberg (1997). doi:10.1007/BFb0053389

43. Rashid, A., Sawyer, P., Moreira, A., Araújo, J.: Early aspects: a model for aspect-oriented requirements engineering. In: RE 2002, pp. 199–202 (2002)

44. Saliber, D., Dey, A.K., Abowd, G.D.: The context toolkit: aiding the development of context-enabled applications. In: CHI 1999, pp. 434–441 (1999)

45. Salifu, M., Nuseibeh, B., Rapanotti, L., Tun, T.T.: Using problem descriptions to represent variability for context-aware applications. In: VaMoS 2007 (2007)

46. Salifu, M., Yu, Y., Nuseibeh, B.: Specifying monitoring and switching problems in context. In: RE 2007, pp. 211–220 (2007)

47. Salvaneschi, G., Ghezzi, C., Pradella, M.: ContextErlang: A language for distributed context-aware self-adaptive applications. Sci. Comput. Program. 102(1), 20–43 (2014)

48. Schärli, N., Ducasse, S., Nierstrasz, O., Black, A.P.: Traits: composable units of behaviour. In: Cardelli, L. (ed.) ECOOP 2003. LNCS, vol. 2743, pp. 248–274. Springer, Heidelberg (2003). doi:10.1007/978-3-540-45070-2_12

49. Sutcliffe, A., Fickas, S., Sohlberg, M.K.M.: PC-RE: a method for personal and contextual requirements engineering with some experience. Requirements Eng. 11(3), 157–173 (2006)

50. Takeyama, F., Chiba, S.: Implementing feature interactions with generic feature modules. In: Binder, W., Bodden, E., Löwe, W. (eds.) SC 2013. LNCS, vol. 8088, pp. 81–96. Springer, Heidelberg (2013). doi:10.1007/978-3-642-39614-4_6

51. Vallejos, J., González, S., Costanza, P., De Meuter, W., D'Hondt, T., Mens, K.: Predicated generic functions: enabling context-dependent method dispatch. In: Baudry, B., Wohlstadter, E. (eds.) SC 2010. LNCS, vol. 6144, pp. 66–81. Springer, Heidelberg (2010). doi:10.1007/978-3-642-14046-4_5

Developing and Verifying Response Specifications in Hierarchical Event-Based Systems

Cynthia Disenfeld$^{(\boxtimes)}$ and Shmuel Katz

Department of Computer Science,
Technion - Israel Institute of Technology, Haifa, Israel
{cdisenfe,katz}@cs.technion.ac.il

Abstract. We introduce a CEGAR-based compositional verification technique for verifying response guarantees and finding the necessary assumptions of the response specification about event detectors in hierarchical event-based systems. By taking advantage of the structure of such systems, only the relevant event specifications are considered, and from these only a part of their specifications is learnt as response assumptions. Whenever a spurious counterexample is found (i.e., the abstract counterexample to a response guarantee property is not consistent with the event specifications), our technique modularly finds the necessary refinements that induce state splitting and add fairness constraints to avoid the counterexample automatically. Eventually, either the response guarantee is proved or a real counterexample is found. In addition, new techniques are presented for more feasible spuriousness checking of counterexamples of liveness response guarantees, and to avoid including unnecessary parts of the event detector alphabet in the model of a response.

1 Introduction

According to [25], reactive systems are activated by the outside world, and they respond and interact with the environment. These outside world occurrences can be thought of as *primitive events* that are immediately detected. In CEP (Complex Event Processing) [21,32], primitive events may occur at different sources, are processed by *event processing agents/detectors* that may trigger new events, which are finally consumed by different *event consumers*. Event detectors observe the system and environment to identify when an event occurs, and can build more complex event occurrences by detecting sequences, filtering, aggregating information, etc. Events have been combined in other software paradigms such as object-oriented programming (OOP) or aspect-oriented programming (AOP) [30]. In [8], event detectors were introduced in the context of AOP so that they can gather information, be hierarchically composed, and triggered (detect an event occurrence) depending on the lower-level events detected and internal state. Event detectors do not directly influence the underlying system during their evaluation and change only their local variables until the event is detected; then the detection is announced

© Springer International Publishing Switzerland 2016
S. Chiba et al. (Eds.): ToMC I, LNCS 9800, pp. 41–79, 2016.
DOI: 10.1007/978-3-319-46969-0_2

and parameter values (possibly including gathered information) are exposed to other event detectors *and* responses that can change the system. Here we consider event detectors and responses as in [8] for hierarchical event-based systems.

In this work we propose a reusable compositional verification technique and associated tool called DaVeRS (Developing and Verifying Response Specifications) that under certain assumptions is fully-automated. DaVeRS can verify properties of responses and learn the necessary assumptions about event detectors that allow a successful proof using model checking. The technique takes advantage of the event specifications and their hierarchical structure to check responses modularly using a compositional CEGAR-like (Counterexample Guided Abstraction Refinement) [11] approach combined with an assume-guarantee mechanism. Assuming that the specifications of the events are correct, the system either learns sufficient assumptions about the event detectors to prove the response guarantee being considered, or shows a counterexample sequence of states that violates the desired guarantee and is consistent with all event specifications.

At each step the response and an abstraction of the relevant event detector specifications is considered. Appropriate refinements are obtained when the property is not proven, and we can show that the problem is the current abstraction (and not the actual system). In this case, the counterexample found for the abstract system is called *spurious* relative to the concrete version.

This work encourages modularity on two levels. First, the result of using our abstract-refinement approach yields a minimal collection of events and conjuncts from their specifications that are needed to verify key properties of a response. This allows the isolation of responses and (only) needed event detectors into reusable modules in a library. Second, as will be shown, the techniques applied are themselves modular, involving checks of many small models, rather than an (unfeasible) global model check.

We also introduce two crucial optimizations, that, as seen in the evaluation section, can often make this approach feasible. In order to compare our abstract counterexample to each event detector separately–essential for the modularity described above, it seems necessary to have all of the shared variables among event detectors present in the abstract model to be checked. This would guarantee that any restrictions to those variables that follow from one event detector will be taken into account when we check the counterexample against another detector. We show that this approach (used in related work) is unnecessary overkill, and present a compositional approach that only adds variables and restrictions as absolutely needed. As shown in Sect. 6, this approach leads to significantly improved performance in many cases. We also show new techniques for checking spuriousness and refining liveness properties without the repeated unwinding of the abstract loop used in previous works. These new techniques are also relevant for other compositional CEGAR approaches where the concrete model is finite.

Therefore, the main contributions of this work are:

– Presenting a set of basic assumptions and formalization of reactive systems with hierarchical event specifications as the parallel composition of finite fair discrete systems so that a compositional CEGAR approach can be applied.

– Introducing an alphabet refinement optimization (applicable to other compositional CEGAR approaches as well) to obtain more accurate refinements and avoid redundant iterations.
– Showing an instrumentation-based technique for checking spuriousness of liveness property counterexamples that avoids unfolding an abstract counterexample a very large number of times.
– Including new techniques to find and refine the model with liveness properties.

Note that we consider responses, but the technique is also applicable to a complex event detector that depends on lower-level detectors and primitive events.

We have implemented a tool – DaVeRS – using the tools presented in this paper to evaluate our ideas over different case studies.

Although most of the paper is devoted to the internal operation of the tool, note that this insight is not needed by a typical user. Only the assume-guarantee specifications of the event detectors and the desired guarantees of the responses, and how they react to detected events must be provided. The DaVeRS tool is then completely automatic.

As a running example, we consider the response that adds a helicopter mission in a Car Crash Crisis Management System (CCCMS) [31]. This response depends, among other conditions, on the occurrence of an accident with serious injuries, ambulances not being close enough or being unable to access the location of the crisis, and weather conditions allowing helicopter flight in the area. Applying formal verification allows proving important properties such as "the helicopter mission will always be proposed whenever the necessary conditions hold", "a helicopter will not be sent whenever an ambulance would arrive sooner", and others, thus improving system reliability.

Our case studies include several guarantees of the CCCMS system, a Discount response depending on a library of complex event detectors determining different marketing strategies, and a set of responses and event detectors related to security concerns in an email application. These examples illustrate the application of the techniques in different contexts. Input files and iteration examples of the case studies are available at a website[1].

Section 2 presents the background and basic definitions to understand our model of events and responses, and modular verification and CEGAR techniques. Section 3 presents the basic assumptions and the formalization which allow us to represent hierarchical reactive systems as parallel components and thus use a compositional CEGAR approach. Section 4 explains the methodology, expanding on how each CEGAR-step is applied in our context. In Sects. 5 and 6, some implementation details, the evaluation, results and discussion are presented. Section 7 presents related work and Sect. 8 concludes.

---

[1] http://www.cs.technion.ac.il/ssdl/research/davers.

2   Background and Basic Definitions

2.1   LTL

For specifications describing computations along time, we use Linear Temporal Logic (LTL).

Given a Kripke structure $M = \langle S, I, R, L \rangle$ over a set of atomic propositions AP with:

– S is the set of states
– $I \subseteq S$ is the set of initial states
– $R \subseteq S \times S$ is the transition relation
– $L : S \rightarrow 2^{AP}$, i.e. the atomic propositions that hold at each state

A state s satisfies an atomic proposition p in AP if and only if $p \in L(s)$. The semantics of the boolean operators is as expected, for example, a state s satisfies $\varphi \wedge \psi$ if and only s satisfies φ and also s satisfies ψ.

A path in the Kripke structure is a sequence $\pi = s_0 s_1 \ldots$ such that $s_0 \in I$ (s_0 is an initial state), and for every i, $(s_i, s_{i+1}) \in R$ (there is a transition according to the transition relation).

In addition to boolean operators, formulas can be built with temporal operators. For example,

– $\mathbf{X}\varphi$ (At the next state φ).
– $\mathbf{G}\varphi$ (From now on, globally φ).
– $\mathbf{F}\varphi$ (Eventually φ).

The semantics of these operators is given by the satisfaction relation ($\vDash$). Given a path $\pi = \pi_0, \pi_1, \ldots$ and i representing a state in the path (π_i):

– $(\pi, i) \vDash \mathbf{X}\varphi$ if and only if $(\pi, i+1) \vDash \varphi$ (the path starting from the next state satisfies φ).
– $(\pi, i) \vDash \mathbf{G}\varphi$ if and only if for all $j \geq i$ $(\pi, j) \vDash \varphi$.
– $(\pi, i) \vDash \mathbf{F}\varphi$ if and only if exists $j \geq i$ $(\pi, j) \vDash \varphi$.

Given a model M and an LTL formula φ, φ holds in M if and only if for every path π in M, $(\pi, 0) \vDash \varphi$. That is, every path starting from the initial states satisfies the given formula.

In Sect. 4.6, we will also use the path quantifiers $\mathbf{A}$ (for every path) and $\mathbf{E}$ (exists path), used in the branching version of temporal logic. Similarly to first order logic quantifiers ($\forall$ and $\exists$), for any formula φ, $\mathbf{A}\varphi$ is equivalent to $\neg\mathbf{E}\neg\varphi$. Formulas in LTL must be satisfied by every path, so they can be considered as having an implicit $\mathbf{A}$ path quantifier at the beginning, and do not include explicit path quantifiers.

Given an LTL formula φ, it is possible to build a state machine containing every possible path satisfying the formula [13]. This state machine is called the *tableau* of φ.

We will consider Kripke structures with fairness constraints ($\mathcal{F}$) which partition the states between those fair and unfair, and the language of the state machine will be given by the *fair* paths (containing infinite fair states) only. For example, the tableau of the formula $\mathbf{F}\,p$ is seen in Fig. 1. In the graphic, p does not hold in the first state (s_1), p holds in the second one (s_2), and p does not hold in the third one (s_3). s_1 and s_2 are initial states, and s_2 and s_3 are the fair states (indicated by the double circle). A path is said to be fair if it has infinite fair states. For example, the path $s_1 s_2 s_3 s_3 s_3 \ldots$ is a fair path (infinite times in s_3) while the path $s_1 s_1 s_1 \ldots$ is not fair (and in particular it does not satisfy $\mathbf{F}\,p$). The fairness constraints can be given by explicitly enumerating the fair states, or by a propositional formula φ so that a state is fair if and only if it satisfies φ.

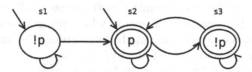

Fig. 1. Fairness example

2.2   Events

We distinguish between event occurrences and their detection. Following the definition of [21]: "An *event* is an occurrence within a particular system or domain; it is something that has happened, or is contemplated as having happened in that domain". We call these *event occurrences* to distinguish them from the programming entities or modules, termed *event detectors*, that analyze and announce complex event occurrences. Primitive event occurrences are immediately detected (without a separate detector).

Examples of events detected in a CCCMS are: "a car crash has just been announced", "an electric storm has begun in the area", "a fire just started from one of the cars in the accident", "there are now no helicopters available", etc. The first three could be considered as primitive input events. A detector of the last event would need to track assignment and release of helicopters from other tasks in order to detect when none are available.

There are several works combining events with existing programming paradigms [3,8,20,22,28,34]. In this case, primitive events are given by the base system (or responses). For example, there could be a system with a module WeatherAnalyzer responsible for analyzing weather conditions and broadcasting particular situations. The primitive event "an electric storm has begun in the area" in such a system would be given by "the base system has a method call to broadcast(electric storm) by WeatherAnalyzer".

Event detectors can update their internal state depending on lower-level event detectors. When an event detector announces detection of an event occurrence (in our version, by executing a *trigger* operation), other detectors and responses can react. This could be implemented by a broadcast mechanism or by having relevant event modules "listening" for the detection of the event. This implementation detail is not treated here.

Another issue to consider is the event duration. Based on [8], two main approaches are (1) event detectors are reevaluated within each response and between responses (2) given the events detected at a certain point, all responses are applied (no matter if some response may disable the event detection or change the data that affects another response).

The first approach is the one following AspectJ semantics, where an aspect may change the joinpoint matching depending on dynamic information. The second approach may be easier to understand (if the event is detected then no matter which other responses are activated, every response reacting to it will be applied), but does not capture the changes done by other responses. Thus, in this work, we consider the first semantics in the context of reactive systems: at each location of the base system or response where primitive events could occur, the different event detectors are evaluated, thus determining whether a response reacting to an event detector should be applied.

Note that in AspectJ [29], the main language used to express aspects in Java, joinpoints given by a method call or a method execution could last an interval of time (e.g., from the time the method is called until it returns). In [33], a fine grained joinpoint model is presented so that each joinpoint takes an instant of time. That is, there is a joinpoint for the actual call, and a different one for the returning point of a method. Between the two possible semantics of primitive events (region-in-time or point-in-time), we will consider primitive events as those given by the point-in-time joinpoint model [33]. This removes any ambiguity regarding when complex event detectors should be evaluated, while still allowing programs considering the region-in-time semantics to be translated to this model.

Specifications of event detectors (called *event specifications*) [17] include assumptions about the system and underlying events, where exactly the event should be detected, and what is expected about the information exposed by the event detector. Primitive event specifications do not assume anything about lower-level events, but provide the event name and exposed information abstractions to be used by higher-level event specifications. In [17], it was observed that expressing how different lower-level event detector sequences affect the current event detector may be easier with state machines or regular expressions. Thus, to represent event assumptions and guarantees including both state machine definitions and LTL properties, event specifications can be formalized by $E = \langle X, I, T, P \rangle$ where X is the set of variables (including those representing the event detection, lower-level events detected, and internal state), I and T are the initial and transition relation constraints, and P is the set of LTL constraints including the event assumptions and guarantees (possibly including safety and liveness formulas). When event detectors are being verified the assumption is used to check the event guarantees. Here we assume that events have already been verified and consider LTL assumptions and guarantees together in P.

Among the variables in X, the subset representing event detectors and their exposed information will be called the interface alphabet of E, since these are the variables possibly affecting or affected by other event specifications.

An abstraction of the event specification E_i that does not add any constraints is given by $E' = \langle \emptyset, \text{TRUE}, \text{TRUE}, \emptyset \rangle$. We denote this as $\text{TRUE}(E_i)$.

By considering event specifications, we are abstracting from the implementation. Thus, the results of our technique are sound (to be justified by the correctness proofs), although not complete. That is, if the verification technique succeeds assuming correct event specifications, then the property holds for the actual event implementations. However, a counterexample may seem consistent with all event specifications (really contradicting the desired guarantee), but if more precise event specifications were available, it might be shown spurious. One advantage of using specifications instead of the actual implementation is that the ideas are relevant both while the software is being modeled (because specifications are used rather than implemented code) and when an implementation is already available (where typical model extraction software is used [14,16]). Other advantages of using event specifications are: (1) proof reusability on any system satisfying the event detectors' and responses' assumptions, (2) abstraction from implementation details, (3) readability of the learnt assumptions, and (4) finer-grained specification dependency understanding: since the learnt assumptions represent a subset of the event specifications needed to prove a property, we can see which event detectors and which parts of their specification may affect that property.

2.3 Responses

In reactive systems, not only the event detectors are relevant but also how the different responses (event consumers) affect the system. In this work we consider responses similar to aspects in AOP. Similar to aspects, responses are activated whenever an interesting event is detected. For instance, given the detection of the event representing reaching a call to a method m, a response can add functionality before or after m or even override the execution of m with its own implementation. Differently from event detectors, responses can affect the execution flow and state of the system.

We will consider responses given by: $A = \langle X_B, X_R, ED, M, P, P_{Ev}, R \rangle$ such that

- X_B is the set of variables of the underlying system.
- X_R is the set of variables local to the response (e.g. response program counter, internal fields).
- ED is a propositional logic formula (on X_B) expressing when the response is applied, i.e., to which event detector it reacts.
- M is a finite state machine representing the actual response. It includes initial response states for each activation, a response transition relation, and return states.
- P is an LTL formula (on X_B) expressing the base system assumption.

- P_{Ev} is a combination of state machine definitions and LTL formulas (Sect. 2.2) expressing the response assumption about underlying events.
- R is an LTL formula (on $X_B \cup X_R$) expressing the guarantee.

We will note the partial specification of a response A as $Spec_A = \langle P, R \rangle$.

2.4   Modular verification

Since reactive systems consist of event detectors and responses, we extend the ideas presented in MAVEN [24] for verifying aspects and adapt and change them to this more general setting while introducing new techniques. In particular the methodology allows the correctness proof of a response guarantee to be reused for different systems by including in its specification an assumption about the underlying system, an assumption about the underlying event detectors, and the guarantee it is expected to satisfy.

As in [24], verification of a response relative to its specification first constructs a model containing the assumption (P) about the base system augmented with the response model given by the state machine (M). This involves *weaving* the response to the tableau of that assumption at the necessary locations: that is, adding the necessary transitions from the tableau of the assumption (T_P) to the response and back at the correct places. The obtained model ($T_P + M$) represents every possible path satisfying the response assumptions augmented with the response behavior and is used to model check temporal logic guarantee properties about the resulting system. If the model check succeeds, the guarantee is true for any system satisfying the response assumptions when the response is woven to it. The given composition does not include P_{Ev}, that is, it represents the response assumption with the response woven when no assumption about the underlying events is needed. In Sect. 3.2 we describe how the response assumption about the event detectors affects the composition.

2.5   CEGAR

CEGAR [11] is an automatic abstraction-refinement technique to verify systems where an overapproximation of the system is considered. The overapproximation represents an abstraction of the concrete system where any path belonging to the concrete system is represented in the abstract one, but more paths may belong as well (the model obtained gets simpler by abstracting from variable values and predicates affecting transitions). When the verification of the abstract system fails, either the counterexample is real or *spurious*, i.e., the counterexample was found because of the overapproximation and not because of the incorrectness of the concrete system. The abstract counterexample is simulated in the concrete model to identify whether the abstract model should be refined. When the counterexample is found spurious, the abstract system is automatically refined by adding information from the concrete system that makes the previous counterexample impossible in the refined version, and a new attempt to verify is initiated.

For example, given the concrete system in Fig. 2, and the property given by the LTL formula (1), a possible initial abstraction (Fig. 3) could include the predicates appearing in the formula. In the figure, each abstract state (a_i) represents a set of concrete states (c_j), e.g. the state a_2 in the abstract model represents both the states c_2 and c_3 of the concrete model. Since there is an edge from c_2 to c_3 in the concrete model, there is a self loop in a_2.

$$\mathbf{G}\,(x > 1.5 \implies \mathbf{F}\,(x = 0)) \tag{1}$$

In general, CEGAR techniques calculate the abstract transition relation, so that for every concrete path there exists an abstract path capturing the same states although the abstract model is less precise and contains spurious paths. When the property is checked in the abstract model, a counterexample is found: $\pi = a_0 a_1 a_2 a_2 a_2 ....$ This counterexample cannot occur in the concrete model (thus it is spurious) and using CEGAR, a refinement that avoids the counterexample is automatically found. For example, in this case, by splitting the state a_2 with the predicate $x = 3$, we obtain the model in Fig. 4 (the transition relation is updated according to the new states). Checking again the property, it is found to be satisfied. Note that in this case the refined model (Fig. 4) contains the same number of states as in the concrete version (Fig. 2). However, in general the number of states required for a CEGAR technique to reach a conclusion is much smaller than in the concrete model.

In this work, we will show how we build the abstract model for event and response specifications, how we verify whether a response property holds in the current abstraction, how given a counterexample we analyze spuriousness in new ways, and how we find the necessary refinements to start a new CEGAR cycle.

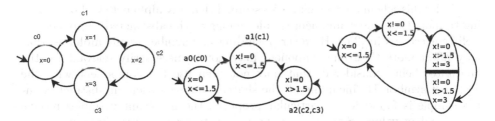

Fig. 2. Concrete model   **Fig. 3.** First abstraction   **Fig. 4.** Refined

Tools implementing CEGAR differ in their program representation for verification, techniques for detecting spuriousness and finding refinements, or the subset of temporal logic considered. Many of these tools interact with SAT or SMT (Satisfiability Modulo Theories) [6] solvers to check spuriousness and to find appropriate refinements. Both SAT and SMT solvers include a tool that obtains the unsat-core of an unsatisfiable set of formulas. The unsat-core is a minimal set of the original set sufficient to prove the model unsatisfiable.

When a counterexample to a safety formula is found in the abstract version, it is sound to consider a finite number of steps (n). Thus, it is enough to simulate the counterexample at most n steps in the concrete version to check whether it is spurious and in case it is, to find the necessary refinements (for example, using the unsat-core tool). The work in [11] shows that there is also a finite number of simulation steps necessary to simulate a liveness property counterexample to check spuriousness given by **unfolding** the loop of the abstract counterexample the maximum number of concrete states represented in an abstract state for each state in the loop. Then it is guaranteed that the worst case scenario of the length of the concrete loop matching the abstract one will be covered, but this leads to a bound which is often impractical. Here, we show a more efficient instrumentation approach to check spuriouness for liveness. Using it, we can efficiently detect whether the counterexample is spurious and find the necessary refinements.

2.6   Compositional CEGAR

There has been previous work applying CEGAR modularly, i.e. checking spuriousness and finding refinements considering one module (of a generalized alphabet parallel composition [35]) at a time. The generalized alphabet parallel composition of two components A and B allows the components to move to their next state asynchronously on non-shared symbols, and requires them to be able to synchronize (both take the same step) on shared symbols that need to be consistent in both components. We will show how hierarchical event-based systems (under certain assumptions) can be reduced to this formal model, allowing almost separate spuriousness checking of an abstract counterexample for each component.

Under this schema, previous work assumed that any alphabet symbol belonging to more than one component should belong to the abstracted component as well (correctness in [35]). However, including any symbol in the alphabet that may affect more than one conponent may not be necessarily relevant for the guarantee being considered, that may not even use the component with the alphabet symbol. By including all the shared symbols, when an abstract counterexample is found for a particular property, the irrelevant variables receive some random values. Since there is no reason to assume that these values are consistent with the component, abstract counterexamples are likely to be found spurious against components because of these arbitrary values, that will be eliminated by refinement. But such refinements are irrelevant for the guarantee being checked, and just delay finding relevant refinements. We will show how to apply CEGAR with only those shared symbols in the abstract version really necessary to ensure consistency, and evaluate the technique in the case studies.

3   Parallel Composition Representation

In this section we present the basic assumptions and formal model to be considered when an assume-guarantee strategy is applied for hierarchical event-based systems.

3.1   Basic Assumptions

The ideas in this paper, though shown for CCCMS, Discount and Security case studies, are applicable to any system where there is a distinction between event detectors and responses. Event detectors observe the system to indicate when interesting things occur. They can be hierarchically composed and have an internal state, but they do not change the state of the underlying system while evaluating. Responses react to an event detected, and may change the state of the underlying system or its control flow. In order to use DaVeRS and apply our approach, correct event specifications (Sect. 2.2), the response state machine and a *partial response specification* (given by the assumption about the base system and desired guarantee) should be available. The response assumption about the events is learnt by our technique.

3.2   Formal Model

Following MAVEN [24], applying verification to a response when only primitive events are considered is done by weaving the response to the tableau of the response assumption and checking whether the response guarantee holds.

Given that complex event evaluations do not affect the underlying system (besides by possibly being detected and causing the response to be applied), the evaluation stage can be modelled as occurring instantaneously, thus having at the same state all the evaluations of event detectors. In this *summarized* version, for each current state of the underlying system and lower-level event detectors, there is one state representing the result of these internal calculations. Given a model of a non-summarized event specification, the summarized version can be obtained by calculating the closure from each possible starting event evaluation point till the end of event evaluation, thus obtaining the summary of changes in one state. When the response guarantee does not have the **X** (next) operator and does not refer to the intermediate states within event evaluation, it can be shown that the summarized and non-summarized version of the event detectors include the same paths (ignoring internal event evaluation states) thus equivalently satisfying LTL formulas with the given conditions.

For example, the event detector indicating that "the crisis location has problematic access", may require some internal calculations and checks. In the summarized version, every state where the lower-level events detected and system state would cause the event detector to be triggered, includes the atomic proposition representing its detection (and every state that would not cause its detection, does not include the atomic proposition).

Now, since every event evaluation is considered instantaneous, a process algebra notation can be used to justify the techniques. By applying a generalized parallel composition ($\|$) over the shared symbols to the event specifications we obtain a model in which at each state – according to the current state of the underlying system, current state of the event detectors, and primitive events detected – we can see which complex events are detected, what information is exposed, and how their internal state is updated.

The generalized parallel composition [35] allows synchronizing on part of the symbols (those shared among components), and interleaved behavior on the remaining ones. If two components share the symbols in X, to apply a transition influencing a symbol in X in one component, the other component must also be able to apply the transition on that symbol. For symbols outside X, the component behaviors are interleaved.

We will note the event specification composition by $E_1\|\ldots\|E_N$ where each E_i is the event specification of the event i.

We want to consider those paths of the system consistent with the event specifications. To do so, we consider the model $(T_P + M)\|E_1\|\ldots\|E_N$, which represents every path satisfying the response assumption with the response woven $(T_P + M)$ (Sect. 2.4) such that it is also consistent with every event specification $(\ldots\|E_1\|\ldots\|E_N)$.

3.3   Running Example

Figure 5 shows a fragment of the library of event detectors relevant to the CCCMS example. The arrows represent dependencies including *temporally* (if e_i has occurred in the past) and *non-occurrence* ones (depending on another event detector not occurring). For instance, the event *shouldSendHeli* depends on the event *problematicAccess* being detected and on *badWeather* **not** being detected at the current state; while *helicoptersAvailable* depends on the history of helicopters that left (*helicopterSent*) and returned (*helicopterBack*). When a box contains multiple names, the first represents the event detection and the rest represent the exposed information. Boxes without exiting arrows represent primitive events.

The response that adds the helicopter mission is activated whenever *shouldSendHeli* is detected (based on a use case of [31]), that is: there is a crisis with serious injuries in a certain location (*shouldGoToLocation*) not easily accessible by normal transportation (*problematicAccess*), the weather conditions do not constrain helicopter flying in the area (*not badWeather*), there are helicopters available (*helicoptersAvailable*) and a response was obtained (*phoneCompanyResponse*) validating the witness information (*phoneCompanyIsValidated*). Each of the complex event detectors has its specification regarding its detection and exposed information. For example, the specification of *badWeather* indicates that this event is detected if and only if there is a snow storm or extreme turbulence.

Following the formal representation of event specifications in Sect. 2.2, the specification of *badWeather* would be given by $Spec_{badWeather} = \langle X, I, T, P \rangle$ where:

– $X = \{badWeather, snowStorm, extremeTurbulence\}$ (i.e. all the variables representing the detection or the lower-level events and exposed information the specification directly depends on).

– I and T are TRUE

– $P = \{\mathbf{G}\,(badWeather \iff (snowStorm \vee extremeTurbulence))\}$

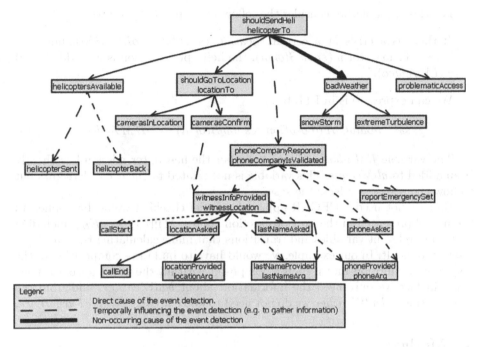

Fig. 5. Event dependency graph example

Note that when the event specifications are composed, we obtain at each state the information from all the event detectors, for instance, any state in the composition including *shouldSendHeli* will also include ¬*badWeather*, ¬*snowStorm* and ¬*extremeTurbulence* (as if the evaluation of *badWeather* were instantaneous).

The event dependency graph illustrates the different components and the hierarchical nature of event-based systems. Each of the boxes will represent a component of a parallel composition, thus getting each component abstracted almost on its own (with only the essential interface from previously checked event detectors); and while in the CEGAR cycle, counterexample spuriousness checking and refinement finding will also be applied considering each component on its own (preserving modularity). The actual input to our technique is the response and the set of event specifications. Since each event specification includes the variables of the lower-level event detectors it depends on, this hierarchy can be inferred automatically.

The following response reacts to *shouldSendHeli* and represents that whenever a helicopter should be sent to a certain location *crisisLocation*, the actual mission of sending an helicopter to that location is added to all the missions to be performed.

```
Response addHelicopterMission
when(Location crisisLocation): shouldSendHeli(crisisLocation)
   allMisions.add(new SendHelicopterMission(crisisLocation));
```

For this example, we consider the following response guarantee:

"If there is a crisis at a certain location (*shouldGoToLocation*), but there is a snow storm (*snowStorm*), the helicopter mission is not added   (2) ($\neg HMAdded$)."

We can express this in LTL by

$$\mathbf{G}((shouldGoToLocation \wedge snowStorm) \rightarrow \neg HMAdded) \tag{3}$$

The variable *HMAdded* indicates whether the helicopter mission has already been added to *allMisions*. This variable is not related to the event detectors but to how the response affects the system.

Had we not used a CEGAR approach, model checking would be applied to the model presented in the previous section $((T_P + M)||E_1|| \ldots ||E_N)$, including multiple irrelevant variables and transitions that make calculating the transition relation difficult. In our example, we would have to build the composition of the response assumption and response composed with all the event specifications, when in fact we only need the information about *badWeather*, and from the specification of *badWeather* we do not need to know about *extremeTurbulence*.

4   Method

To avoid applying direct verification to the model in the previous section, the abstract model we consider is $(T_P + M)||E'_1|| \ldots ||E'_N$ where E'_i is an overapproximation of E_i (i.e. $I \rightarrow I'$, $T \rightarrow T'$, and $P' \subseteq P$) representing the assumption of the response A about E_i, and thus making the composition much simpler (at the first iteration $E'_i = \text{TRUE}(E_i)$ - as presented in Sect. 2.2). As long as these assumptions are refined (refining some E_i), since the $N+1$ components are composed, the refinement affects the paths of the augmented response model.

Given a system that satisfies the mentioned assumptions, a CEGAR-like algorithm can be applied (Algorithm 1). The input to the algorithm is the response definition (A) and partial response specification $\langle P, R \rangle$ (P initially not including any assumption about the event specifications, R the desired response guarantee), and the event specifications S.

Initially (line 1), we obtain from all the possible events those from which possible refinements may be obtained (Sect. 4.1), and (line 2) initialize E' with TRUE (every event specification abstraction is TRUE(E_i), in the first iteration $(T_P + M)||E' = (T_P + M)$). At each iteration, E' includes partial information obtained from the event specifications necessary to check the response. In line 4 we build the model and in line 5 we check whether it satisfies R (Sect. 4.2). Since the actual abstraction represents an overapproximation of the actual model to be checked, if it is satisfied with the current refinements, then it is satisfied in the actual model (line 6). Otherwise, in line 6 we check whether the counterexample is due to the abstraction (spurious) or real (Sect. 4.3). If found spurious (line 10), refinements to avoid the current abstract counterexample are obtained (Sect. 4.7). Otherwise, the counterexample is real (line 12) and the CEGAR cycle ends.

Algorithm 1. Compositional CEGAR for Hierarchical Reactive Systems

---

    input : $M, \langle P, R \rangle$: Response model and response partial specification
             $S : Set[E]$: Event Specification Library
    output: $satisfied?$: Indicates whether the response guarantee is guaranteed
             with the given assumptions so far
             E': Event specifications' abstraction
1 $S' = $ "get subset of relevant events from S";
2 $E' = $ TRUE;
3 **while** (True) **do**
4     $modelToCheck = (T_P + M) || E'$;
5   **if** $modelToCheck \vDash R$ **then**
6        $satisfied? = $ True;
7   **return**
8   **else**
9        $spurious? = $ "check spuriousness using S'";
10   **if** $spurious?$ **then** $E' = E' \cup$ "get spuriousness reasons" ;
11   **else**
12         $satisfied? = $ False;
13   **return**
14   **end**
15   **end**
16 **end**

At each step, the event specification abstractions (response assumption about the events) are refined by adding constraints to I, T, or P and refining X accordingly. Since P_{Ev} is an abstraction of the event specifications, at every step any path in $E_1 || \ldots || E_N$ is a path in P_{Ev}.

If every call to the model checker or SMT solver terminates (in reasonable time), the technique terminates: every iteration includes at least one refinement (if spurious) and there is a finite number of refinements (obtained from the event specifications). The technique is sound: if verification (after a number of refining iterations) succeded, then the guarantee indeed holds for the concrete model (every step preserves soundness).

When the CEGAR cycle ends, either the response guarantee holds (and the necessary assumptions about the event detectors have been obtained) or a real counterexample has been obtained.

On success, knowing the fine-grained dependencies (which part of which event specifications are required for a guarantee) allow us to change event detectors or specifications and know exactly which response guarantees are affected. Moreover, the assume-guarantee model used for response and event specifications implies that given any concrete system S, it is enough to check whether S satisfies the response assumption about the underlying system, and the learnt event assumptions required to prove the response guarantee (R) to assure that S *with* the response activated at the correct places will satisfy R.

On failure, due to the essential-alphabet strategy contribution (Sect. 4.3), in most cases only a few iterations are necessary to find that there is a real counterexample consistent with all the event specifications. This counterexample contains only the variables of the response and those included in the refinements. Then, the counterexample becomes easier to understand (there are fewer variables to be considered).

4.1   Relevant Events

The input contains a library of event specifications. However, not every event may be necessary to check the response guarantee and DaVeRS automatically considers only those potentially relevant. The only event specifications that may include relevant refinements are those sharing some alphabet symbol with the response and those affecting (directly or indirectly) these event detectors. Lower-level event detectors must be considered because the necessary refinements may be in their specifications.

All other event specifications do not share the alphabet symbols with the response nor affect higher-level events sharing some alphabet symbol with the response, and thus do not add any path restriction that would imply a refinement.

In our example, all the event detectors in the fragment of the library presented are relevant (affect the detection of *shouldSendHeli* and are potential sources of refinements to prove the guarantee). However, other events such as "fire started", "heat wave", "police at location" are not relevant according to the current definition: they do not affect *shouldSendHeli* or the event detectors relevant to the response guarantee.

4.2   Verification

To apply verification, the model $(T_P + M)||E'$ is built. $T_P + M$ is built as in Sect. 2.4. In each step, E' represents partial information of the event specifications, that is, $E'_1|| \ldots ||E'_N$. If E'_i contains LTL formulas, the state machine representation of these formulas is considered. Therefore, building the state machine $(T_P + M)||E'$ is done by including all the constraints of both $(T_P + M)$ and all the current response assumptions about the events (E').

The response guarantee is an LTL formula, thus can be checked for the built model with any LTL model checker.

Figure 6 shows the helicopter response model on its own and Fig. 7 shows the response model after weaving it to its assumption (that the base system does not itself add the helicopter mission). The response model indicates that whenever *shouldSendHeli* is detected, after that state the variable *allMissions* includes the helicopter mission. In the woven model (Fig. 7, as in line 4 of Algorithm 1), the system can remain at the initial state (performing actions irrelevant to our response) until *shouldSendHeli* is detected. At those locations the response is *woven*, and at the return state the execution continues from the base system where it should with the updated state. Note that this model is very simple (almost trivial): it does not include any information about the remaining events. Any atomic proposition not appearing can have any value.

Fig. 6. Response: Helicopter mission   **Fig. 7.** Assumption + Helicopter mission

In the given example, our desired property (Property (3)) is not initially satisfied: there could be a path where *shouldSendHeli* (which activates the response) is detected together with *shouldGoToLocation* and *snowStorm*, causing the response to be activated, even when there is a snow storm. The unexpected behavior is due to the initial overapproximation of the system that does not include (yet) the *indirect* connection where both *shouldSendHeli* and *snowStorm* cannot be detected in the same state.

4.3   Checking Spuriousness

As mentioned before (Sect. 2.6), contrary to previous work we allow the abstract version not to automatically include the concrete model alphabet. We will

---

Algorithm 2. Checking spuriousness - essential-shared alphabet

    input : $E_1, \ldots, E_n$: Event specifications
            $V_1, \ldots, V_n$: Variables determining the needed abstractions
            π: Abstract counterexample
    output: spurious: indicates whether π is spurious with $E_1 \| \ldots \| E_n$
1   prevAbstractModel = M_{True};
2   **for** i in 1..n **do**
3   currModel = prevAbstractModel —— E_i;
4   spurious = not "π is consistent with currModel";
5   **if** spurious **then** break;
6   **else** prevAbstractModel = "currModel abstracted to COI(currModel,
         $V_i \cup \Sigma_\pi$)" ;
7 **end**

---

call the strategy of including all the shared symbols of the concrete components in their abstractions as *full-shared alphabet strategy*, and the strategy we present as *essential-shared alphabet strategy*, i.e. we only include the symbols essential to prove the guarantee. When the abstract version does not contain all the shared symbols of the concrete components (the event specifications), and if no further steps are taken, a counterexample could be consistent with every event specification but not with their composition. For example, given $G\,(snowStorm \rightarrow badWeather)$ belonging to $Spec_{badWeather}$ (as in Sect. 3.3) and $G\,(shouldSendHeli \rightarrow \neg badWeather)$ in $Spec_{shouldSendHeli}$ (similarly specified), then there cannot be a state satisfying $shouldSendHeli \wedge snowStorm$. However, if the abstract version of the response does not include in its alphabet $badWeather$, then the problematic state is consistent with each event specification (for each modular check there is an assignment of $badWeather$ making the state possible), but not with their composition. The problem has to do with the shared alphabet among event specifications not being included in the abstract counterexample. Our approach to deal with this situation is to sequentially consider each event specification with a needed subset of the alphabet interface of other event specifications. That way, we can abstract the response alphabet (i.e. not include variables that do not affect the current guarantee).

Given an event specification sequence, we first compute $\{V_i\}$: V_0 is empty and V_i $(i > 0)$ contains V_{i-1} and the variables of E_i that some event specification appearing later in the sequence includes. The event specification sequence, $\{V_i\}$ (representing the variables to which each event model should be abstracted), and the abstract counterexample are the input to Algorithm 2 which checks spuriousness for the essential-shared alphabet strategy.

The first event specification of the sequence does not need to be composed with a previous event specification abstracted, thus *prevAbstractModel* is initialized as M_{True} (i.e., the model accepting every path). Every other event specification E_i is composed with the Cone of Influence (COI) [13] reduction of the previous model to the variables that may affect following events in the sequence.

When a model is given by a set of variables V (i.e. the set of states is every combination of the values of the variables in V), an initial constraint (which values are allowed for each variable at the initial states), and a transition relation constraint given by how each variable is affected by the values of the variables at the previous state (i.e. $v'_i = f_i\,(V)$, where v'_i represents the value of v_i at the next state), the Cone of Influence C of a set of variables $V' \subseteq V$ is the minimal set of variables such that:

- $V' \subseteq C$
- if for some $v_l \in C$, its f_l depends on v_j, then $v_j \in C$

Then, the COI reduction of the system is built considering only the variables in V' and the equations determining their next value. The COI reduction is obtained syntactically from the model definition. Therefore, it does not depend on the size of the model, but on the size of the model description, making it very feasible in practice. Moreover, due to the hierarchical structure of the event detectors, in general only a small set of variables will be required to be included in the abstraction.

At each step, we abstract $currModel$ (last composed with E_i) to the COI of V_i and the alphabet of the counterexample to guarantee that events appearing later in the sequence will be affected by the shared symbols appearing in the current event specification (when composed with the abstraction of the previous model).

If the counterexample is found spurious, then it is inconsistent with $currModel$, which contains the composition of the necessary interfaces with the last event specification considered. This model will be used later to find the appropriate refinements. In the worst case scenario, the COI reduction of the model is the actual model. If this is the case for all the event specifications till step i, then we are checking spuriousness against the actual composition of these event specifications. However, we are considering hierarchical reactive systems with multiple event detectors, and since not every event specification depends on every other event specification, the obtained model is much smaller than the full composition.

In our running example, $shouldSendHeli$ implies that there is not $badWeather$ (within the specification of $shouldSendHeli$).

With our algorithm (essential-shared alphabet), $badWeather$ does not belong to the initial alphabet. Then, in the first CEGAR cycle the counterexample is:

$$\pi = (\neg HMAdded), \begin{pmatrix} shouldSendHeli \\ shouldGoToLoc \\ snowStorm \\ \neg HMAdded \end{pmatrix}, \begin{pmatrix} shouldGoToLoc \\ snowStorm \\ HMAdded \end{pmatrix}$$

That is, the event $shouldSendHeli$ is detected in the second state of the abstract counterexample, and in the third state the helicopter mission is added to the set of missions. In the first iteration of Algorithm 2, the counterexample is checked with the specification of $shouldSendHeli$ as given (`prevAbstractModel` does not add any restrictions in the first iteration of Algorithm 2). Since the specification of $shouldSendHeli$ does not refer directly to $snowStorm$, the abstract counterexample is possible (not spurious so far), and `prevAbstractModel` is updated. Among the variables within the specification of $shouldSendHeli$, there is $badWeather$ which appears later in the sequence of events. Since $badWeather$ is part of the variables to calculate the COI reduction (it is required by a future event specification in the sequence, the property referring to $badWeather$ and $shouldSendHeli$ ($\mathbf{G}\,(shouldSendHeli \implies \neg badWeather)$) is preserved in `prevAbstractModel`. In the second iteration of the algorithm, the abstraction of the previous model is composed with the specification of $badWeather$. Checking the counterexample with the composition shows the abstract counterexample spurious. From this composition the necessary refinements will be obtained (Sect. 4.7): ($shouldSendHeli$ implies not $badWeather$, and $snowStorm$ implies $badWeather$) which prevent future counterexamples with $shouldSendHeli$ and $snowStorm$ in the same state.

Had we not used our optimization, variables shared among components would have been included in the abstract model, and the model checker would have given random values to those variables in the abstract counterexample, thus adding potentially irrelevant refinements. For example, given the following abstract counterexample

$$\pi = (\neg HMAdded), \begin{pmatrix} shouldSendHeli \\ shouldGoToLoc \\ \neg \mathbf{helicoptersAvailable} \\ snowStorm \\ \neg HMAdded \end{pmatrix}, \begin{pmatrix} shouldGoToLoc \\ snowStorm \\ HMAdded \end{pmatrix}$$

may add the refinement that there must be helicopters available for the event *shouldSendHeli* to be detected, but that refinement is irrelevant for the property being checked.

Event Ordering. In both approaches (full-shared, essential-shared alphabet) the order in which the event specifications are considered can significantly affect the performance. Since the goal is to find the refinements as soon as possible, we have observed that a good event ordering is a prioritized search such that starting from the response event detector, we next consider the root of the unexplored subtree in the event dependency graph with the greatest number of atomic predicates in common with the desired response guarantee.

4.4   Modular Approach - Correctness

This section is more technical and proves correctness of Algorithm 2.

Compositional CEGAR approaches in which the abstraction of the components includes the alphabet of the concrete components (without alphabet refinement) has been proven to be correct in [9] based on Lemma 1.

Lemma 1 (from [35]). *A path belongs to the parallel composition of a set of components if and only if its projection to the alphabet of each component C_i is a path in C_i.*

We have shown in Sect. 3.2 that our model represents hierarchical reactive systems as the parallel composition of the event specifications and the response augmented model, making those ideas applicable.

We now show correctness of our optimization for alphabet refinement, by showing that a path belongs to the alphabet of the composition of two components if it belongs to the COI reduction of the first one composed with the second one. This can then be easily extended to any number of components by induction.

We first present some auxiliary notations, definitions and propositions that we will use to prove the correctness of our approach.

Notation

- We will use M to represent any model.
- For any path π and alphabet Σ, $\pi \upharpoonright_\Sigma$ represents the path projected to include only the symbols appearing in Σ.
- For any model M and alphabet Σ, $M \upharpoonright_\Sigma$ represents M abstracted to the variables appearing in Σ.
- For any model M and alphabet Σ, $COI(M, \Sigma)$ represents the variables of M that belong to the cone of influence of Σ.
- Given a model M, path π, alphabet Σ, $[M]_\Sigma$ represents $M \upharpoonright_{COI(M,\Sigma)}$ and $[\pi]^M_\Sigma$ represents $\pi \upharpoonright_{COI(M,\Sigma)}$. The superscript representing the model will be omitted when clear.

Definition 1. *A path π over an alphabet Σ_π is consistent with a model M over an alphabet Σ_M if and only if there exists a path $\hat\pi \in M$ such that $\hat\pi \upharpoonright_{\Sigma_\pi} = \pi \upharpoonright_{\Sigma_M}$. $\hat\pi$ will be called the* witness *of π being consistent with M.*

The next two propositions are trivial but will be used to prove the correctness of our approach.

Proposition 1 expresses that for a path π and model M, if $\pi \in M$, taking the COI reduction of the path and of M with any alphabet, maintains the membership relation.

Proposition 1. *If π is a path of a model M, then for an alphabet Σ, $[\pi]^M_\Sigma$ is a path of $[M]_\Sigma$.*

This is a corollary from the theorem in [13]: Let f be a CTL* formula with atomic propositions in C (where $C = COI(M, Vars(f))$). Then $M \models f \iff [M]_{Vars(f)} \models f$.

Proposition 2 expresses that if a path belongs to the cone of influence reduction of a composition, then the path belongs to the cone of influence reduction of each component (restricted to the corresponding alphabet). This can be proven using a (weak) simulation relation among the two models.

Proposition 2. *Given a path π, two models M_1, M_2, and alphabet Σ, $\pi \in [M_1 \| M_2]_\Sigma \implies \pi \upharpoonright_{COI(M_i, \Sigma)} \in [M_i]_\Sigma$ for $i = 1, 2$.*

The following lemma explains why it is enough to consider the abstraction of the previous model with the concrete version of the current model to check whether an abstract path is consistent with the composition of two components.

Lemma 2. *Given M_1, M_2 two models and M_1', M_2' their respective overapproximations - not necessarily with the same alphabet, i.e. $\Sigma_{M_i'} \neq \Sigma_{M_i}$ - then, for any path π in $M_1' \| M_2'$, π is consistent with $M_1 \| M_2$ if and only if π is consistent with $[M_1]_{\Sigma_{M_2} \cup \Sigma_\pi} \| M_2$*

Proof. Let $M^{abs} = [M_1]_{\Sigma_{M_2} \cup \Sigma_\pi}$. Then, $M^{abs} \| M_2$ represents the composition of two components when using alphabet refinement.

Note that $\Sigma_{M^{abs}} = COI(M_1, \Sigma_{M_2} \cup \Sigma_\pi)$.

$\Rightarrow$) Assuming π is consistent with $M_1\|M_2$, we want to see that π is consistent with $M^{abs}\|M_2$.

Since π is consistent with $M_1\|M_2$, then there exists $\overline{\pi} \in M_1\|M_2$ such that $\overline{\pi}\lceil_{\Sigma_\pi} = \pi\lceil_{\Sigma_{M_1\|M_2}}$ (from the definition of *being consistent with*).

Since $\overline{\pi} \in M_1\|M_2$, then by the traces definition of composed components [35], $\overline{\pi}\lceil_{\Sigma_{M_1}} \in M_1$ and $\overline{\pi}\lceil_{\Sigma_{M_2}} \in M_2$. Therefore, $\overline{\pi}\lceil_{\Sigma_{M_1}}$ is a witness of π being consistent with M_1 and $\overline{\pi}\lceil_{\Sigma_{M_2}}$ is a witness of π being consistent with M_2.

We now show that $\boxed{\pi} = \overline{\pi}\lceil_{\Sigma_{M^{abs}}\cup\Sigma_{M_2}}$ (the witness of π being consistent with $M_1\|M_2$, restricted to the alphabet of $M^{abs}\|M_2$) is a witness for π being consistent with $M^{abs}\|M_2$.

1. We first show that $\boxed{\pi}$ is a trace of $M^{abs}\|M_2$, i.e. $\boxed{\pi}\lceil_{\Sigma_{M^{abs}}} \in M^{abs}$ and $\boxed{\pi}\lceil_{\Sigma_{M_2}} \in M_2$.

   $\boxed{\pi}\lceil_{\Sigma_{M^{abs}}} \in M^{abs}$:

   (a) $\boxed{\pi}\lceil_{\Sigma_{M^{abs}}} = \left(\overline{\pi}\lceil_{\Sigma_{M^{abs}}\cup\Sigma_{M_2}}\right)_{\lceil_{\Sigma_{M^{abs}}}} = \overline{\pi}\lceil_{\Sigma_{M^{abs}}}$ (by definition of $\boxed{\pi}$ and $\lceil$).

   (b) Since $\overline{\pi} \in M_1\|M_2$, $[\overline{\pi}]_{\Sigma_{M_2}\cup\Sigma_\pi}$ is a path in $[(M_1\|M_2)]_{\Sigma_{M_2}\cup\Sigma_\pi}$ (by Proposition 1).

   (c) Then, by Proposition 2, $([\overline{\pi}]_{\Sigma_{M_2}\cup\Sigma_\pi})\lceil_{COI(M_1,\Sigma_{M_2}\cup\Sigma_\pi)}$ is a path in $[M_1]_{\Sigma_{M_2}\cup\Sigma_\pi}$.

   (d) By definition, $([\overline{\pi}]_{\Sigma_{M_2}\cup\Sigma_\pi})\lceil_{COI(M_1,\Sigma_{M_2}\cup\Sigma_\pi)} = \overline{\pi}\lceil_{COI(M_1,\Sigma_{M_2}\cup\Sigma_\pi)} = \overline{\pi}\lceil_{\Sigma_{M^{abs}}}$.

   (e) From 1a and d, $\boxed{\pi}\lceil_{\Sigma_{M^{abs}}} = ([\overline{\pi}]_{\Sigma_{M_2}\cup\Sigma_\pi})\lceil_{COI(M_1,\Sigma_{M_2}\cup\Sigma_\pi)}$ and from 1c, $\boxed{\pi}\lceil_{\Sigma_{M^{abs}}}$ is a path in $[M_1]_{\Sigma_{M_2}\cup\Sigma_\pi} = M^{abs}$.

   $\boxed{\pi}\lceil_{\Sigma_{M_2}} \in M_2$:

   $\boxed{\pi}\lceil_{\Sigma_{M_2}} = \left(\overline{\pi}\lceil_{\Sigma_{M^{abs}}\cup\Sigma_{M_2}}\right)_{\lceil_{\Sigma_{M_2}}} = \overline{\pi}\lceil_{\Sigma_{M_2}}$. We already have that $\overline{\pi}\lceil_{\Sigma_{M_2}}$ is a witness of π being consistent with M_2. Therefore, $\boxed{\pi}\lceil_{\Sigma_{M_2}}$ is a witness of π being consistent with M_2.

2. We now show that $\boxed{\pi}\lceil_{\Sigma_\pi} = \pi\lceil_{\Sigma_{M^{abs}\|M_2}}$:

   – $\boxed{\pi}\lceil_{\Sigma_\pi} = \left(\overline{\pi}\lceil_{\Sigma_{M^{abs}}\cup\Sigma_{M_2}}\right)_{\lceil_{\Sigma_\pi}} = \left(\overline{\pi}\lceil_{\Sigma_{M^{abs}\|M_2}}\right)_{\lceil_{\Sigma_\pi}}$ by the definition of $\boxed{\pi}$.

   – $\left(\overline{\pi}\lceil_{\Sigma_{M^{abs}\|M_2}}\right)_{\lceil_{\Sigma_\pi}} = (\overline{\pi}\lceil_{\Sigma_\pi})\lceil_{\Sigma_{M^{abs}\|M_2}}$ by the definition of $\lceil$.

   – $(\overline{\pi}\lceil_{\Sigma_\pi})\lceil_{\Sigma_{M^{abs}\|M_2}} = \pi\lceil_{\Sigma_{M^{abs}\|M_2}}$ due to $\overline{\pi}$ being the witness of π being consistent with $M_1\|M_2$.

$\Leftarrow$) Assuming that π is consistent with $M^{abs}\|M_2$, we want to see that π is consistent with $M_1\|M_2$.

By assumption, there exists $\overline{\pi} \in M^{abs}\|M_2$ witness of π being consistent with $M^{abs}\|M_2$. Thus, $\overline{\pi}\lceil_{\Sigma_{M^{abs}}}$ belongs to M^{abs}. Since M^{abs} is an abstraction of M_1, there exists a concrete path $\overline{\pi}_1^c$ in M_1 such that restricted to

$COI\,(M_1, \Sigma_{M_2} \cup \Sigma_\pi)$ is equal to $\bar{\pi} \restriction_{\Sigma_{Mabs}}$, i.e. $[\bar{\pi}_1^c]\,\Sigma_{M_2 \cup \Sigma_\pi} = \bar{\pi} \restriction_{\Sigma_{Mabs}}$.
Let $\pi^c = (\bar{\pi}_1^c \times \bar{\pi})$, that is, the labels at each state are obtained from the current state at $\bar{\pi}_1^c$ and $\bar{\pi}$. From the way $\bar{\pi}_1^c$ was obtained, any shared symbols between the states of the two paths are consistent.
We will now show that π^c ils a witness of π being consistent with $M_1||M_2$.
$\pi^c \in M_1||M_2$: To prove this, we just need to prove that restricted to the corresponding alphabets it belongs to both components.

1. $\pi^c \restriction_{\Sigma_{M_1}}$ is equivalent to restricting to the variables of $\bar{\pi}_1^c$. By construction $\bar{\pi}_1^c \in M_1$, therefore $\pi^c \restriction_{\Sigma_{M_1}} \in M_1$.
2. $\pi^c \restriction_{\Sigma_{M_2}}$ is equivalent to considering $\bar{\pi} \restriction_{\Sigma_{M_2}}$. Since $\bar{\pi}$ is the witness of π being consistent with $M^{abs}||M_2$, $\bar{\pi} \restriction_{\Sigma_{M_2}}$ belongs to M_2.

$\pi^c \restriction_{\Sigma_\pi} = \pi \restriction_{\Sigma_{M_1||M_2}}$: Both sides of the equation are equal to π, thus the paths obtained by each restriction are equal. $\qquad\square$

Corollary 1. *Given n components $M_1, \ldots, M_n$ and their abstractions $M_1', \ldots, M_n'$, for any path π in $M_1'||\ldots||M_n'$, π is consistent with $M_1||\ldots||M_n$ if and only if:*

1. *π is consistent with M_1*
2. *π is consistent with $[M_1]\,\Sigma_{M_2} \cup \Sigma_\pi ||M_2$*
3. *π is consistent with $\left[([M_1]\,\Sigma_{M_2} \cup \Sigma_{M_3} \cup \Sigma_\pi ||M_2)\right]\,\Sigma_{M_3} \cup \Sigma_\pi ||M_3$*

$\ldots$

n. *π is consistent with $\left[\ldots\left[[M_1]_{\bigcup_{i=2}^n \Sigma_i \cup \Sigma_\pi}||M_2\right]_{\bigcup_{i=3}^n \Sigma_i \cup \Sigma_\pi} \ldots\right]_{\Sigma_n \cup \Sigma_\pi}||M_n$*

The proof is applying the previous lemma inductively on the number of elements in the composition.

The previous proof almost provides the basis of Algorithm 2. We will now show how each iteration is obtained from the composition of n components.

We use the following auxiliary proposition (provable with the definitions given and showing that there is a simulation relation such that $[M]_{\Sigma \cup \Sigma'} \leq [M]_\Sigma$).

Proposition 3. *Given a path π, a component M and two alphabets Σ and Σ', if π is consistent with $[M]_\Sigma$, then π is consistent with $[M]_{\Sigma \cup \Sigma'}$.*

In Corollary 1, we saw that a path π is consistent with the composition of the concrete components by proving the n items in the list. However, it would seem that each proof item requires calculating a new abstraction of the previous components. For instance in 1. we use M_1 as is. In 2. M_1 is abstracted to the COI of $\Sigma_{M_2} \cup \Sigma_\pi$. In 3. M_1 is abstracted to the COI of $\Sigma_{M_2} \cup \Sigma_{M_3} \cup \Sigma_\pi$.

We now show that each component can be abstracted only one time.

Corollary 2. *Given n components $M_1, \ldots, M_n$ and their abstractions $M_1', \ldots, M_n'$, for any path π in $M_1'||\ldots||M_n'$, all the conditions in Corollary 1 hold if and only if all the following are satisfied*

1. π *is consistent with* M_1
2. π *is consistent with* $[M_1]_{\bigcup_{i=2}^{n} \Sigma_i \cup \Sigma_\pi} || M_2$
3. π *is consistent with* $\left[\left([M_1]_{\bigcup_{i=2}^{n} \Sigma_i \cup \Sigma_\pi} || M_2 \right) \right]_{\bigcup_{i=3}^{n} \Sigma_i \cup \Sigma_\pi} || M_3$

   $\cdots$

n. π *is consistent with* $\left[\cdots \left[[M_1]_{\bigcup_{i=2}^{n} \Sigma_i \cup \Sigma_\pi} || M_2 \right]_{\bigcup_{i=3}^{n} \Sigma_i \cup \Sigma_\pi} \cdots \right]_{\Sigma_n \cup \Sigma_\pi} || M_n$

Proof. Each item in this corollary implies the corresponding item in Corollary 1 because of Proposition 3. Therefore if all the conditions in Corollary 2 are satisfied, then all the conditions in Corollary 1 hold.

For every condition in Corollary 2 proving π consistent with some $\tilde{M}_1 || \tilde{M}_2$, there are conditions in Corollary 2 in which each $\tilde{M}_i$ appears (perhaps abstracted, but due to Proposition 1, it still is consistent). Therefore when all the conditions in Corollary 1 hold, in particular π is consistent with every $\tilde{M}_i$ appearing in any condition of Corollary 2. Thus, all the conditions in Corollary 2 are satisfied. $\square$

The last condition of Corollary 2 includes as sub-expressions the previous conditions, from here we infer the algorithm.

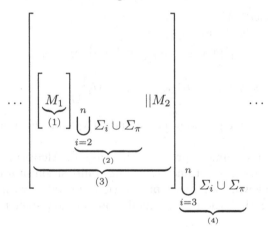

Part (1) (matching the first condition of Corollary 2), is when the algorithm executes line 3 during the first iteration. The first event specification is composed with M_{True}, leaving the specification as is.

If not spurious, we abstract the model to the Cone of Influence of $V_1 \cup \Sigma_\pi$. Recall that V_i contains the symbols of E_i that appear in some event specification later in the sequence. When abstracting the current model to the COI $\bigcup_{i=2}^{n} \Sigma_i$, we are in fact abstracting M_1 to the variables that may appear later in the sequence. This is line 6 of Algorithm 2, first iteration.

Part (3) represents line 3 of the second iteration: composing the previous abstracted model with the current one. The resulting model is checked and if not spurious the algorithm continues by abstracting this resulting model to V_2 (4). This continues until either the abstract counterexample is found spurious (one of the conditions in Corollary 2 does not hold) or it is consistent with every event specification, making the counterexample real.

4.5   Liveness Abstract Counterexample Spuriousness Checking

In this section we describe in more detail line 4 of Algorithm 2.

Depending on whether the property is a safety or liveness guarantee, different techniques are used. Our tool interacts with the model checker NuSMV [1], whose LTL counterexamples are always given by infinite paths, thus we cannot infer from these whether the original property is safety or liveness. To distinguish between safety (a prefix is enough) and liveness properties (counterexample given by an infinite path), in [4] it was shown that given a Büchi automata representing a property m, the automata represents a safety formula if and only if $L(m) = L(Cl(m))$ where $Cl(m)$ is the same as m but with every state being an accepting state. When the translation of an LTL formula to a state machine does not include fairness constraints, there are no restrictions regarding the states that should occur infinite times thus all states are accepting states (therefore, the state machine represents a safety formula).

Then, when the translation of the formula does not have any fairness constraints we infer that the formula is safety. For safety it is enough to simulate the counterexample (there is a finite path which contains the violation of the safety property) with currModel. For liveness, we propose the new instrumentation technique below in place of the usual unfolding seen in Sect. 2.5.

The abstract counterexample (that shows a liveness formula unsatisfied) looks like: $\underbrace{s_0, \ldots, s_i,}_{prefix} \underbrace{s_{i+1}, \ldots, s_j,}_{loop} s_{i+1}, \ldots$. The prefix can be empty, and the loop may contain one or more abstract states.

When the counterexample is real, the abstract loop might have to be unfolded multiple times to find the concrete counterexample. In order to avoid this unfolding, given the abstract counterexample, we know that each abstract loop iteration contains $j - i$ states. Each event specification state machine (that is, considering the initial and transition relation constraints together with the state machine translation of the LTL formulas of the specification) is instrumented with a counter that represents the states within the loop. To check spuriousness we check whether there is a concrete path that is consistent with the abstract counterexample.

Given a concrete model $M = \langle X, I, T, F \rangle$, where X is the set of variables and the different values of the variables determine the set of states, the instrumented model is given by $\tilde{M} = \langle \tilde{X}, \tilde{I}, \tilde{T}, F \rangle$ with:

$$\tilde{X} = X \cup \{prefix : 0..i; cnt : 0..j - i\}$$
$$\tilde{I} = I \wedge prefix = 0 \wedge cnt = 0$$
$$\begin{aligned}\tilde{T} = T &\wedge (prefix < i \rightarrow (prefix' = prefix + 1 \wedge cnt' = cnt)) \text{ (part 1)}\\ &\wedge (prefix = i \rightarrow prefix' = prefix) \text{ (part 2)}\\ &\wedge ((prefix = i \wedge cnt < j - i) \rightarrow (cnt' = cnt + 1)) \text{ (part 3)}\\ &\wedge ((prefix = i \wedge cnt = j - i) \rightarrow (cnt' = 1)) \text{ (part 4)}\end{aligned}$$

That is, we add a variable $prefix$ to identify while in the abstract counterexample prefix, and the counter cnt to identify the different states of the abstract loop. Both counters are initialized as 0 and the following transition relation constraints are added:

part 1. While in the prefix part of the abstract counterexample, increment *prefix*.

part 2. While in the loop part of the abstract counterexample, do not return to the prefix part.

part 3. While in the loop part of the abstract counterexample, if it is not yet the end of the abstract loop, increment the counter.

part 4. While in the loop part of the abstract counterexample, if it is the end of the abstract loop, reset the counter to represent the beginning of the abstract loop.

Note that if the number of states of the concrete model is $|S|$, the number of different states in the instrumented model will be at most $|S| \cdot (j+1)$: in the worst case scenario, every abstract state of the counterexample is matched by every concrete state.

Once the event state machine is instrumented according to the abstract counterexample, the LTL formula to be checked is

$$
\neg \left(s_0 \wedge X s_1 \wedge \cdots \wedge \underbrace{X \ldots X}_{i} s_i \wedge \underbrace{X \ldots X}_{i+1} G \left(\bigwedge_{k=1}^{j-i} (cnt = k \implies s_{i+k}) \right) \right) \quad (4)
$$

The first $i+1$ conjuncts characterize each state of the abstract prefix and the remainder what every state within the abstract loop satisfies. Therefore, this property expresses that no path of the concrete model is consistent with the abstract counterexample (the formula within the brackets represents a path consistent with the counterexample). If this formula is satisfied, the counterexample is found spurious with respect to the current event specification; otherwise, a path has been found showing the counterexample consistent with the current event specification and the abstract counterexample is checked against the remaining event specifications. Note that, as before, this formula is checked against each (concrete) event specification modularly, and not the whole concrete system.

In our case study, one possible guarantee could be that whenever the location is provided (*locationProvided*) by a witness of a crisis within a witness call (*inCall*), then that phone call will eventually end (*callEnd*).

$$
\mathbf{G} \left((locationProvided \wedge inCall) \rightarrow \mathbf{F} \; callEnd \right) \quad (5)
$$

When we try to verify the guarantee (5) with the abstract model, we may obtain the following abstract counterexample:

$$
\begin{array}{ccc}
\pi = callStart, & locationProvided, & (\neg callEnd)^{\omega} \\
\neg callEnd & inCall & \\
& \neg callEnd &
\end{array}
$$

That is, there is a witness call starting in the first state, in the second one the location of the crisis is provided, and then there is no state ending the current call. Then, to check spuriousness with each event specification (and previous abstractions), we build the formula (6) as in the general formula (4). Since there is only one abstract loop state, the counter is not necessary.

$$\neg \left(\begin{array}{l} (callStart \wedge \neg callEnd) \\ \wedge \mathbf{X}\,(locationProvided \wedge inCall \wedge \neg callEnd) \\ \wedge \mathbf{X}\,\mathbf{X}\,\mathbf{G}\,(\neg callEnd) \end{array} \right) \tag{6}$$

This formula holds whenever the counterexample is spurious (i.e., there is no concrete path matching the abstract counterexample), and does not hold whenever the counterexample is real (i.e., there is a concrete path matching the abstract counterexample).

In Sect. 4.7, we will show how the spuriousness reason of this example is found (and thus used to refine the model).

4.6 Instrumentation Correctness

To see that instrumenting and checking Formula (4), which is $\neg \left(\underbrace{\overbrace{\vphantom{G}\cdots}^{prefix} \wedge \overbrace{G\,(\dots)}^{loop}}_{\phi} \right)$, is indeed sound, we prove that the counterexample is consistent with the concrete model if and only if the property is not satisfied in the instrumented model.

Let $\tilde{M}$ be the instrumented model M (i.e. M with the counter instrumentation). $M \vDash E\pi$ represents whether π is a path in the model M.

$$M \vDash E\pi \underbrace{\Longleftrightarrow}_{(a)} \tilde{M} \vDash E\pi \underbrace{\Longleftrightarrow}_{(b)} \tilde{M} \vDash E\phi \iff \tilde{M} \vDash \neg E\phi \iff \tilde{M} \nvDash A\neg\phi$$

Relation (a) holds since the instrumentation added to the model does not restrict nor add paths to M (over the variables of M), and has no effect in the counterexample. The $\Longrightarrow$ part of (b) is easy to see: if π is a path in $\tilde{M}$, then there is an assignment to cnt such that the formula holds in $\tilde{M}$. The remaining steps are trivial logic identities. Thus we have obtained that $M \vDash E\pi \Longrightarrow \tilde{M} \nvDash A\neg\phi$, therefore $\tilde{M} \vDash A\neg\phi \Longrightarrow M \nvDash E\pi$. If the instrumented model satisfies formula (4), then the path is not consistent with the model and is found spurious.

We now show the other direction of (b), that $\tilde{M} \vDash E\phi \Longrightarrow \tilde{M} \vDash E\pi$:

Let $\tilde{\pi} = \tilde{s}_0, \tilde{s}_1, \tilde{s}_2, \tilde{s}_3, \tilde{s}_4, \tilde{s}_4, \tilde{s}_5, \dots$ be the witness path of $\tilde{M} \vDash E\phi$. Since $\tilde{\pi}$ is a path in $\tilde{M}$, then $\tilde{s}_0$ must satisfy the initial conditions defined in M and for every pair of consecutive states $\tilde{s}_i$ and $\tilde{s}_{i+1}$, M's transition relation constraints must hold. Using this idea and the ϕ definition, we observe that ϕ is also consistent with π: It is clear that any state before the loop of the witness is also at the same position within π (satisfying any initial and transition constraints); and for every state within the loop, the state has a value of the *cnt* variable, and therefore should be both consistent with the corresponding abstract state and respect the transition relation. Therefore we have found an actual path in M consistent with π. Note that the formula does not force the concrete loop proving the *globally* part of the ϕ to be of the same length as the abstract counterexample. Instead, it could correspond to k abstract loop iterations. Once this loop has been found in the concrete instrumented model, every iteration of the concrete loop will be consistent with k iterations of the abstract one.

Thus, we have obtained that $M \vDash E\pi \iff \tilde{M} \nvDash \varphi$, determining whether the error is spurious by checking Formula (4) over the instrumented model.

4.7   Refining

Refinement is obtained from an event specification (composed with the previous event abstractions) against which the counterexample has been found spurious. Let *modelFindRefs* be this model from which the refinement will be obtained. The refinement consists of information (initial or transition relation constraints, or LTL properties) and variables appearing in these constraints obtained from the event specifications that the current path (the spurious abstract counterexample) does not satisfy, but any path behaving consistently with the events does.

Safety Refinement. For safety guarantees, one SMT unsat-core activation simulating the finite counterexample with *modelFindRefs* is enough to find the necessary refinements. Recall that the unsat-core gives a small subset of the constraints enough to show unsatisfiability. The part from the event specifications in that core should be added to the assumption of the response, in order to prevent obtaining the same abstract counterexample in the future. This part may strengthen the initial states constraints or the relation transition constraints.

Recall that event specifications can include both safety and liveness properties. The state machine representation of a safety formula does not include any fairness constraints (i.e. every path belongs to the language of the state machine), while the state machine representation of liveness formulas must include fairness constraints (restricting the language of the state machine to include only fair paths, c.f. Sect. 2.1). When checking a counterexample with an event specification, we are actually checking it with the state machine representing the event specification. Therefore, for every liveness property φ, the state machine includes the transition relation and fairness constraints representing φ. When translating the liveness formulas into their corresponding state machine, we save what fairness constraints are introduced by each liveness formula within the event specifications.

For example, given our running example, when the abstract counterexample was checked with the COI reduction of *shouldSendHeli* composed with *badWeather*, it was found spurious. This composition included the formula $G(shouldSendHeli \implies \neg badWeather)$ translated to a state machine, that is:

$$(shouldSendHeli \implies \neg badWeather) \in I$$

$$(shouldSendHeli' \implies \neg badWeather') \in T$$

The SMT model checked includes these assertions, and when simulating the abstract counterexample, $(shouldSendHeli' \implies \neg badWeather')$ is found as a part of the unsat-core. Since we have saved how each LTL formula is translated to a state machine, we know that this constraint was introduced by the property $G(shouldSendHeli \implies \neg badWeather)$ within the specification of $shouldSendHeli$, and this property is then added to refine the current abstract model.

Liveness Refinement. For liveness guarantees, the refinement to avoid a spurious abstract counterexample is also obtained from $modelFindRefs$. This refinement either includes transition relation constraints (refine the model by splitting the abstract states – including the initial states – so that the current path is no longer feasible in the model) or liveness properties (finding the necessary refinement first finds the missing fairness constraints, and then the refinement is given by the liveness formulas within the event specifications introducing those fairness constraints).

This must be handled differently from safety guarantees since finite path simulation does not capture fairness refinements. Previous work either considered only safety formulas (making simulation enough) or considered predicate abstraction or well-founded sets refinement for which the fairness constraints are not part of the refinements.

If the abstract counterexample is consistent when checked against $modelFindRefs$ but without any fairness constraints (there is a concrete path τ matching the abstract path in the model without fairness), we know that some fairness constraint would avoid the abstract counterexample (and the refinement will be the liveness property whose state machine representation introduced that fairness constraint).

That is, if $\mathcal{F}$ is the set of fairness constraints, then there exists a path τ witness of π being consistent with $modelFindRefs \setminus \mathcal{F}$. From τ, we can obtain how many times the abstract loop has to be unfolded to represent a concrete loop. Thus, $modelFindRefs$ and the counterexample can be translated to SMT to find the unsat-core that makes the counterexample spurious. The counterexample loop is translated in the standard way (the last state of the loop is followed by the first state of the loop) and each fairness constraint f is translated to "at least one state of the (concrete) loop satisfies f".

The counterexample was shown consistent with the model without any fairness constraints but spurious otherwise. Thus, the unsat-core of this translation (that includes the fairness constraints) will include at least one of those fairness constraints. Since we have saved for each liveness formula what fairness constraints it introduces, from the fairness constraints in the unsat-core we can easily get the liveness formulas that introduced those constraints and add them as refinements to the abstract assumption of the response, thus avoiding any concrete counterexample with a loop matching n times the abstract loop. Any abstract counterexample found in a future iteration will not match these concrete paths. This is similar to other CEGAR work: when an abstract counterexample is found, a predicate splitting a problematic state is added so as to avoid the counterexample. Our fairness refinement "splits" paths when fairness constraints are added.

For instance, let π be the counterexample obtained in the example of Sect. 4.5.

One of the event specifications ($witnessInfoProvided$) assumes that every call that starts eventually ends: $\mathbf{G}\,(callStart \rightarrow \mathbf{F}callEnd)$ and that a call does not start and end at the same state $\mathbf{G}\neg\,(callStart \wedge callEnd)$. This can be represented by the state machine in Fig. 8. In the initial state either there is or there is not a call start (states s_1 and s_2 respectively). It is possible to stay in s_2 indefinitely (no matter if there is a call end), but when there is call start it moves to s_1, which is not a fair state. Therefore, the only way to achieve a fair path is by eventually reaching s_4 (guaranteeing that every call that has started, eventually ends).

To find that this information from the event specifications avoids the current counterexample (π), our technique first detects that the fairness constraint of this assumption is required.

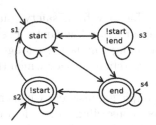

Fig. 8. State machine representing part of WitnessInfoProvided's specification

When π is checked with this event specification, π is found to be spurious. If we check this same abstract counterexample with the event specification without including any fairness constraints, then the abstract counterexample is consistent (the state machine without any fairness constraints would allow staying infinitely in s_1 or s_3). Thus, we can conclude that the refinement required includes fairness constraints.

The translation of the current model to an SMT instance includes the fairness constraint translation that it cannot stay forever in a state where callStart has occurred, but callEnd does not occur. This constraint will be part of the unsat core, and since it originated from the liveness property $\mathbf{G}\,(callStart \rightarrow \mathbf{F}callEnd)$, this property is added to the assumptions of the response.

Transition Relation Refinement. Now we describe how we find the necessary refinements when we have identified that no fairness constraint avoids the abstract counterexample, i.e. there is some transition (or initial state constraint)

in the abstract model that is not allowed according *modelFindRefs* and the refinement will be a transition relation constraint.

For liveness guarantees not requiring liveness property refinements, instead of simulating the counterexample through repeated SMT activations, we take advantage of the formula representing the counterexample. If the abstract counterexample is spurious, then there must be some state reachable from the initial states but without any actual successor in the concrete model (*modelFindRefs*) consistent with the abstract counterexample. If we consider the product of *modelFindRefs* and the state machine representation of the formula representing the abstract counterexample, then the resulting model will not contain any infinite path. Thus the model checker outputs that the model is empty and returns the diameter needed to reach this conclusion. This diameter serves as the bound for which the state to be split is sure to be found. A single activation of an SMT solver with that bound can then find the needed refinement using the unsat-core option.

A possible response guarantee could express that whenever the conditions for *shouldSendHeli* to be detected hold, then the helicopter mission will be added (Property (7)).

$$\mathbf{G}((shouldGoToLoc \wedge \neg badWeather \wedge helicoptersAvailable \wedge problematicAccess)$$
$$\rightarrow \mathbf{F}\ HMAdded) \tag{7}$$

If we try to verify the guarantee (7), we may obtain the counterexample

$$\pi = \begin{pmatrix} \neg shouldSendHeli \\ shouldGoToLoc \\ \neg badWeather \\ helicoptersAvailable \\ problematicAccess \\ \neg HMAdded \end{pmatrix}^{\omega}$$

That is, all the conditions for the event *shouldSendHeli* are satisfied but the event is not detected with the current abstractions.

In this case, we find the abstract counterexample spurious with the specification of *shouldSendHeli*, even when removing any fairness constraints of the concrete *modelFindRefs*. Therefore we conclude that in this case we need a transition relation refinement.

Composing the model representing the abstract counterexample with *modelFindRefs* shows that there is no infinite path (by considering a diameter of one state the problematic situation is found) and by simulating one step of *modelFindRefs* and the abstract counterexample the necessary refinement (Property (8)) that belongs to the specification of *shouldSendHeli* is found and added to the response assumptions.

$$\mathbf{G}((shouldGoToLoc \wedge \neg badWeather \wedge helicoptersAvailable \wedge problematicAccess)$$
$$\iff shouldSendHeli) \tag{8}$$

5   DaVeRS

As noted before, many CEGAR tools use SMT solvers to build the abstract model or find predicate refinements. In this work, DaVeRS also interacts with an SMT solver (SMTInterpol [2]) whenever a bound is known (for example, once the counterexample is known to be spurious because of a missing transition definition). Otherwise DaVeRS interacts with a BDD-based unbounded model checking tool (NuSMV [1]).

Recall that event specifications are given by $E = \langle X, I, T, P \rangle$ (Sect. 2.2) representing the state machine and temporal logic constraints for the event assumptions and guarantees. Responses are given by $\langle X_B, X_R, ED, M, P, P_{Ev}, R \rangle$ (Sect. 2.3), representing the variables of the underlying system and response, the event detector to which the response reacts, the state machine definition of the response, and the response partial specification.

The response and event specification are given by text files expressing the contents of each of the categories in their representation, where P_{Ev} could initially be empty. We use the NuSMV language to express variable domains (boolean, integer range, enumerated types); state machine definitions (initial and transition relations constraints); and LTL formulas (for the temporal logic assumptions and guarantees of event detectors and responses). This is the only input required from the user. DaVeRS automatically applies the techniques presented in this paper.

NuSMV includes a tool (ltl2smv) that allows building the state machine matching a linear temporal logic formula, in particular for liveness properties it introduces the fairness constraints required. We interact with this tool both to build the tableau of the assumption Sect. 4.2, and to obtain the state machine representation of the LTL properties within event specifications. By saving which event specification formula introduced which fairness constraints, following the ideas in Sect. 4.7, we obtain the actual formula that introduced the fariness refinement.

Once we have obtained the LTL to state machine translation of each event specification, we can see every event specification given by a state machine where we can calculate the value of the variables of the next state according to the value of the variables at the previous state, and thus NuSMV can easily calculate the cone of influence of an event specification reduced to a set of variables.

For each response guarantee, the relevant events are obtained and if the full-shared alphabet configuration is used, all the relevant event interface alphabets are added to the response alphabet, otherwise only the symbols directly necessary for building the augmented model and checking the property are added. Then, the application executes the CEGAR cycle as explained in the previous sections until the guarantee has been checked or a real counterexample has been found, and the assumptions learnt about the events are saved.

When DaVeRS terminates, it outputs whether it succeeded or failed, saves the response file with the refinements that led to that conclusion, and in case of failure, outputs the real counterexample.

6   Evaluation

We have implemented the DaVeRS tool using these techniques and evaluated it with three extensive case studies: a Car Crash Crisis Management System (CCCMS) [31], a Discount library (as in [18]) and a security concern in an email application. These represent contrasting examples of reusable systems with many options based on event detectors and responses. The goals of the Car Crash Crisis Management System are to receive information about a possible crisis, assess and propose the necessary missions, assign internal/external resources, update the state of the missions, etc. At any moment any of a large number of events occur possibly causing many events to be detected by the event detectors, and appropriate responses (often with guarantees verified in advance) can react and be activated. The Discount case applies discounts according to the events detected (such as buying a product for which sales have not been enough in the last period, discounts for the loyalty program customers, or detecting whenever two of a certain family of products is bought, so that the second one is free). This case study resembles more a library of reusable event detectors and response specifications (and implementations). A user involved in e-commerce can decide which events and responses (that apply discounts of various types) to use over his existing software for handling purchases. The email application includes event detectors triggering when user authorization is required and a response that encrypts any password to be sent. The security concerns in the email application represent the application of a reusable library to a particular domain.

We have considered 34 guarantees for each case study, including assertions about the future and past, identifying when the response should be activated or should not, checking assertions that refer only to the higher-level event or also to lower-level ones, and referring only to the event detection or also to the exposed information.

The CCCMS event dependency graph contains seven complex event specifications relying on 16 primitive events such as a phone call just started, there is a snow storm, etc. The Discount event dependency graph contains six complex event specifications relying on 12 primitive events. The security concern for the email application event dependency graph contains 12 complex event specifications relying on 24 primitive events.

Examples of guarantees of the CCCMS case study include checking (1) that the location parameter with which the helicopter sending mission is created is the one exposed by lower-level event detectors, (2) that if a helicopter mission is added then *shouldSendHeli* must have occurred, and the other way around, or (3) the guarantee considered as a running example.

The Discount response we have considered gives priority to the "buy one, get one free" Discount, and only in case this discount is not applied, the other discounts are considered. Some examples of guarantees of the Discount case study are checking that indeed the indicated discount is prioritized, or that loyalty customers receive the appropriate discounts.

The security concern in the email application requires authentication, for instance, whenever preparing to write an email or accessing the inbox and the user has not yet authenticated; or when intending to change the account settings. During authentication, a password is sent, and our concern encrypts this password (or any other password sent within the application).

Recall that in classical compositional CEGAR all potentially relevant variables are included in advance (full-shared alphabet strategy), and loop unfolding is used to check liveness. We compared this with our new techniques for adding only needed variables and instrumenting loops with a counter for liveness spuriousness checking.

We compared the different strategies against the different guarantees measuring the time taken by each. All the experiments were carried out on a 2.5 GHz Intel Core i5 (quad-core) with 4 GB RAM running 64-bit Ubuntu 14.04.

For all the case studies, if all the relevant event specifications are included as initial assumptions of the response (CEGAR not applied), the technique takes more than 15 min for each example.

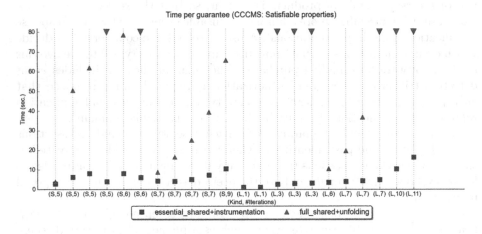

Fig. 9. CCCMS - satisfiable properties

Figure 9 shows the time taken by the classical compositional CEGAR techniques full_shared+unfolding (triangles) and our essential_shared+instrumentation (boxes) for CCCMS satisfiable guarantees. The x axis represents the kind of guarantee (S: Safety, L: Liveness) and the number of iterations required to reach the conclusion when the essential-shared alphabet + instrumentation strategy was used (full-shared alphabet + unfolding always took the same or more iterations). The y axis shows the time in seconds. The inverse triangle on the top of the figure represents when the classical techniques were off the scale of the figure. All such cases took more than 15 min, except for two liveness properties that took 3 and 10 min, respectively. Both for safety and liveness guarantees, our approach works significantly better. In particular, the improvement is even more noticeable for liveness formulas, where our technique took less than 20 s for every guarantee considered.

Figure 10 shows the time taken for unsatisfiable CCCMS guarantees (including safety and liveness formulas). Here too, our technique improved over the classical techniques considerably, due to the irrelevant variables needed in classical techniques, and the unfolding strategy used for liveness spuriousness checking. Some guarantees considered giving very similar results to the ones presented in the graphic were not included.

Figure 11 shows the time taken for satisfiable safety guarantees belonging to the Discount (D) and Security (S) case studies. Both techniques show a significant performance improvement when applying our optimizations.

The Discount case study event specifications are more complex than in the other case studies (include information about the customers, products, counters). For this example, liveness and unsatisfiable guarantees reached timeout (15 min) for most guarantees when checking with classical techniques, while our techniques provided results in less than three minutes. For the only two liveness guarantees where the classical techniques terminated, it took around 7 min with the classical techniques and less than two minutes with ours.

The Security case study contains more event detectors (primitive and complex) than the other case studies, making the bound for unfolding liveness guarantee counterexamples significantly larger when using classical techniques. Thus, classical techniques reached timeout for every liveness guarantee in the Security case study (satisfiable and unsatisfiable), while our technique took less than 15 s. For unsatisfiable safety guarantees considered, our technique took less than 20 s, while classical techniques took between 40 s and 2 min (depending on the complexity of the guarantee).

The results in the graphics (and the timeout results) suggest scalability improvements over existing techniques, since now fewer iterations are required to check guarantees, and liveness spuriousness checking can be applied, and terminate in reasonable time. As long as many event specifications are involved, our alphabet refinement optimizations avoids automatically including the interface alphabet of all these, thus considering only the necessary refinements.

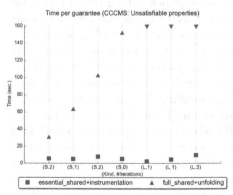

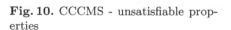

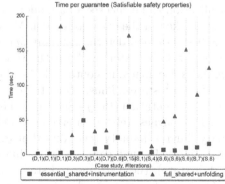

Fig. 10. CCCMS - unsatisfiable properties

Fig. 11. Discount, security - satisfiable safety properties

7 Related Work

In [18], the idea of using CEGAR for event systems is proposed, but here we formalize the model and assumptions, show the mechanism and elaborate a tool implementation, including new techniques for handling liveness and reducing the state space that were not presented there.

There are several CEGAR approaches, each with its own way of building the abstract model, verifying, analyzing counterexamples and refining. Among the non-compositional ones, [5,12,27] consider only safety formulas, simulate abstract counterexamples against the system's implementation, and learn new predicates that refine the abstract model. The work in [11,15] present non-compositional CEGAR approaches for also checking liveness formulas. The bound to which liveness counterexamples can be simulated to detect spuriousness in [11] can be very large, and refinements consist of predicates that make the spurious counterexample unreachable, but fairness constraints are not added to the abstract model. As seen in the evaluation section, using instrumentation instead of unfolding the abstract counterexample loop to this bound gives better performance results. In [15], Terminator uses predicate abstraction-refinement for safety formulas and well-founded sets abstraction refinement to prove program fair termination and check liveness specifications. Although we use a symbolic model checker to verify liveness formulas, the fair binary reachability algorithm presented in that work could also be used and then spuriousness checking and refinement finding applied as we have presented. One could argue that from the ranking functions variables and current predicates, one can obtain which of the event specification parts are relevant (that we obtain by translating the event specification to SMT and obtaining the unsat-core). Future work will analyze performance differences between these.

Instrumenting a model to check properties has been considered before [7,15]. In both works, the model is instrumented to check liveness properties as safety. Though our instrumentation is based on the same principle as theirs (every liveness counterexample consists of a prefix and a loop), the problem addressed and instrumentation itself are different. In those papers, the input is a liveness specification to be checked in a model, in ours it is a path of the abstract model to be checked in the concrete model. Moreover, the instrumentation proposed in [7] is based on non-deterministically *guessing* the initial loop state and checking if it is reachable later in the path (thus checking every possible state). If the original state machine contained $|S|$ states, the instrumented state machines contains $|S|^2$ states. Thus, the obtained state machine is much larger than with our instrumentation ($|S| \cdot j$ - Sect. 4.5). The work in [15] instruments the program to include fairness related assertions as well and reduces the problem to analyzing binary fair reachability (checking that every possible cycle satisfies the fairness constraints). In that paper as well, due to the instrumentation used (guessing the fair state), the instrumented state machines contains more than $|S|^2$ states.

Other works have considered compositional CEGAR approaches [9,10,23,26] for safety guarantees. The abstract components in [9,10,26] have to include every symbol shared among components, only [23] includes a way to refine the alphabet of the composition of two components.

Our work is mostly useful for event-based systems relying on complex events. That is, our approach is most useful for approaches including hierarchically composed events [3,8,19] rather than related work adding events to existing paradigms including limited composition (at most boolean composition) as [22,34]. For example, tracematches and trace-based aspects [3,19] trigger the execution of a response depending on a regular pattern of events (detected). These regular patterns include the lower-level events they rely on (described by pointcuts) and the regular expressions to which a method reacts (response). For each regular expression, an event dependency graph can be built. The event dependency graph includes two levels: the one of the joinpoints captured by pointcuts, and the one of the regular expression. We could apply DaVeRS to understand which of the pointcuts are relevant to which guarantees.

8 Conclusions

We have presented a practical tool and a CEGAR-based compositional verification technique for verifying response guarantees and finding the necessary assumptions of the response specification about event detectors in hierarchical event-based systems.

The responses and event detectors are specified with state machines and temporal logic formulas, that can either represent a design stage (before implementing in a programming language), or an abstraction of an implemented system.

The basic assumptions about hierarchical event-based systems allow the system to be represented as a parallel composition and thus apply a compositional CEGAR technique. At each step, the response augmented model is built considering only an abstraction of the event specifications, and when a counterexample is found, spuriousness checking and refinement finding is done modularly.

We have presented improvements to state of the art CEGAR techniques for checking spuriousness of liveness property counterexamples, and for including alphabet refinement (even over shared alphabet symbols). The results in the evaluation section validated these as really improving performance with respect to techniques in related work.

References

1. NuSMV. http://nusmv.fbk.eu/
2. SMT. http://ultimate.informatik.uni-freiburg.de/smtinterpol/
3. Allan, C., Avgustinov, P., Christensen, A.S., Hendren, L., Kuzins, S., Lhoták, O., De Moor, O., Sereni, D., Sittampalam, G., Tibble, J.: Adding trace matching with free variables to AspectJ. ACM SIGPLAN Not. **40**, 345–364 (2005)
4. Alpern, B., Schneider, F.B.: Recognizing safety and liveness. Distrib. Comput. **2**(3), 117–126 (1987)

5. Ball, T., Rajamani, S.K.: Automatically validating temporal safety properties of interfaces. In: Dwyer, M. (ed.) SPIN 2001. LNCS, vol. 2057, pp. 102–122. Springer, Heidelberg (2001). doi:10.1007/3-540-45139-0_7

6. Barrett, C., Stump, A., Tinelli, C.: The Satisfiability Modulo Theories Library (SMT-LIB) (2010). www.SMT-LIB.org

7. Biere, A., Artho, C., Schuppan, V.: Liveness checking as safety checking. Electron. Notes Theoret. Comput. Sci. **66**, 160–177 (2002)

8. Bockisch, C., Malakuti, S., Akşit, M., Katz, S.: Making aspects natural: events and composition. In: AOSD 2011. ACM (2011)

9. Chaki, S., Clarke, E., Groce, A., Ouaknine, J., Strichman, O., Yorav, K.: Efficient verification of sequential and concurrent C programs. Formal Meth. Syst. Des. **25**, 129–166 (2004)

10. Chucri, F.: Exploiting model structure in CEGAR verification method. Ph.D. thesis, University of Bordeaux I (2012)

11. Clarke, E., Grumberg, O., Jha, S., Lu, Y., Veith, H.: Counterexample-guided abstraction refinement. In: Emerson, E.A., Sistla, A.P. (eds.) CAV 2000. LNCS, vol. 1855, pp. 154–169. Springer, Heidelberg (2000). doi:10.1007/10722167_15

12. Clarke, E., Kroening, D., Sharygina, N., Yorav, K.: SATABS: SAT-based predicate abstraction for ANSI-C. In: Halbwachs, N., Zuck, L.D. (eds.) TACAS 2005. LNCS, vol. 3440, pp. 570–574. Springer, Heidelberg (2005). doi:10.1007/978-3-540-31980-1_40

13. Clarke, E.M., Grumberg, O., Peled, D.: Model Checking. MIT Press, Cambridge (2001)

14. Cobleigh, J.M., Clarke, L.A., Osterweil, L.J.: FLAVERS: a finite state verification technique for software systems. IBM Syst. J. **41**, 140–165 (2002)

15. Cook, B., Gotsman, A., Podelski, A., Rybalchenko, A., Vardi, M.Y.: Proving that programs eventually do something good. ACM SIGPLAN Not. **42**, 265–276 (2007)

16. Corbett, J.C., Dwyer, M.B., Hatcliff, J., Laubach, S., Păsăreanu, C.S., Robby, Zheng, H.: Bandera: Extracting finite-state models from java source code. In: ICSE 2000 (2000)

17. Disenfeld, C., Katz, S.: Compositional verification of events and observers (summary). In: FOAL 2011. ACM (2011)

18. Disenfeld, C., Katz, S.: Specification and verification of event detectors and responses. In: AOSD 2013. ACM (2013)

19. Douence, R., Fradet, P., Südholt, M., et al.: Trace-based aspects. Aspect-Oriented Software Development (2004)

20. Douence, R., Südholt, M.: A model and a tool for event-based aspect-oriented programming (EAOP). Techn. Ber., Ecole des Mines de Nantes. TR, vol. 2(11) (2002)

21. Etzion, O., Niblett, P.: Event Processing in Action, 1st edn. Manning Publications Co., Greenwich (2010)

22. Gasiunas, V., Satabin, L., Mezini, M., Núñez, A., Noyé, J.: Escala: modular event-driven object interactions in scala. In: Proceedings of the Tenth International Conference On Aspect-Oriented Software Development. ACM (2011)

23. Bobaru, M.G., Păsăreanu, C.S., Giannakopoulou, D.: Automated assume-guarantee reasoning by abstraction refinement. In: Gupta, A., Malik, S. (eds.) CAV 2008. LNCS, vol. 5123, pp. 135–148. Springer, Heidelberg (2008). doi:10.1007/978-3-540-70545-1_14

24. Goldman, M., Katz, E., Katz, S.: MAVEN: modular aspect verification and interference analysis. Formal Meth. Syst. Des. **37**, 61–92 (2010)

25. Harel, D., Pnueli, A.: On the development of reactive systems. In: Apt, K.R. (ed.) Logics and Models of Concurrent Systems, pp. 477–498. Springer, New York (1985)
26. Henzinger, T.A., Jhala, R., Majumdar, R., Qadeer, S.: Thread-modular abstraction refinement. In: Hunt, W.A., Somenzi, F. (eds.) CAV 2003. LNCS, vol. 2725, pp. 262–274. Springer, Heidelberg (2003). doi:10.1007/978-3-540-45069-6_27
27. Henzinger, T.A., Jhala, R., Majumdar, R., Sutre, G.: Lazy abstraction. In: POPL 2002. ACM (2002)
28. Kamina, T., Aotani, T., Masuhara, H.: EventCJ: a context-oriented programming language with declarative event-based context transition. In: Proceedings of the Tenth International Conference On Aspect-Oriented Software Development
29. Kiczales, G., Hilsdale, E., Hugunin, J., Kersten, M., Palm, J., Griswold, W.G.: An overview of aspectj. In: ECOOP (2001)
30. Kiczales, G., Lamping, J., Mendhekar, A., Maeda, C., Lopes, C., Loingtier, J.-M., Irwin, J.: Aspect-oriented programming. In: Akşit, M., Matsuoka, S. (eds.) ECOOP 1997. LNCS, vol. 1241, pp. 220–242. Springer, Heidelberg (1997). doi:10.1007/BFb0053381
31. Kienzle, J., Guelfi, N., Mustafiz, S.: Crisis management systems: a case study for aspect-oriented modeling. In: Katz, S., Mezini, M., Kienzle, J. (eds.) Transactions on Aspect-Oriented Software Development VII. LNCS, vol. 6210, pp. 1–22. Springer, Heidelberg (2010). doi:10.1007/978-3-642-16086-8_1
32. Luckham, D.C.: The Power of Events: An Introduction to Complex Event Processing in Distributed Enterprise Systems. Addison-Wesley Longman Publishing Co. Inc., Boston (2001)
33. Masuhara, H., Endoh, Y., Yonezawa, A.: A fine-grained join point model for more reusable aspects. In: Kobayashi, N. (ed.) APLAS 2006. LNCS, vol. 4279, pp. 131–147. Springer, Heidelberg (2006). doi:10.1007/11924661_8
34. Rajan, H., Leavens, G.T.: Ptolemy: a language with quantified, typed events. In: Vitek, J. (ed.) ECOOP 2008. LNCS, vol. 5142, pp. 155–179. Springer, Heidelberg (2008). doi:10.1007/978-3-540-70592-5_8
35. Roscoe, A.W., Hoare, C.A.R., Bird, R.: The Theory and Practice of Concurrency. Prentice Hall PTR, Upper Saddle River (1997)

Programming with Emergent Gummy Modules

Somayeh Malakuti[✉]

Software Technology Group, Technical University of Dresden, Dresden, Germany
somayeh.malakuti@tu-dresden.de

Abstract. Emergent behavior is generally defined as the appearance of complex behavior out of multiplicity of relatively simple interactions. Although significant amount of research has been dedicated to develop algorithms for detecting emergent behavior, there is no specific attempt to provide suitable linguistic abstractions to modularize emergent behavior and its related concerns. This results in the implementations that are complex and hard to maintain. In this paper, we identify three characteristic features of emergent behavior from the perspective of programming languages, and accordingly outline the shortcomings of current languages to properly program and modularize emergent behavior. We introduce emergent gummy modules, which are dedicated linguistic abstractions to define the appearance and disappearance conditions of emergent behavior as well as its utilization operations as one holistic module. We explain the implementation of emergent gummy modules in the GummyJ language, and illustrate that they improve the modularity of implementations. We represent the event processing semantics of GummyJ in UPPAAL simulation and model checking toolset.

Keywords: Emergent behavior · Cyber-physical systems · Event-based modularization · Event-based composition

1 Introduction

Emergent behavior is generally defined as the appearance of complex behavior out of multiplicity of relatively simple interactions [1–3]; it is an effect that is caused by the properties and relations characterizing its simpler constituents. Nowadays, there are various kinds of (cyber-physical) software systems that deal with detecting the emergence of certain behavior in the environment, representing it in the software and providing means to manipulate the behavior.

There has been significant amount of research to develop suitable algorithms for detecting emergent behavior in various domains. However, suitable programming languages to implement the algorithms and to modularize the implementations have not been studied.

In this paper, we take an initial step towards filling this gap. We identify three characteristic features of emergent behavior that must be respected by a language: (a) Emergent behavior may have transient nature, because it appears and disappears when certain effect occurs due to the interactions among its

© Springer International Publishing Switzerland 2016
S. Chiba et al. (Eds.): ToMC I, LNCS 9800, pp. 80–119, 2016.
DOI: 10.1007/978-3-319-46969-0_3

constituents; (b) it may have elastic nature, because the number of constituents may change in due time; and (c) it may have crosscutting nature, because it is the result of interactions among multiple constituents.

Object-oriented (OO) programming can be regarded as a dominating paradigm for modularizing complex software systems. Historically, objects are regarded as abstractions over data and a set of operations that can be performed on the data. In an OO modularization of software, there are structural dependencies among objects, which are imposed by the application domain and requirements. In most mainstream OO languages, the lifetime of objects is influenced by the structural dependency of objects; an object is destroyed if there is no reference to it from other objects.

These characteristics of OO modularization do not directly match the characteristics of emergent behavior. Emergent behavior is structurally decoupled to its constituents; instead, there is a behavioral dependency, which is transient. It has also been extensively studied by the aspect-oriented (AO) community [4] that OO modularization falls short in separating and modularizing the concerns that crosscut multiple concerns in software. Due to the mentioned mismatch, workarounds must be provided to support the transient, elastic and crosscutting nature of emergent behavior, which significantly increase the complexity of implementations.

AO programming has been introduced to facilitate modularizing crosscutting concerns. AO offers the notion of aspects as means to modularly represent a concern that crosscuts multiple concerns. Although AO languages have been successfully applied to various kinds of crosscutting concerns including object interactions [5], we observe that they significantly fall short in modularizing emergent behavior. This is mainly because, inspired from OO languages, AO languages also impose a tight structural coupling between aspects and their base objects; an aspect is bound to a specific set of base objects. Consequently, workarounds must be provided to program the transient and elastic nature of emergent behavior, which significantly increase the complexity of implementations.

Context-oriented programming (COP) [6] has been introduced to facilitate modular implementations of context-aware applications. Emergent behavior can be regarded as a special kind of context, which dynamically appears and disappears; it crosscuts multiple constituents, where the multiplicity of the constituents may change over the time. Current COP languages also fall short in expressing such a complex and dynamic context as a first-entity in software.

In [7], we introduced **emergent gummy modules** as novel linguistic abstractions to modularly represent emergent behavior as a first-class entity in software. To respect the transient nature of emergent behavior, emergent gummy modules encapsulate the condition under which their instances must be constructed and destructed. To respect the elastic nature of emergent behavior, emergent gummy modules adopt an event-based communication mechanism to acquire data from the relevant constituents; if an event matches the specified event selection predicates, it is selected for further processing, without limiting the constituents that publish events. To respect the crosscutting nature of emergent behavior, emergent gummy modules facilitate representing emergent behavior, its appearance and disappearance conditions and its utilization operations as one holistic module.

In this paper we extend our previous work from practical, functional and theoretical points of view. From a practical point of view, we show the use of emergent gummy module in two example domains. In addition, we explain the possible ways of acquiring necessary environmental data via events; the events can be produced directly in a Java program or can be received from external entities via a third-party event processing engine such as Esper [8]. The possible ways of accessing the instances of emergent gummy modules from Java objects are also explained in details. From a functional point of view, we extend GummyJ to support concurrent event processing by emergent gummy modules, and publishing events in both synchronous and asynchronous manners. The latter is particularly important in some utilization scenarios. From a theoretical point of view, we extend the formal models of GummyJ to represent these extensions.

This paper is organized as follows: Sect. 2 provides background information about emergent behavior. Section 3 outlines our illustrative case studies. Section 4 defines a set of requirements for implementing and modularizing emergent behavior. Section 5 discusses the shortcomings of current languages in fulfilling these requirements. Section 6 explains emergent gummy modules, and Sect. 7 illustrates the implementations of our illustrative examples in the GummyJ language. Section 8 explains possible ways of utilizing emergent gummy modules in Java programs. Section 9 discusses the formal semantics of the GummyJ language. Section 10 discusses the suitability of emergent gummy modules for representing emergent behavior. Section 11 outlines conclusion and future work.

2   Background on Emergent Behavior

There have been several attempts to define the phenomenon of emergent behavior and its types [1–3]. Independently of the type of emergent behavior, it is generally accepted that emergent behavior is an effect that is caused by the properties and relations characterizing its simpler constituents [1].

Various classifications and forms of emergent behavior have been defined in the literature. In this paper, we consider the classification proposed in [1,2], which is also represented in Fig. 1.

The type I of emergent behavior is characterized by a feed-forward process from constituents to emergent behavior, where the constituents are put together to form a system as a whole. In this type, the state of each constituent is independent of the state of other constituents, emergent behavior or the environment. An example of type I is a car in which each constituent part has a specific functionality, and together they provide the overall functionality of the car. Another example is a software program, in which each statement carries out a specific functionality, and the statements together provide the overall functionality of the program.

In the type II, emergent behavior appears from the interactions of constituents, and in turn influences the interactions of the constituents through

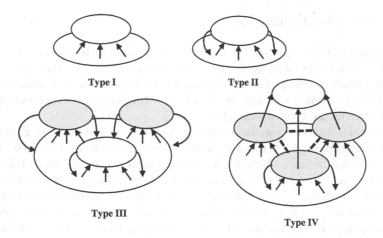

Fig. 1. Types of emergence [1]

a feedback process. In this case, the constituents can have flexible roles to be able to adapt themselves according to the feedback. An example of this case is traffic congestion, which is a pattern formed from the interactions of multiple drivers, and in turn it influences the way the drivers continue driving.

The type III deals with emergent behavior in complex adaptive systems, where there are multiple levels of feedback processes. For example, traffic congestion in a road segment may cause air pollution to emerge in the road segment. The type IV is the strongest form of emergence, which appears as the result of evolution, for example, in human genes, life, nature, and culture. In this type, a whole new world of new roles may appear.

Significant amount of research is dedicated to develop suitable algorithms for detecting the appearance and disappearance of emergent behavior. The existing methods for this can be classified to (a) variable-based, (b) event-based, and (c) grammar-based.

In variable-based methods [9], a set of variables are chosen to represent emergence; usually, emergence is measured numerically based on information theory and probability theory. In the event-based methods [10], the behavior of constituent elements is defined as a set of events; emergent behavior is defined as a complex event that can be reduced to a sequence of simpler events.

In the variable-based and event-based methods, a prior definition of variables, event types and emergence is required. To overcome the problem of a prior definition of emergence, the grammar-based methods [11] make use of an extended cooperating array grammar system to formalize the environment, agents and the cooperation among the agents.

3 Illustrative Examples

Various kinds of (cyber-physical) software systems deal with detecting the emergence of certain behavior in the environment, representing it in the software and providing means to manipulate the behavior. Traffic monitoring/simulation systems, air traffic control systems, weather forecasting systems, and stock market analysis systems are typical examples.

In air traffic control systems, traffic in both routes and airports is detected and necessary support is provided to air traffic controllers so that suitable rerouting decisions can be made. Weather forecasting systems reason about the occurrence of certain atmospheric conditions based on the data observed from sensors. Stock market monitoring systems observe the sales rate and the price of stocks, and reason about the fluctuation of every price. In traffic monitoring systems, traffic congestion is regarded as behavior that emerges as a result of interactions and decisions of individual drivers, and the conditions of road segments.

In this paper, we take systems in the banking domain and in the traffic domain and as our illustrative examples.

3.1 The Fraud Detection Software

For our first case study, we are inspired from the example provided in [12] for detecting frauds when using ATMs. It is considered a fraud if in less than 60 min, a user withdraws from two ATMs that are located more than 100 miles from each other. As Fig. 2 symbolically depicts, there are several ATMs, and *Fraud Detector* entities that gather information about cash withdrawals from the ATMs.

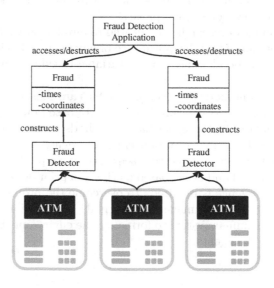

Fig. 2. An example fraud detection software

Frauds are regarded as emergent behavior that appears when the above-mentioned criteria holds; in this case, users, ATMs and the cash withdrawal transactions are the constituents of the emergent behavior. Frauds are represented as runtime entities in the system. Frauds do not disappear by themselves; instead, the system administrator can request for the explicit removal of the fraud runtime entities.

3.2   The Traffic Simulation Software

The traffic simulation software offers the functionality to represent road segments, cars and traffic congestion in the road segments. As Fig. 3 symbolically depicts, there are several road segments and cars passing these segments. Whenever a car enters and/or exists a road segment, it sends its coordinates and its entrance/exit time to the *Congestion Detector* entities. These entities calculate the time to pass the road segment for each car. If in the time duration T, the average travel time of cars exceeds the threshold W, it is concluded that there is a congestion in the road segment. If the average travel time goes below W, it is concluded that traffic congestion has disappeared.

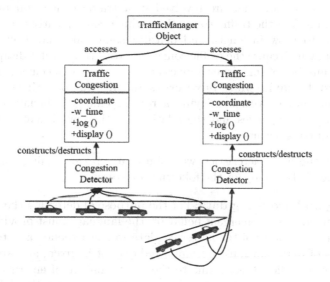

Fig. 3. An example traffic simulation software

In case of congestion, a runtime entity is created to represent the emergent behavior traffic congestion in the road segment. This entity maintains information about the road segment and the average waiting time of cars in the segment. In addition, it defines the operations (e.g. log and display), which can be performed on traffic congestion information by other entities in the software. If the traffic congestion disappears in the road segment, this runtime entity is destroyed by the *Congestion Detector* entities.

4   Requirements for Representing Emergent Behavior

In addition to developing suitable algorithms for detecting emergent behavior, we require suitable programming abstractions to implement the algorithms such that desired quality attributes are fulfilled in the implementations. In this regard, we identify the following characteristics of emergent behavior from the programming languages perspective:

- **Emergent behavior may have transient nature:** Emergent behavior appears when a certain effect becomes present, and may eventually disappear when the effect is no longer present. This implies that emergent behavior is *structurally decoupled* to its constituents; instead, there is a *behavioral dependency*. For example, traffic congestion in a road segment is neither a property of the road segment nor the cars passing the road segment; it is a transient effect caused by the individual decisions of drivers, road conditions, etc.
- **Emergent behavior may have elastic nature:** By definition, the effect cannot easily be reduced to individual constituents. One reason for this, which we consider in this paper, is that the multiplicity of the constituents may vary in due time. For example consider the emergent behavior traffic congestion. The number of cars that are involved in a traffic congestion may change; new cars may join the traffic congestion, which consequently cause the traffic congestion to grow in length and density; some cars may leave the traffic congestion, which cause the traffic congestion to shrink until it disappears. The changing number of constituents gives an elastic nature to emergent behavior.
- **Emergent behavior may have crosscutting nature:** Since there can be more than one constituent playing a role in emergent behavior, the effect caused by the properties and the relations of the constituents crosscuts the behavior of constituents.

Based on these characteristics, we claim that a programming language must offer suitable abstractions for the following matters:

- **Defining and acquiring data:** For the purpose of detecting the appearance and disappearance of emergent behavior, the language must provide means to detect the availability of the necessary data in constituents, and to receive it. The kinds of data that must be supported cannot be fixed, and are in general application specific. Besides, due to the elastic nature of emergent behavior, the constituents that provide the data may change in due time. These imply that the language must facilitate defining various data providers as well as various kinds of data that must be acquired from them.
- **Detecting the appearance and disappearance of emergent behavior:** In all four types of emergent behavior, the initial step is to detect the appearance and disappearance of certain behavior at runtime.
  Due to the inherent causal relation between emergent behavior and its constituents, the conditions for the appearance and disappearance of emergent behavior are defined as correlations among the data that is acquired from the constituents [13,14]. Therefore, to be able to program the transient nature of

emergent behavior, the language must provide suitable constructs to express the conditions for the appearance and disappearance of emergent behavior, to acquire the necessary data, and to evaluate the conditions.

- **Utilizing emergent behavior:** For each kind of emergent behavior, the language must facilitate maintaining necessary state information, and must offer means to define desired operations to access and manipulate this information. For example in the traffic simulation software, the language must facilitate maintaining information about the road segment and the average waiting time, in addition to defining necessary operations such as *display* and *log* to access and possibly manipulate this information.

  Emergent behavior goes through various states during its lifetime: it appears, it is represented in software as a runtime entity, the entity may be utilized in the software until the behavior disappears. To achieve a correct implementation of software, the language must offer suitable means to define and enforce desired synchronization rules. For example, emergent behavior cannot be considered as appeared and disappeared at the same time, or the runtime entity must no longer be utilized in the software when the emergent behavior has disappeared.

  In the types II, III and IV of emergent behavior, there is feedback from emergent behavior to its constituents as well as feed-froward from the constituents to the emergent behavior. These indicate the need for advanced techniques to adapt the behavior of constituents and the states of the emergent behavior during the execution of software. Such techniques are out of the scope of this paper; we mainly focus on suitable abstractions for defining synchronization rules and for accessing the states of emergent behavior.

- **Modularizing emergent behavior:** Software systems dealing with emergent behavior are complex because they usually need to consider multiple cases of emergent behavior [14]. Therefore, like in any complex software system, it is also necessary to properly modularize the concerns that exist in such software systems.

  Due to the crosscutting nature of emergent behavior and the structural decoupling to its constituents, the language must offer suitable means to separate and modularize emergent behavior and its corresponding concerns (e.g. appearance and disappearance conditions, utilization operations and synchronization rules). Consequently, if the definition of emergent behavior and its relevant concerns evolve, ripple modification effects on irrelevant parts of the software can be prevented.

5   Obstacles in Representing Emergent Behavior

The current trend in simulating emergent behavior in software is to adopt agent-oriented programming [15], where the constituents are represented as agents, and emergent interactions among the agents are detected. These solutions mainly focus on the detection of emergent behavior, rather than providing means to explicitly represent emergent behavior in applications and to utilize it.

	Transient Nature	Elastic Nature	Crosscutting Nature
AO languages with pointcut-based instantiation	Aspects' lifetime depends on the lifetime of base objects. Workarounds are needed to define aspect instantiation and destruction conditions.	Workarounds are needed to support a dynamic group of base objects.	Emergent behavior and its relevant concerns can be defined as one aspect module.
OO languages/ AO Languages unifying aspects and objects	Objects' lifetime depends on the lifetime of other objects. Application code is needed to program transient nature.	An aspect/ object is bound to a predefined set of base objects. Workarounds are needed to support a dynamic group of base objects.	Multiple objects and aspects are needed to program emergent behavior and its relevant concerns.
COP Languages	Complex appearance and disappearance conditions for contexts cannot be defined.	Contexts are defined for predefined sets of objects.	Some languages offer constructs to represent contexts as first-class entities.
Emergent gummy modules	An emergent gummy module is loosely coupled to the base objects. It encapsulates its appearance and disappearance conditions.	An emergent gummy module can receive events from several base objects.	An emergent behavior and its relevant concerns are modularized via emergent gummy modules.

Fig. 4. An evaluation of languages for representing emergent behavior

Therefore, one has to adopt OO, AO and/or COP languages to represent emergent behavior in software. In this section, we evaluate these languages in detail. Figure 4 summarizes our evaluation.

5.1   OO Languages

Historically, objects are regarded as abstractions over data and the set of operations that can be performed on the data. In an OO modularization of software, there are structural dependencies among objects, which are imposed by application requirements. In most mainstream languages such as Java, the lifetime of objects is influenced by the structural dependency of objects on each other; an object is destroyed if there is no reference to it from other objects.

These characteristics of OO modularization do not directly match the characteristics of emergent behavior. Emergent behavior is structurally decoupled to its constituents; instead, there is a behavioral dependency, which is transient. Due to the mentioned mismatch between the characteristics of emergent behavior and objects, application code must be provided to program emergent behavior. Like any other complex software system, we face the challenge of selecting the implementation that offers better software qualities such as adaptability and evolvability.

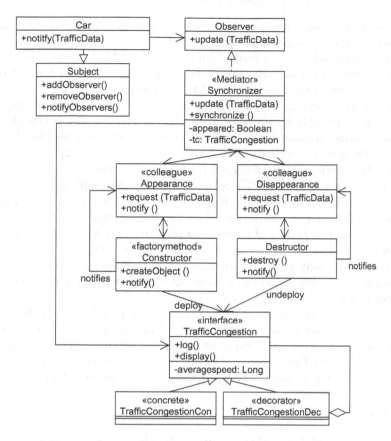

Fig. 5. An OO modularization of emergent behavior

For example, adopting the OO design patterns seems to be a proper choice since adaptability and evolvability of software is considered important. Figure 5 schematically represents an example implementation, in which the Observer, Mediator, Factory Method and Decorator patterns are adopted.

The Observer pattern is adopted to gather traffic data from the instances of *Car*, which represent cars entering and exiting a road segment.

The Mediator pattern is adopted to implement the synchronization rules between the classes *Appearance* and *Disappearance*, which implement the functionality to compute the appearance and disappearance conditions of traffic congestion. A synchronization rule is implemented as follows: if traffic congestion has not appeared in a road segment, the observed traffic data is forwarded from *Synchronizer* to *Appearance* to compute the appearance condition; otherwise, it is forwarded to *Disappearance*.

The classes *Constructor* and *Destructor* implement the functionality to instantiate and destroy an instance of the *TrafficCongestion* object. Depending on the adopted OO language, various implementation mechanisms such as object pooling, strong, weak and safe references can be adopted to construct and destruct the instances of *TrafficCongestion*. It is outside the scope of this paper to discuss all possible implementation mechanisms. The Decorator pattern is adopted to enforce that no method can be executed on the instance of *TrafficCongestion* if traffic congestion has disappeared.

Most design patterns emphasize reusability and evolvability of implementations. However, this comes with the price of increasing the complexity of implementations, because each pattern requires its own classes, its class hierarchies with specific methods, and its constraints. The complexity increases further where various association relations must be defined among the classes to facilitate exchanging data. Therefore, adopting such implementations significantly increases the overall complexity of the software that has to deal with various kinds of emergent behavior. Moreover, workarounds may still be needed to overcome the constraints of patterns in programming emergent behavior. For example, due to the elastic nature of traffic congestion, the cars that constitute traffic congestion may change; this means that workarounds must be provided to dynamically bind/un-bind the instance of *Synchronizer* to the corresponding instances of *Car*.

Another alternative to the Observer pattern is to adopt event-based communication to gather necessary information. Various proposals exist to extend existing languages to support event-based communications. The event-delegate mechanisms of C#, Ptolemy [16], EScala [17] and DominoJ [18] are examples. The above-mentioned complexity and problems exist in these languages too.

5.2   AO Languages

Due to the crosscutting nature of emergent behavior, an obvious choice is to adopt AO languages to modularly represent emergent behavior in software. AO languages offer the so-called *aspects* as means to modularize behavior that crosscuts multiple entities. To modularly represent emergent behavior via aspects, one may consider the constituents as *base objects*. The changes in the behavior of the constituents and the corresponding data can be represented via *join points*. *Pointcut designators* facilitate selecting the data of interest; *advice code* can be adopted to implement the functionality to process the data and compute the appearance or disappearance conditions of emergent behavior. Most AO languages facilitate defining various attributes and methods for utilizing aspects.

We classify AO languages into the languages that support explicit instantiation of aspects and the languages that support pointcut-based aspect instantiation. The languages in the first category [19,20] unify the notion of aspects and objects; as a result, an aspect is instantiated and treated in a similar way as objects. Where conventional objects can also be adopted instead of aspects to represent emergent behavior, aspects help to cope with the crosscutting nature of emergent behavior.

In these languages, aspects can dynamically be deployed/undeployed on base objects; this may facilitate programming the transient nature of emergent behavior. However, similar to OO languages, the appearance and disappearance conditions of emergent behavior as well as the necessary synchronization rules must be programmed via several classes. Moreover, these AO languages also have limitations to cope with the elastic nature of emergent behavior because an aspect instance can be deployed on a fixed set of objects.

In the AO languages that support pointcut-based aspect instantiation such as [4,21], emergent behavior and its relevant concerns can modularly be represented via an aspect. The appearance condition of emergent behavior may be expressed via a pointcut designator; if the pointcut is evaluated to TRUE, an aspect instance is constructed to represent emergent behavior. These languages, however, have two limitations to program the transient nature of emergent behavior.

Firstly, the pointcut designators have limited expression power to define various kinds of appearance conditions of emergent behavior. As a result, workaround code must be provided via advice code. Secondly, aspect instances remain active as long as their corresponding base objects are not destroyed. However, the lifetime of emergent behavior does not usually depend on the lifetime of its constituents; it conditionally depends on the behavior and properties of the constituents. For example the lifetime of traffic congestion is independent of the actual lifetime of a road segment and cars in the road segment. Instead, it depends on the average travel time of the cars in a given time period. These two shortcomings oblige programmers to provide workarounds, which may not fulfill application requirements and may increase the complexity of implementations.

These AO languages also fall short in programming the elastic nature of emergent behavior. An aspect can be instantiated as a singleton object, or it can be bound to one or a specific group of objects [20]. Therefore, workarounds must be provided to bind an aspect to a group with dynamically changing constituents. Such workarounds naturally increase the complexity of implementations.

Let us illustrate these shortcomings by means of an example. We adopt AspectJ, which is a widely-used AO language, for the purpose of presentation; however, the discussions are generic to other AO languages in this category. To compute the appearance of traffic congestion in a road segment, we need to collect information from each individual car that enters and exits the road segment. This requires binding an aspect instance to multiple base objects (i.e. car objects) and being able to coping with the dynamically changing number of base objects. Since AspectJ cannot support this dynamic nature in the base objects, as a workaround we assume that there is the Java class *Segment* whose individual instances represent individual road segments and provide corresponding traffic data from the cars passing the road segment.

Figure 6 shows the aspect *TrafficCongestion*, which provides a modular representation of traffic congestion. The pointcut designator *selecting* in lines 4–6 implements the functionality to collect traffic data which is provided via the argument *data* of the method *notify*. The pointcut designators and instantiation strategy of AspectJ are not expressive enough to accumulate data; therefore, we have to adopt advice code as a workaround. The advice code in lines 7–14 implements the functionality for accumulating the data and detecting the appearance

```
1. public aspect TrafficCongestion pertarget(selecting (SensorData, Segment)){
2.    private boolean constructed;
3.    private static long T = 10, W = 30;
4.    pointcut selecting(TrafficData data, Segment s):
5.        execution(void Segment.notify(TrafficData))
6.        && target(s) && args(data);
7.    after(TrafficData data, Segment s): selecting (data, s){
8.        if (!constructed) {
9.            //compute the appearance condition
10.           if (computeAverageWaitingTime(data) >= W){
11.               this.constructed = Boolean.TRUE;
12.               //initialize the fields
13.           }
14.       }
15.       else
16.           if (computeAverageWaitingTime(data) < W)
17.               this.constructed = Boolean.FALSE;
18.   }
19.   private static long computeAverageWaitingTime (TrafficData data){...}
20.   private long w_time;
21.   public void log(){ if (this.constructed){ … }}
22.   public void display (){ if (this.constructed){ … }}
23.}
```

Fig. 6. An AO modularization of emergent behavior

of traffic congestion. The pointcut designator *selecting* is consequently specified in line 1 as the instantiator pointcut; an aspect instance is constructed for each instance of *Segment* as soon as traffic data is available in a road segment.

AspectJ does not offer explicit language constructs to destruct aspect instances; an aspect instance remains alive as long as its corresponding base object is alive. For this reason, we define the workaround variable *constructed* to mark the aspect instance as destructed if it is concluded that traffic congestion has disappeared in a road segment. The advice code in lines 15–18 is provided to compute the disappearance condition and to mark the aspect instance as destructed. Since the aspect instance is not destroyed, the instantiation strategy in line 1 is not executed to compute the re-appearance of traffic congestion; instead the advice code in lines 7–14 marks the aspect instance as *constructed*.

To facilitate utilizing traffic congestion in the software, lines 20–22 define a set of attributes and methods for the aspect. The extra checks in the methods *log* and *display* are to define the synchronization rules; if an aspect is marked as destructed, its utilization must be prevented.

Adopting an AspectJ-like language to represent emergent behavior gives the advantage of defining the emergent behavior and its relevant concerns (i.e. appearance and disappearance conditions, utilization operations, and synchronization rules) in one module. Therefore, evolutions of these can be encapsulated within the aspect module. However, as the red lines in Fig. 6 show, significant workarounds are needed to program the transient and elastic nature of emergent behavior. Such workarounds increase the complexity of implementations; besides the implementations may not fulfill application requirements. For example, an instance of *TrafficCongestion* is constructed as soon as the first traffic data is observed in a road segment even if no traffic congestion has appeared in the road segment.

There are several proposals to increase the expression power of pointcut designators, for example via history-based pointcuts [22,23]. As we have extensively studied in [24], such extensions also have limited expression power to define various appearance conditions. Moreover, these extensions are not integrated with the instantiation strategy of the AO languages.

5.3 COP Languages

Emergent behavior can be considered a fundamental concept in developing self-adaptive/context-aware applications. In the types II and III, emergent behavior can be seen as a transient situation (*context*); as long as it exists, its constituents must be able to handle feedback from the emergent behavior and adapt their behavior within the context of the emergent behavior. Such adaptations may in turn influence the states of the emergent behavior; for example, it may cause the emergent behavior to disappear.

Context-oriented programming (COP) [6] has been introduced to facilitate modular implementation of context-aware applications. Considering emergent behavior as a special kind of context, we also study the suitability of COP languages in representing emergent behavior.

A large number of COP languages have been proposed in the literature. Due to the crosscutting nature of emergent behavior, we focus on the COP languages that benefit from AO features to modularize context activation and layer composition [25–28].

JCop [25] offers predicates, which are similar to conditional pointcut expressions, to specify the methods to whose dynamic extent a layer composition must be applied. JCop also provides a dedicated construct for representing contexts as first-class entities. These are special singleton types that cannot be instantiated. Therefore, JCop falls short in supporting the elastic and transient nature of emergent behavior.

In ECaesarJ [26], a context is defined as a class implementing two events representing the activation and the deactivation of the context. Events can be defined explicitly, or via AspectJ-like pointcut expressions. Complex events can also be defined via composing simpler events. ECaesarJ supports quantification on a list of objects, where an event can be defined as a disjunction of the events that occur on different objects. ECaesarJ partially copes with the transient nature of emergent behavior, because only the disjunction operator is supported to define complex appearance/disappearance conditions over the events published by a group of constituent objects. ECaesarJ has the same shortcomings as its predecessor AO language CaesarJ [19] in supporting the elastic nature of emergent behavior.

EventCJ [27] is another COP language that benefits from AspectJ-like pointcut expressions to define contextual events that must trigger a layer activation. Here, events and layer transition rules are supported to specify when and how layer switching should happen, respectively. Via two available operators in EventCJ, contextual situations can be specified as conditions in layer transition rules. Due to the limited expression power of these operators, complex appearance/disappearance conditions cannot be programmed. Moreover, contexts are defined per object; as a result, the elastic nature of emergent behavior in which multiple objects incorporate in the appearance/disappearance of the emergent behavior cannot be supported.

ServalCJ [28] offers dedicated constructs to define context groups, which facilitate grouping related specifications of layer activation into one module. ServalCJ offers a limited set of constructs to define layer activation conditions for each context groups. Context groups can be instantiated explicitly in a similar way as conventional objects. Each instance of context group contains a set of so-called subscribers that are objects to which the specified layer activation is applied. Objects must explicitly subscribe to context groups in a similar way as in the Observer pattern. Due to these similarities of ServalCJ to conventional OO languages, it suffers from the same shortcomings explained in Sect. 5.1 in implementing emergent behavior.

6   Emergent Gummy Modules

During the past years, we have been developing the concept of **event-based modularization** [7, 24, 29, 30], which offers novel linguistic abstractions for modular representation of (emergent) behavior in software.

Our recent development is **emergent gummy modules** [7], which facilitate defining emergent behavior, its appearance and disappearance conditions, its utilization operations and necessary synchronization rules as one holistic module. Figure 7 represents the abstract syntax of emergent gummy modules. Note that this is a description of emergent gummy modules, not the syntax of a particular language in which this concept is implemented.

A *Program* consists of a set of events, emergent gummy modules, and ordinary objects communicating with emergent gummy modules. We consider the notion of events fundamental to represent emergent behavior and to achieve loose coupling to constituent objects. An event represents a state change of interest in the environment, and is used to represent and convey necessary information about behavior in the environment. As the expressions *Event* and *Attribute* show, an event can convey necessary information about the state changes via its attributes. An attribute is recognized by its unique identifier, type, and value.

As the expression *EmergentGummyModule* shows, an emergent gummy module is recognized by its unique identifier, and may define a set of static and instance-level local variables and methods. An emergent gummy module may consist of three kinds of code blocks, which interact with the environment; these are identified as *Appearance*, *Disappearance* and *Utilization* code blocks.

The *Appearance* code block implements the functionality to compute appearance conditions of emergent behavior. To this aim, it filters the events of interest from the environment; as the expression *EventSelector* shows the event selection semantics are defined as predicates over events and their attributes.

Before an emergent gummy module is instantiated, the *Appearance* code block cannot access instance-level variables and methods defined in the module.

Program ::= (e: Event| m: EmergentGummyModule | o: Object)*
Event ::= Attribute*
Attribute ::= id: Identifier; t : Type; v : Value
                       where *Value* is an acceptable value for *Type*
EmergentGummyModule ::= id: Identifier; Variable*; Method*;
                            Appearance; Disappearance; Utilization*
Appearance ::= EventSelector; Initializer*; AppearanceStatement*; (**construct**; Statement*)?
Disappearance ::= EventSelector; Statement*; (**destruct**; Statement*)?
Utilization ::= EventSelector; Statement*
EventSelector ::= q $\in$ Q
               where *Q* is a set of acceptable logical predicates
Initializer ::= Variable (= initialization statement)?
Variable ::= id: Identifier; t: Type
Method ::= Signature; Statement*
Identifier ::= an acceptable identifier in the language
Signature ::= an acceptable signature in the language
Type ::= t $\in$ T
          Where *T* is a set of acceptable types in the language
AppearanceStatement ::= s $\in$ S\M
               Where *S* is the set of supported statements in the language
               M is the set of supported statements modifying the
               local variables of emergent gummy module
Statement ::= s $\in$ S\{**construct, destruct**}
               where *S* is the set of supported statements in the language

Fig. 7. The abstract syntax of emergent gummy modules

Necessary local variables for computing the appearance conditions can be defined and initialized via a set of *Initializer* statements. These statements are executed only once, when the *Appearance* code block is executed for the first time.

The *Appearance* code block contains a set of statements for computing the appearance conditions, which eventually may lead to a request to *construct* an instance of the corresponding emergent gummy module. The construction request may be followed with more statements to perform necessary operations after the instantiation of an emergent gummy module; for example, to initialize its local variables.

Likewise, the *Disappearance* code block implements the functionality to compute disappearance conditions of emergent behavior. It may eventually request to *destruct* the instance of the corresponding emergent gummy module. This request may be followed by more statements that must be executed upon destruction, for example to release the acquired resources.

An emergent gummy module may define zero or more *Utilization* code blocks. These blocks are means to perform desired operations on the local variables of the module. They receive the requests to perform an operation via events, which are filtered using the specified event selection predicates. Within these code blocks, various operations can be performed on the events, except for requesting to construct or destruct the instance of emergent gummy module.

The semantic constraints of emergent gummy modules are shown in Fig. 8 in which white and gray rectangles are active and inactive parts of emergent

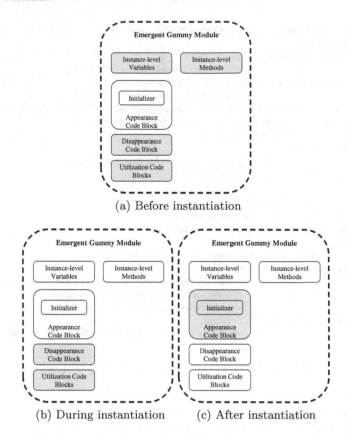

(a) Before instantiation

(b) During instantiation   (c) After instantiation

Fig. 8. The activation time of each code block

gummy modules, respectively. As Fig. 8a shows, before an instance of an emergent gummy module is constructed, its appearance code block is the only active code block of the module, which responds to the events in the environment. This code block can access the local variables that are defined in its *Initializer*; however, the instance-level variables and methods that are defined within the enclosing emergent gummy module are not accessible. Besides, the *Disappearance* and *Utilization* code blocks are inactive.

Figure 8b shows the case where the *construct* statement in the *Appearance* code block is executed, and an instance of the emergent gummy module is under construction. In this case, the instance-level variables and methods in the enclosing emergent gummy module are accessible within the *Appearance* code block, for example to initialize the instance-level variables. However, the *Disappearance* and *Utilization* code blocks remain inactive until the execution of the *Appearance* code block terminates successfully.

Figure 8c shows the case where the execution of the *Appearance* code block has successfully terminated. In this case, the *Appearance* code block is deactivated and the *Disappearance* and *Utilization* code blocks are finally activated.

In responding to the environmental events, the disappearance code block has a higher priority over the utilization code blocks that select the same set of events. This means that upon arrival of an event, if it matches the event selection predicate of the disappearance block, it is first processed by this block. If the event processing causes the module instance to be destructed, the *Disappearance* and *Utilization* code blocks are deactivated after the execution of the *Disappearance* terminates successfully. This will also cause the *Appearance* code block of the emergent gummy module to be activated.

If the event processing in the *Disappearance* code block does not cause the module instance to be destructed, the event is processed by the utilization code blocks whose event selection predicates matches the event.

7   The GummyJ Language

In this paper, we explain an implementation of emergent gummy modules in the GummyJ 1.0 language[1]. We provide an implementation of our illustrative examples to explain the language. The implementation makes use of some helper Java classes to implement the necessary functionality of our examples; due to the page limit we do not explain the details of these classes.

7.1   The Fraud Detection Software

In the following, we represent how frauds can be represented via emergent gummy modules.

Modular Definition of Event Types. In GummyJ, we consider events as typed entities. An event type is a data structure defining a set of attributes, where an event is an instance that contains the values of these attributes. There can be an inheritance relation among event types. Listing 1 shows an excerpt of the specified event types. Here, EventType is the default super type of all event types, which defines the attributes publisherID, targetID and stacktrace. These keep the unique identifier of the event publisher, the target emergent gummy module, and information about the active stack frames at the time events are published, respectively.

```
1  eventtype EventType{
2      String publisherID; String targetID; gummy.types.StackTrace stacktrace;}
3  eventtype WithdrawalEvent extends EventType{
4      String account; Long amount; Long time; Fraud.ATMCoordinate coordinate;}
5  eventtype RemoveEvent extends EventType{ String account;}
```

Listing 1. The modular definition of fraud-related event types

---

[1] https://github.com/malakuti/gummyj.

For our fraud detection software we define the type WithdrawalEvent, which has four attributes account, amount, time and coordinate. The events of type RemoveEvent are used to issue requests for destroying fraud objects.

Modular Representation of Frauds. Listing 2 shows the definition of the module Fraud, which is defined for modular representation of frauds in software Since frauds must be detected for each bank account, the gummy module receives the account number via its parameter account.

Lines 4–5 define the local variables coordinates and times to keep the ATM coordinates and the cash withdrawal times.

Lines 8–39 define the appearance code block for Fraud. The appearance keyword indicates that this code block may request to instantiate the emergent gummy module Fraud. This code block is executed when there is no instance of the module for the given bank account, and when an event matches the specified predicate in lines 8–9. This predicate filters the withdrawal events issued for account.

In GummyJ, the event selection expressions are defined as Boolean predicates over event attributes. The keyword input in the language refers to the current event being processed by the language, and is of the type EventType.

Before a module is instantiated, its instance-level variables and methods cannot be accessed within its appearance code block. One can define local variables for the appearance code block via the initializer block. This block is executed only once, when the appearance code block is executed for the first time. In our example, the local variables counter, first_coordinate and first_time are defined in lines 11–13. These variables keep the number of cash withdrawals, the ATM coordinate and the time when the first cash withdrawal has occurred, respectively.

Lines 16–20 are executed upon the first cash withdrawal attempt, and initialize the variables first_coordinate and first_time. In lines 22–25, the criteria for fraud detection is checked by the help of Java methods checkDistance and checkTime. If this criteria holds, a request for constructing an instance of the gummy module Fraud for the account number represented by account is issued in line 27. Afterwards, the instance-level variables of the gummy modules are initialized in lines 28–31.

If the fraud criteria does not hold, the variables counter, first_coordinate and first_time are reset in lines 34–36 to take the next cash withdrawal attempt into account.

Lines 42–45 define the disappearance code block for the module Fraud. Here the condition is to receive events of the type RemoveEvent for instance of Fraud whose parameter account matches the attribute account of the events. Such events can be published by the administrator of the software, when she/he decides to remove specific instances of the module Fraud.

```
1  import Fraud.*;
2  emergentgummymodule Fraud (String account) {
3    // The specification of instance−level variables
4    ATMCoordinate [] coordinates = new ATMCoordinate [2];
5    Long [] times = new Long [2];
6
7    // The specification of the appearance code block
8    appearance (input in [WithdrawalEvent]
9           && input.get("account") == account) {
10     initializer{
11          int counter = 0;
12          ATMCoordinate first_coordinate;
13          Long first_time;
14      }
15      counter ++;
16      if (counter == 1)
17      {
18          first_coordinate = input.get("coordinate");
19          first_time = input.get("time");
20      }
21      else {
22          if ((FraudHelper.checkDistance(
23                  input.get("coordinate"),first_coordinate) > 100)
24              && (FraudHelper.checkTime(
25                  input.get("time"), first_time) < 3600000))
26          {
27              construct;
28              coordinates [0] = first_coordinate;
29              coordinates [1] = input.get("coordinate");
30              times [0] = first_time;
31              times [1] = input.get("time");
32          }
33          else {
34              counter = 1;
35              first_coordinate = input.get("coordinate");
36              first_time = input.get("time");
37          }
38      }
39   }
40
41   // The specification of the disappearance code block
42   disappearance (input in [RemoveEvent]
43          && input.get("account") == account) {
44     destruct;
45   }
46 }
```

Listing 2. The modular representation of frauds

7.2   The Traffic Simulation Software

In the following, we represent how our second case study is implemented in GummyJ.

Modular Definition of Event Types. For our traffic simulation software we define the following event types. The events of type `CarEvent` are published by the cars when they enter or exit a road segment; they carry along the coordinates of the corresponding road segment, the time of entrance or exit as well as the speed of the car. The events of type `LogEvent` and `DisplayEvent` are means to represent the requests to log and display traffic congestion information, respectively. The events of type `GetInfoEvent` are means to get information about the average waiting time of traffic congestion.

```
1  eventtype CarEvent extends EventType{TMS.CarCoordinate coordinate; Long time;}
2  eventtype LogEvent extends EventType{}
3  eventtype DisplayEvent extends EventType{}
4  eventtype GetInfoEvent extends EventType{Long waitingtime;}
```

Listing 3. The modular definition of traffic-related event types

Modularization of Emergent Behavior. For our illustrative example, we would like to represent traffic congestion that appears in each road segment as individual instances of an emergent gummy module. In this case, we consider the cars that enter or exit a road segment as the constituents of the emergent behavior traffic congestion, whose events are processed by `TrafficCongestion`. The road segments are means to limit the scopes of the emergent behavior traffic congestion.

Listing 4 shows the definition of the module `TrafficCongestion`, which is defined for this matter. The gummy module receives the coordinates of the corresponding segment via its parameter `s_coordinate`.

Line 5 defines the static variable `W`, which maintains the threshold for average waiting time. Line 6 defines the instance-level variable `w_time`, which maintains the average speed of traffic congestion for each instance of `TrafficCongestion`. Lines 7–8 define the instance-level variables `cars` and `times` to accumulate information about the cars in a road segment, and the time that each car took to travel across the segment.

Lines 11–24 define the appearance code block for `TrafficCcongestion`. The keyword **appearance** indicates that this code block may request to instantiate the emergent gummy module `TrafficCongestion`. This code block is executed when there is no instance of the module for the given road segment, and when an event matches the specified predicate. The expression in lines 11–12 filters the events whose type matches `CarEvent`, and via the helper method `inSegment` filters the events whose coordinate is within the road segment specified by `s_coordinate`.

```
1  import TMS.*;
2  emergentgummymodule TrafficCongestion (TMS.SegmentCoordinate s_coordinate)
3  {
4     // The specification of the instance-level variables
5     static Long W = new Long(30);
6     Long w_time;
7     HashMap<Object, CarInfo> cars = new HashMap<Object, CarInfo>();
8     ArrayList<Long> times = new ArrayList<Long>();
9
10    // The specification of the appearance code block
11    appearance (input in [CarEvent]
12       && TMSHelper.inSegment(input.get("coordinate"), s_coordinate)) {
13       initializer {
14          HashMap<Object, CarInfo> a_cars = new HashMap<Object, CarInfo>();
15          ArrayList<Long> a_times = new ArrayList<Long>();
16       }
17       Long avg = TMSHelper.computeAverageWaitingTime (a_cars, a_times, input);
18       if (avg >= W){
19          construct;
20          w_time = avg;
21          cars.putAll(a_cars);
22          times.putall(a_times);
23       }
24    }
25
26    // The specification of the disappearance code block
27    disappearance (input in [CarEvent]
28      && TMSHelper.inSegment(input.get("coordinate"), s_coordinate)){
29      Long avg = TMSHelper.computeAverageWaitingTime (cars, times, input);
30    if (avg < W) destruct;
31    }
32
33    // The specification of the utilization code blocks
34    update (input in [CarEvent]
35       && TMSHelper.inSegment(input.get("coordinate"), s_coordinate)) {
36       w_time = TMSHelper.computeAverageWaitingTime (cars, times, input);
37    }
38
39    log (input in [LogEvent]) { TMSHelper.log(w_time); }
40    display (input in [DisplayEvent]) { TMSHelper.display(w_time); }
41    getWaitingTime (input in [GetInfoEvent]) {
42       input.set("waitingtime", w_time);
43    }
44 }
```

Listing 4. The modular representation of traffic congestion

The local variables `a_cars` and `a_times` are defined in lines 14 and 15, respectively, to maintain necessary information about the cars and their travel time.

In line 17, the helper method `computeAverageWaitingTime` is invoked to compute the average travel time of the cars in the road segment within the time period T. If the average travel time is equal or above W, a request to instantiate `TrafficCongestion` is issued to the runtime environment of GummyJ. After the instantiation, the control of execution returns to line 20, in which local variables of `TrafficCongestion` are updated.

Lines 27–31 define a code block encapsulating the condition for the disappearance of traffic congestion. The keyword `disappearance` indicates that this code block may request to destroy an instance of `TrafficCongestion`. This code block is executed after `TrafficCongestion` is instantiated for the given road segment, and when an event is selected by its predicate.

Lines 34–37 define the code block `update` to update the information about the average waiting time in the road segment; this code block is executed in the time interval after an instance of `TrafficCongestion` is constructed, and before it is destroyed. Since both `disappear` and `update` react to the same set of events, according to the semantics explained in Sect. 9, `disappear` has higher priority to process the events. This is because processing the events may cause the instance of `TrafficCongestion` to be destroyed.

The code blocks `log`, `display` and `getWaitingTime` show three utilization examples, which define the functionality to log, display and get average waiting time of traffic congestion, respectively.

8   Utilization of Emergent Gummy Modules

If emergent behavior is represented as a first-class entity in software, suitable linguistic abstractions are required to utilize the entity in the software, for example, by accessing it, manipulating its internal variables, passing it as an argument of method calls, etc. In this section, we explain possible ways of utilizing emergent gummy modules in Java programs.

8.1   Introducing Emergent Gummy Modules in GummyJ Runtime

An emergent gummy module is defined in two steps: (1) its semantics is defined as shown in Listing 4, and (2) it is introduced in the GummyJ runtime, so that it can start processing events and be instantiated. In this step, the actual value of the module's parameters is also defined.

Assume for example that we have two road segments and at runtime we want to have two instances of the emergent gummy module `TrafficCongestion` to represent traffic congestion in these segments. As lines 1–5 of Listing 5 shows, we define the class `Segment`, whose instances represent road segments. Lines 12–14 of Listing 5 make use of the method `introduce` of GummyJ to introduce two variables of the type `TrafficCongestion` to represent traffic congestion in the road segments `segment_1` and `segment_2`, respectively.

It is worth mentioning that at this step, the `TrafficCongestion` module is not instantiated yet, only it is introduced that two instances of the module may exist at runtime. The actual instantiation takes place when the `construct` statement in the appearance code block of these is executed.

As the argument `TrafficCongestion_Segment_2` in line 14 shows, it is possible to define a unique index for a module instance to communicate with that instance later on (see lines 5 and 13 in Listing 8). If not specified by programmers, by default, the index key is a string literal concatenating the type of emergent gummy module with a unique random number.

```
1  public class Segment{
2    public TMS.SegmentCoordinate coordinate;
3    public Long segmentID;
4    ...
5  }
6  ...
7  public class Initializer {
8    public void initialize (){
9      Segment segment_1 = new Segment ();
10     Segment segment_2 = new Segment ();
11     ...
12     GummyJ.introduce(TrafficCongestion.class, segment_1.coordinate);
13     GummyJ.introduce(TrafficCongestion.class,
14            "TrafficCongestion_Segment_2", segment_2.coordinate);
15   }
16 }
```

Listing 5. An example definition of variables

8.2   Communicating with Emergent Gummy Modules

Communications with emergent gummy modules are performed via events, which are published in a synchronous or asynchronous manner. There are two main kinds of entities that may publish events to emergent gummy modules. (a) Environmental entities, which provide necessary data to reason about the appearance and disappearance of emergent behavior. The transient, elastic and crosscutting nature of emergent behavior is related to these entities. (b) Application entities, which utilize emergent gummy modules in software.

In GummyJ, Java objects can be adopted to represent both environmental and application entities. Nevertheless, it is also possible to support other kinds of external environmental entities, provided that there are means to publish and receive necessary events from them. In the following we illustrate various examples of communicating with emergent gummy modules.

Communicating from Environmental Entities: In GummyJ, each event type is translated to a Java class, whose instances are means to represent specific events. Events can be published from various sources; for example, we have shown that via utilizing Java-JNI [31], events can be published from software implemented in various languages [24].

Events can be broadcast to all instances of emergent gummy modules, or to a specific instance specified by its index key. For the latter case, the target emergent gummy module of an event must be specified in the attribute `targetID` of the event.

Listing 6 shows an example code publishing events in an asynchronous manner from a Java program. Here, we assume that each instance of the class `Car` represents a car passing a road segment. Each instance publishes an event of the type `CarEvent` upon entering a road segment. For this matter, an instance of `CarEvent` is constructed, its attributes are initialized, and is published to the runtime manager of GummyJ via the method `publish`.

```
1  public class Car{
2    private TMS.SegmentCoordinate coordinate;
3    private String ID;
4    ...
5     public void enter (){
6     CarEvent event = new CarEvent();
7     event.setPublisherID(this.ID);
8     event.setTime(getCurrentTime());
9     event.setCoordinate(this.coordinate);
10    GummyJ.publish(event, Mode.Asynchronous);
11   }
12   ...
13  }
```

Listing 6. An example event publishing code

The formal semantics of GummyJ in processing events is explained in Sect. 9. Assume for example that `TrafficCongestion(segment_1.coordinate)` and `TrafficCongestion(segment_2.coordinate)` are introduced in the GummJ runtime via Listing 5, but not instantiated yet.

The runtime manager of GummyJ receives the event that is published in line 10 of Listing 6. Since no specific target is specified for this event, the runtime manager provides it to both `TrafficCongestion(segment_1.coordinate)` and `TrafficCongestion(segment_2.coordinate)`. The appearance code block is the only active block to process the event. If the event matches the event selection expression of the appearance code block, it will be further processed in the code block. Other input events are processed likewise. If any of these modules is eventually instantiated, its appearance code block is deactivated, and its disappearance and other utilization blocks are activated.

To reason about the appearance and disappearance of emergent behavior, it may be needed to deal with a large amount of environmental events. There are various kinds of event processing engines that offer means to gather events, to reason about correlation of events, to define spanning time windows over event streams, and to filter events [8]. GummyJ can be adopted in combination with these engines to receive environmental events.

Assume for example that we would like to reason about the emergence of traffic congestion only during day time, between 6:00 a.m. and 5:59 p.m. We would like to adopt a complex event processing engine to filter out the events that occur before or after this time. Listing 7 shows an example usage of the complex event processing engine Esper [8] in combination with GummyJ.

```
1  final EPStatement statement;
2  String stmt = "select carId, t_hour, t_minute, x_coordinate,
3                 y_coordinate" + "from CarEntity" +
4                 "where t_hour in [6:17] and t_minute in [0:59]" ;
5  statement = epService.getEPAdministrator().createEPL(stmt);
6  statement.addListener(new UpdateListener() {
7    public void update(EventBean[] newEvents, EventBean[] oldEvents) {
8      CarEvent c_event = new CarEvent();
9      c_event.setPublisherID(newEvents[0].get("carId"));
10     c_event.setTime(TimeConverter.convert(
11         newEvents[0].get("t_hour"), newEvents[0].get("t_minute")));
12     c_event.setCoordinate(CoordinateConverter.convert(
13         newEvents[0].get("x_coordinate"),newEvents[0].get("y_coordinate")));
14     GummyJ.publish(c_event, Mode.Asynchronous);
15   }
16 }
```

Listing 7. An example integration with Esper

In Esper, events can be represented as JavaBean classes, legacy Java classes, an XML document or java.util.Map. SQL-like statements are supported to query the events of interest from event streams. In Listing 7, we assume that there is a JavaBean class named as `CarEntity`, which defines the attributes carId, t_hour, t_minute, x_coordinate and y_coordinate. Each instance of this class represents an event indicating that a car has entered or exited a road segment.

Lines 2–4 define an expression to query the events occurring between 6:00 a.m. and 5:59 p.m. This expression is translated to an Esper statement object in line 5. Lines 6–16 define a so-called listener, which implements the functionality to react to each selected event. Here, we define c_event as an instance of `CarEvent`, update its attribute with the related attributes of the selected event, and publish c_event to GummyJ.

Communicating from Application Objects: Lines 3–7 of Listing 8 show an example utilization of emergent gummy modules, in which a request to display traffic congestion information is broadcast to all emergent gummy modules whose index key matches the expression `"TrafficCongestion*"`. In our example, the runtime manager of GummyJ provides this event to both `TrafficCongestion` (`segment_1.coordinate`) and `TrafficCongestion(segment_2.coordinate)` in the order they are introduced to the language. The `display` code block of the ones that are already instantiated reacts to this event.

```
 1  public class Utilizer (){
 2    ...
 3    public void displayInfo (){
 4      DisplayEvent event = new DisplayEvent();
 5      event.setTargetID("TrafficCongestion*");
 6      GummyJ.publish(event, Mode.Asynchronous);
 7    }
 8    public void logInfoAll (){
 9      HashMap<String, EmergentGummyModule> modules =
10              GummyJ.retrieveall("TrafficCongestion*");
11      for (String key: modules.keySet()) {
12          GetInfoEvent event = new GetInfoEvent();
13          event.setTargetID(key);
14          GummyJ.publish(event, Mode.Synchronous);
15          if (event.getWaitingTime() != null)
16              System.out.println(event.getWaitingTime());
17      }
18    }
19    ...
20  }
```

Listing 8. An example utilization of emergent gummy modules

Lines 8–18 of Listing 8 show another usage example, which retrieves the current waiting time of traffic congestion in each road segment. Here, via the method `retreiveall` of GummyJ, references to modules whose index key matches the pattern "`TrafficCongestion*`" are retrieved. The results are stored in `modules`. Here, `EmergentGummyModule` is the super type of all emergent gummy modules in GummyJ.

In lines 12–14, an event of the type `GetInfo` is prepared and published to each emergent gummy module in a synchronous manner. If the target module is not instantiated yet, the event is provided to its `appearance` code block. In our example, this event does not match the event selection expression of the code block and is ignored by the emergent gummy module. As a result, the attribute `waitingtime` of the `event` will have the `null` value. If the target gummy module is already instantiated, this event is processed by its `getWaitingTime` code block, which sets the current waiting time in the attribute `waitingtime` of the input event.

8.3   Communicating from Emergent Gummy Modules

Emergent gummy modules can also refer to Java objects and interact with them via method invocation. Java objects can be provided to emergent gummy module via the parameters of the module and/or attributes of the events. Line 2 of Listing 4 shows an example, in which an instance of `SegmentCoordinate` is provided to `TrafficCongestion` via the parameter of the module.

9   Event Processing Semantics of GummyJ

An application developed in GummyJ consists of a set of emergent gummy modules, environmental objects and application objects that communicate with emergent gummy modules via events. Due to the support for asynchronous event publishing, the objects and emergent gummy modules are executed concurrently. Although not shown in this paper, emergent gummy modules may also publish events like ordinary application objects. This is useful when it is necessary to infer more complex emergent behavior from simpler ones.

As for any other general-purpose abstraction, the ways that emergent gummy modules are defined, communicate with each other and with their environment depends on application requirements. Nevertheless, to get an insight about the behavior of applications developed in GummyJ, we adopt the UPPAAL toolbox [32] to formally simulate possible behavior of emergent gummy modules independently from any specific application.

In UPPAAL, behavior of a system can modularly be represented via a set of automata, which execute concurrently and communicate with each other via channels and/or global variables. An automaton consists of a set of states and labelled transitions. Local variables, data structures and C-style functions can be defined and used in the automata, to maintain and manipulate necessary state information. In channel-based communications, an automaton may send the channel $c!$, which is received by another automaton via $c?$ through a state transition.

Figures 9, 10, 11, and 12 show the automata for the coordinator entitics, the appearance, disappearance and utilization code blocks, respectively. There is a separate instance of the automata in Figs. 9, 10, 11, and 12 for each emergent gummy module that is introduced in the GummyJ language (see lines 12–14 in Listing 5 for introducing emergent gummy modules in the GummyJ runtime). These instances are distinguished by the variable gm_id in the models. In the following we explain the runtime behavior of GummyJ in detail.

9.1   Data Structures and Variables

Listing 9 shows an example set of data structures and variables that are defined for our models. We define the data structure *BaseEventType* to represent event types, and the variable *input* of this type. The variable *input* represents an event that is retrieved to be processed by each introduced emergent gummy module. We define the variable *local_eventqueue* to maintain a queue of the input events for each introduced emergent gummy module.

The variable *statement* represents the *construct* statement, the *destruct* statement, or the statements to access local variables/methods in emergent gummy modules. The variables *counter* and *block* represent the number of active code blocks and the current code block that must process events, respectively. The variables *constructing* and *constructed* indicate whether an instance of an emergent gummy module is under construction or constructed, respectively. Likewise, the variables *destructing* and *destructed* represent the destruction state of an emergent gummy module. In addition to these variables, we define a set of channels and helper functions, which are explained throughout the paper.

```
1  typedef int[0,1] GMDID;
2  typedef struct {
3    TYPE type;
4    TargetID target;
5    PublisherID publisher;
6    int timestamp;
7  } BaseEventType;
8
9  BaseEventType input[GMDID];
10 BaseEventType local_eventqueue[GMDID][10];
11 int statement[GMDID];
12 int counter[GMDID];
13 int block[GMDID];
14 int[0,1] constructing[GMDID], destructing[GMDID],
15          constructed[GMDID], destructed[GMDID];
```

Listing 9. Example set of data structures and variables

9.2 The Runtime Manager

The runtime manager of GummyJ has a pool in which reference to the emergent gummy modules that are introduced in the GummyJ runtime are maintained. These references are sorted in this pool based on the order in which they are introduced in the GummyJ runtime.

The runtime manager receives events from application objects and external entities, and maintains them in a queue. It dispatches the events to all emergent gummy modules in a FIFO manner. This is done by copying the event in the local event queue of each introduced emergent gummy module.

9.3 Coordinator Entities

If an emergent gummy module is not instantiated yet, its appearance code block is the only active code block. After the instantiation, this code block is deactivated, and the disappearance and utilization code blocks are activated.

Each emergent gummy module that is introduced in the GummyJ runtime (see lines 12–14 in Listing 5) has a coordinator entity, which implements the functionality to activate and deactivate the code blocks of the module, and to construct/destruct the instances of the module.

The coordinator object is instantiated by the runtime manager when an emergent gummy module is introduced in the runtime manager. Each coordinator has a local queue (represented by *local_eventqueue[gm_id]*) to maintain the events that are dispatched to the corresponding emergent gummy module by the runtime manager. This implies that if multiple modules are introduced in the language, the input events are processed by them concurrently.

Figure 9 shows the semantics of the coordinator entities. The runtime manager issues the request to instantiate the coordinator of the emergent gummy module *gm_id* via the channel synchronization *instantiate_coordinator[gm_id]?*. As a result, the coordinator is instantiated and the local event queue is initialized via the function *initialize(gm_id)*. Via the channel synchronization *instantiate_coordinator_return[gm_id]!*, the runtime manager is informed that the coordinator is instantiated, which also result in a transition to the location *Get_Event*.

In this location, the event at the head of the local event queue is retrieved, if any, and is stored in the variable *input[gm_id]*. If there is an event to process, *!NULL(input[gm_id])*, the number of code blocks and the information about active code blocks of the corresponding module are retrieved in the variables *counter[gm_id]* and *blocks[gm_id]*, respectively, and a transition is taken to the location *Processing_Event*.

In this location if there is any code block to process the event, *counter[gm_id] > 0*, the type of the active code block is checked. If the code block is an appearance code block, a transition is taken to the location *Start_App*, and the event is provided to the appearance code block via the channel synchronization *process_app[gm_id]!*.

While an event is being processed by the appearance code block, requests to construct an instance of the module may be issued via the *construct* statements. These requests are received by the corresponding coordinator via the channel synchronization *statement_call[gm]?*, which leads to a transition to the location *Special_Cmd*, and eventually to the location *Constructing*. Here, the coordinator marks the module to be under instantiation, by setting the variable *constructing[gm_id] = 1*. If there are multiple requests to instantiate a module, the requests are ignored.

After handling the *construct* statement, the coordinator informs the appearance code block to proceed with the next statement via the channel synchronization *statement_call_return[gm]!*. When the appearance code block finishes processing the input event, it synchronizes with the coordinator via *process_app_return[gm_id]?*, which results in a transition to the location *Get_Event*.

On this transition the function *finish_constructing()* is invoked, which results in the following. If the module has been set to be under instantiation, *constructing[gm_id] == 1*, the coordinator marks the module to be fully instantiated. Besides, if the module is instantiated, its disappearance and utilization code blocks become active, and its appearance code block becomes inactive. Since a transition is taken to the location *Get_Event*, the input event will not be processed by the disappearance and utilization blocks of the constructed instance. This is because the event processing may lead to an infinite number of consequent instantiation and destruction of the module.

In the location *Select_Block* of Fig. 9, if the active code block is the disappearance block, *block[gm_id] == DISAPPEARANCE*, the coordinator synchronizes with the automaton in Fig. 11 via the channel *process_disapp[gm_id]!*. As a result, the disappearance code block starts processing the input event. When the event

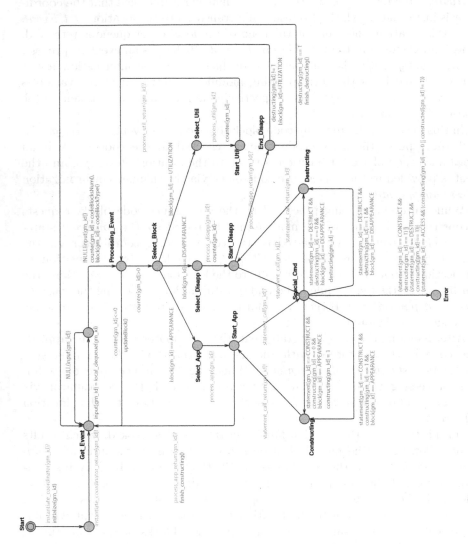

Fig. 9. A model for coordinating the activation of code blocks

processing terminates, the disappearance code block synchronizes with the coordinator via *process_disapp_return[gm_id]?*, which results in a transition to the location *End_Disapp*.

If the execution of the disappearance block terminates and it does not result in destructing the module instance, *destructing[gm_id] != 1*, the input event must be processed by the utilization blocks of the module. This is modelled by taking a transition from *End_Disapp* to *Processing_Event*. Otherwise, via invoking the function *finish_destructing()*, the appearance code block is activated, and other code blocks are deactivated. Afterwards, a transition is taken to the location *Get_Event*, so that the module starts processing the next input event.

It is considered erroneous if before a module is fully constructed (destructed), a destruction (construction) request for it is issued. This is modeled in the coordinator automaton in Fig. 9 by the location *Error*. Moreover, it is considered erroneous, if there is an attempt to access any instance-level variable or method of the module before there is a request to instantiate the module.

9.4   Appearance Code Blocks

Figure 10 models the runtime semantics of appearance code blocks. In this automaton, the event selection criteria is evaluated via the method *matches(input)*. If the event does not match the event expression, it is ignored and the automaton stays in the location *Start*. If the event is of interest, and it is the first time that the appearance code block is executed, its initializer part is executed by assigning the value *1* to the variable *initialized*.

The event processing takes place in the location *Processing*; the automaton stays in this location for maximum $c <= MAX$ time unit to represent a time consuming event processing operation. Various kinds of operations can be performed in this location. As the sub-graph starting with the transition *statement[gm_id] = ACCESS* shows, the appearance code block may try to access the instance-level variables or methods of the module, which is erroneous behavior reported by the corresponding coordinator.

As the sub-graph starting with the transition *p_event = produceEvent()* shows, the appearance code block may publish new events in an asynchronous manner, which are inserted in the event queue and the execution of the appearance automaton continues by taking a transition to the location *Processing*.

In Fig. 10, as the sub-graph starting with the *statement[gm_id] = CONSTRUCT* shows, a request to instantiate the emergent gummy module may be issued via the channel *statement_call[gm_id]!*, which is received by the automaton in Fig. 9. As a result, the corresponding coordinator marks the emergent gummy module as being constructed by taking a transition to the location *Constructing* and updating the variable *constructing[gm]* with *1*. Afterwards, the control returns to the appearance automaton, which continues with event processing, for example, by publishing new events. To keep the models simple, we only show the case events are published asynchronously.

After the execution of the appearance block terminates successfully, it informs the coordinator via the channel *process_app_return[gm_id]!*. In case the execution

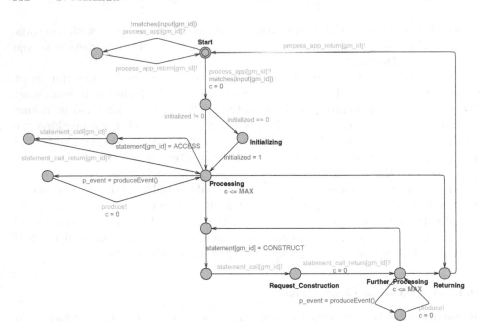

Fig. 10. A model for the appearance code blocks

of the appearance terminates unsuccessfully due to runtime exceptions, the coordinator removes the previously constructed module instance, if any, and keeps the appearance block active. To keep the models simple, we did not show exceptional cases in the models.

9.5   Disappearance Code Blocks

After the instantiation of a module, the corresponding coordinator updates *block[gm_id]* with the value *DISAPPEARANCE*. Therefore, if the coordinator automaton in Fig. 9 receives an event, it directs the event to the disappearance automaton in Fig. 11. The event is processed in the disappearance automaton, which may request to destroy the instance of the emergent gummy module. This request is handled by the coordinator in a similar way as the request for instantiation. As the figure shows, similar to appearance code blocks, events may also be published from within disappearance code blocks.

9.6   Utilization Code Blocks

As Fig. 9 shows, after an event is processed by the disappearance automaton, and if this has not resulted in the destruction of the emergent gummy module, *destructing[gm_id] != 1*, the request is provided to the utilization code blocks, sequentially in the order they are defined in the emergent gummy module. The semantics of utilization code blocks is shown in Fig. 12. Like other code blocks, new events may be published from within utilization code blocks.

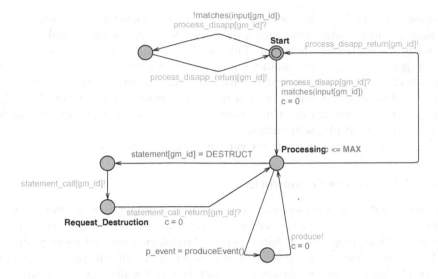

Fig. 11. A model for the disappearance code blocks

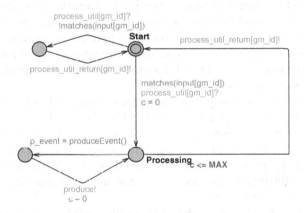

Fig. 12. A model for the utilization code blocks

10   Discussions

Emergent gummy modules are new kinds of modules, which are orthogonal
to other kinds of modules such as objects and aspects. They have two main
characteristics: (a) they encapsulate their lifetime semantics, and (b) they have
pure event-based interfaces. As summarized in Fig. 4, these characteristics help
to overcome the shortcomings of objects and aspects in representing emergent
behavior.

To express the transient nature of emergent behavior, various appearance
and disappearance conditions of emergent behavior can be programmed and
modularized from the rest of emergent gummy modules via appearance and

disappearance code blocks, respectively. Through adopting an event-based communication mechanism, emergent gummy modules are loosely coupled to the constituents of emergent behavior. This facilitates supporting the elastic nature of emergent behavior; if an event matches the specified event selection predicates, it is selected for further processing without being bound to a specific type and number of event publishers (e.g. cars in our example). This feature also helps to support the crosscutting nature of emergent behavior, because events can be received from multiple constituents.

In the following, we explain our various design alternatives.

10.1   DSLs versus Frameworks

An important design choice was to propose a new type of module and its implementation in a language versus proving a framework using existing module abstractions (e.g. objects and aspects). Modularization and reuse problems of frameworks have been extensively discussed in the literature. For example in [33, 34], frameworks are classified as black-box and white-box frameworks. In black-box frameworks, the programmers only rely on the interfaces and as such they do not need to extend or modify the implementation of classes. Black-box frameworks are preferred because of their lower complexity but unfortunately their expression power is restricted; certain applications cannot be effectively modularized and extended using black-box frameworks. In white-box frameworks, the programmer has the full-freedom, but the complexity of software increases after each extension attempt.

In the literature, various publications have compared domain specific languages (DSLs) with application frameworks [35]. In general, DSLs are considered superior to application frameworks. Disadvantages of DSLs are, however, defined as the extra effort necessary in designing and implementing a DSL and the tools associated with it. Nevertheless, as motivated by this paper, we think that it is worthwhile to introduce new language constructs that are more expressive in programming emergent behavior.

For example, in a framework-based implementation, one can push the abstract classes implementing the design patterns into the framework. However, for each example application, programmers have to define sub-classes of these classes to represent application-specific information (e.g. classes `Car`, `Segment`, `TrafficCongestion`, `TrafficData`) about emergent behavior. Consequently, one may get the same class diagram as depicted in Fig. 5.

10.2   Instance Management Strategies

Another design decision was how to express the instantiation strategy of emergent gummy modules so that the transient nature of emergent behavior is respected. In programming languages, there are two main ways of expressing the instantiation strategy of a module: (1) By an external module, for example via a constructor call or cloning as in OO languages; (2) By the module itself, for example via pointcut-based instantiation as in AO languages. There are also two main ways of expressing the destruction semantics of module instances: (1) Implicitly by letting the garbage collector destroy the instances that are not referenced; (2) Explicitly by invoking the so-called destructor method.

As we have shown in Figs. 5 and 6, the instantiation of the module by itself results in less classes and dependencies; hence, leads to more concise implementations. However, current AO languages have limited expression power in specifying different kinds of instantiation policies. To overcome this limitation, emergent gummy modules have appearance code block in which desired instantiation strategy can be programmed. In addition, emergent gummy modules define their destruction semantics via the disappearance code block. Via this design, we introduce the third form of instance destruction, where instances encapsulate their destruction semantics. We claim that this model is particularly useful in cyber-physical systems, where the life of objects in software must be independent of the lifetime of the long-living entities in the physical environment.

Various utilization code blocks can be defined as well as local variables and methods to facilitate utilizing emergent gummy modules in applications. Unlike current AO languages, GummyJ has built-in synchronization rules to activate the code blocks. This eliminates the need for extending the code blocks with extra synchronization checks as it was needed in AO languages.

10.3 Explicit versus Implicit Events

As for any other module system, modules must provide suitable interfaces to communicate with each other. To respect the characteristic of emergent behavior, we use events as the interfaces of base objects and emergent gummy modules. There are two major ways to define event-based interfaces for application objects: (1) similar to most AO languages, by providing a fixed set of events that can be mapped to a set of predefined state changes in programs (i.e. join points), or (2) by offering construct to explicitly publish events.

The first case has the advantage that event detection and publishing can be performed automatically by the language compiler. However, providing a fixed set of events in a language may complicate programs if the programmer needs different events than the ones that are supported. In this case, the programmer may end up defining workarounds to map the desired events to a set of supported events in the language. This topic has been discussed within the AO community as extensible join point models [36–38].

The second case is more generic, and is supported in GummyJ. As we show in Listing 3 new types of events and attributes can be defined depending on the application requirements. As Listing 7 shows, using explicit events, we can easily integrate GummyJ with complex event processing engines. Nevertheless, adopted from AO languages, GummyJ can also be extended to support a predefined set of events.

In GummyJ, event predicates are defined over the attributes of the input event; i.e. the event that is retrieved from the queue to be processed. As modelled in Sect. 9, the predicates are evaluated in an atomic way for each input event. History-based predicates or predicates that need to evaluate multiple events are defined within the body of code blocks. An example is shown in the appearance code block in Listing 4, where we accumulate information from multiple events that are published in a specific time period. We would like to extend the language with declarative constructs such as regular expressions and temporal logic formula, to support history-based event filtering.

10.4   The Scope of Emergent Behavior in the Environment

Another design decision was related to limiting the scope of emergent behavior that appears in the environment. As shown in Listing 4, we can limit the scope of emergent behavior via defining parametric emergent gummy modules, and introducing multiple emergent gummy modules in the GummyJ runtime as shown in Listing 5. This means that the appearance and the disappearance of emergent behavior is reasoned from the constituents that exist in the specified scope; e.g. the cars enter or exit a specific road segment.

11   Conclusion and Future Work

In various application domains, it is necessary to consider certain behavior that emerges in the environment as the concern of interest, and to represent the concern in software. For example, various monitoring systems such as traffic monitoring and control systems, various smart cyber physical systems, and context-aware applications in some ways deal with detecting and manipulating the emergence of certain behavior in their environment.

Although developing suitable algorithms for detecting emergent behavior is being widely studied, to the best of our knowledge there is no attempt to provide suitable programming languages to implement these algorithms and to modularize emergent behavior. We believe that since the applications of monitoring systems, smart systems, cyber physical systems and context-aware systems increase in various domains, it is necessary to provide suitable programming abstractions to represent emergent behavior in a modular way.

This paper took the initial step to fill this gap. We studied that emergent behavior has three main characteristics: transient nature, elastic nature and crosscutting nature. These make emergent behavior distinctive from conventional kinds of concerns which have tight structural coupling to each other. We have shown that emergent behavior cannot be properly modularized by OO and AO modularization mechanisms due to these distinctive characteristics.

We introduced emergent gummy modules as dedicated linguistic abstractions to modularly represent emergent behavior by encapsulating the appearance and disappearance conditions, the utilization operations and the synchronization rules.

Through explicit and modular representation of emergent behavior, a program contains ordinary objects that have tight coupling to each other in terms of their lifetime, and emergent objects that encapsulate their lifetime semantics.

The interplays and communications of these two kinds of objects with each other require further study.

For example, we would like to extend the GummyJ language such that conventional application objects can communicate with emergent gummy modules via explicit method invocations. This implies that emergent gummy modules must support concurrent operations; the lifetime and the internal states of an emergent gummy module are updated according to the events that are acquired from the environment, and the module can concurrently be utilized by other application objects.

A naïve example of representing an erroneous behavior as a module is the exception handling mechanism of advanced programming languages, where the behavior, its related data, and the set of operations that can be performed on it is represented as an object. Advanced programming languages offer means to utilize this object in programs. Emergent gummy modules can be considered useful in the domains of runtime verification and exception handling to modularly represent erroneous emergent behavior, and provide means to control the behavior.

Another interesting topic is to adopt emergent gummy modules for representing emergent patterns in Big Data applications. A common practice in such applications is to adopt a middleware to process large amount of data (e.g. streams of events) and to detect certain patterns among the data. Modular representations of such patterns in various Big Data applications is our other topic of research for future.

Acknowledgements. The author is supported by the German Research Foundation (DFG) in the Collaborative Research Center 912 "Highly Adaptive Energy-Efficient Computing". The author thanks Prof. Mehmet Aksit and Prof. Uwe Aßmann for their valuable feedback on this work. The author would like to also thank Christian Fraß and Raphael Urmoneit for their support in implementing GummyJ.

References

1. Fromm, J.: Types and forms of emergence. arXiv:nlin/0506028
2. Holland, O.T.: Taxonomy for the modeling and simulation of emergent behavior systems. In: Proceedings of the 2007 Spring Simulation Multiconference, vol. 2. Society for Computer Simulation International (2007)
3. Resnick, M.: Turtles, Termites, and Traffic Jams: Explorations in Massively Parallel Microworlds (Complex Adaptive Systems). A Bradford Book, Cambridge (1997)
4. Kiczales, G., Hilsdale, E., Hugunin, J., Kersten, M., Palm, J., Griswold, W.G.: An overview of AspectJ. In: Knudsen, J.L. (ed.) ECOOP 2001. LNCS, vol. 2072, pp. 327–354. Springer, Heidelberg (2001). doi:10.1007/3-540-45337-7_18
5. Aksit, M., Wakita, K., Bosch, J., Bergmans, L., Yonezawa, A.: Abstracting object interactions using composition filters. In: Guerraoui, R., Nierstrasz, O., Riveill, M. (eds.) ECOOP 1993. LNCS, vol. 791, pp. 152–184. Springer, Heidelberg (1994). doi:10.1007/BFb0017540
6. Hirschfeld, R., Costanza, P., Nierstrasz, O.: Context-oriented programming. J. Object Technol. **7**(3), 125–151 (2008)

7. Malakuti, S., Aksit, M.: Emergent gummy modules: modular representation of emergent behavior. In: GPCE 2014. ACM, New York (2014)

8. Esper. http://esper.codehaus.org/

9. Fisch, D., Janicke, M., Sick, B., Muller-Schloer, C.: Quantitative emergence - a refined approach based on divergence measures. In: SASO 2010, pp. 94–103, September 2010

10. Chen, C.C.: Complex event types for agent-based simulation. Ph.D. thesis, University College London (2009)

11. Kubík, A.: Toward a formalization of emergence. Artif. Life 9(1), 41–65 (2002)

12. Schutz, W.M.: Getting started with complex event processing nodes. White paper, IBM Software Services for WebSphere

13. Sen, R., Cross, A., Vashistha, A., Padmanabhan, V.N., Cutrell, E., Thies, W.: Accurate speed and density measurement for road traffic in India. In: ACM DEV 2013. ACM (2013)

14. Bouarfa, S., Blom, H., Curran, R., Everdij, M.: Agent-based modeling and simulation of emergent behavior in air transportation. Complex Adapt. Syst. Model. 1(1), 1–15 (2013)

15. Shoham, Y.: Agent-oriented programming. Artif. Intell. 60(1), 51–92 (1993)

16. Rajan, H., Leavens, G.T.: Ptolemy: a language with quantified, typed events. In: Vitek, J. (ed.) ECOOP 2008. LNCS, vol. 5142, pp. 155–179. Springer, Heidelberg (2008). doi:10.1007/978-3-540-70592-5_8

17. Gasiunas, V., Satabin, L., Mezini, M., Núñez, A., Noyé, J.: EScala: modular event-driven object interactions in scala. In: AOSD 2011. ACM (2011)

18. Zhuang, Y., Chiba, S.: Method slots: supporting methods, events, and advices by a single language construct. In: AOSD 2013. ACM (2013)

19. Mezini, M., Ostermann, K.: Conquering aspects with Caesar. In: AOSD 2003. ACM Press (2003)

20. Sakurai, K., Masuhara, H., Ubayashi, N., Matsuura, S., Komiya, S.: Association aspects. In: AOSD 2004. ACM Press (2004)

21. Compose*. http://composestar.sourceforge.net/

22. Vanderperren, W., Suvée, D., Cibrán, M.A., Fraine, B.: Stateful aspects in JAsCo. In: Gschwind, T., Aßmann, U., Nierstrasz, O. (eds.) SC 2005. LNCS, vol. 3628, pp. 167–181. Springer, Heidelberg (2005). doi:10.1007/11550679_13

23. Pavel, C.A., Allan, C., Avgustinov, P., Christensen, A.S., Hendren, L., Kuzins, S., Moor, O.D., Sereni, D., Sittampalam, G., Tibble, J.: Adding trace matching with free variables to AspectJ. In: OOPSLA 2005. ACM (2005)

24. Malakuti, S., Akşit, M.: Event modules: modularizing domain-specific crosscutting RV concerns. In: Chiba, S., Tanter, É., Bodden, E., Maoz, S., Kienzle, J. (eds.) Transactions on Aspect-Oriented Software Development XI. LNCS, vol. 8400, pp. 27–69. Springer, Heidelberg (2014). doi:10.1007/978-3-642-55099-7_2

25. Appeltauer, M., Hirschfeld, R., Masuhara, H., Haupt, M., Kawauchi, K.: Event-specific software composition in context-oriented programming. In: Baudry, B., Wohlstadter, E. (eds.) SC 2010. LNCS, vol. 6144, pp. 50–65. Springer, Heidelberg (2010). doi:10.1007/978-3-642-14046-4_4

26. Núñez, A., Noyé, J., Gasiūnas, V.: Declarative definition of contexts with polymorphic events. In: COP 2009. ACM (2009)

27. Kamina, T., Aotani, T., Masuhara, H.: EventCJ: a context-oriented programming language with declarative event-based context transition. In: AOSD 2011. ACM (2011)

28. Kamina, T., Aotani, T., Masuhara, H.: Generalized layer activation mechanism through contexts and subscribers. In: MODULARITY 2015. ACM, New York (2015)

29. Malakuti, S.: Event composition model: achieving naturalness in runtime enforcement. Ph.D. thesis, University of Twente (2011)

30. Malakuti, S., Aksit, M.: Event-based modularization: how emergent behavioral patterns must be modularized? In: FOAL 2014. ACM (2014)

31. Java-JNI. http://download.oracle.com/javase/1.5.0/docs/guide/jni/spec/jnitoc.html

32. UPPAAL. http://www.uppaal.org/

33. Gonzlez, S., Mens, K., Cdiz, A.: Designing reusable classes. J. Object Oriented Program. 1(5), 22–35 (1988)

34. Fayad, M., Schmidt, D.C.: Object-oriented application frameworks. Commun. ACM 40(10), 32 (1997). Special Issue on Object-Oriented Application Frameworks

35. Johansen, M.F.: Domain specific languages versus frameworks. Master thesis, Department of Informatics, University of Oslo (2009)

36. Malakuti, S., Aksit, M.: Event-based modularization of reactive systems. In: Agha, G., Igarashi, A., Kobayashi, N., Masuhara, H., Matsuoka, S., Shibayama, E., Taura, K. (eds.) Concurrent Objects and Beyond: Papers dedicated to Akinori Yonezawa on the Occasion of His 65th Birthday. LNCS, vol. 8665, pp. 367–407. Springer, Heidelberg (2014). doi:10.1007/978-3-662-44471-9_16

37. Cazzola, W., Vacchi, E.: Fine-grained annotations for pointcuts with a finer granularity. In: SAC 2013. ACM (2013)

38. Hoffman, K., Eugster, P.: Cooperative aspect-oriented programming. Sci. Comput. Program. 74, 333–354 (2009)

Selected Papers from *Modularity 2015*

Generalized Layer Activation Mechanism for Context-Oriented Programming

Tetsuo Kamina[1]($\boxtimes$), Tomoyuki Aotani[2], and Hidehiko Masuhara[2]

[1] Ritsumeikan University, 1-1-1 Noji-higashi, Kusatsu, Shiga 525-8577, Japan
kamina@acm.org
[2] Tokyo Institute of Technology, 2-12-1 Ohokayama, Meguro, Tokyo 152-8550, Japan
aotani@is.titech.ac.jp, masuhara@acm.org

Abstract. Context-oriented programming (COP) languages modularize context-dependent behaviors in multiple classes into layers. These languages have *layer activation mechanisms* so that the behaviors in layers take effect on a particular unit of computation during a particular period of time. Existing COP languages have different layer activation mechanisms, and each of them has its own advantages. However, since these mechanisms interfere with each other in terms of extent (time duration) and scope (a set of units of computations) of activation, combining them into a single language is not trivial. We propose a generalized layer activation mechanism based on *contexts* and *subscribers* to implement the different activation mechanisms in existing COP languages in a single language called ServalCJ. We formalize the operational semantics of ServalCJ as a small calculus and prove *priority preservation*, i.e., ensuring that layer prioritization, which resolves the interference between layers, is preserved during computation. To prove this property, we give a formal definition of layer priority that is general so that we can discuss the priorities of layers in other COP calculi and implementations. We implement a ServalCJ compiler, and demonstrate its effectiveness through several example applications.

Keywords: Contexts and subscribers · ServalCJ · Priorities of layers · Priority preservation

1 Introduction

A large number of software systems, such as ubiquitous computing systems, adaptive user interfaces, and self-adaptive systems, as well as their associated computations, require the ability to change behavior with respect to context. For example, for some computations comprising a system, a specific system state that affects such computations may be considered a context. For the system itself, a specific state of the external environment can be considered a context. Dynamic changes in behavior with respect to context changes result in complicated system structures and behaviors that are difficult to predict with traditional programming abstractions.

© Springer International Publishing Switzerland 2016
S. Chiba et al. (Eds.): ToMC I, LNCS 9800, pp. 123–166, 2016.
DOI: 10.1007/978-3-319-46969-0_4

Context-oriented programming (COP) [17] addresses this difficulty in that it can abstract behavior depending on the same context as a module called a *layer*, and it provides *layer activation mechanisms* so that the behavior in the layer takes effect on a particular unit of computation during a particular period of time. A number of COP languages have been developed to date, and they have successfully modularized such context-dependent behavior [6,8,12,14,21,24,29,32].

However, existing COP languages have different layer activation mechanisms, making them rather use-case-specific. These layer activation mechanisms have been developed to specify context changes such that they are triggered by internal state changes in the program or external events, or are encoded in the application frameworks. Programmers must select an appropriate mechanism based on use cases. Furthermore, existing layer activation mechanisms are hardwired into the language and thus do not provide means to extend themselves when combined with other mechanisms in other languages. For example, the per-control-flow activation in ContextJ [6] and JCop [8] is strongly coupled with the current execution thread. Similarly, the implicit activation mechanism in PyContext [32] cannot represent per-instance layer activation. This issue is exacerbated by the fact that different use cases can coexist in the same application. Thus, there is a natural requirement to generalize existing layer activation mechanisms into a single mechanism.

This paper aims to propose a generalized model of layer activation mechanisms that covers all existing COP languages, and to develop a COP language based on that model. To do this, we must solve two problems. First, we must provide a general model to specify a context and the units of computation to which it is applied. Generally, a context can be defined as "everything that exists *outside* the particular unit of computation on which we are focused." However, this definition is too vague when discussing a model on which a particular COP language is based. Second, when developing a generalized COP language, we must unify existing COP mechanisms that may interfere with each other. Thus, we must resolve this interference in order to satisfy programmer expectations.

We tackle these problems by proposing a model based on two concepts: *contexts*, which specify the extent (time duration) of layer activation, and *subscribers*, which specify the scope (a set of units of computations) of activation. These concepts reveal that existing layer activation mechanisms can be explained uniformly using a single model. Furthermore, we define the dynamic semantics of layer activation in the model that satisfy programmer expectations when different existing activation mechanisms coexist in the same application. In the proposed model, the interferences between existing COP mechanisms are resolved by unifying per-instance and global activations, as well as by determining the priority of active layers that are activated synchronously as well as asynchronously.

Based on this model, we have designed the ServalCJ language. A context in ServalCJ is defined as a term of simple temporal logic with a call stack that can represent the extent of layer activation specified by all existing layer activation mechanisms (to the best of our knowledge). Each context can also be parameterized, which allows us to easily specify the behavioral changes reactively triggered by state changes in the system. A subscriber in ServalCJ is the object on which we focus when considering the context. A set of subscribers can also be global (i.e., all objects are implicitly subscribed to a specific set of contexts when created). A *context group* in ServalCJ specifies a combination of contexts and subscribers.

We demonstrate the effectiveness of ServalCJ through several example applications. The first example is a context-aware program editor, where each construct in ServalCJ is explained. We also present a case study of a maze-solving robot simulator to study the usefulness of ServalCJ. This simulator has different layer activation scenarios, some of which are supported by existing languages, but others are not. We demonstrate that such scenarios are represented uniformly by ServalCJ.

We formalize the dynamic semantics of ServalCJ as a small calculus, Featherweight ServalCJ (FSCJ), to describe how the generalized layer activation is performed. We formulate the *priority preservation* property by stating that the priorities of layers assigned for different layer activation mechanisms are preserved during computation, and prove this property. This formulation is general so that we can discuss the priorities of layers in FSCJ and other COP calculi such as ContextFJ [18,19] and context holders [4], as well as in other COP implementations with multiple layer activation mechanisms, such as ContextJS [24]. We also show that FSCJ is parameterized over the priority assignment, i.e., we can obtain another calculus that conforms to another priority assignment by changing only some auxiliary definitions and without changing the main part of the reduction rules.

To study ServalCJ's feasibility, we implemented a ServalCJ compiler. The compiler translates ServalCJ programs into standard Java bytecode; thus, they can be run on standard Java virtual machines. We evaluated method dispatch performance in ServalCJ by comparing the time of method calls with and without active layers in ServalCJ against that in plain Java. The results show that our compiler does not impose a serious overhead on the running application.

The remainder of this paper is organized as follows. In Sect. 2, we introduce an example of a context-aware program editor and review existing COP mechanisms. In Sect. 3, we argue the necessity of a generalized activation mechanism and explain the challenges in achieving this. In Sect. 4, we present a model of a unified activation mechanism, and discuss the appropriate dynamic semantics of layer activation. In Sect. 5, ServalCJ, an instantiation of the model discussed in Sect. 4, is proposed. In Sect. 6, we present a case study of a maze-solving robot simulator, compare COP with other implementation techniques, and compare ServalCJ with existing COP languages. In Sect. 7, we formalize the operational semantics of ServalCJ, provide a definition of layer priority, and prove the priority preservation. In Sect. 8, we discuss the implementation of the ServalCJ compiler and evaluate its performance. Section 9 discusses related work and Sect. 10 concludes the paper.

2   Existing COP Mechanisms

In this section, we use an example to explain the commonalities and differences among existing COP languages.

2.1   Example

CJEdit, first implemented by Appeltauer et al. [7], is a program editor that enhances the readability of programs by providing different text formatting techniques for code and comments. The code part is rendered in a typewriter format with syntax highlighting and the comment part is rendered in rich text format that supports multiple fonts, text sizes, decorations, and alignments. Furthermore, CJEdit provides different GUI components depending on which part of the code or comments the programmer is currently editing. For example, when the programmer is editing code, CJEdit displays an outline view of the program so that they can easily determine the structure of the program; when the programmer is editing comments, it displays tools and menus for changing text fonts, sizes, etc.

We extend the CJEdit program editor to make it is multi-tabbed so that the programmer can open multiple files simultaneously. As in the original CJEdit, each tab displays the source code rendered in different text format for code and comments, and different GUI components are provided depending on the cursor's position on the focused tab. A tab displaying an unsaved file shows a mark indicating that the file has not been saved. If the programmer attempts to close a tab that displays an unsaved file, a dialog stating that the programmer is attempting to close an unsaved file is displayed.

We also extend this editor with a couple of features. First, when the editor is used online, the files are stored in a remote repository. When no networks are available, an icon is displayed indicating that the system is operating offline and files are stored on the local disk. Second, we have added a find-name function to CJEdit that can be used to search for the names of variables, methods, and classes throughout the entire source code. During the search, the mouse cursor changes, and a new widget that displays the status bar is added.

2.2   Overview of COP

In the above example, there are a number of behavioral variations that depend on situations, such as the position of the cursor, rendering of text regions, status of the opened file (saved or unsaved), and the availability of a network. In the following, we refer to such situations as contexts. A COP language provides a modularization mechanism for implementing related context-dependent behavior into a single layer and a layer activation mechanism for dynamically composing and decomposing layers with the application.

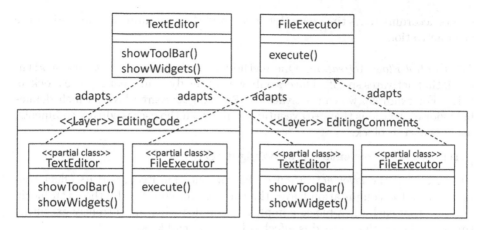

Fig. 1. Relationships among layers and classes

Layers. Figure 1 shows how the related context-dependent behavior is modularized into a layer using a class diagram. The diagram uses two layers, `EditingCode` and `EditingComments`, to represent behavioral variations that are executable only when the cursor is on code or comments, respectively. A COP layer contains a set of partial methods. In Fig. 1, we represent a set of partial methods as a class stereotyped as `<<partial class>>`. A partial method is executable only when the enclosing layer is *active*, i.e., the layer is composed with the application and changes the behavior of the class to which it is applied (Fig. 1). For example, when the `EditingCode` layer is active, at the `TextEditor.showWidgets()` call, the `showWidgets` partial method declared in `EditingCode` is called instead of the original method. In fact, a partial method runs before or after the execution of the original method when it has a `before` or `after` modifier, respectively. If a partial method has no such modifiers, it is called an *around* partial method and runs instead of the original method. Within an around partial method, we can invoke a special `proceed` method to execute the original method. As discussed in Sects. 2.3 and 4.2, multiple layers can be active simultaneously, and in that case, when `proceed` is invoked, the partial method in the layer with lower priority is executed.

Layer Activation. As mentioned above, a layer can be composed and decomposed dynamically with the running application. These processes are called *layer activation* and *layer deactivation*, respectively. Each COP language provides different linguistic mechanisms to perform activation and deactivation, and this is discussed in the following.

2.3 Different Mechanisms for Layer Activation

Whereas most COP languages provide similar mechanisms for layers, for layer activation, existing COP languages provide a variety of mechanisms. Each mechanism

differs according to its time period, trigger, and the computations affected by the
layer activation.

Per-Control-Flow Activation. One method to activate layers is to use a with-
block that activates specified layers only within the dynamic scope of the block [6,
8,12]. For example, we can activate the `EditingComments` layer, which defines
behavioral variations that are executable only when the user is editing comments,
using the with-block.

```
with (EditingComments) { showWidgets(); }
```

The trigger of the layer activation is the computation itself, and its effect continues until the computation leaves the control flow specified by the with-block.
We note that each with-block is implicitly coupled with the currently executing
thread and only that thread is affected by the with-block.

Another feature of the per-control-flow activation is that, in this model, a
programmer is likely aware of the activation order of layers. For example, we can
write the following nested with-blocks.

```
with(EditingComments) {
   with(RenderingCode) { format(..); }
}
```

This code activates both the `EditingComments` and `RenderingCode` layers, and
the inner with-block supersedes the outer one. Thus, if these layers define the
same partial methods, those defined in `RenderingCode` have priority, i.e., the
`before` partial methods in `RenderingCode` are executed first, `after` partial
methods in `RenderingCode` are executed last, and around partial methods in
`RenderingCode` override those defined in other layers.

Imperative Activation. Some COP languages provide *imperative activation* that
uses imperative operations to activate behavior that indefinitely affects the rest
of the execution [14,15]. For example, in Subjective-C [14], the activation and
deactivation of a layer is written as follows.

```
[CONTEXT activateContextWithName: @"EditingCode"];
[CONTEXT deactivateContextWithName: @"EditingComments"];
```

The first line activates the `EditingCode` layer, and the second line deactivates the
`EditingComments` layer. The activation continues indefinitely, or until another
imperative operation that explicitly deactivates the layer is executed. In existing
COP languages that support this mechanism, the effect of the activation is *global*,
i.e., the entire application is affected by the activation. In general, however, we
may consider another variation such that the effect is restricted to within the
execution thread.

Event-Based Activation. In this model, the trigger of layer activation is an event,
and the activation continues until another event that deactivates the layer is

generated. Unlike activation with an imperative model, this activation can be per-instance and the event receivers may differ from the event senders.

EventCJ [21] supports this model. In EventCJ, an event is declaratively defined using AspectJ-like pointcut language.

```
event MoveOnCode(TextEditor e)
  :after call(void TextEditor.onCsrPosChanged())
    && target(e) && if(e.isCursorOnCode())
  :sendTo(e);
```

This event definition specifies that the `MoveOnCode` event is generated immediately after the `onCsrPosChanged` method call declared in the `TextEditor` class and only if the `isCursorOnCode` call on the receiver object of the former call returns `true`. The `sendTo` clause specifies that this event is sent to only `e`, the receiver of the `onCsrPosChanged` call as specified by the `target` pointcut. In other words, EventCJ supports *per-instance* layer activation. If the `sendTo` clause is omitted, the event is sent to the entire application. Thus, EventCJ also supports global layer activation.

Layer switching upon event is specified declaratively using the layer transition rule.

```
transition MoveOnCode:
  EditingComments ? EditingComments -> EditingCode
  | -> EditingCode;
```

This rule is interpreted as follows. When `MoveOnCode` is generated, if the `EditingComments` layer is active, it is deactivated and `EditingCode` is activated; otherwise, no layers are deactivated and `EditingCode` is activated.

One problem with per-instance activation in EventCJ is that it can only specify instances that are accessible from the join-point where the event is generated. If these instances cannot be obtained from the join-point directly, we must either specify a complex chain of method calls or provide a workaround to access the receiver instances in the base program.

Implicit Activation. In contrast to the above activation mechanisms, where variations of context-dependent behavior are *explicitly* activated, in the *implicit activation* model, the trigger and time period of activation are implicitly specified by a condition. This mechanism is supported by PyContext [32], where the activation is specified by implementing the `active` method, which is implicitly evaluated when the layer activation is tested. We show this in Java-like syntax as follows.

```
class TextEditor {
  .. boolean isCursorOnCode() { .. } ..
  layer EditingCode {
    boolean active() {
      return isCursorOnCode(); } ..
  }
}
```

This code fragment illustrates the `TextEditor` class and `EditingCode` layer in the *layer-in-class* manner [5]. The `EditingCode` layer implements the `active` method that is evaluated whenever, for example, a method that consists of a set of partial methods is called, and, if `active` returns `true` (i.e., if the `isCursorOnCode` call returns `true`), the `EditingCode` layer becomes active.

In PyContext, only the currently executing thread is affected by the implicit activation, as in per-control-flow activation.

3   Problem Statements

In this section, we present the expressibility problem in existing COP mechanisms and the interference problem that exists between the mechanisms.

3.1   Expressibility Problem

When we choose one COP language to implement context-dependent behavior, we sometimes encounter difficulties because each mechanism fits only specific cases of behavioral changes in the application. For example, in the CJEdit example, if we choose the per-control-flow model, it becomes difficult to implement event-driven behavioral changes triggered by, for example, a change in the position of the cursor. On the other hand, if we choose the event-based model, it is difficult to implement the find-name function, which recursively searches the name in the entire source code, because the state transition model of the event-based activation cannot represent the call stack. Furthermore, the set of entities affected by the layer activation also varies within the application. For example, the arrangement of widgets and tools in the toolbar and the behavior depending on the network availability are applied to the entire application, while the status of opened files can vary for each tab.

We face similar problems in other context-aware applications. For example, in a multi-tabbed Twitter client, each tab displays the user's timeline, which is updated after a followed person posts a tweet. Each tab behaves differently with respect to contexts, such as tab focus (focused or unfocused) and the content displayed on the timeline (all tweets from all followed accounts, tweets only from a specific account, or all tweets that match a search keyword). The trigger of a context change can be an event, such as clicking a tab, and can be defined implicitly relative to timeline content. The effect of behavior changes may also vary. Each tab can change its behavior dynamically, and its effect is restricted to only the instances contained within the tab. We can also consider other cases, such as behavior changes with respect to battery status, which can affect the entire application. Another example is a pedestrian navigation system that changes behavior with respect to changes in situation, such as moving from an indoor to an outdoor environment, which is triggered by an event. In addition, such a system can change behavior based on changes in computation, such as "during map download," which is activated only within the control-flow.

We also argue that some COP mechanisms provide incomplete abstractions. For example, EventCJ supports per-instance activation, where we can specify only instances accessible from the join-point where the event was generated. Similarly, events in event-based activation in EventCJ are only join-points, and thus EventCJ does not provide any way to abstract the event sender.

3.2 Interference Problem

Some COP languages support multiple activation mechanisms and thus support some combination of different behavioral change use cases in the application. For example, EventCJ supports global activation as well as per-instance activation so that the effect of the behavioral change is exerted on the entire application. Similarly, ContextJS [24] supports global activation as well as per-control-flow activation as pre-defined activation mechanisms. Although these languages allow us to represent different cases of behavioral changes uniformly to some extent, the activations that they support are still limited. For example, neither language supports implicit activations.

A more serious problem with existing approaches is that an activation mechanism sometimes interferes with an activation triggered by another mechanism. There are two interference problems, i.e., between global and per-instance activations and between synchronous and asynchronous activations.

Global-Per-Instance Interference. We explain the former interference problem using an example of a mobile application written in EventCJ that uses both global and per-instance activation mechanisms. Suppose that the layer Battery-Low, which implements the "energy-saving mode" behavior that uses less precise computation and fewer resources, is globally active because the battery power of the executing machine is low. Also suppose that activation on some instances is controlled in a per-instance manner to allow the user to control the behavioral changes of these instances manually. For example, the user may require some objects to produce precise computation results in short periods even when the battery is on the verge of running out.

In fact, EventCJ does not support such a situation because global activation always cancels a per-instance deactivation. In EventCJ, the layers activated by global activation and those activated by per-instance activation are stored in different arrays, and the partial method dispatch uses both arrays. Thus, the layer stored in the global activation array is effective even when it is removed from the per-instance activation array. A similar problem also occurs in ContextJS. Although this may be an implementation issue, this kind of interference is likely to arise if the different linguistic mechanisms were "piled up" into a single language.

Synchronous-Asynchronous Interference. Another type of interference occurs when we unify activation mechanisms from different languages. In the per-control-flow model, the order of active layers is explicit for the programmer, i.e., the inner-most layer always precedes other layers. Although in other models, such an order is not explicit for the programmer, the order of active layers is also well-defined to make the execution result universal. For example, in EventCJ, the most recently activated layer always precedes the others [3]. This semantics of EventCJ conflict with those of the per-control-flow model in ContextJ. For example, in the following with-block, the programmer expects the text block stored in textBlock to be formatted with syntax highlighting.

```
SyntaxHighlighter sh = ..
with(EditingCode) {
  with(RenderingCode) {
    // forcing text to be formatted with
    // syntax highlighting
    sh.format(text);    } }
```

However, the event-based layer activation may not meet this expectation because an event activating EditingComments may be generated after the activation of EditingCode and before the call of format, thereby causing the syntax highlighting to be switched off.

The source of this conflict is the mixing of the synchronous layer activation, where the trigger is the computation itself, and the asynchronous layer activation, where the trigger is the external event. If the layer activation is synchronous with the execution of the application described in the base program, the programmer is aware of the execution point when the specified layer becomes active. On the other hand, we cannot foresee when layer activation will be triggered asynchronously by events.

4 Model of Generalized Layer Activation

To address the aforementioned problems, we propose a generalized model of the existing COP mechanisms and provide the semantics of layer activation to define activation order uniformly.

4.1 Contexts and Subscribers

To develop the generalized activation model, we coordinate the different layer activation mechanisms in existing COP languages using the following concepts, i.e., *context*, which specifies the time and duration of the layer activation[1], and *subscribers*, which specifies which computations the activation affects. A number of layer activations represented by contexts affect a specific set of subscribers. We combine a set of contexts with a set of subscribers and call this combination a *context group*. When an object subscribes to a context group, method dispatch on the object includes the partial methods in the active layers with respect to the context group. In other words, when we activate a layer with respect to

---

[1] We use the term "context" to indicate the temporal context.

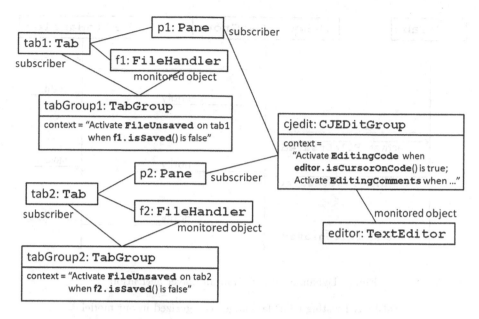

Fig. 2. Unified model of COP in an object diagram. We abbreviate insignificant edges, i.e., every object is a subscriber of the instance `cjedit`. This is not represented in the diagram because only specific instances (`p1` and `p2`) provide context-dependent behavior for `cjedit`.

a context group, all the objects subscribing to that group will begin searching partial methods in that layer upon method dispatch. For example, the contexts that specify when the cursor is on code or comments affect the entire application with respect to the behavior of the toolbar and menubar; thus, they are grouped into a single context group. The context specifying when the opened file in a tab is unsaved affects only a limited subset of instances in the application; thus, they are grouped into another context group.

We illustrate this model in Fig. 2 using a UML instance diagram. In this diagram, the instance `cjedit` of the context group `CJEditGroup` specifies contexts for activating `EditingCode`, which implements the code-editing functions, and `EditingComments`, which implements the comment-editing functions. All instances in the entire application subscribe to this context group. These contexts are parameterized over the objects on which the layer activation depends, e.g., in `cjedit`, this parameter is bound to `editor`, an instance of `TextEditor`. When the state of `editor` changes, the layer activation of all subscribed instances also changes. Similarly, the instance `tabGroup1` of the `TabGroup` context group specifies the contexts for activating `FileUnsaved`, which implements the behavior related to unsaved files. Only the instance `tab1` of `Tab` subscribes to that context group. The context specified in `TabGroup` is also parameterized, and this parameter is bound to `f1`, an instance of `FileHandler`.

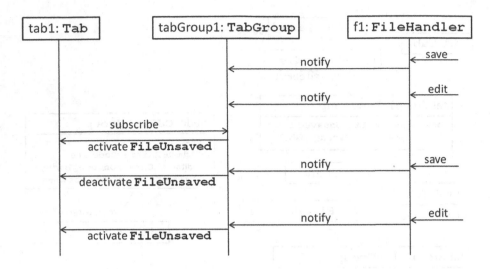

Fig. 3. Dynamic subscription and layer activation

Table 1. Existing COP languages categorized in our model

	Global	Thread	Instance
Control-flow		ContextJ [6], PyContext [32]	ContextErlang [29]
Imperative	Subjective-C [14]		ContextErlang
Event-based	EventCJ [21]		EventCJ
Implicit	Flute [10]	PyContext	

We further illustrate the dynamic semantics of this model using the UML sequence diagram in Fig. 3. When the instance `f1` of `FileHandler` changes its state according to outside operations such as the "save" and "edit" commands, it also notifies these changes to the instance `tabGroup1` of the context group `TabGroup`, which refers to `f1`. If no instances subscribe to `tabGroup1`, these notifications do not trigger any layer activation. After an instance of `Tab`, i.e., `tab1`, subscribes to `tabGroup1`, it immediately activates `FileUnsaved` on `tab1` if `f1` is not saved after editing. After this subscription, the notifications from `f1` triggered by the state changes on `f1` trigger the activation and deactivation of `FileUnsaved` on `tab1`.

We show that each existing COP language falls into one specific case of this model, as illustrated in Table 1. In Table 1 the methods that specify contexts are categorized into four variants, i.e., per-control-flow, imperative, event-based, and implicit, that correspond to each layer activation model discussed in Sect. 2.3. In the table, the methods that specify subscribers are also categorized into three variants, i.e., global (the "world"), thread (the currently executing thread), and instance (a limited set of instances). Each cell represents the COP languages that support the specific combination of these methods. In addition to the languages discussed in the previous section, we also list the COP languages mentioned in Sect. 10. For example, EventCJ supports event-based specification of contexts that are applicable to both all instances in the application and a limited set of instances. Some cells indicate that no existing COP languages support such a combination. For example, implicit activation of a limited set of instances is not supported by any existing COP language.

4.2   Model of Activation Order

The synchronous-asynchronous interference explained in Sect. 3.2 implies that we must manage synchronous and asynchronous layer activation separately. To satisfy programmer expectations, in our model, synchronous layer activation always precedes asynchronous activation. More precisely, the semantics of layer activation in our model are defined as follows.

First, we define synchronous and asynchronous layer activation.

- Layer activation is *synchronous* if and only if its context is specified as a control-flow and it is statically known that its subscribers contain the thread that will execute the control-flow. For example, global and per-thread activation with the per-control-flow model are considered synchronous.
- Layer activation that is not synchronous is *asynchronous*.

We then define the order of active layers as follows.[2] Let $\bar{L}_S = L_1, \cdots, L_n$ be a sequence of layers that are activated synchronously, and let $\bar{L}_A = L'_1, \cdots, L'_n$ be a sequence of layers that are activated asynchronously. We assume that there are no duplicate layers in a sequence of activated layers. We define the function *actSync* that takes a concatenation of sequences of activated layers $\bar{L}_A; \bar{L}_S$ and a layer L and returns a new concatenation of the sequences of activated layers.

$$actSync(\bar{L}_A; \bar{L}_S, L) = (\bar{L}_A \setminus L); (\bar{L}_S \setminus L)L$$

This function models synchronous layer activation. If L is not contained in both $\bar{L}_A$ and $\bar{L}_S$, it is added at the head of sequence $\bar{L}_S$, indicating that L has the highest priority. Otherwise, L is removed from the original position and is moved to the head of the sequence $\bar{L}_S$.

Similarly, asynchronous layer activation is modeled by the *actAsync* function.

$$actAsync(\bar{L}_A; \bar{L}_S, L) = \begin{cases} (\bar{L}_A \setminus L)L; \bar{L}_S & \text{if } L \notin \bar{L}_S \\ \bar{L}_A; \bar{L}_S & \text{if } L \in \bar{L}_S \end{cases}$$

If L is not contained in both $\bar{L}_A$ and $\bar{L}_S$, it is added at the head of the sequence $\bar{L}_A$, indicating that L has higher priority than all layers in $\bar{L}_A$ but has lower priority than all layers in $\bar{L}_S$. If L is contained in $\bar{L}_A$, it is moved to the head

---

[2] As illustrated in Sect. 3.2, we believe that this ordering is preferable in many cases. However, we also acknowledge that it is preferable for programmers to configure the ordering policy in particular cases. This configuration mechanism is discussed in Sect. 7.

of $\bar{L}_A$. If L is contained in $\bar{L}_S$, the order of the active layers does not change, because this case indicates that L has already been activated with higher priority than the layers in $\bar{L}_A$.

We define the function *deact* to model layer deactivation.

$$deact(\bar{L}_A; \bar{L}_S, L) = (\bar{L}_A \setminus L); (\bar{L}_S \setminus L)$$

The above functions are used when we describe the operational semantics shown in Sect. 7. For example, *actSync* is always used when the with-block is applied, and *actAsync* is always used when event-based activation is applied. The order of active layers $\bar{L}_A; \bar{L}_S$ is used when dispatching a partial method. The search for a partial method begins from the right-most layer of $\bar{L}_S$ and proceeds to the left-most layer of $\bar{L}_A$. If no partial methods are found, the original method is dispatched.

To address global-per-instance interference, every activation is performed in a per-instance manner. This means that, when a layer becomes globally active, that layer is added to the active layers for all instances that have that layer. This mechanism ensures that global activation does not interfere with per-instance activation at the cost of activating the layer for all of these instances.

5   COP Language with Contexts and Subscribers

We have designed the COP language ServalCJ to be an instance of the generalized activation model discussed in Sect. 4. ServalCJ provides the following linguistic constructs: *activate declaration*, which specifies when the layer is active in terms of *contexts* that identify the extent of layer activation, and *context group declaration*, which modularizes these declarations and specifies the set of *subscribers* where they are applied. In ServalCJ, a subscriber is the object on which we focus when considering the context.

ServalCJ is a layer-based COP language that provides a modularization mechanism for context-dependent behavior using layers. ServalCJ supports the class-in-layer syntax of layer declarations as well as the layer-in-class syntax [5], where we can define a set of partial methods and activate/deactivate blocks. This paper focuses on how layer activation is specified by ServalCJ; how layers are declared in ServalCJ is beyond the scope of this paper.

We formalize the dynamic semantics of ServalCJ in Sect. 7. While the formal model provides semantics based on primitive linguistic constructs, ServalCJ provides a more convenient syntax.

5.1   Context Group Declarations

In ServalCJ, a context group is declared using a *context group declaration*. A context group groups related specifications of layer activation into one module, and can be instantiated. Each context group instance contains subscribers, i.e., a set of instances where the specified layer activation is applied. A context group

```
1  contextgroup EachTabGroup(FileHandler f) {
2    subscriberTypes: Pane, FileHandler;
3    activate FileUnsaved if(!f.isSaved());
4  }
```

Fig. 4. Context group declaration for CJEdit specifying the layer activation for each tab

can also declare parameters that can be referred to from the layer activation specification.

Figure 4 shows an example of layer activation for CJEdit that specifies the layer activation for each tab. Line 1 specifies the name of the context group and its parameter. We can replace this parameter with an argument when this context group is instantiated. A context group is instantiated using the standard **new** expression. We can also declaratively specify when the instance of context group is created using the AspectJ pointcut and advice mechanism. For simplicity, we do not use this mechanism in this paper.

```
FileHandler file = new FileHandler(..);
EachTabGroup etg = new EachTabGroup(file);
etg.subscribe(file);
Pane pane = new Pane();
etg.subscribe(pane);
```

An object can dynamically subscribe to the instance of a context group, thereby becoming one of the subscribers of that context group. This subscription is performed by calling the subscribe method on the instance of context group. For example, in the above code fragment, instances of **FileHandler** and **Pane** subscribe to **etg**, which is an instance of **EachTabGroup**. The current version of ServalCJ requires that each context group declares the types of instances that can subscribe to it (Line 2, Fig. 4). We can also declaratively specify which instance subscribes to this context group when using the AspectJ pointcut and advice mechanism. This flexible subscription mechanism addresses the problem of per-instance activation in EventCJ, where any receivers of an event must be accessible from the specified join-point.

Line 3 of Fig. 4 declares when the layer **FileUnsaved** is active, which occurs whenever the **isSaved** method call on **f** returns **false**. We further discuss the specification of layer activation in Sect. 5.2.

Global Context Groups. In the aforementioned example, we explicitly specified which instances subscribe to the context group. In ServalCJ, we can also declare a context group that affects all instances in the application. Such a group is called a *global context group*.

Figure 5 shows an example of a global context group declaration. To make the context group global, we must provide the **global** modifier. A global context group does not contain any specifications for subscribers. Instead, every object is implicitly considered to have subscribed to the global context group. As for other

```
1 global contextgroup CJEditGroup(TextEditor e) {
2   activate EditingCode if(e.isCursorOnCode());
3   activate EditingComments if(e.isCursorOnComments());
4 }
```

Fig. 5. Example of a global context group

context groups, we can create an instance of the global context group, which becomes effective only after instance creation. The context group `CJEditGroup` in Fig. 5 declares two layer activation rules: (1) the layer `EditingCode` is active whenever the `isCursorOnCode` method call on `editor` returns `true` and (2) the layer `EditingComments` is active whenever the `isCursorOnComments` method call on `editor` returns `true`.

5.2   Declaring Layer Activation

In ServalCJ, we define when the layer is active by specifying the name of the layer and a Boolean term, i.e., when the Boolean term is `true`, the layer is active. This specification is performed using an *activate declaration*, which has the following syntax.

    activate *LayerName Context*;

This declaration begins with the keyword `activate` followed by the name of the layer. Next, we specify a context, which has the `boolean` type in Java.

In particular, in ServalCJ, a context is declared using a temporal logic term with call stacks. This term consists of *if expressions* that specify the condition under which the context is active, *from-to expressions* that specify the from-event and to-event that activate and deactivate the context, respectively, *cflow expressions* that specify the control flows where that context is active, *named contexts* that are contexts identified by name, and *composite contexts* that are contexts combined by using logical-OR, logical-AND, and NOT expressions. We discuss each of these terms in the following.

Conditional Expressions. The first way to specify layer activation is to use a conditional (`if`) expression that corresponds to implicit activation (Sect. 2.3). To support implicit activation, ServalCJ provides `if` expressions that specify the condition under which the context is active. We have provided an example in Fig. 4, which contains the following activate declaration.

```
activate FileUnsaved if(!f.isSaved());
```

Within `if` expressions, we can use any Boolean-type Java expression. Note that ServalCJ can represent implicit activation that is applied per-instance. As shown in Fig. 4, we can create a different instance of `EachTabGroup` for each tab that contains distinct instances of `Pane` and `FileHandler`. Each instance of `EachTab-Group` refers to a distinct instance of `FileHandler` through the variable `f`, which

```
1 class TextEditor {
2   event MoveOnCode;
3   event MoveOnComments;
4   void onCursorPositionChanged() {
5     if (isCursorOnCode()) { MoveOnCode(); }
6     else if(isCursorOnComments()) { MoveOnComments(); }
7   }
8 }
```

Fig. 6. Publishing events in ServalCJ

is referenced from the `if` expression. Thus, we can control the activation of layers for each tab independently.

From-to Expressions. A from-to expression specifies the *events* that activate and deactivate the context. This expression makes it possible to represent event-based layer activation. An event in ServalCJ is declared as a member of a class and triggered like a method invocation. For example, in Fig. 6, two events, `MoveOnCode` and `MoveOnComments`, are declared in the class `TextEditor`. These events are triggered during the execution of `onCursorPositionChanged` and if the `isCursorOnCode` (`isCursorOnComments`, resp.) call returns `true`. We can also declare an event using the AspectJ pointcut language.

Using these events, we can specify when the `EditingCode` layer becomes active and inactive as follows.

```
activate EditingCode
  from MoveOnCode to MoveOnComments;
```

This declaration specifies a *from-event* that activates `EditingCode` and a *to-event* that deactivates the layer. Here, the `EditingCode` layer is activated whenever the `MoveOnCode` event is triggered and is deactivated whenever the `MoveOnComments` event is triggered.

As in the case of implicit activation, we can specify the *sender* of the event by referring to the parameter of the enclosing context group.

```
contextgroup CJEditGroup(TextEditor editor) {
  activate EditingCode
    from editor.MoveOnCode
    to editor.MoveOnComments;
}
```

This activate declaration specifies that `EditingCode` is activated when `MoveOnCode` is triggered and is deactivated when `MoveOnComments` is triggered *only when these events are triggered by* `editor`. Note that we cannot specify an event sender in EventCJ.

Cflow Expressions. A cflow expression specifies a control-flow in which the layer is active. This expression makes it possible to represent per-control-flow layer activation. An example of a cflow expression is as follows.

```
activate SearchingName
  in cflow(call(void FileHandler.find(*)));
```

This context declaration specifies that the `SearchingName` layer is active only under the control flow specified by the `cflow` expression, which is the entire execution of the `find` method declared in the `FileHandler` class. Note that cflow expressions are not a particular case of from-to expressions, because we cannot represent a control-flow using a from-to expression when the control-flow under the specified method call contains the same method call specified in the cflow expression.

Per-Thread Activation. The `with`-block-based COP languages, such as ContextJ, activate layers in a per-thread manner. Note that most useful cases of ContextJ are easily encoded by a combination of a global context group and cflow activation. To restrict the effects of layer activation to the currently executing thread, we may introduce another modifier, `perthread`, that limits the set of subscribers to the subscribers accessed from the thread executing the control flow.

```
global contextgroup AContextGroup(..) {
  perthread activate ALayer in cflow(..);
}
```

The `perthread` modifier does not have any effect when it is used with other expressions.

Named Contexts. The same contexts are sometimes used in different activate declarations. To improve the reusability of contexts, ServalCJ provides a *named context*, which is a mechanism that provides a name to a context to make it possible to reference it from several activate declarations. A named context in ServalCJ is declared using the following syntax.

`context ContextName is Context;`

This declaration begins with the keyword `context` followed by the name and specification of the context. The syntax of the context is the same as that specified in activate declarations. The name of the context is used in activate declarations and should be enclosed within a `when` clause. For example, the context group declaration:

```
contextgroup Highlighter(SyntaxHighlighter sh) {
  context RenderCode is
    if(sh.getBlock().isCodeBlock());
  activate Highlighting when RenderCode;
}
```

is identical to the following declaration.

```
contextgroup Highlighter(SyntaxHighlighter sh) {
  activate Highlighting
    if(sh.getBlock().isCodeBlock());
}
```

ServalCJ also provides a way to compose contexts to represent more complex layer activation. This composition was originally known as *composite layers* [22]. To compose contexts, we can use the logical operators || (logical-OR), && (logical-AND), and ! (NOT).

6   Case Study

The program editor example described above shows how different COP mechanisms coexist in the same application, thereby justifying the design of the generalized layer activation mechanism in ServalCJ.

To provide more evidence, we conducted another case study to implement a maze-solving simulator.[3] This application simulates how a line-tracing robot solves a maze. The following code skeleton illustrates how the robot solves a maze.[4]

```
void run() {
  while (!isGoal()) {
    followSegment();
    printPath();
    turn();
    simplify();
  }
}
```

The `followSegment` method performs line-tracing until the robot reaches an intersection, a corner, or a dead-end (in the following, we refer to these as *intersections*). The robot detects an intersection using sensors. The `printPath` method prints some debugging information on the LCD attached to the robot. The `turn` method selects one path from the outgoing paths at an intersection by applying a specific rule (e.g., the left-hand rule selects the left-most path) and controls the motors to make the robot turn accordingly. The `simplify` method calculates a potentially optimized path from the start point to the current intersection by eliminating dead-ends. The robot repeats these behaviors until it reaches the goal. After solving the maze, the robot can run the optimized path from the start point to the goal by simply following the path calculated by `simplify`.

---

[3] The simulator source code is available at https://github.com/ServalCJ/mazesimula
tor.git.

[4] This case study was inspired by the real maze-solving Pololu 3pi Robot (http://
www.pololu.com/product/975). The simulator's behavior follows the sample program provided by the 3pi Robot distribution.

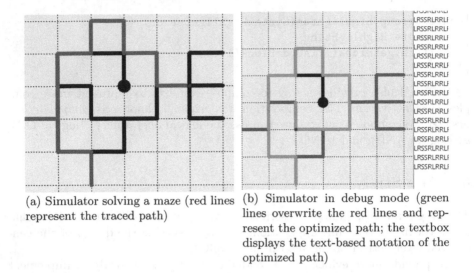

(a) Simulator solving a maze (red lines represent the traced path)

(b) Simulator in debug mode (green lines overwrite the red lines and represent the optimized path; the textbox displays the text-based notation of the optimized path)

Fig. 7. The maze-solving simulator (the lines indicate paths within the maze; the black circle represents the goal) (Color figure online)

If the maze contains loops, the robot must remember all visited intersections and/or segments (i.e., a path from one intersection to one of the neighbors) to detect such loops. There are several algorithms to solve mazes; some can only solve mazes that contain no loops, and others can solve mazes with loops.

The simulator emulates the behavior of a maze-solving robot. In this simulator, the maze is modeled as a graph where each node representing an intersection provides coordinates to indicate its position. The instance `robot` of `Robot` emulates maze-solving in this model, e.g., the `followSegment` method simply updates the current position of the `robot` according to the destination of the edge that models the segment. The simulator provides three algorithms to solve the maze, i.e., the left-hand rule, right-hand rule, and Trémaux's algorithm.[5] The selection of these algorithms changes the behavior of `turn` and possibly that of `simplify`.

For the user, this simulator provides a number of functions, i.e., edits a maze, simulates how the robot solves the maze, and simulates how the robot follows the optimized path after solving the maze. These functions are exclusive, i.e., when we are editing a maze, we cannot run any simulations for solving the maze or following the optimized path. These functions are switched when the user finishes editing the maze (or loads a pre-edited maze) and when the robot finishes solving the maze. The simulator provides GUI tools, such as a menubar and menu buttons, that are switched automatically when the functions are switched. During maze-solving, visited intersections and segments are colored to visualize the traced path (Fig. 7(a)). Furthermore, while the robot is solving the maze,

---

[5] Among them, only the last algorithm can solve mazes with loops.

the user can select a debug mode to display the currently calculated optimized path by printing text that represents the optimized path and changing the color of intersections and segments in the optimized path (Fig. 7(b)).

We implemented this simulator using ServalCJ, and a number of layers were defined to implement context-dependent behavior:

- EditingMaze provides GUI tools for editing the maze, such as inserting segments and intersections, saving the maze to a file, opening a maze from a file, and finishing editing the maze.
- SolvingMaze provides GUI tools for starting the simulation, solving the maze, stopping the simulation, switching to debug mode, and selecting the algorithm to solve the maze (the default is the left-hand rule).
- RunningMaze provides GUI tools for starting the simulation, following the optimized path and stopping the simulation.
- RightHandRule solves the maze using the right-hand rule.
- Tremaux solves the maze using Trémaux's algorithm.
- Debugging provides a textbox to display the currently calculated optimized path.
- UnderDebugging changes the color of segments and intersections in the maze only if they are in the optimized path and debug mode is selected.

All of these layers crosscut multiple classes. Even RightHandRule and Tremaux, which seem to be related to only a single instance of a robot, affect both a robot instance and the GUI tools. Note that the debugging feature is divided into two layers, Debugging and UnderDebugging, because they are applied in slightly different situations, as will be explained below.

These layers change the behavior of multiple classes. For example, Solving-Maze and RunningMaze change the appearance of the GUI components and the behavior of the simulator. The simulator is executed in a different thread from the GUI components, and the behavior of the run method is switched when the active layer is changed (Fig. 8).

To specify layer activation, we implemented two context groups. The first context group manages layer activations that are applied globally, and the other context group manages layer activations that are applied only to specific instances.

Figure 9 shows the context group for managing globally activated layers. It specifies activate declarations for five layers. The activation of the first four layers is controlled by from-to expressions. The events that activate and deactivate the layers correspond to the GUI events generated by the operations taken by the user. The UnderDebugging layer is a composite layer; it is active only when the Debugging layer is active and the additional condition specified by the named context Print holds. As Fig. 10 shows, the UnderDebugging layer changes how the color of visited segments and intersections is set. First, this behavior is applicable only when the application is in the debug mode. Second, this behavior is applicable only to the intersections and segments in the shortest path. Thus, UnderDebugging is activated only in the control flow where the shortest path is printed (which also calls the setTraced methods on Edge and Node). In this case, we apply the cflow expression.

```
layer SolvingMaze {
  class Robot {
    public void run() {
      /* maze solving behavior */
    }
  }
  class View {
    public void setMenuBar() { .. }
    public void setButtons() { .. }
  }
}
layer RunningMaze {
  class Robot {
    public void run() {
      /* running the optimized path */
    }
  }
  class View {
    public void setMenuBar() { .. }
    public void setButtons() { .. }
  }
}
```

Fig. 8. Example layers in the maze-solving simulator

```
1 global contextgroup MazeUI() {
2   activate EditingMaze
3     from startEditor to startSolver;
4   activate SolvingMaze from startSolver to solved;
5   activate RunningMaze from solved to neverMatchingEvent;
6   activate Debugging from startDebug to endDebug;
7   context Print is in cflow(call(void Simulator.print()));
8   activate UnderDebugging when Debugging && when Print;
9 }
```

Fig. 9. Context group for globally activating layers

Figure 11 shows the context group for managing activations that are applicable to a specific robot instance. Although there is only one robot instance in this application, we apply per-instance activation in this case for future extensibility (e.g., supporting multiple robots that execute different algorithms). In this case, we apply conditional (if) expressions rather than from-to expressions to specify the activate declarations because, in the base program, the value indicating the algorithm is set to the robot instance when the user selects the algorithm, which is useful for determining which layer should be activated. Note that the program structure of the base program may affect how the programmer selects the activation mechanism.

```
layer UnderDebugging {
  class Edge { // segments
    public void setTraced() {
      proceed();
      color = Color.GREEN; //the default is RED
      src.setTraced();
      dst.setTraced();
    }
  }
  class Node { // intersections
    public void setTraced() {
      proceed();
      color = Color.GREEN;
    }
  }
}
```

Fig. 10. The UnderDebugging layer

```
1  contextgroup Algorithm(Robot robot) {
2    activate RightHandRule if(robot.isRightHandRule());
3    activate Tremaux if(robot.isTremaux());
4  }
```

Fig. 11. Context group applicable to the robot instance

Discussion. We first discuss the appropriateness of applying COP to implement this simulator.[6] First, the variations of context-dependent behavior in this simulator crosscut multiple classes and are modularized by corresponding layers in COP. For example, the SolvingMaze and RunningMaze layers change the behavior in both the simulator and the GUI components. Debugging changes the appearance of the GUI (showing or hiding the textbox that prints the shortest path) and the behavior of the simulator (whether the shortest path stored in the simulator instance is printed). UnderDebugging changes the color of intersections and segments. The algorithms applied to the simulator instance also change the appearance of the GUI components (e.g., the currently selected algorithm is disabled for selection in the menu). Thus, it is appropriate to use layers to implement these behavioral variations.

Second, COP supports disciplined changes of context-dependent behavior. We can apply meta-programming techniques to implement dynamic changes of behavioral variations. However, in such techniques, it is difficult to mechanize reasoning about some properties among these variations. For example, in this simulator, the variations of behavior implemented in EditingMaze, SolvingMaze, and RunningMaze should be exclusive. The algorithms executed by the simulator are also exclusive. The behavior implemented in UnderDebugging

---

[6] The same discussion is also applicable to the program editor example.

should be applicable only when the system is in debug mode. It is difficult for meta-programming to mechanically check such properties. On the other hand, by using COP, we can easily generate a state transition model from the event-driven layer switching to perform model checking [21]. The exclusiveness of algorithms can be checked by checking only the exclusiveness of the simulator states that affect the value of the expressions used in the if expressions (e.g., the value of the isRightHandRule call). The dependency between UnderDebugging and Debugging is obtained immediately from the context specification of the activate declaration.

Finally, COP supports modularization of the specification that determines when behavior changes occur. If we apply other approaches to implement such behavior changes (e.g., the state design pattern), the behavior changes may be hardwired and scattered in the base program. Using the declarative specification of layer switching in COP languages, e.g., JCop [8] and EventCJ [21], such behavior changes are specified separately. Although the examples shown in this paper are written using imperative events for brevity, ServalCJ also supports declarative events using AspectJ-like pointcut language.

We further compared ServalCJ with existing COP languages. The case study showed that different activation mechanisms can be used in the same application. As discussed in Sect. 2.3, no existing COP language supports such a variety of activation mechanisms. There are no existing COP languages that support all event-based, per-control-flow, and implicit activation mechanisms, while ServalCJ supports all activation mechanisms (the imperative activation in Subjective-C can also be represented by from-to expressions where the until clause specifies an event that will never happen). Furthermore, the case study demonstrated how several *combinations* of activation mechanisms and sets of subscribers are used in the same application. In particular, the combination of global and per-control-flow activation and per-instance and implicit activation are used in the application. As Table 1 summarizes, existing COP languages do not support such combinations. Even combining these languages, where we can apply workarounds to represent such combinations, does not provide a sufficient solution. For example, when combining Subjective-C and ContextJ, the imperative activation can be used to globally activate and deactivate some layer L at the beginning and end of a with-block, respectively. In this workaround, it is the programmer's responsibility not to forget the deactivation of L. The errors caused by forgetting this deactivation can be avoided in ServalCJ by declaring a cflow in a global context group. Furthermore, ServalCJ provides a more expressive mechanism for representing per-instance and event-based activation than existing languages. In ServalCJ, there are no limitations for objects to dynamically subscribe to the context group, and we can specify the sender of the event.

7   Formal Model of Layer Activation

In this section, we formalize the semantics of layer activation in our model to precisely describe how generalized layer activation discussed in Sect. 4 is performed.

We present a formal calculus Featherweight ServalCJ (FSCJ), which unifies different layer activation mechanisms (synchronous and asynchronous activation mechanisms and global and per-instance activation mechanisms) by combining two existing COP calculi, i.e., Featherweight EventCJ (FECJ) [3], which provides per-instance and asynchronous activation, and ContextFJ [18], which provides global and synchronous activation.

To prove that the activation policy discussed in Sect. 4 is always satisfied in FSCJ, we formally define the priority of a layer and describe a safety property, which we refer to as *priority preservation*. Intuitively, we consider that the priority of layer L_1 is higher than that of layer L_2 at the invocation of method $C.m$ if (1) both L_1 and L_2 override $C.m$ and (2) if the body of $L_2.C.m$ is executed, there must be an execution of $L_1.C.m$ prior to the execution of $L_2.C.m$. The priority preservation ensures that, if there are multiple layer activation mechanisms (e.g., synchronous and asynchronous) and some policy is defined between them (e.g., synchronously activated layers always have higher priority than asynchronously activated layers), this policy is satisfied during computation.

Based on these definitions, we prove priority preservation in FSCJ. Furthermore, we show that these definitions are not specific to FSCJ but are useful for discussing layer priority in other calculi for COP such as ContextFJ and context holders [4]. We believe that these definitions are also applicable to discuss the priorities of layers activated by the imperative activation mechanism and the dynamic scoping mechanism in ContextJS [24].

We also show that FSCJ is parameterized over the activation policies. The activation policy determined in Sect. 4 is application specific, and it is desirable for programmers to configure it for specific cases. FSCJ allows activation policies to be switched by switching only the definitions of some auxiliary functions without changing the reduction rules. The proof of priority preservation for different policies is obtained in a straightforward manner.

7.1 The Calculus

Syntax. The abstract syntax of FSCJ is shown in Fig. 12. Metavariable C ranges over class names; L ranges over layer names; f ranges over field names; m ranges over method names; ℓ ranges over labels, which include an empty label ϵ; ι ranges over instance labels; γ ranges over global labels; v and w range over values; and x ranges over variables, which include a special variable $this$. Overlines denote sequences: e.g., $\bar{f}$ stands for a possibly empty sequence $f_1, \cdots, f_n$. We also abbreviate a sequence of pairs by writing "$\overline{Cf}$" for "$C_1 f_1, \cdots, C_n f_n$," where n denotes the length of $\bar{C}$ and $\bar{f}$. Similarly, we write "$\overline{Cf};$" as shorthand for the sequence of declarations "$C_1 f_1; \ldots C_n f_n;$" and "$this.\bar{f}=\bar{f};$" as shorthand for "$this.f_1 = f_1; \ldots; this.f_n = f_n;$". We use commas and semicolons for concatenations. We abbreviate a concatenation $\bar{L}_A; \bar{L}_S$ of asynchronously activated layers $\bar{L}_A$ and synchronously activated layers $\bar{L}_S$ simply as a sequence of layers $\bar{L}$ when such distinction is not important. It is assumed that sequences of field declarations, parameter names, layer names, and method declarations contain no duplicate names.

$$
\begin{aligned}
\text{CL} &::= \text{class C} \vartriangleleft \text{C \{ } \overline{\text{C}} \ \overline{\text{f}}; \ \text{K} \ \overline{\text{M}} \ \} && (\textit{classes}) \\
\text{K} &::= && (\textit{constructors}) \\
&\quad \text{C}(\overline{\text{C}} \ \overline{\text{f}})\{ \ \text{super}(\overline{\text{f}}); \ \text{this.}\overline{\text{f}} = \overline{\text{f}}; \ \} \\
\text{M} &::= \text{C m}(\overline{\text{C}} \ \overline{\text{x}})\{ \ \text{return e}; \ \} && (\textit{methods}) \\
\text{e,d} &::= \text{x} \mid e^{\ell}.\text{f} \mid e^{\ell}.\text{m}(\overline{e^{\ell}}) \mid \text{new C}(\overline{\text{e}}) && (\textit{expressions}) \\
&\quad \mid \text{proceed}(\overline{\text{e}}) \mid \text{with L e} \\
&\quad \mid \text{v} \mid \text{v<C,}\overline{\text{L}}\text{,}\overline{\text{L}}\text{>.m}(\overline{\text{v}}) \mid \{\text{e}\} \\
\text{t} &::= \ \uparrow \text{L} \mid \downarrow \text{L} && (\textit{activation rules}) \\
\ell &::= \iota \mid \gamma && (\textit{event labels}) \\
\text{p} &::= \text{v} \mapsto \text{new C}(\overline{\text{v}})\text{<}\overline{\text{L}}\text{>} && (\textit{partial stores}) \\
\mu &::= \overline{\text{p}} && (\textit{stores}) \\
\text{st} &::= \cdot \mid \text{st} \gg \overline{\text{L}} && (\textit{stack})
\end{aligned}
$$

Fig. 12. FSCJ: abstract syntax

A class declaration CL consists of its name, its superclass name, field declarations $\overline{\text{C}} \ \overline{\text{f}}$, a constructor K, and method definitions $\overline{\text{M}}$. A constructor K is trivial; it only sets the initial values to the corresponding fields. A method M takes arguments $\overline{\text{x}}$ and returns the value of expression e. An expression can be a variable, field access, method invocation, object instantiation, synchronous layer activation with, proceed call, and special runtime expressions, such as a location v, $\{\text{e}\}$, and $\text{v<C,}\overline{\text{L}}\text{,}\overline{\text{L}}\text{>.m}(\overline{\text{v}})$. These runtime expressions are explained in the following. Note that FSCJ is a functional calculus; thus, all constructs (including with) return values.

A value v is a location. A store μ is a sequence of pairs of a location and an object. We write this pair as $\text{v} \mapsto \text{new C}(\overline{\text{v}})\text{<}\overline{\text{L}}\text{>}$, which is read as "object new $\text{C}(\overline{\text{v}})\text{<}\overline{\text{L}}\text{>}$ is stored at location v." This store is used to destructively update the set of layers associated with each object during computation. The runtime expression $\{\text{e}\}$ appears only as a subterm of with under reduction. A stack st remembers a sequence of layers $\overline{\text{L}}$ before the reduction of with starts so that the computation can restore that sequence after it finishes the reduction of with. The runtime expression $\text{new C}(\overline{\text{v}})\text{<C,}\overline{\text{L}}'\text{,}\overline{\text{L}}\text{>.m}(\overline{\text{e}})$, where $\overline{\text{L}}'$ is assumed to be a prefix of $\overline{\text{L}}$, means that m is going to be invoked on $\text{new C}(\overline{\text{v}})$. The annotation $\text{<C,}\overline{\text{L}}'\text{,}\overline{\text{L}}\text{>}$ indicates the cursor where method lookup should start. As explained in the following, this form allow us to give the semantics of proceed by simple substitution-based reduction.

A label attached to an expression denotes an event receiver that simplifies the asynchronous layer activation; e^{ι} represents a situation in which an event (that activates some layer) is received by e, and e^{γ} represents a situation in which an event that globally activates some layer is sent by e. To represent an expression that does not receive or send any events, we introduce an empty label ϵ. Typically, we write e to mean e^{ϵ}.

As in ContextFJ, the calculus does not provide syntax for layers because the syntactical details of layers, such as the difference between class-in-layer and layer-in-class styles [5], are not relevant. Partial methods are registered in a partial method table PT that maps a triple C, L, and m of class, layer, and method names, respectively, to a method definition. The calculus also provides an activation rule table TT that maps a label to an activation rule that is either an activation $\uparrow$ L (activating L) or a deactivation $\downarrow$ L (deactivating L). Note that $TT(\epsilon) = \emptyset$ (no layers are activated and deactivated).

FSCJ supports the multiple layer activation mechanisms described in Sect. 5.2. Intuitively, asynchronous layer activation triggered by the activation rules in TT corresponds to layer activation using conditionals and from-to expressions in ServalCJ. Synchronous layer activation represented by the `with` expressions in FSCJ corresponds to layer activation using `cflow` in ServalCJ. A value with a label v^ℓ corresponds to a subscriber in ServalCJ, and the global label γ indicates the global layer activation.

A program (CT, PT, TT, e) consists of a class table CT (that maps a class name to a class definition), a partial method table PT, an activation rule table TT, and an expression e that corresponds to the body of the main method. We assume CT, PT, and TT are fixed and satisfy the following sanity conditions:

1. $CT(C) = $ class C... for any $C \in dom(CT)$.
2. Object $\notin dom(CT)$.
3. For every class name C (except Object) appearing anywhere in CT, we have $C \in dom(CT)$.
4. There are no cycles in the transitive closure of $\lhd$ (extends).
5. $PT(m,C,L) = $ ... m(...){...} for any $(m,C,L) \in dom(PT)$.
6. $TT(\ell) = \bar{t}$ for every label ℓ that appears in e, CT, and PT.

Auxiliary Functions. The operational semantics of FSCJ use auxiliary functions to look up field and method definitions. These lookup functions are defined in Fig. 13. The function $fields(C)$ returns a sequence $\bar{C}\ \bar{f}$ of pairs of a field name and its type declared in class C and its superclasses. The function $mbody(m,C,\bar{L}_1,\bar{L}_2)$ returns a pair $\bar{x}.e$ of parameters and the body of method m in class C when the search starts from $\bar{L}_1$. The other layer names $\bar{L}_2$ keep track of the layers that are active when the search initially started. It also returns the information where the method has been found. This information will be used in the reduction rules to handle `proceed`. The method definition is searched for in class C in all activated layers and then in the base definition. If no method definition is found, then the search continues to C's superclass. Note that in MB-Super, which shows a case whereby the search proceeds to C's superclass D, $\bar{L}$ is copied to the third argument in the premise in order to consider all activated layers.

Operational Semantics. The operational semantics are given by a reduction relation of the form $e \mid \mu \mid \bar{L} \mid st \longrightarrow e' \mid \mu' \mid \bar{L}' \mid st'$, which is read as "expression e under a store μ, globally activated layers $\bar{L}$, and a stack st reduces to e' under μ', $\bar{L}'$, and st'." We assume that neither μ nor μ' contain duplicate names.

$$\boxed{\mathit{fields}(\texttt{C}) = \overline{\texttt{C}}\ \overline{\texttt{f}}}$$

$$\mathit{fields}(\texttt{Object}) = \bullet \qquad\qquad\qquad \text{(F-Object)}$$

$$\frac{\texttt{class C} \lhd \texttt{D \{ } \overline{\texttt{C}}\ \overline{\texttt{f}}; \ \ldots\ \texttt{\}} \qquad \mathit{fields}(\texttt{D}) = \overline{\texttt{D}}\ \overline{\texttt{g}}}{\mathit{fields}(\texttt{C}) = \overline{\texttt{D}}\ \overline{\texttt{g}}, \overline{\texttt{C}}\ \overline{\texttt{f}}} \qquad \text{(F-Class)}$$

$$\boxed{\mathit{mbody}(\texttt{m},\texttt{C},\overline{\texttt{L}}',\overline{\texttt{L}}) = \overline{\texttt{x}}.\texttt{e in D}, \overline{\texttt{L}}''}$$

$$\frac{\texttt{class C} \lhd \texttt{D \{ } \ldots\ \texttt{C}_0\ \texttt{m}(\overline{\texttt{C}}\ \overline{\texttt{x}})\{ \texttt{ return e; } \}\ \ldots\ \texttt{\}}}{\mathit{mbody}(\texttt{m},\texttt{C},\bullet,\overline{\texttt{L}}) = \overline{\texttt{x}}.\texttt{e in C}, \bullet} \qquad \text{(MB-Class)}$$

$$\frac{PT(\texttt{m},\texttt{C},\texttt{L}_0) = \texttt{C}_0\ \texttt{m}(\overline{\texttt{C}}\ \overline{\texttt{x}})\{ \texttt{ return e; } \}}{\mathit{mbody}(\texttt{m},\texttt{C},(\overline{\texttt{L}}';\texttt{L}_0),\overline{\texttt{L}}) = \overline{\texttt{x}}.\texttt{e in C},(\overline{\texttt{L}}';\texttt{L}_0)} \qquad \text{(MB-Layer)}$$

$$\frac{PT(\texttt{m},\texttt{C},\texttt{L}_0) \text{ undefined} \qquad \mathit{mbody}(\texttt{m},\texttt{C},\overline{\texttt{L}}',\overline{\texttt{L}}) = \overline{\texttt{x}}.\texttt{e in D}, \overline{\texttt{L}}''}{\mathit{mbody}(\texttt{m},\texttt{C},(\overline{\texttt{L}}';\texttt{L}_0),\overline{\texttt{L}}) = \overline{\texttt{x}}.\texttt{e in D}, \overline{\texttt{L}}''}$$
$$\text{(MB-NextLayer)}$$

$$\frac{\texttt{class C} \lhd \texttt{D \{ } \ldots\ \overline{\texttt{M}}\ \texttt{\}} \qquad \texttt{m} \notin \overline{\texttt{M}} \qquad \mathit{mbody}(\texttt{m},\texttt{D},\overline{\texttt{L}},\overline{\texttt{L}}) = \overline{\texttt{x}}.\texttt{e in E}, \overline{\texttt{L}}'}{\mathit{mbody}(\texttt{m},\texttt{C},\bullet,\overline{\texttt{L}}) = \overline{\texttt{x}}.\texttt{e in E}, \overline{\texttt{L}}'}$$
$$\text{(MB-Super)}$$

Fig. 13. FSCJ: lookup functions

The reduction rules for layer activation and deactivation are shown in Fig. 14. The rule R-LabelActI represents the reduction that occurs when a value v receives an event denoted by label ι. This rule obtains the corresponding layer activation rule stored in TT and calculates the order of active layers by applying $actAsync$. The store μ is updated by inserting the location of the instance with new active layers. The layer deactivation is provided by R-LabelDeactI, which is obtained by replacing $\uparrow$ and $actAsync$ in R-LabelActI with $\downarrow$ and $deact$, respectively.

Similarly, the rule R-LabelActG represents the reduction that occurs when a value v sends an event denoted by label γ, which triggers the global layer activation. This rule updates the sequence of globally activated layers $\overline{\texttt{L}}$. It also applies $actAsync$ to all the elements in μ using the auxiliary function $actAsync_\mu$, which is defined as follows.

$$\frac{\mu' = \{\texttt{v} \mapsto \texttt{new C}(\overline{\texttt{v}})\texttt{<}\overline{\texttt{L}}'\texttt{>} \mid \texttt{v} \mapsto \texttt{new C}(\overline{\texttt{v}})\texttt{<}\overline{\texttt{L}}\texttt{>} \in \mu, \overline{\texttt{L}}' = actAsync(\overline{\texttt{L}},\texttt{L})\}}{actAsync_\mu(\overline{\texttt{L}},\texttt{L}) = \mu'}$$

$$\boxed{\texttt{e} \mid \mu \mid \overline{\text{L}} \mid st \longrightarrow \texttt{e}' \mid \mu' \mid \overline{\text{L}}' \mid st'}$$

$$\frac{TT(\iota) = \uparrow \text{L} \quad \mu(\texttt{v}) = \texttt{new } \texttt{C}(\overline{\texttt{v}})\texttt{<}\overline{\text{L}}'\texttt{>}}{actAsync(\overline{\text{L}}', \text{L}) = \overline{\text{L}}'' \quad \mu' = (\texttt{v} \mapsto \texttt{new } \texttt{C}(\overline{\texttt{v}})\texttt{<}\overline{\text{L}}''\texttt{>}, \mu)}{\texttt{v}^{\iota} \mid \mu \mid \overline{\text{L}} \mid st \longrightarrow \texttt{v} \mid \mu' \mid \overline{\text{L}} \mid st} \qquad \text{(R-LABELActI)}$$

$$\frac{TT(\iota) = \downarrow \text{L} \quad \mu(\texttt{v}) = \texttt{new } \texttt{C}(\overline{\texttt{v}})\texttt{<}\overline{\text{L}}'\texttt{>}}{deact(\overline{\text{L}}', \text{L}) = \overline{\text{L}}'' \quad \mu' = (\texttt{v} \mapsto \texttt{new } \texttt{C}(\overline{\texttt{v}})\texttt{<}\overline{\text{L}}''\texttt{>}, \mu)}{\texttt{v}^{\iota} \mid \mu \mid \overline{\text{L}} \mid st \longrightarrow \texttt{v} \mid \mu' \mid \overline{\text{L}} \mid st} \qquad \text{(R-LABELDEACTI)}$$

$$\frac{TT(\gamma) = \uparrow \text{L} \quad actAsync_{\mu}(\mu, \text{L}) = \mu'}{actAsync(\overline{\text{L}}, \text{L}) = \overline{\text{L}}' \quad actAsync_{st}(st, \text{L}) = st'}{\texttt{v}^{\gamma} \mid \mu \mid \overline{\text{L}} \mid st \longrightarrow \texttt{v} \mid \mu' \mid \overline{\text{L}}' \mid st'} \qquad \text{(R-LABELActG)}$$

$$\frac{TT(\gamma) = \downarrow \text{L} \quad deact_{\mu}(\mu, \text{L}) = \mu'}{deact(\overline{\text{L}}, \text{L}) = \overline{\text{L}}' \quad deact_{st}(st, \text{L}) = st'}{\texttt{v}^{\gamma} \mid \mu \mid \overline{\text{L}} \mid st \longrightarrow \texttt{v} \mid \mu' \mid \overline{\text{L}}' \mid st'} \qquad \text{(R-LABELDEACTG)}$$

$$\frac{actSync(\overline{\text{L}}, \text{L}) = \overline{\text{L}}'}{\texttt{with L e} \mid \mu \mid \overline{\text{L}} \mid st \longrightarrow \{\texttt{e}\} \mid \mu \mid \overline{\text{L}}' \mid st \gg \overline{\text{L}}} \qquad \text{(R-ActSync)}$$

$$\frac{\texttt{e} \mid \mu \mid \overline{\text{L}} \mid st \longrightarrow \texttt{e}' \mid \mu' \mid \overline{\text{L}}' \mid st'}{\{\texttt{e}\} \mid \mu \mid \overline{\text{L}} \mid st \longrightarrow \{\texttt{e}'\} \mid \mu' \mid \overline{\text{L}}' \mid st'} \qquad \text{(R-ActSyncCont)}$$

$$\{\texttt{v}\} \mid \mu \mid \overline{\text{L}} \mid st \gg \overline{\text{L}}' \longrightarrow \texttt{v} \mid \mu \mid \overline{\text{L}}' \mid st \qquad \text{(R-ActSyncFin)}$$

Fig. 14. FSCJ: reduction rules (1)

i.e., for each sequence of active layers $\overline{\text{L}}_i$ in the range of μ is updated by applying $actAsync(\overline{\text{L}}_i, \text{L})$. Similarly, R-LABELActG applies $actAsync$ to the stack st using the following auxiliary function.

$$actAsync_{st}(\cdot) = \cdot$$

$$\frac{actAsync_{st}(st) = st' \quad actAsync(\overline{\text{L}}) = \overline{\text{L}}'}{actAsync_{st}(st \gg \overline{\text{L}}) = st' \gg \overline{\text{L}}'}$$

The rule R-LABELDEACTG defines the global layer deactivation. This rule is obtained by replacing $actAsync$ in R-LABELActG with $deact$. The auxiliary functions $deact_{\mu}$ and $deact_{st}$ are defined as follows.

$$\frac{\mu' = \{v \mapsto \text{new } C(\overline{v}) <\overline{L}'> \mid v \mapsto \text{new } C(\overline{v}) <\overline{L}> \in \mu, \overline{L}' = deact(\overline{L}, L)\}}{deact_\mu(\overline{L}, L) = \mu'}$$

$$deact_{st}(\cdot) = \cdot$$

$$\frac{deact_{st}(st) = st' \qquad deact(\overline{L}) = \overline{L}'}{deact_{st}(st \gg \overline{L}) = st' \gg \overline{L}'}$$

Note that there is a subtle problem here; that the global layer deactivation can deactivate a layer that has been activated by `with`, which may contradict our proposal that synchronous layer activation dominates asynchronous layer activation, because, in FSCJ (and in the implementation of ServalCJ), there is no runtime information that retains the synchronously activated layers (the stack does not remember the layer activated by synchronous activation but remembers the layers activated prior to synchronous activation). This problem can be resolved if we manage the synchronous layer activation separately, similar to context holders [4].

The R-ACTSYNC rule defines synchronous layer activation. The *actSync* function places L on top of the sequence of activated layers $\overline{L}'$ and ensures it is activated during the evaluation of body e, which is reduced to the runtime expression {e}. Stack *st* is updated so that it can pop $\overline{L}$, i.e., the globally activated layers before the evaluation of `with`, when the evaluation of the body e is finished. The reduction rules for this runtime expression are given as rules R-ACTSYNCCONT and R-ACTSYNCFIN, and the R-ACTSYNCFIN rule ensures that the pop operation can be applied only when the expression is in the form of {v}, i.e., it preserves the push-pop correspondence in the nested `with`-blocks.

The reduction rules for field access, method invocation, and instance creation are shown in Fig. 15. The rule R-FIELD for field access is straightforward, i.e., *fields* tells which argument to `new C(..)` corresponds to f_i. The next three rules are for method invocation. In the method lookup, we must include layers that are activated globally and synchronously in the search sequence, as shown in the R-INVK, R-INVKB and R-INVKP rules. The cursor for the method lookup is set as a concatenation of the asynchronously activated layers in a per-instance manner $\overline{L}''_A$ and globally and synchronously activated layers $\overline{L}_S$. The auxiliary definition *o* represents concatenation of the asynchronously activated layers and synchronously activated layers, and is defined as follows.

$$o(\overline{L}_A, \overline{L}_S) = \overline{L}_A; \overline{L}_S$$

This definition, along with *actSync* and *actAsync*, can be parameterized. As discussed in Sect. 7.4, giving different definitions for them results in another calculus that conforms to another activation policy, e.g., asynchronously activated layers always supersede synchronously activated layers.

The R-NEW rule explains the reduction of an instance creation. Note that globally and asynchronously activated layers $\overline{L}_A$ are prospectively activated in

$$\boxed{e \mid \mu \mid \overline{L} \mid st \longrightarrow e' \mid \mu' \mid \overline{L}' \mid st'}$$

$$\frac{\mu(v) = \text{new } C(\overline{w})<\overline{L}'> \qquad \mathit{fields}(C) = \overline{C}\ \overline{f}}{v.f_i \mid \mu \mid \overline{L} \mid st \longrightarrow w_i \mid \mu \mid \overline{L} \mid st} \qquad \text{(R-Field)}$$

$$\frac{\mu(v_0) = \text{new } C(\overline{w})<\overline{L}''_A> \qquad \overline{L}'' = o(\overline{L}''_A, \overline{L}_S) \qquad \overline{L} = o(\overline{L}_A, \overline{L}_S)}{v_0<C,\overline{L}'',\overline{L}''>.m(\overline{v}) \mid \mu \mid \overline{L} \mid st \longrightarrow e \mid \mu' \mid \overline{L}' \mid st'}{v_0.m(\overline{v}) \mid \mu \mid \overline{L} \mid st \longrightarrow e \mid \mu' \mid \overline{L}' \mid st'} \qquad \text{(R-Invk)}$$

$$\frac{\mathit{mbody}(m, C, \overline{L}'', \overline{L}') = \overline{x}.e \text{ in } C', \bullet}{v<C,\overline{L}'',\overline{L}'>.m(\overline{w}) \mid \mu \mid \overline{L} \mid st \longrightarrow [v/\text{this}, \overline{w}/\overline{x}]e \mid \mu \mid \overline{L} \mid st} \qquad \text{(R-InvkB)}$$

$$\frac{\mathit{mbody}(m, C, \overline{L}'', \overline{L}') = \overline{x}.e \text{ in } C', (\overline{L}'''; L_0)}{v<C,\overline{L}'',\overline{L}'>.m(\overline{w}) \mid \mu \mid \overline{L} \mid st \longrightarrow [v/\text{this}, \overline{w}/\overline{x}, v<C',\overline{L}''',\overline{L}'>.m/\text{proceed}]e \mid \mu \mid \overline{L} \mid st}{\qquad \text{(R-InvkP)}}$$

$$\frac{w \notin \mathit{dom}(\mu) \qquad \overline{L} = o(\overline{L}_A, \overline{L}_S)}{\text{new } C(\overline{v}) \mid \mu \mid \overline{L} \mid st \longrightarrow w \mid (w \mapsto \text{new } C(\overline{v})<\overline{L}_A>, \mu) \mid \overline{L} \mid st} \qquad \text{(R-New)}$$

Fig. 15. FSCJ: reduction rules (2)

the new instance. Also note that each instance new $C(\overline{v})<\overline{L}>$ only has asynchronously activated layers.

Finally, we provide a straightforward congruence rule that reduces a subexpression with a label.

$$\frac{e \mid \mu \mid \overline{L} \mid st \longrightarrow e' \mid \mu' \mid \overline{L}' \mid st'}{G[e^{\ell}] \mid \mu \mid \overline{L} \mid st \longrightarrow G[e'^{\ell}] \mid \mu' \mid \overline{L}' \mid st'} \qquad \text{(RC-Label)}$$

$G[\cdot]$ forms evaluation contexts, which is defined as follows.

$$G ::= [] \mid G.m(\overline{e}^{\ell}) \mid v^{\ell}.m(\overline{w}^{\ell}, G, \overline{e}^{\ell}) \mid G.f \mid \text{new } C(\overline{v}, G, \overline{e})$$

We write $G[e^{\ell}]$ for the ordinary expression obtained by replacing the hole in G with e^{ℓ}. As in FECJ, FSCJ requires the receiver and all arguments on the left of the redex to be values.

Example. In the piece of code in Sect. 3.2, the layers activated by synchronous layer activation are pushed to list $\overline{L}_S$, and the layer activated by an event is pushed to list $\overline{L}_A$. Thus, the resulting order of the active layers is as follows.

```
EditingComments;EditingCode,RenderingCode
```

Thus, the priority of the `EditingCode` layer is higher than that of the `Editing-Comments` layer, ensuring that syntax highlighting is always applied when the `sh.format(textBlock)` method call is executed.

Since FSCJ does not provide layer-introduced base methods (i.e., methods defined in layers but not defined in base classes) [19], the type system of FSCJ is trivial. It is a straightforward adaptation of the type system of (an earlier version) of ContextFJ [18]. The type soundness of FSCJ is also obtained by straightforward adaptation of the proof of type soundness in ContextFJ, which is also a straightforward adaptation of the proof of type soundness in Featherweight Java [20]. In this paper, we omit the type system and type soundness for simplicity.

7.2 Definition of Priority

In the previous example, the priorities of layers are as expected with respect to the activation policy discussed in Sect. 4. A formal study is a promising approach to ensure that this activation policy is preserved during computation.

In this section, we formally provide a definition of layer priority. To make the definition general and language-independent, we do not define priority in terms of language-specific features, such as the ordering of activated layers. Instead, we consider the history of activation and deactivation to define priority. To describe such a history, we first define a trace of the execution. Let $e_0 \longrightarrow^* e_n$ be the transitive closure of the smallstep reduction of some COP calculus.[7] A trace t is a sequence $e'_0|\Lambda_0, \cdots, e'_n|\Lambda_n$ of a pair of an expression and a set of activated layers[8], where each e'_i is the redex in e_i replaced with a subexpression in e_{i+1} in one reduction step. Each Λ_i is a set of activated layers of a particular computation unit on which we focus when e_i is to be evaluated. For example, for a *trace of the application* in ContextFJ, each Λ_i is a set of activated layers in the runtime environment where e_i is to be evaluated. Similarly, for a *trace of value* v in FSCJ, each Λ_i is a set of activated layers associated with $\mu(v)$ in the runtime environment where e_i is to be evaluated. We also define an activation sequence for t, written $act(t)$, which is a sequence $\alpha_0, \cdots, \alpha_{n-1}$, where each α_i is either ϕ (no layers are activated and deactivated), $\uparrow L$ (L is activated), or $\downarrow L$ (L is deactivated). We assume that a trace t satisfies the following conditions.

$$\Lambda_i = \Lambda_{i+1} \qquad \text{if } \alpha_i = \phi, \alpha_i \in act(t)$$
$$\Lambda_i \cup \{L\} = \Lambda_{i+1} \text{ if } \alpha_i = \uparrow L, \alpha_i \in act(t)$$
$$\Lambda_i \setminus \{L\} = \Lambda_{i+1} \text{ if } \alpha_i = \downarrow L, \alpha_i \in act(t)$$

---

[7] While we consider the definitions that are independent from the activation mechanisms, we still assume that layers and constructs of the host language are based on ContextFJ-like calculi, e.g., we assume the existence of *mbody* and substitution-based reduction for `proceed`.

[8] To speak of the layer priority, we focus on *which partial method executes first* rather than the ordering of the activated layers.

In other words, at most one layer is added to (removed from) Λ_i to obtain Λ_{i+1}, and each α_i is constructed by taking the difference between Λ_i and Λ_{i+1}. Note that each *act* does not correspond to each activation operation in the reduction steps. It represents an observed activation when focusing on the set of activated layers. For example, an activation operation that does not change the set of activated layers (i.e., an operation activating an already activated layer) is not captured in the trace.

Example. Let $(CT, PT, TT, \texttt{new C()}^\gamma.\texttt{m(withL'new C())})$ be a well-typed FSCJ program where $TT(\gamma) = \uparrow \texttt{L}$. We have the following reduction steps for this program (each subexpression with an underline is replaced with another expression in each reduction step).

$$
\begin{aligned}
&\underline{\texttt{new C()}^\gamma}.\texttt{m(with L'new C())} \\
&\longrightarrow \underline{\texttt{v}^\gamma}.\texttt{m(with L'new C())} \text{ where } \mu(\texttt{v}) = \texttt{new C()} \\
&\longrightarrow \texttt{v.m(}\underline{\texttt{with L'new C()}}\texttt{)} \\
&\longrightarrow \texttt{v.m(}\underline{\texttt{\{new C()\}}}\texttt{)} \\
&\longrightarrow \texttt{v.m(}\underline{\texttt{\{v'\}}}\texttt{)} \qquad\qquad \text{where } \mu(\texttt{v'}) = \texttt{new C()} \\
&\longrightarrow \texttt{v.m(}\underline{\texttt{v'}}\texttt{)} \\
&\longrightarrow \cdots
\end{aligned}
$$

By listing each underlined subexpression, we have the trace t of the value v and its activation sequence as follows.[9]

$$
\begin{aligned}
t &= \texttt{new C()}^\gamma \mid \emptyset, \texttt{v}^\gamma \mid \emptyset, \texttt{with L'new C()} \mid \{\texttt{L}\}, \texttt{new C()} \mid \{\texttt{L}, \texttt{L'}\}, \\
&\quad \{\texttt{v'}\} \mid \{\texttt{L}, \texttt{L'}\}, \texttt{v.m(v')} \mid \{\texttt{L}\}, \cdots \\
act(t) &= \phi, \uparrow \texttt{L}, \uparrow \texttt{L'}, \phi, \downarrow \texttt{L}, \phi, \cdots
\end{aligned}
$$

A trace contains a history of layer activation, as well as a history of field accesses and method invocations, including partial method invocations (of the form $\texttt{v<C}, \overline{\texttt{L}}, \ \overline{\texttt{L'}}\texttt{>.m(..)}$) for each value. We can define the relation between layers at an execution point, i.e., the relation by which "the priority of layer L is higher than the priority of L' at e_m," in terms of the positions of the partial method invocations in the trace. Note that, if multiple occurrences of the same value v exist in the expression e_i in the reduction steps, each such value is uniquely renamed to make each value identical in the trace. This renaming prevents us from mixing multiple calls of the same method in the same expression. For example, assuming the expression $\texttt{v<C}, \overline{\texttt{L}}, \overline{\texttt{L'}}\texttt{>.m(}\underline{\texttt{v.m(v')}}\texttt{)}$, the underlined expression is reduced to $\texttt{v} < \texttt{C}, \overline{\texttt{L''}}, \overline{\texttt{L''}} > \texttt{.m(..)} = e_{m'}$, which is added to the trace. Then, it becomes difficult to determine which method call, i.e., the outer or inner call of m, was evaluated to produce $e_{m'}$. To avoid this, the inner v is renamed as another value, e.g., $\texttt{v1}$, in the trace.

---

[9] All Λ_i are empty before v is created.

Definition 1. *Suppose we have a trace* $t = e_0 \mid \Lambda_0, \cdots, e_n \mid \Lambda_n$ *and an expression* $e_m = \text{v.m}(..)$ *in* t *where* v *is a value of type* C. *Assume that* $\text{L}, \text{L}' \in \Lambda_m$ *and both* L *and* L' *provide a partial method* m *that overrides the method* m *in* C. *We say that* L*'s priority is higher than the priority of* L' *at* e_m *iff, if* $mbody(\text{m}, \text{C}, \cdots) = \overline{y}.e' \text{inD}, (\cdots; \text{L}')$ *for some* $\overline{y}$, e', *and* D *on the reduction of* $\text{v} < \text{C}, .. > .\text{m}(..) = e_{o'}$ *where* $m < o'$ *and* $\forall i'$ *such that* $m < i' < o', \alpha_{i'} \neq\uparrow \text{L}'$, *then there is some* o *such that* $m < o < o'$ *and* $mbody(\text{m}, \text{C}, \cdots) = \overline{x}.e \text{ in E}, (\cdots; \text{L})$ *for some* $\overline{x}$, e *and* E *on the reduction of* $\text{v} < \text{C}, .. > .\text{m}(..) = e_o$.

While existing COP calculi express the precedence of layers in terms of layer ordering, this definition of priority is applicable to other COP models that do not incorporate the notion of ordering (e.g., a (imaginary) COP model where layer priorities are defined statically). Of course, this definition of priority is applicable to existing COP calculi. For example, ContextFJ [18] applies the semantics that the most recently activated layer has the highest priority, which is expressed by the following example (we write $\{\overline{L}_i\}$ when we regard a sequence $\overline{L}$ as a set).

Example. Let (CT, PT, e_0) be a well-typed ContextFJ program and $\bullet \vdash e_0 \longrightarrow^* e_n$ be a transitive closure of reduction steps in ContextFJ. Let $t = e_0 \mid \{\overline{L}_0\}, \cdots, e_n \mid \{\overline{L}_n\}$, where each $\overline{L}_i$ is an environment in which reduction of e_i is performed, be a trace of the application in ContextFJ (rather than applying the original ContextFJ dynamic semantics, we apply FSCJ-like semantics; i.e., a with expression is reduced using R-ACTSYNC in FSCJ), and both $\uparrow \text{L} = \alpha_i$ and $\uparrow \text{L}' = \alpha_j \in act(t)$ are the most recent activations of L and L' from the method invocation $e_m = \text{v.m}(..)$, respectively. It is easy to show that, if $i < j$, the priority of L is higher than the priority of L' at e_m.

In the calculus that supports multiple activation mechanisms, such as FSCJ and context holders [4], it is desirable to discuss the priorities of layers activated by different activation mechanisms. For this purpose, we distinguish the different categories of activation mechanisms, and extend the definition of a trace to express the activation sequence with multiple activation mechanisms. A trace t with multiple activation mechanisms X_j $(1 < j < m)$ is a sequence $e_0 \mid \{\Lambda_{01}, \cdots, \Lambda_{0m}\}, \cdots, e_n \mid \{\Lambda_{n1}, \cdots, \Lambda_{nm}\}$ of a pair of an expression and a set of sets of activated layers where each Λ_{ij} is a set of activated layers at e_i that are activated by X_j.

7.3 Property

We show that the activation policy discussed in Sect. 4 holds in FSCJ, which is represented by the following priority preservation theorem.

Theorem 1 (priority preservation). *For all* $e_m = \text{v.m}(..)$ *in a trace* $t = e_0 \mid \{\{\overline{L}_{S0}\}, \{\overline{L}_{A0}\}\}, \cdots, e_n \mid \{\{\overline{L}_{Sn}\}, \{\overline{L}_{An}\}\}$ *of* v *in FSCJ,* $\forall \text{L}, \text{L}'$ *where* $\text{L} \in \{\overline{L}_{Sm}\}$ *and* $\text{L}' \in \{\overline{L}_{Am}\}$, L*'s priority is higher than that of* L' *at* e_m.

Proof. By the definitions of *actSync* and *actAsync*, and the fact that trace t is constructed from a transitive closure of reduction steps in FSCJ, there is a store μ in the runtime environment where an expression that has e_m as a subexpression to be evaluated, and $\mu(v) = $ new $C(..)<\overline{L}>$ where $\overline{L} = \overline{L}_{Am}; \overline{L}_{Sm}$. Since $L \in \{\overline{L}_{Sm}\}$ and $L' \in \{\overline{L}_{Am}\}$, we can also write $\overline{L} = \overline{L}'; L'; \overline{L}'''; L; \overline{L}''$. We prove this theorem by induction on the length of $\overline{L}'''$.

Base case: $\overline{L} = \overline{L}'; L'; L; \overline{L}''$.

By the definition of priority, we only consider the case where both $PT(\mathtt{m}, \mathtt{C}, \mathtt{L})$ and $PT(\mathtt{m}, \mathtt{C}, \mathtt{L}')$ are defined. Then, $mbody(\mathtt{m}, \mathtt{C}, \overline{L}'; L', \overline{L}) = \overline{y}.e'$ in D, $(\overline{L}; L')$ for some $\overline{y}$, e', and D. By the definition of *mbody* and R-INVKP, there must be $e_p = v < \mathtt{C}, \overline{L}_0, \overline{L} > .\mathtt{m}(..)$ for some $\overline{L}_0 = \overline{L}'; L'; \cdots$ and $\overline{L} = \overline{L}_0; \cdots$ and $p < o'$ and $mbody(\mathtt{m}, \mathtt{C}, \overline{L}_0, \overline{L}) = \overline{y}'.e''$ in E, $(\cdots; L'')$. Without loss of generality, we can let $\overline{L}_0 = \overline{L}'; L'; L$. Then, by the definition of *mbody*, $L'' = L$, finishes the case.

Case: $\overline{L} = \overline{L}'; L'; \overline{L}'''; L; \overline{L}''$.

Let $\overline{L}''' = \overline{L}_1; L'''$.

By the hypothesis of the induction, the priority of L''' is higher than L'. The base case tells us that L's priority is higher than the priority of L'''. It is obvious that this priority relation has transitivity; thus, L's priority is higher than L'''s, which finishes the case. □

7.4 Changing the Activation Policy

In Sect. 4, we determined the activation policy, i.e., synchronously activated layers always have higher priorities than asynchronously activated layers. Although this policy seems preferable in many cases, there may be other cases in which asynchronous layer activation should supersede synchronous layer activation. For example, some urgent behavior triggered by an external event should supersede the currently executing synchronously activated behavior.

This section demonstrates that the activation policy in FSCJ is configurable. By changing the auxiliary definitions used in the reduction rules, we obtain a calculus that conforms to another activation policy, i.e., asynchronously activated layers always have higher priorities than synchronously activated layers, without changing the reduction rules.

The auxiliary functions that we need to change when switching the activation policies are *actSync* and *actAsync*, which are defined in Sect. 4.2. Assume that their definitions are overridden as follows.

$$actSync(\overline{L}_S; \overline{L}_A, L) = \begin{cases} (\overline{L}_S \setminus L)L; \overline{L}_A & \text{if } L \notin \overline{L}_A \\ \overline{L}_S; \overline{L}_A & \text{if } L \in \overline{L}_A \end{cases}$$

$$actAsync(\overline{L}_S; \overline{L}_A, L) = (\overline{L}_S \setminus L); (\overline{L}_A \setminus L)L$$

We also override the auxiliary function o that is used in rules R-INVK and R-NEW.

$$o(\overline{L}_A, \overline{L}_S) = \overline{L}_S; \overline{L}_A$$

The calculus obtained by applying these auxiliary functions conforms to another activation policy. In fact, the proof is obtained immediately by switching $\{\overline{L}_{Sm}\}$ and $\{\overline{L}_{Am}\}$ in Theorem 1.

8 Implementation

The ServalCJ compiler is built on top of the AspectBench Compiler (abc) [9] by extending the front-end. The compiler eventually generates bytecode that is executable on the standard Java virtual machine by first translating a ServalCJ program into an AspectJ program, and then by having the AspectJ compiler generate bytecode.[10]

8.1 Overview of Translation

The translation processes manipulate the following four constructs separately: partial and base methods, conditional layer activation, global layer activation, and events. The main differences between the ServalCJ and EventCJ compilers are the implementations of layer activation using conditional expressions and global layer activation.

We first explain how layers are translated. The translation is similar to that performed in the EventCJ compiler [21]. A layer is translated into an inner class, and each partial method in that layer is translated into a method in that inner class. The body of the base method for that partial method is translated to code that first obtains the list of instances of active layers (i.e., instances of the inner classes) and then calls the instance method at the tail position of the list. The proceed call is translated to code that calls the method on the instance at the preceding position in the list. Every class extended by partial methods will have a new field, lm, to store a list of active layers.

The conditional expressions are evaluated just before a partial method call. The ServalCJ compiler inserts checking code at the beginning of the layered method. The checking code (1) tests whether the instance executing the method subscribes to some context groups and (2) collects a list of context groups where the instance subscribes. For each context group, the checking code evaluates a conditional expression (associated with that context group). If any of the conditions hold and the corresponding layer is inactive, the code activates the layer. On the other hand, if they do not hold and the corresponding layer is active, the code deactivates the layer.

ServalCJ implements global layer activation using the per-instance layer activation mechanism. It places globally active layers in the list of active layers in every instance. To do so, the runtime manages a list of all instances in a program.[11] When a global layer is activated, that layer is added to the lm field of

---

[10] The source code of the compiler is available at https://github.com/ServalCJ/pl.git. Per-thread activation is currently not implemented.

[11] Precisely, only instances that have globally activated layers are added to the list to reduce the performance degradation.

every instance in the list. The runtime also manages a list of globally activated layers (that correspond to the global active layers $\bar{L}$ that appear in the reduction relation in Appendix 7). This is used as an initial value of the list of active layers for a newly created instance.

Events in ServalCJ are translated into pointcuts in AspectJ. As in EventCJ, for each join point, the compiler inserts the advice code to update the lm field of each subscriber and the list of globally activated layers to perform layer activation and deactivation. Cflow expressions are also implemented in a similar manner, except that, in this case the advice code counts the number of method calls to handle recursive calls appropriately. For layer activations with multiple contexts using the && and || operators, the compiler resolves which layers should be active on each join-point specified by the pointcuts.

8.2 Microbenchmarks

In this section, we evaluate the performance of method dispatch in ServalCJ by comparing the duration of method calls with and without active layers in ServalCJ with the duration of method calls in plain Java. To evaluate the overhead imposed on the compiled program, we conducted two experiments. The first experiment was performed to verify that ServalCJ does not degrade the execution performance significantly when we do not use the ServalCJ specific features that impose additional overhead. The objective of the second experiment was to measure the overhead of layered method calls with implicit and global activations.

We used JGFMethodBench in the Java Grande Forum Benchmark Suite [11] version 2 as the benchmark. We extended this benchmark to evaluate the layered method. For example, each target method in the program was extended using an around partial method that contained only the proceed call. All experiments were performed using the Oracle Java HotSpot VM 1.7.0_65 running on an Intel Core i5-4440 (4 cores, 3.10 GHz) with Linux kernel version 2.6.32. To prohibit the JIT compiler from eliminating the entire target method call, which is always performed in the server VM (the default setting of the Java HotSpot VM) and prohibits measuring overhead with respect to method calls, we used the client VM setting. This avoids such elimination in the benchmark.

Figure 16 summarizes the method dispatch time in Java and ServalCJ *without active layers*. The benchmark program measured the execution time of eight types of method calls. The labels "same" and "other" indicate that the caller and callee methods belong to the same or another instance/class, respectively. "Instance" indicates that the method is an instance method, and "class" indicates that it is a class method. "Synchronized" and "ofAbstract" indicate that the method is either synchronized or abstract, respectively. In the ServalCJ version, we defined a layer with a partial method for the instance methods that is inactive during measurement. We did not provide any partial methods for the class methods because ServalCJ does not currently support this.

Figure 16 shows that, when no layers are active, the performance of method calls in ServalCJ is comparable to that of plain Java if implicit activation is

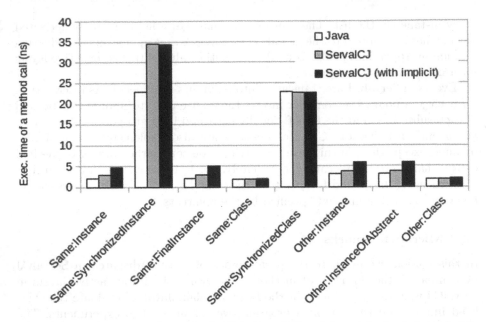

Fig. 16. Execution time of a method call in ServalCJ and Java (shorter is better). We ran the benchmarks 10 times; the range of error was approximately 0.007 % – 1 %.

not used. The primary reason for this is that, in this case, ServalCJ does not impose overhead on the program except, with the exception of the overhead incurred when it checks the number of currently active layers. The method call is approximately two times slower if we use implicit activation where the conditional expression in `if` is always evaluated just prior to the call of the partial method; this overhead is also comparable to other COP languages.

Figure 17 shows the results of measuring the method dispatch time in ServalCJ *with 1 to 15 active layers*. In this experiment, we defined 15 identical layers, each of which declared an around partial method that contained only one single `proceed` call for the "same:instance" method. As can be seen, each additional active layer adds an approximately constant amount of time to the execution time of a call, and thus the overhead is linear with the number of layers. This result is similar to the performance of EventCJ [21] and ContextJ [6].

Finally, we show the execution time of global activation. As explained above, global activation manipulates all instances of classes that have layers controlled by the global context group; thus, the number of such instances affects the execution time of the global activation. The execution time of global activation is measured similarly to the method used in the JGFMethodBench to measure the execution time of a method call. We repeatedly generated an event that activates a layer and an event that deactivates the layer within a loop (we assume that both layer activation and deactivation take the same amount of time). We repeated this experiment while changing the number of target instances.

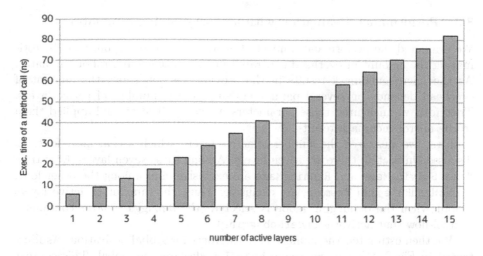

Fig. 17. Execution time of a method call in ServalCJ when increasing the number of active layers. We ran the benchmarks 10 times; the range of error was approximately 0.04 % – 0.1 %.

Figure 18 shows the results. We can observe that each additional target instance adds a constant amount of time to the execution time of an activation. In the case of a large number of target instances, the layer activation may take more than 1 ms. This overhead will not produce a severe problem if the number of instances with layers is not very large, or if the layer activation does not occur frequently. We consider that most COP applications satisfy these conditions. For example, the environment or a user's current task does not change frequently within a very short period.

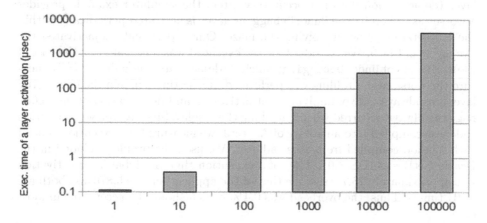

Fig. 18. Execution time of a global activation in ServalCJ when increasing the number of target instances. We ran the benchmarks 10 times; the range of error was approximately 0.01 % – 0.08 %.

8.3 Performance Evaluation with a Maze-Solving Simulator

We evaluated the performance impact of ServalCJ on a real application by esti-
mating the amount of overhead generated in the maze-solving robot simulator.
As the microbenchmark results in the previous section show, the amount of
overhead depends on several parameters such as the number of active layers.
Therefore, we measured those parameters in the application and applied them
to the microbenchmark results.

First, we measured the number of active layers, which was at most four. As
discussed in Sect. 6, there are seven layers. Among these seven layers, `Editing-
Maze`, `SolvingMaze` and `RunningMaze` are exclusive, and among the other four,
`RightHandRule` and `Tremaux` are exclusive. Thus, the number of active layers
is four when the debugging mode is selected (the `Debugging` layer contains a
control-flow that activates `UnderDebugging`).

We then estimated the number of subscribers for global activation. As illustrated in Fig. 9, the context group `MazeUI` is declared as global. This context
group has five activate declarations. Among them, `UnderDebugging` changes the
behavior of the instances of classes `Edge` (segment) and `Node` (intersection), and
the other four activate declarations change the behavior of `Robot` and `View`
(Fig. 8). While each instance of the latter two classes are singletons, the number
of instances of the former two classes depends on the size of the maze. When
we used the maze-solving robot in our classroom, the amount of `Edge` and `Node`
instances for the most complicated maze were 43 and 39, respectively. Thus, the
total number of subscribers for global activation was 84 (including two singleton
instances). According to the microbenchmarks, the overhead of each global layer
(de)activation in this case should be less than $3.0\,\mu$s.

To determine the actual overhead of global activation in the maze-solving
simulator, we measured the total execution time of global activation using a
profiler. We conducted this experiment because, even though we believe that
layer (de)activation does not occur very often, the simulator example provides
a worse case whereby the `UnderDebugging` layer is activated periodically within
the loop statement when solving the maze. Our experiment (de)activated the
five layers in Fig. 9. We consider that the overhead was dominated by the cost of
(de)activation of `UnderDebugging`, which is (de)activated periodically.[12] To measure the worst case, profiling was performed in a setting wherein the `Debugging`
layer was always active, implying that activation and deactivation of `UnderDe-
bugging` always occurred when refreshing the display. Since each layer activation
code was compiled into an advice of AspectJ, we measured the execution time of
each method compiled from those advices. We used the profiler included in the
Oracle NetBeans IDE 8.01. The total execution time of global layer activation
was approximately 25.7 ms, while that of the application was 5,870 ms (both are
CPU times). Thus, the overhead was 0.4 %, which should be acceptable in most
cases.

---

[12] By "overhead," we mean the overhead against the mechanism where the global
activation time is constant with respect to the number of instances.

9 Related Work

COP Related Mechanisms. ContextJS [24] supports user-definable activation mechanisms using the meta-programming features in JavaScript. This is sufficiently powerful to realize any type of layer activation. However, it is nearly impossible to reason about it mechanically because that constitutes meta-programming. Due to its ability to change behavior dynamically, context-aware applications are occasionally error-prone, and providing control of layer activation to the programmer may easily lead to poor application design. Thus, it is preferable to support a more disciplined layer activation mechanism implemented in the programming language.

There are several linguistic mechanisms similar to conditionals in ServalCJ. In LEAD/LEAD++ [1,2], a method consists of a number of implementations with a condition, and only the implementation where this condition holds is selected for execution. The condition changes with respect to the states of the so-called *metaobjects*, and the programmer can change these states. Tanter et al. proposed context-aware aspects [30], i.e., aspects whose behaviors depend on contexts. This concept is realized as a framework where a context is defined as a pointcut. This is similar to AspectJ's `if` pointcut, but it can also restrict the *past* contexts. Contexts are composable, because they are realized as pointcuts.

Context traits [16] mix the mechanism of trait composition with COP. Context traits take a different approach from that of layer-based COP in that the order of layers is resolved by the programmer. They provide primitive layer activation mechanisms; however, only global activation is supported.

Related Mechanisms Beyond COP. There are also language mechanisms beyond COP, such as aspect-oriented programming (AOP) and event-based programming mechanisms. Generally, there are two major differences between them: (1) while COP emphasizes on changing the behavior of multiple modules *simultaneously*, many of the other mechanisms are essentially intended to change the behavior of each module, and (2) while COP separates context changes from the execution of behavior that depends on contexts, the other mechanisms focus on control of the execution points where such behavior is executed. We further discuss the similarities and differences between our approach and each of the related mechanisms in the following.

A ServalCJ's event is equivalent to a join-point in AOP. In this sense, ServalCJ's layer activation mechanism is similar to typical AspectJ pointcuts [23] because it provides declarative events using a pointcut language. However, ServalCJ's events can also be conditional. Although layer activation using a conditional expression can be encoded in an AspectJ pointcut, e.g., "`call(* *.*(..)) && if(..)`," this may lead to serious performance degradation.

EventJava [13] is an extension of Java that integrates events with methods. In EventJava, events are broadcast as in the case of global layer activation in ServalCJ. Dynamic subscription of event receivers in event-based languages was proposed in Ptolemy [28]. ServalCJ integrates such event-based mechanisms with dynamic activation of layers in COP. However, a more complex event composition mechanism [25,26] is currently not supported by the event model in ServalCJ.

Method slots [33] unify event-based programming and AOP by extending the "slots" in Self [31] to hold multiple function closures for each method slot. We can add function closures to each method slot dynamically. Unlike COP mechanisms, this addition is performed in a per-method manner.

To represent context-dependent behavior, other approaches can be taken by representing contexts as objects that are explicitly (or indirectly through dependency injections like Scala's cake pattern [27]) passed to a method. Even though the obliviousness of the layer activation in our approach may make it difficult to predict the base program behavior, it has its own advantage in that it can modularize dynamic behavior changes. The reasoning about properties of context-dependent behaviors described in the discussion part of Sect. 6 may alleviate this disadvantage.

10 Conclusions

This paper has summarized the differences and commonalities of existing COP languages and proposed a unified model of COP mechanisms and a new COP language, ServalCJ, based on the proposed model. The model represents contexts that specify the duration of layer activation and a set of subscribers that specifies which targets the activation affects. The order of active layers is defined such that synchronous layer activation always has higher priority than asynchronous layer activation. ServalCJ implements this model by providing context groups that can be used to define layer activation based on contexts. ServalCJ covers all the use cases that can be implemented by existing COP mechanisms as well as some other cases that existing COP mechanisms cannot address. The feasibility of the proposed approach has been validated through implementation of a ServalCJ compiler and a performance evaluation.

References

1. Amano, N., Watanabe, T.: LEAD: a linguistic approach to dynamic adaptability for practical applications. In: Proceedings of the IFIP TC2 WG2.4 Working Conference on Systems Implementation 2000: Languages, Methods and Tools, pp. 277–290 (1998)
2. Amano, N., Watanabe, T.: LEAD++: an object-oriented language based on a reflective model fordynamic software adaptation. In: Technology of Object-Oriented Languages and Systems (TOOLS31), pp. 41–50 (1999)
3. Aotani, T., Kamina, T., Masuhara, H.: Featherweight EventCJ: a core calculus for a context-oriented language with event-based per-instance layer transition. In: COP 2011 (2011)
4. Aotani, T., Kamina, T., Masuhara, H.: Context holders: realizing multiple layer activation mechanisms in asingle context-oriented language. In: FOAL 2014, pp. 3–6 (2014)

5. Appeltauer, M., Hirschfeld, R., Haupt, M., Lincke, J., Perscheid, M.: A comparison of context-oriented programming languages. In: COP 2009, pp. 1–6 (2009)
6. Appeltauer, M., Hirschfeld, R., Haupt, M., Masuhara, H.: ContextJ: context-oriented programming with Java. Comput. Softw. **28**(1), 272–292 (2011)
7. Appeltauer, M., Hirschfeld, R., Masuhara, H.: Improving the development of context-dependent Java application with ContextJ. In: COP 2009 (2009)
8. Appeltauer, M., Hirschfeld, R., Masuhara, H., Haupt, M., Kawauchi, K.: Event-specific software composition in context-oriented programming. In: Baudry, B., Wohlstadter, E. (eds.) SC 2010. LNCS, vol. 6144, pp. 50–65. Springer, Heidelberg (2010). doi:10.1007/978-3-642-14046-4_4
9. Avgustinov, P., et al.: *abc*: an extensible AspectJ compiler. In: Rashid, A., Aksit, M. (eds.) Transactions on Aspect-Oriented Software Development I. LNCS, vol. 3880, pp. 293–334. Springer, Heidelberg (2006). doi:10.1007/11687061_9
10. Bainomugisha, E., Vallejos, J., De Roover, C., Carreton, A.L., De Meuter, W.: Interruptible context-dependent executions: a fresh look atprogramming context-aware applications. In: Onward! 2012, pp. 67–84 (2012)
11. Bull, J.M., Smith, L.A., Westhead, M.D., Henty, D.S., Davey. R.A.: A methodology for benchmarking Java Grande applications. In: Proceedings of ACM 1999 Java Grande Conference, pp. 81–88 (1999)
12. Costanza, P., Hirschfeld, R.: Language constructs for context-oriented programming - an overview of ContextL. In: Dynamic Language Symposium (DLS) 2005, pp. 1–10 (2005)
13. Eugster, P., Jayaram, K.R.: EventJava: an extension of Java for event correlation. In: Drossopoulou, S. (ed.) ECOOP 2009. LNCS, vol. 5653, pp. 570–594. Springer, Heidelberg (2009). doi:10.1007/978-3-642-03013-0_26
14. González, S., Cardozo, N., Mens, K., Cádiz, A., Libbrecht, J.-C., Goffaux, J.: Subjective-C: bringing context to mobile platform. In: Malloy, B., Staab, S., Brand, M. (eds.) SLE 2010. LNCS, vol. 6563, pp. 246 265. Springer, Heidelberg (2011). doi:10.1007/978-3-642-19440-5_15
15. González, S., Mens, K., Cádiz, A.: Context-oriented programming with the ambient object systems. J. Univ. Comput. Sci. **14**(20), 3307–3332 (2008)
16. González, S., Mens, K., Colacioiu, M., Cazzola, W.: Context traits: dynamic behaviour adaptation through run-time traitrecomposition. In: AOSD 2013, pp. 209–220 (2013)
17. Hirschfeld, R., Costanza, P., Nierstrasz, O.: Context-oriented programming. J. Object Technol. **7**(3), 125–151 (2008)
18. Hirschfeld, R., Igarashi, A., Masuhara, H.: ContextFJ: a minimal core calculus for context-orientedprogramming. In: FOAL 2011, pp. 19–23 (2011)
19. Igarashi, A., Hirschfeld, R., Masuhara, H.: A type system for dynamic layer composition. In: FOOL 2012 (2012)
20. Igarashi, A., Pierce, B., Wadler, P.: Featherweight Java: a minimal core calculus for Java and GJ. ACM TOPLAS **23**(3), 396–450 (2001)
21. Kamina, T., Aotani, T., Masuhara, H.: EventCJ: a context-oriented programming language with declarative event-based context transition. In: AOSD 2011, pp. 253–264 (2011)
22. Kamina, T., Aotani, T., Masuhara, H.: Introducing composite layers in EventCJ. IPSJ Trans. Program. **6**(1), 1–8 (2013)
23. Kiczales, G., Hilsdale, E., Hugunin, J., Kersten, M., Palm, J., Griswold, W.G.: An overview of AspectJ. In: Knudsen, J.L. (ed.) ECOOP 2001. LNCS, vol. 2072, pp. 327–354. Springer, Heidelberg (2001). doi:10.1007/3-540-45337-7_18

24. Lincke, J., Appeltauer, M., Steinert, B., Hirschfeld, R.: An open implementation for context-oriented layer composition in ContextJS. Sci. Comput. Program. **76**(12), 1194–1209 (2011)

25. Malakuti, S., Akşit, M.: Event modules: modularizing domain-specific crosscutting RV concerns. In: Chiba, S., Tanter, É., Bodden, E., Maoz, S., Kienzle, J. (eds.) Transactions on AOSD XI. LNCS, vol. 8400, pp. 27–69. Springer, Heidelberg (2014). doi:10.1007/978-3-642-55099-7_2

26. Malakuti, S., Akşit, M.: Evolution of composition filters to event composition. In: SAC 2012, pp. 1850–1857 (2012)

27. Odersky, M., Zenger, M.: Scalable component abstractions. In: OOPSLA 2005, pp. 41–57 (2005)

28. Rajan, H., Leavens, G.T.: Ptolemy: a language with quantified, typed events. In: Vitek, J. (ed.) ECOOP 2008. LNCS, vol. 5142, pp. 155–179. Springer, Heidelberg (2008). doi:10.1007/978-3-540-70592-5_8

29. Salvaneschi, G., Ghezzi, C., Pradella, M.: ContextErlang: introducing context-oriented programming in theactor model. In: AOSD 2012 (2012)

30. Tanter, É., Gybels, K., Denker, M., Bergel, A.: Context-aware aspects. In: Löwe, W., Südholt, M. (eds.) SC 2006. LNCS, vol. 4089, pp. 227–242. Springer, Heidelberg (2006). doi:10.1007/11821946_15

31. Ungar, D., Smith, R.B.: Self: the power of simplicity. In: OOPSLA 1987, pp. 227–241 (1987)

32. von Löwis, M., Denker, M., Nierstrasz, O.: Context-oriented programming: beyond layers. In: ICDL 2007: Proceedings of the 2007 International Conference on Dynamic Languages, pp. 143–156 (2007)

33. Zhuang, Y.Y., Chiba, S.: Method slots: supporting methods, events, and advices by a singlelanguage construct. In: AOSD 2013, pp. 197–208 (2013)

Modular Reasoning in the Presence of Event Subtyping

Mehdi Bagherzadeh[1]([✉]), Robert Dyer[2], Rex D. Fernando[3], José Sánchez[4],
and Hridesh Rajan[1]

[1] Iowa State University, Ames, USA
{mbagherz,hridesh}@iastate.edu
[2] Bowling Green State University, Bowling Green, USA
rdyer@bgsu.edu
[3] University of Wisconsin, Madison, USA
rex@cs.wisc.edu
[4] University of Central Florida, Orlando, USA
sanchez@eecs.ucf.edu

Abstract. Separating crosscutting concerns while preserving modular reasoning is challenging. Type-based interfaces (event types) separate modularized crosscutting concerns (observers) and traditional object-oriented concerns (subjects). Event types paired with event specifications were shown to be effective in enabling modular reasoning about subjects and observers. Similar to class subtyping, organizing event types into subtyping hierarchies is beneficial. However, unrelated behaviors of observers and their arbitrary execution orders could cause unique, somewhat counterintuitive, reasoning challenges in the presence of event subtyping. These challenges threaten both tractability of reasoning and reuse of event types. This work makes three contributions. First, we pose and explain these challenges. Second, we propose an event-based calculus to show how these challenges can be overcome. Finally, we present modular reasoning rules of our technique and show its applicability to other event-based techniques.

1 Introduction

Separation of crosscutting concerns has generated significant interest over the past decade or so [2–22]. An interesting challenge in separation of crosscutting concerns is to preserve modular reasoning and its underlying modular type checking. Recently some consensus has been formed that a notion of explicit interfaces between modularized crosscutting concerns and traditional object-oriented (OO) concerns enables modular type checking [11–16,19,20,23], modular reasoning [3,6–15] as well as design stability [24–26].

Previous work, such as join point types (JPT) [20], join point interfaces (JPI) [19] and Ptolemy's typed events [27], just to name a few, propose a type-based formulation of these interfaces to enable modular type checking. These type-based interfaces could be thought of as *event types* which are announced, implicitly or explicitly, by traditional

---

The work described in this article is the revised and extended version of an article in the proceedings of Modularity 2015 [1].

© Springer International Publishing Switzerland 2016
S. Chiba et al. (Eds.): ToMC I, LNCS 9800, pp. 167–223, 2016.
DOI: 10.1007/978-3-319-46969-0_5

OO concerns, or *subjects*, where modularized crosscutting concerns, or *observers*, register for the events and run upon their announcement [28,29]. Announcement of an event type could cause *zero or more* of its observers to run in a chain where observers can invoke each other. This event announcement and handling model for separation of concerns has been popularized by AspectJ [2] and is different from models in which the subject is responsible for invoking all of its observers, as in Java's event model and the Observer pattern [30].

Similar to OO subtyping, where a class can subtype another class, an event type can subtype another event type. *Event subtyping* enables structuring of event types and allows for code reuse [19,20,27]. Code reuse allows *an observer of an event to run upon announcement of any of its subevents*, i.e. observer reuse, and makes the data attributes of the event accessible in its subevents, i.e. event inheritance. Modular type checking of subjects and observers in the presence of event subtyping has been explored by previous work [19,20,27].

Modular reasoning about subjects and observers, unlike their modular type checking, is focused on understanding their behaviors [6,31], control effects [8,10,32], data effects [3,33] and exception flows [9]. In modular reasoning [34], a system is understood one module at a time and in isolation using only its implementation and the interfaces, not implementations, of other modules it references [13,14]. Previous work, such as crosscutting programming interfaces (XPI) [6], crosscutting programming interfaces with design rules (XPIDR) [32] and translucid contracts [8–10,35], enables modular reasoning about subjects and observers using *event specifications*, however, they do not support event subtyping.

Modular reasoning about behaviors of subjects and observers, using event specifications of event types that can subtype each other, where announcement of an event allows not only observers of the event but also observers of *all* of its superevents, with possibly *unrelated behaviors* run in an *arbitrary order*, faces the following unique challenges:

- *Problem ❶ – Combinatorial reasoning*: unrelated behaviors of observers may require a factorial number of combinations of execution orders of observers of the event and observers of all of its superevents, up to $n!$ for n observers, to be considered in reasoning about the subject, which makes reasoning intractable;
- *Problem ❷ – Behavior invariance*: arbitrary execution orders of observers may force observers of the event and observers of all of its superevents to satisfy the same behavior, which prevents reuse of event types, their specifications and observers.

In this work, we solve problem *(1)* by imposing a novel *refining relation* among specifications of an event and its superevents such that for each event in a subtyping hierarchy its greybox specification [36] refines both behaviors and control effects of the greybox specification of its superevent. Our refining relation is the inverse of the classical refining for blackbox specifications [37] and extends it to greybox specifications with control effect specifications. We solve problem *(2)* by imposing a *non-decreasing relation* on execution orders of observers of an event and observers of its superevents, such that for each event in a subtyping hierarchy observers of an event run before observers of its superevents. With the refining and non-decreasing relations combined, subjects and observers of an event could be understood modularly and in a tractable manner using only the specification of their event, independent of observers of the event, observers of its superevents and their execution orders, while allowing reuse. This is only sound when we impose a *conformance relation* on subjects and observers of an event such that each subject and observer of the event respects behaviors and control effects of their event specifications.

We illustrate problems *(1)–(2)* in the event-based language Ptolemy [27] by adding greybox event specifications to it, and propose our solution in the context of a new language design called *Ptolemy$_S$*. The language *Ptolemy$_S$* has built-in support for the refining, non-decreasing and conformance relations that together enable modular reasoning about behaviors and control effects of subjects and observers. Our proposed solution could be applied to other event-based systems especially those with event announcement and handling models similar to AspectJ [2] including join point types [20] and join point interfaces [19].

Contributions. We make the following contributions:

- identification and illustration of problems *(1)–(2)* of modular reasoning about subjects and observers in the presence of event subtyping (Sect. 2);
- the refining relation for greybox event specifications, the non-decreasing relation for execution orders of observers and the conformance relation for behaviors and control effects of subjects and observers of an event hierarchy, to solve problems *(1)–(2)* and enable modular reasoning (Sects. 3 and 4);
- *Ptolemy$_S$*, a language design with support for refining, non-decreasing and conformance relations;
- *Ptolemy$_S$*'s Hoare logic [38] for modular reasoning (Sect. 4);
- applicability of *Ptolemy$_S$*'s reasoning to AspectJ-like event-based systems including join point types [20] and join point interfaces [19] (Sect. 5);
- modular reasoning about control effects of observers and subject-observer control interference (Sect. 6);
- event specification inheritance to statically enforce the refining relation for greybox event specifications and enable specification reuse (Sect. 7);
- *Ptolemy$_S$*'s sound static and dynamic semantics (Sects. 8 and 9);
- binary compatibility rules for *Ptolemy$_S$*'s event types and their specifications to enable binary reuse (Sect. 10).

Implementation of *Ptolemy$_S$*'s compiler is publicly available at http://sf.net/p/ptolemyj/ code/HEAD/tree/pyc/branches/event-inheritance/. Section 11 discusses the implementation and limitations of our approach. Section 12 presents related work and Sect. 13 discusses future work and concludes. Appendix A and B present full proofs for soundness of *Ptolemy$_S$*'s modular reasoning and type system.

2   Problems

In this section we illustrate problems *(1)–(2)*, discussed in Sect. 1, using the event-based language Ptolemy [27].

As an example of modular reasoning about the behavior of a subject, consider *static* verification of the JML-like [39] assertion Φ on line 8 of Fig. 1. The assertion says that

```
 1  /* subject */
 2  class ASTVisitor {
 3    void visit(AndExp e) {
 4      announce AndEv(e, e.left, e.right) {
 5        e.left.accept(this);
 6        e.right.accept(this);
 7      }
 8      assert e.equals(old(e)); Φ
 9    }
10    void visit(TrueExp e) { announce TrueEv(e) {} } ..
11  }
```

Fig. 1. Static verification of Φ in subject `ASTVisitor`.

```
12  /* event types */
13  void event ExpEv                 { Exp node; }
14  void event BinEv   extends ExpEv {
15    BinExp node; Exp left, right;
16  }
17  void event AndEv   extends BinEv { AndExp node; }
18  void event UnEv    extends ExpEv { UnExp node; }
19  void event TrueEv extends UnEv  { TrueExp node; }
20  /* data types */
21  class Exp {
22    Exp parent;
23    void accept(ASTVisitor v) { v.visit(this); }
24  }
25  class BinExp extends Exp     { Exp left, right; .. }
26  class AndExp extends BinExp { .. }
27  class UnExp  extends Exp     { .. }
28  class TruExp extends UnExp  { .. }
```

Fig. 2. Event `AndEv` and its superevents `BinEv` and `ExpEv`.

the expression e and its state remain the same after announcement and handling of the event type `AndEv`, *on lines 4–7*, where `AndEv` is a subevent of `BinEv` and `ExpEv`, in the event subtyping hierarchy of Fig. 2. The assertion assumes that `e`, `e.left` and `e.right` are not null. The method `equals` checks for equality of two objects and their states, e.g. two expressions of type `AndExp` are equal if their object references, `parents` and their `left` and `right` children are equal. The expression *old* refers to values of variables at the beginning of method `visit`, on line 3. To better understand the problems of modular reasoning we first provide a short background on Ptolemy.

2.1 Ptolemy in a Nutshell

Ptolemy [27] is an extension of Java for separation of crosscutting concerns [16]. It has a unified model like Eos [17,40–43] with support for event types, event subtyping and explicit announcement and handling of events. In Ptolemy, a subject announces an event and observers register for the event and run upon its announcement. Announcement of an event causes observers of the event and observers of its superevents to run in a chain according to their *dynamic registration order*, where observers can invoke each other.

Written in Ptolemy, Figs. 1, 2 and 3 together show a simple expression language with a tracer, type checker and evaluator for boolean expressions such as `AndExp`,

```
29  /* observers */
30  class Tracer {
31    Tracer() { register(this); }
32    void printExp(ExpEv next) {
33      next.invoke();
34      logVisitEnd(next.node()); }
35    when ExpEv do printExp;
36  }
37  class Checker{
38    Stack<Type> typeStack = ..
39    Checker() { register(this); }
40    void checkBinExp (BinEv next) {
41      next.invoke();
42      Bool t1 = (Bool) typeStack.pop();
43      Bool t2 = (Bool) typeStack.pop();
44      typeStack.push(new Bool()); }
45    when BinEv do checkBinExp;
46    void checkUnExp(UnEv next) {
47      next.invoke();
48      typeStack.push(new Bool()); }
49    when UnEv do checkUnExp;
50  }
51  class Evaluator {
52    Stack<Value> valStack = ..
53    Evaluator() { register(this); }
54    void evalAndExp (AndEv next) {
55      next.invoke();
56      BoolVal b1 = (BoolVal) valStack.pop();
57      BoolVal b2 = (BoolVal) valStack.pop();
58      valStack.push(new BoolVal(b1.val && b2.val)); }
59    when AndEv do evalAndExp;
60    void evalTrueExp (TrueEv next) {
61      next.invoke();
62      valStack.push(new BoolVal(true)); }
63    when TrueEv do evalTrueExp; ..
64  }
```

Fig. 3. Observers Tracer, Checker and Evaluator.

OrExp and numerical expressions. We focus on the code for boolean expressions but the complete code can be found elsewhere[1]. A parser generates abstract syntax trees (AST) for expressions of the language and provides a visitor to visit these abstract syntax trees.

The subject ASTVisitor, in Fig. 1, uses *announce* expressions to announce event types for each node type in the AST of an expression upon its visit. For example, it announces the event type AndEv for visiting AndExp, on lines 4–7, with its event body on lines 5–6. Observers Tracer, Checker and Evaluator, in Fig. 3, show interest in events and register to run upon their announcement. For example, Evaluator shows interest in AndEv using a *when − do* binding declaration, on line 59, and registers for it using a *register* expression, on line 53. Evaluator runs the observer handler method[2]

---

[1] http://sf.net/p/ptolemyj/code/HEAD/tree/pyc/branches/event-inheritance/examples/
   100-Polymorphic-Expressions.

[2] Phrases 'observer' and 'observer handler method' are used interchangably.

evalAndExp, on lines 54–58, upon announcement of AndEv. The handler pops values of the left and right children of the visited AndExp node from a value stack conjoins them together to evaluate the value of the conjunct expression and pushes the result back to the stack. For a binary boolean expression, Checker ensures that its children are boolean expressions by popping and casting their boolean values from a type stack. Types Type and Value and their subtypes, e.g. Bool and BoolVal, denote types and values of boolean and numerical expressions.

Announcement of AndEv, on lines 4–7, could cause the observer Evaluator of the event and observers Checker and Tracer of its superevents BinEv and ExpEv to run in a chain, if they are registered. An observer of an event is bound to the event through a binding declaration. For example, Evaluator is an observer of AndEv because of its binding declaration whereas Checker is not, though it may run upon announcement of AndEv. Observers are put in a chain of observers as they register for an event with the event body as the last observer. For example, the event body for AndEv is the last observer of the event in the chain. The chain of observers is stored inside an event closure represented by a variable *next* and the chain is passed to each observer handler method. For example, the chain is passed to evalAndExp on line 54. An observer of an event can invoke the next observer in the chain using an *invoke* expression which is similar to AspectJ's *proceed*. Dynamic registration allows observers to register in any arbitrary order which in turn means that an observer of an event can invoke another observer of the same event, an observer of any of its superevents or any of its subevents. For example, the observer Evaluator for the event AndEv can invoke, on line 55, another observer of AndEv or any of its superevents or subevents.

Event types must be declared before they are announced by subjects or handled by observers. An event declaration names a superevent in its *extends* clause and a set of context variables in its body. Context variables are shared data between subjects and observers of an event. An event inherits contexts of its superevents via event inheritance, can redeclare contexts of its superevents via depth subtyping or add to them via width subtyping. For example, the declaration of AndEv extends BinEv as its superevent, inherits its context variables left and right and redeclares its context node. The declaration of BinEv, on lines 14–16, adds contexts left and right, using width subtyping, to node that it inherits from its superevent ExpEv. Contexts left and right serve illustration purposes only, otherwise they could be projected from node. Values of context variables of an event are set upon its announcement and stored in its event closure. For example, the contexts node, left and right of AndEv are set with values e, e.left and e.right upon announcement of AndEv, on line 4.

Event Type Specifications. To verify Φ in Fig. 1, the behavior of the announce expression for AndEv, on lines 4–7, must be understood, which in turn is dependent on behaviors of observers of AndEv and observers of its superevents, running upon its announcement. For such understanding to be modular, only the implementation of the subject ASTVisitor, on lines 2–11, and interfaces of modules it references, including the event types AndEv and its superevents BinEv and ExpEv, are available. However, neither ASTVisitor nor AndEv, BinEv or ExpEv say anything about the behaviors of their observers, which in turn makes modular verification of Φ difficult.

Previous work [8–10] proposes translucid contracts as event type specifications to specify behaviors and control effects of subjects and observers of an event and enables their modular reasoning in the *absence* of event subtyping. We add translucid contracts to Ptolemy's event types and illustrate how unrelated event specifications in a subtyping hierarchy and arbitrary execution of their observers could cause problems *(1)–(2)* in modular reasoning about subjects and observers in the *presence* of event subtyping.

```
1  void event ExpEv { ..
2   requires node != null
3   assumes {
4    next.invoke();
5    requires true
6    ensures next.node().parent==old(next.node().parent);
7   }
8   ensures node.equals(old(node))
9  }
10 void event BinEv extends ExpEv { ..
11  requires left != null && right != null && node != null
12  assumes {
13   next.invoke();
14   requires next.node().left!=null&&next.node().right!=null
15   ensures next.node().parent==old(next.node().parent);
16  }
17 ensures true
18 }
19 void event AndEv extends BinEv { ..
20  requires left != null && right != null && node != null
21  assumes {
22   next.invoke();
23   requires next.node().left!=null&&next.node().right!=null
24   ensures next.node().parent==old(next.node().parent);
25  }
26  ensures node.equals(old(node))
27 }
```

Fig. 4. Unrelated contracts of subtyping events.

In its original form [8], a translucid contract of an event is a greybox specification [36] that specifies behaviors and control effects of individual observers of the event with *no relation* to behaviors and control effects of its superevents or subevents. Figure 4 shows translucid contracts of a few event types of Fig. 2. The translucid contract of AndEv, on lines 20–26, specifies behavior and control effects of the observer Evaluator of AndEv and especially its observer handler method evalAndExp. The behavior of evalAndExp is specified using the precondition *requires*, on line 20, and the postcondition *ensures*, on line 26, which says that the execution of the observer starts in a state in which the context node, left and right are not null, i.e. *left! = null &&* *right! = null && node ! = null*, and if the execution terminates it terminates in a state in which the node is the same as before the start of the execution of the observer, i.e. *node.equals(old (node))*.

Control effects of evalAndExp are specified by the *assumes* block, on lines 21–25, that limits its implementation structure. The assumes block is a combination of program and specification expressions. The program expression *next.invoke*(), on line 22, specifies and exposes control effects of interest, e.g. occurrence of the invoke expression in the implementation of `evalAndExp`, and the specification expression *requires next.node*().*left*! $= null$ && *next.node*().*right*! $= null$ *ensures next.node*().*parent* $== old$ (*next.node*().*parent*), on lines 23–24, hides the rest of the implementation of `evalAndExp`, allowing it to vary as long as it respects the specification. The assumes block of `AndEv` says that an observer `evalAndExp` of `AndEv` must invoke the next observer in the chain of observers, on line 22, and then can do anything as long as it does not modify the `parent` field of the context variable `node`, on lines 23–24. The expression *next.node*() in the contract retrieves the context `node` from the event closure *next* for `AndEv` and the expression *old* refers to values of variables before event announcement.

Through the specification of behaviors of observers of an event, the translucid contract of an event also specifies the behavior of an invoke expression in the implementation of an observer of the event. This is true because in the absence of event subtyping the invoke expression causes the invocation of the next observer of the same event. For example, the contract of `AndEv` specifies the behavior of the invoke expression in the implementation of the observer handler method `evalAndExp` to have the precondition *left*! $= null$ && *right*! $= null$ && *node*! $= null$ and the postcondition *node.equals*(*old* (*node*)). The precondition of the invoke expression must hold right before its invocation and its postcondition must hold right after it.

2.2   Combinatorial Reasoning, Problem (1)

Various execution orders of observers of an event and observers of its superevents could yield different behaviors, especially if there is no relation between behaviors of observers of the event and its superevents and no known order of their execution. Combinatorial reasoning forces all such variations of execution orders to be considered in reasoning about a subject of an event, which makes the reasoning intractable [29].

To illustrate, reconsider static verification of Φ for announcement of `AndEv`, on lines 4–7 of Fig. 1, with an observer instance `evaluator` registered to handle `AndEv` and an observer instance `checker` registered to handle `BinEv`. Translucid contracts of `AndEv` and `BinEv` in Fig. 4 specify the behaviors of `evaluator` and `checker`, respectively. Announcement of `AndEv` could cause the observers `evaluator` and `checker` to run in two alternative execution orders χ_1: `evaluator` $\rightarrow$ `checker` or χ_2: `checker` $\rightarrow$ `evaluator`, depending on their dynamic registration order. In χ_1, `evaluator` runs first, where it invokes `checker` using its invoke expression, on line 55 of Fig. 3, and the opposite happens in χ_2. The body of `AndEv` runs as the last observer in χ_1 and χ_2 (not shown here).

For χ_1, the assertion Φ could be verified using the contract of `AndEv` for `evaluator`, on lines 20–26 of Fig. 4, using its postcondition *node.equals*(*old* (*node*)), on line 26. Recall that the precondition and postcondition of `AndEv` are the precondition and postcondition of its observer `evaluator`. To verify Φ, the postcondition of `AndEv` is copied right after the announce expression, using the copy rule [44], and its context variables `node`, `left` and `right` are replaced respectively with parameters e, e.left and e.right of the announce expression [8]. This allows use of the postcondition of the contract of AndEv in the scope of the method visit. Replacing the context variables in the postcondition of AndEv produces the predicate *e.equals(old (e))*, which is exactly the assertion Φ that we wanted to prove.

In χ_1, the assertion Φ could be verified using the postcondition of the translucid contract of AndEv alone. An example of a more subtle interplay of behaviors of evaluator and checker is a scenario in which translucid contracts of AndEv and BinEv look like *requires true assumes* { *establishes true; next.invoke();* } *ensures true* and *requires true assumes* {*establishes node.equals (old (node)); next.invoke();* } *ensures true*, respectively. The specification expression *establishes q* is a sugar for *requires true ensures q*. With these contracts, neither the postcondition of AndEv nor BinEv alone are enough to verify Φ, but their interplay results in a postcondition that implies and consequently verifies Φ.

In contrast, Φ cannot be statically verified for χ_2 because neither the postcondition *true* of the contract of BinEv, on line 17 of Fig. 4, nor the interplay of behaviors of observers evaluator and checker in χ_2 provides the guarantees required by Φ.

As illustrated, in reasoning about a subject of an event, various execution orders of its observers and observers of its superevents must be considered. Generally for n observers of events in a subtyping hierarchy there can be up to $n!$ possible execution orders [9,29] which in turn makes the reasoning intractable. Also, dependency of the reasoning on execution orders of observers *threatens the modularity* of the reasoning. This is because any changes in execution orders of observers could invalidate any previous reasoning. For example, the already verified assertion Φ for the execution order χ_1 is invalidated by changing the execution order to χ_2.

2.3 Behavior Invariance, Problem (2)

In reasoning about an observer of an event, arbitrary execution orders of observers of the event and observers of its superevents in a chain could force observers of the event and observers of all of its superevents in a subtyping hierarchy to satisfy the same behavior. This could prevent reuse of event types, their specifications [45] and their observers [19,20].

To illustrate, consider reasoning about the behavior of the invoke expression in the observer evaluator, in Fig. 3 line 55, with an observer instance evaluator registered to handle AndEv and observer instance tracer registered to handle its transitive superevent ExpEv. Translucid contracts of AndEv and ExpEv in Fig. 4 specify behaviors of evaluator and tracer, respectively. Upon announcement of AndEv, observers evaluator and tracer could run in two alternative execution orders χ_1: evaluator $\rightarrow$ tracer or χ_2: tracer $\rightarrow$ evaluator.

Recall that the translucid contract of an event also specifies behaviors of invoke expressions in implementations of its observers. In other words, the contract of AndEv specifies the behavior of the invoke expression in its observer evaluator, on line 55. That is, the precondition *left!* = *null && right!* = *null && node!* = *null* of AndEv must hold right before the invoke expression in evaluator and the postcondition *node.equals(old (node))* must hold right after the invoke expression.

In χ_1, for the invoke expression of evaluator to invoke tracer, its precondition must imply the precondition *node!* = *null* of tracer and the postcondition

$node.equals(old\ (node))$ of `tracer` must imply the postcondition of the invoke expression in `evaluator`. In other words, χ_1 requires $\omega_1 : \mathscr{P}(\texttt{AndEv}) \Rightarrow \mathscr{P}(\texttt{ExpEv}) \wedge \mathscr{Q}(\texttt{ExpEv}) \Rightarrow \mathscr{Q}(\texttt{AndEv})$ to hold for `evaluator` to invoke `tracer`. Auxiliary functions $\mathscr{P}$ and $\mathscr{Q}$ return the precondition and postcondition of an event type, respectively. In contrast, χ_2 requires $\omega_2 : \mathscr{P}(\texttt{ExpEv}) \Rightarrow \mathscr{P}(\texttt{AndEv}) \wedge \mathscr{Q}(\texttt{AndEv}) \Rightarrow \mathscr{Q}(\texttt{ExpEv})$ to hold for `tracer` to invoke `evaluator`. To allow both execution orders χ_1 and χ_2, both conditions ω_1 and ω_2 must hold which in turn requires preconditions and postconditions of `AndEv` and `ExpEv` and consequently preconditions and postconditions of their observers `evaluator` and `tracer` to be the same, i.e. invariant.

3   Solution

To solve combinatorial reasoning and behavior invariance problems we propose to *(1)* relate behaviors of observers of an event and its superevent by a refining relation among greybox event specifications in an event subtyping hierarchy and to *(2)* limit arbitrary execution order of observers by a non-decreasing relation on execution orders of observers. This proposal constitutes a new language design called *Ptolemy$_S$* with support for these relations. Figure 5 shows an overview of these relations in *Ptolemy$_S$*.

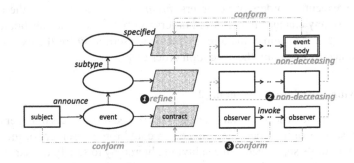

Fig. 5. Refining, non-decreasing and conformance relations.

In Fig. 5, for an event subtyping hierarchy, the refining relation guarantees that the specification (contract) of an event refines the specification of its superevent and the non-decreasing relation guarantees that upon announcement of an event by a subject, an observer of the event runs before an observer of its superevent. The conformance relation guarantees that each subject and observer of an event conform to and respect their event specification.

Detailed formalization of *Ptolemy$_S$*'s sound static and dynamic semantics can be found in Sects. 8 and 9.

3.1   *Ptolemy$_S$*'s Syntax

Figure 6 shows the expression-based core syntax of *Ptolemy$_S$* with focus on event types, event subtyping and event specifications. Hereafter, *term** means a sequence of zero or more terms and *[term]* means zero or one term.

A *Ptolemy$_S$* program is a set of declarations followed by an expression, which is like a call to the main method in Java. There are two kinds of declarations: class and event type declarations. A class can extend another class and it may have zero or more fields, methods and binding declarations.

Similarly, an event type declaration can extend (subtype) another event type and has a return type, a set of context variable declarations and an optional translucid contract. The return type of an event specifies the return type of its observers. An interesting property of return types of subtyping events is that, because of the non-decreasing relation, the return type of an event is a supertype of the return type of the event it extends, see Sect. 9. An event type declaration inherits context variables of the event types it extends and can declare more through width subtyping. It can also redeclare the context variables of the event types it extends through depth subtyping [27], as long as the type of the redeclaring context is a subtype of the type of the redeclared context. Figure 2 illustrates the declaration of the event type AndEv, on line 17.

$$prog ::= decl^* \ e$$
$$decl ::= \text{class } c \text{ extends } d \ \{ \ form^* \ meth^* \ binding^* \ \}$$
$$\mid c \text{ event } ev \text{ extends } ev' \ \{ \ form^* \ [contract] \ \}$$
$$meth ::= t \ m \ (form^*) \ \{ \ e \ \}$$
$$binding ::= \text{when } ev \text{ do } m$$
$$e, se ::= var \mid \text{null} \mid \text{new } c \ () \mid \text{cast } c \ e \mid \text{if } (e) \ \{e\} \text{ else } \{e\}$$
$$\mid e.m \ (e^*) \mid e.f \mid e.f = e \mid form = e \ ; \ e$$
$$\mid \text{announce } ev \ (e^*) \ \{ \ e \ \} \mid e.\text{invoke} \ ()$$
$$\mid \text{register} \ (e) \mid \text{unregister} \ (e)$$
$$\mid \text{refining } spec \ \{ \ e \ \} \mid spec \mid \text{either } \{e\} \text{ or } \{e\}$$
$$p, q ::= var \mid p.f \mid p == p \mid p < p \mid \ ! \ p \mid p \ \&\& \ p \mid \text{old} \ (p)$$
$$contract ::= \text{requires } p \ [\text{assumes } \{ \ se \ \}] \text{ ensures } q$$
$$spec ::= \text{requires } p \text{ ensures } q$$
$$t ::= c \mid \text{thunk } ev$$
$$form ::= t \ var$$

$$c, d \in \mathscr{C} \cup \{\textbf{\textit{Object}}\} \qquad \text{set of class names}$$
$$ev, ev' \in \mathscr{E} \cup \{\textbf{\textit{Event}}\} \qquad \text{set of event names}$$
$$f \in \mathscr{F} \qquad \text{set of field names}$$
$$var \in \mathscr{V} \cup \{\textbf{\textit{this}}, \textbf{\textit{next}}\} \ \text{set of variable names}$$

Fig. 6. *Ptolemy$_S$*'s core syntax, based on [8,16,27].

3.2 Refining Relation of Event Specifications

Ptolemy$_S$ relates behaviors and control effects of observers of events in a subtyping hierarchy by relating their greybox event specifications through a refinement relation $\lhd$. In the refining relation, the specification of an event refines the specification of its super-event, for both behaviors and control effects. *Ptolemy$_S$*'s refinement among greybox event specifications is the inverse of classical behavioral subtyping for blackbox method specifications [37], however, blackbox specifications do not specify control effects.

In *Ptolemy*$_S$, a translucid contract [8,9] of an event is a greybox specification that, *in relation* to its superevents, specifies behaviors and control effects of individual observers of the event and their invoke expressions. A translucid contract of an event specifies behaviors using the precondition *requires* and the postcondition *ensures*. The behavior *requires p ensures q* says that if the execution of an observer of the event starts in state σ satisfying p, written as $\sigma \models p$, and it terminates normally, it terminates in a state σ' that satisfies q, i.e. $\sigma' \models q$.

A translucid contract specifies control effects of its individual observers using its *assumes* block. An assumes block is a combination of program and specification expressions. A program expression exposes control effects of interest, e.g. invoke expressions, in the implementation of an observer whereas a specification expression *spec* hides the rest of its implementation allowing it to vary as long it respects its specification. The contract of an event only names the context variables of the event and must expose invoke expressions in the implementation of its observers. Figure 4 illustrates the translucid contract of AndEv, on lines 20–26, with its precondition, on line 20, postcondition, on line 26, program expression, on line 22 and specification expression, on lines 23–24. *Ptolemy*$_S$ relates translucid contracts of an event and its superevents through the refining relation $\trianglelefteq$.

Definition 1 (*Refining translucid contracts*). *For event types ev and ev', where ev is a subevent of ev', written as ev $\ll$: ev'[3], and their respective translucid contracts $\mathcal{G} = ($requires p assumes $\{se\}$ ensures $q)$ and $\mathcal{G}' = ($requires p' assumes $\{se'\}$ ensures $q'),$ $\mathcal{G}'$ is refined by $\mathcal{G}$, written as $\mathcal{G}' \trianglelefteq \mathcal{G}$, if and only if:*

(i) requires p' ensures $q' \trianglelefteq$ requires p ensures q
(ii) se' $\trianglelefteq$ se

Figure 7 defines the refinement relation $\trianglelefteq$ for Ptolemy$_S$ expressions.

In Definition 1, for a translucid contract of an event to refine the contract of its superevent, *(i)* its behavior must refine the behavior of the contract of the superevent and *(ii)* its assumes block must refine the assumes block of the contract of its superevent.

In Fig. 7, the rule (R-SPEC) shows the refinement of the behavior *spec' = requires p' ensures q'* by the behavior *spec = requires p ensures q*. For the behavior *spec* to refine *spec'*, its precondition p must imply the precondition p', i.e. $p \Rightarrow p'$, and the opposite must be true for their postconditions, i.e. $q' \Rightarrow q$. That is the subevent can *strengthen* the precondition of its superevent and *weaken* its postcondition which is the inverse of classical refinement in class subtyping [37] where a subclass weakens the precondition of its superclass and strengthens its postcondition. Such inverse relation of behaviors is necessary in *Ptolemy*$_S$ to allow an observer of a superevent to run upon announcement of its subevents. Also unlike *Ptolemy*$_S$'s refining, the classical refining is for blackbox contracts and does not directly apply to greybox translucid contracts [36] and especially their assumes block [46] with control effect specifications.

The assumes block *se* of the translucid contract of an event refines the assumes block *se'* of the contract of its superevent, i.e. *se' $\trianglelefteq$ se*, if: *(a)* each specification expression in

---

[3] The class subtyping relation $\preccurlyeq$ is different from *Ptolemy*$_S$'s event subtyping relation $\ll$:, as discussed in Sect. 9.

Event specification refinement relation: $\boxed{\Gamma \vdash se' \trianglelefteq se}$

(R-SPEC)

$$\frac{spec = \textbf{\textit{requires}}\ p\ \textbf{\textit{ensures}}\ q \quad spec' = \textbf{\textit{requires}}\ p'\ \textbf{\textit{ensures}}\ q' \quad p \Rightarrow p' \quad q' \Rightarrow q}{\Gamma \vdash spec' \trianglelefteq spec}$$

(R-INVOKE)

$$\frac{\Gamma \vdash se' \trianglelefteq se}{\Gamma \vdash se'.\textbf{\textit{invoke}}() \trianglelefteq se.\textbf{\textit{invoke}}()}$$

(R-VAR)

$$\frac{textualMatch(var', var)}{\Gamma \vdash var' \trianglelefteq var}$$

(R-DEFINE)

$$\frac{\Gamma \vdash se'_1 \trianglelefteq se_1 \quad \Gamma, t : var \vdash se'_2 \trianglelefteq se_2}{\Gamma \vdash t\ var = se'_1 ; se'_2 \trianglelefteq t\ var = se_1 ; se_2}$$

(R-IF)

$$\frac{\Gamma \vdash sp' \trianglelefteq sp \quad \Gamma \vdash se'_1 \trianglelefteq se_1 \quad \Gamma \vdash se'_2 \trianglelefteq se_2}{\Gamma \vdash \textbf{\textit{if}}(sp')\{se'_1\}\ \textbf{\textit{else}}\{se'_2\} \trianglelefteq \textbf{\textit{if}}(sp)\{se_1\}\ \textbf{\textit{else}}\{se_2\}}$$

Fig. 7. Select rules for the refining relation $\trianglelefteq$.

se refines its *corresponding* specification expression in *se'* and *(b)* each program expression in *se* refines its corresponding program expression in *se*. The rule (R-SPEC) for refinement of behaviors also applies for refinement of specification expressions since they similarly are behavior specifications with a precondition and postcondition [46]. A specification expression in a subevent can strengthen the precondition of its corresponding specification expression in its superevent and weaken its postcondition. For a program expression to refine another program expression, they must textually match. The rule (R-VAR) checks for textual matching of variable names using the auxiliary function *textualMatch*. For other program expressions, such as invoke and conditional, their refinement boils down to the refinement of their subexpressions, as in rules (R-INVOKE), (R-DEFINE) and (R-IF).

To illustrate, the translucid contract of AndEv, on lines 20–26 in Fig. 4, refines the contract of ExpEv, on lines 2–8. This is because *(i)* the precondition *left*! $= $ *null* && *right*! $= $ *null* && *node*! $= $ *null* of AndEv implies the precondition *node*! $= $ *null* of ExpEv and the postcondition *node.equals*(*old* (*node*)) of ExpEv implies the same postcondition of AndEv, and therefore using the rule (R-SPEC) the behavior of AndEv refines the behavior of ExpEv; *(ii)* the program expression *next.invoke*() of AndEv, on line 22, refines its corresponding program expression of ExpEv, on line 4, using (R-INVOKE) and (R-VAR), and specification expression *requires next.node*().*left* $==$*old* (*next.node*().*left*) && *next.node*().*right* $==$ *old* (*next.node*().*right*) *ensures* *next.node*().*parent* $==$ *old* (*next.node*().*parent*) of AndEv, on lines 23–24, refines its corresponding specification expression *requires* *true ensures* *next.node*().*parent* $==$*old* (*next.node*().*parent*) in ExpEv, on lines 5–6, using the rule (R-SPEC).

However, the translucid contract of AndEv does not refine the contract of BinEv, on lines 11–17, because the postcondition *true* of BinEv does not imply the postcondition of AndEv. Changing the postcondition of BinEv to *next.node().parent* ==*old* (*next.node().parent*) makes the contract of BinEv refine the contract of ExpEv.

Textual matching of program expressions is a simpler alternative to complex higher order logic or trace verification techniques with its tradeoffs [46]. Textual matching works because *Ptolemy$_S$*'s semantics enforces depth subtyping, ensuring that a redeclaring context variable in an event is a subtype of the redeclared context in its superevents and a *next* variable in the contract of an event is a subtype of the next variable in the contract of its superevent.

The refining relation ⊴ defines the refinement for corresponding program and specification expressions. That is, only *structurally similar* contracts may refine each other. Two translucid contracts are structurally similar if for each specification (program) expression in the assumes block of one, a possibly different specification (program) expression exists in the assumes block of the other at the same location. *Ptolemy$_S$*'s structural similarity for the refining relation allows definition of *Ptolemy$_S$*'s event specification inheritance, see Sect. 7, such that it statically guarantees the refining relation by combining translucid contracts of an event and its superevents in a subtyping hierarchy.

3.3 Non-Decreasing Relation of Observers' Execution

Ptolemy$_S$ limits the arbitrary execution order of observers of an event and its superevents by enforcing a non-decreasing relation on execution orders of observers. In the non-decreasing order, an observer of an event runs before an observer of its superevent. *Ptolemy$_S$*'s semantics for *announce*, *invoke*, *register* and *unregister* expressions and the relation of return types of events in an event hierarchy guarantee the non-decreasing order on execution of the observers.

In *Ptolemy$_S$*, a subject announces an event *ev* using the announce expression *announce* $ev(e^*)\{e'\}$. The announce expression evaluates parameters e^* to values v^*, creates an event closure for the event *ev* and binds values v^* to context variables of *ev* in the closure. The announce expression also creates, in the event closure, a chain containing registered observers of *ev* and observers of *all its superevents* and runs the first observer in the chain. To construct the chain, the announce expression adds observers of the event *ev* to an empty chain followed by adding observers of the direct superevent of *ev* and recursively continues until it reaches the root event *Event*[4]. The event body e' is added to the end of the chain.

By construction, the announce expression ensures that an observer of an event shows up before an observer of its superevent in the chain, which basically is the non-decreasing order of observers. Observers of the same event in the chain *maintain* among themselves the same order as their dynamic registration order, i.e. an observer registered earlier shows up in the chain before the ones registered later. This makes *Ptolemy$_S$* backward compatible with its earlier versions [8, 9, 16] that do not support event subtyping.

---

[4] *Event* is not accessible to programmers and does not have observers, as a simple design choice, to not allow programmers to affect behaviors of events of a system by defining a specification for *Event*.

The expression *next* is a placeholder for an event closure and the type *thunk ev* is the type of the event closure of an event *ev*.

After construction of the chain and running the first observer in the chain, by the announce expression, observers in the chain can invoke each other using an invoke expression *e.invoke*(). The invoke expression evaluates *e* to an event closure containing the chain of observers and runs the next observer in the chain, which is according to the non-decreasing order. For observers to run according to the non-decreasing order, the return type of an observer of an event must be a supertype of the return type of the observers of its superevent. *Ptolemy*$_S$'s static semantics, in Sect. 9, guarantees this by ensuring that the return type of an event is a supertype of the return type of its superevent.

Upon announcement of an event, only registered observers of the event and its superevents run. In *Ptolemy*$_S$, observers show interest in events through binding declarations and register to handle the events. A binding declaration **when** *ev* **do** *m* in an observer says to run the observer handler method *m* when an event of type *ev* is announced. The expression *register*(*e*) evaluates *e* to an object and adds it to the list of observers *A*[*ev*] for each event type *ev* that is named in binding declarations of the observer, and *unregister*(*e*) removes the object *e* from the list of observers of those events. Announce expression for an event *ev* recursively concatenates the list of observers *A*[*ev*] and the list of observers of its superevents to construct the chain of observers.

3.4 Refining + Non-decreasing Relations

Any of refining or non-decreasing relations alone cannot solve both combinatorial reasoning and behavior invariance problems. With the refining relation alone, because of the arbitrary execution order of observers, still up to *n*! possible execution orders of *n* observers of the event and observers of its superevents should be considered in reasoning, which threatens its tractability; changes in execution orders of observers of the event or observers of its superevents can still invalidate any previous reasoning, which threatens modularity of reasoning; and observers of events in a subtyping hierarchy still could be forced to satisfy the same behavior, which threatens reuse. A trivial refining relation in which events of a hierarchy satisfy the same behavior enables modular reasoning, however, it is undesirable as it prevents reuse of event types, their specifications [45] and observers [19, 20].

With the non-decreasing relation alone, because of unrelated behaviors of observers, observers of events in a subtyping hierarchy may still be forced to satisfy the same behavior and any changes in behaviors of superevents of an event could invalidate any previous reasoning about subjects and observers of the event.

Interestingly, reversing both refining and non-decreasing relations still allows modular reasoning. To reverse these relations, the translucid contract of a superevent refines the contract of its subevent and an observer of a superevent runs before any observer of its subevent. We chose the current design, as it seemed more natural, to us, for observers of an already announced event to run before observers of its superevents.

4 Modular Reasoning

This section formalizes $Ptolemy_S$'s Hoare logic for modular reasoning, its conformance relation for subjects and observers and soundness of its reasoning technique.

$Ptolemy_S$'s refining and non-decreasing relations enable its modular reasoning about subjects and observers of an event, as shown in Fig. 8. The main idea is to use the translucid contract of an event as a sound approximation of the behaviors of its observers and observers of its superevents to reason about:

(1) a subject of the event, especially its ***announce*** expression, independent of its observers and observers of its superevents and their execution orders; and

(2) an observer of the event, especially its ***invoke*** expressions, independent of its subjects as well as observers it may invoke and their execution orders.

Reasoning judgement: $\boxed{\Gamma \vdash \{p\}\, e\, \{q\}}$

(V-ANNOUNCE)
$$\frac{\begin{array}{c}(c\ \textbf{\textit{event}}\ ev\ \textbf{\textit{extends}}\ ev'\{(t\ var)^*\ contract\}) \in CT \\ contract = \textbf{\textit{requires}}\ p\ \textbf{\textit{assumes}}\ \{se\}\ \textbf{\textit{ensures}}\ q \\ topContract(ev) = \textbf{\textit{requires}}\ p'\ \textbf{\textit{assumes}}\ \{se'\}\ \textbf{\textit{ensures}}\ q' \\ \Gamma \vdash \{p'[e^*/var^*]\}\ e'\ \{q'[e^*/var^*]\}\end{array}}{\Gamma \vdash \{p[e^*/var^*]\}\ \textbf{\textit{announce}}\ ev(e^*)\ \{e'\}\ \{q[e^*/var^*]\}}$$

(V-INVOKE)
$$\frac{\textbf{\textit{thunk}}\ ev = \Gamma(\textbf{\textit{next}}) \qquad (c\ \textbf{\textit{event}}\ ev\ \textbf{\textit{extends}}\ ev'\{form^*\ contract\}) \in CT \\ contract = \textbf{\textit{requires}}\ p\ \textbf{\textit{assumes}}\ \{se\}\ \textbf{\textit{ensures}}\ q}{\Gamma \vdash \{p\}\ \textbf{\textit{next.invoke}}()\ \{q\}}$$

(V-REFINING)
$$\frac{\Gamma \vdash \{p\}\, e\, \{q\}}{\Gamma \vdash \{p\}\ (\textbf{\textit{refining requires}}\ p\ \textbf{\textit{ensures}}\ q\ \{\, e\, \})\ \{q\}}$$

(V-SPEC)   (V-CONSEQ)
$$\Gamma \vdash \{p\}\ \textbf{\textit{requires}}\ p\ \textbf{\textit{ensures}}\ q\ \{q\} \qquad \frac{p \Rightarrow p' \qquad q' \Rightarrow q \qquad \{p'\}\, e\, \{q'\}}{\Gamma \vdash \{p\}\, e\, \{q\}}$$

Fig. 8. Select reasoning rules in $Ptolemy_S$'s Hoare logic [38], inspired by [10,46].

Figure 8 shows $Ptolemy_S$'s Hoare logic [38] for modular reasoning about behaviors of subjects and observers. $Ptolemy_S$'s reasoning rules use a reasoning judgement of the form $\Gamma \vdash \{p\}\, e\, \{q\}$ that says the Hoare triple $\{p\}\, e\, \{q\}$ is provable using the variable typing environment Γ, which maps variables to their types. The judgement $\Gamma \vdash \{p\}\, e\, \{q\}$ is valid, written as $\Gamma \models \{p\}\, e\, \{q\}$, if for every state σ that agrees with type environment Γ, if p is true in σ, i.e. $\sigma \models p$, and if the execution of e terminates in a state σ', then $\sigma' \models q$. This definition of validity is for partial correctness where termination is not guaranteed. *Ptolemy_S*'s reasoning rules use a fixed class table *CT*, which is a set of the program's class and event type declarations. The notation $ep[e^*/var^*]$ denotes replacing variables var^* with e^* in the expression ep. *Ptolemy_S*'s rules for reasoning about standard object-oriented expressions remain the same as in previous work [38, 46–48] and are omitted.

In Fig. 8, the rule (V-ANNOUNCE) reasons about the behavior of an announce expression in a subject. The rule says that the behavior of an announce expression announcing an event *ev* is the behavior *requires p ensures q* of the translucid *contract* of the event *ev*. To use the precondition *p* of the contract and its postcondition *q* in the scope of the announce expression, their context variables var^* are replaced by arguments e^* of the announce expression [44]. The rule (V-ANNOUNCE) does not require and is independent of any knowledge of individual observers of *ev* or observers of its superevents, their implementations or execution orders which in turn makes it modular and tractable.

To illustrate (V-ANNOUNCE), reconsider verification of the assertion Φ for the announce expression of AndEv, on lines 4–7 of Fig. 1. Using the translucid contract of AndEv, on lines 20–26, the conclusion of (V-ANNOUNCE) replaces parameters e, e.left and e.right of the announce expression for context variables of node, left and right of AndEv in the precondition and postcondition of the contract of AndEv and yields the following Hoare triple:

$$\Gamma \vdash \{e.left! = null \ \&\& \ e.right! = null \ \&\& \ e! = null\}$$
$$announce \ AndEv(e, \ e.left, \ e.right)$$
$$\{e.left.accept(\textbf{this}); \ e.right.accept(\textbf{this}); \}$$
$$\{e.equals(\textbf{old} \ (e))\}$$

The above judgement says, if e, e.left and e.right are not null, the expression *e* and its state remain the same after announcement and handling of AndEv, i.e. *e.equals(old (e))*, which is exactly the assertion Φ we wanted to verify.

The rule (V-INVOKE) reasons about the behavior of an invoke expression, in an observer. The rule says that the behavior of an invoke expression in an observer of the event *ev*, is the behavior of the translucid *contract* of *ev*. The type of the event that the observer handles, i.e. *ev*, is part of the type of the event closure *next*. The function $\Gamma(\textit{next})$ returns the type of the *next* expression in the typing environment Γ. Recall that the event closure next is passed as a parameter to each observer handler method. Again, the rule (V-INVOKE) does not require and is independent of any knowledge about subjects of the event *ev* or observers it may invoke in the chain of observer *next* and therefore is modular and tractable.

The rule (V-REFINING) says that the behavior of the body *e* of a refining expression is the behavior of its specification expression *requires p ensures q*. This is true, because the body of the refining expression claims to refine its specification. The rule (V-SPEC) is straightforward [46] and the rule (V-CONSEQ) is standard [38].

4.1 Soundness of Reasoning

In *Ptolemy_S*, the translucid contract of an event is a sound approximation of behaviors of its subjects and observers independent of observers of the event, observers of its superevents and their execution orders. This is sound because of the following:

1. conformance of each observer and subject of an event to the translucid contract of the event;
2. refining relation among specifications of the event and its superevents; and
3. non-decreasing relation on execution orders of observers of the event and observers of its superevents.

For a greybox translucid contract of an event, *all* subjects and observers of the event must conform to the contract of the event. This is different from a blackbox method specification, e.g. in JML, in which only a single method has to respect a contract [9,37]. *Ptolemy*$_S$'s semantics, in Sects. 8 and 9, guarantees the conformance using a combination of type checking and runtime assertion checking. *Ptolemy*$_S$'s event specification inheritance, in Sect. 7, statically guarantees the refining relation and *Ptolemy*$_S$'s dynamic semantics guarantees the non-decreasing relation. Figure 5 shows the interplay of conformance, refining and non-decreasing relations.

Conforming Observers

Definition 2 *(Conforming observer). For an event type ev with a translucid contract* $\mathscr{G} = ($**requires** *p* **assumes** *{se}* **ensures** *q), its observer handler method m with its implementation e is conforming if and only if there exists a typing environment* Γ *such that:*

(i) $\Gamma \models \{p\} \, e \, \{q\}$
(ii) $se \sqsubseteq_s e$

where Fig. 9 defines the structural refinement relation $\sqsubseteq_s$ *between the assumes block se and the body e of its observer.*

Definition 2 says that for an observer handler method of an event *ev* to be conforming, its implementation *e* must satisfy the precondition *p* and postcondition *q* of the translucid contract of the event, i.e. requirement *(i)*. An expression *e* satisfies a precondition *p* and a postcondition *q* in a typing environment Γ, written as $\Gamma \models \{p\} \, e \, \{q\}$, if and only if for every program state σ that agrees with the type environment Γ, if the precondition *p* is true in σ, and if the execution of *e* terminates in a state σ', then *q* is true in σ'. Currently *Ptolemy*$_S$ uses runtime assertions to check for satisfaction of preconditions and postconditions of a contract by its observers. Static verification techniques could also be used to check for such satisfaction [10]. Figure 10 shows the conforming observer `Evaluator` and its observer handler method `evalAndExp`, on lines 21–32. In `evalAndExp`, assertions on lines 22 and 31 check for preconditions and postconditions of the contract of AndEv on lines 2 and 8.

Definition 2 also requires the implementation *e* of a conforming observer to structurally refine the assumes block *se* of its translucid contract, i.e. requirement *(ii)*. The structural refinement $\sqsubseteq_s$ guarantees that an observer of an event, in its implementation has the control effects exposed in its translucid contract [8,9] using its program expressions. Figure 9 shows select rules for *Ptolemy*$_S$'s structural refinement.

The implementation *e* of an observer handler method structurally refines the assumes block *se* of its translucid contract if: *(a)* for each specification expression *spec* in *se* there is a corresponding **refining** expression in *e* with the same specification

Structural refinement relation: $\boxed{\Gamma \vdash se \sqsubseteq_s e}$

(S-REFINING)
$$\Gamma \vdash spec \sqsubseteq_s \textbf{refining } spec \; \{e\}$$

(S-INVOKE)
$$\frac{\Gamma \vdash se \sqsubseteq_s e}{\Gamma \vdash se.\textbf{\textit{invoke}}() \sqsubseteq_s e.\textbf{\textit{invoke}}()}$$

(S-VAR)
$$\frac{textualMatch(var', var)}{\Gamma \vdash var' \sqsubseteq_s var}$$

(S-ANNOUNCE)
$$\frac{\Gamma \vdash se^* \sqsubseteq_s e^* \qquad \Gamma \vdash se \sqsubseteq_s e}{\Gamma \vdash \textbf{announce } ev(se^*)\{se\} \sqsubseteq_s \textbf{announce } ev(e^*)\{e\}}$$

(S-EITHEROR)
$$\frac{\Gamma \vdash se_1 \sqsubseteq_s e \vee \Gamma \vdash se_2 \sqsubseteq_s e}{\Gamma \vdash \textbf{either } \{se_1\} \textbf{ or } \{se_2\} \sqsubseteq_s e}$$

(S-DEFINE)
$$\frac{\Gamma \vdash se_1 \sqsubseteq_s e_1 \qquad \Gamma, var : t \vdash se_2 \sqsubseteq_s e_2}{\Gamma \vdash t \; var = se_1; se_2 \sqsubseteq_s t \; var = e_1; e_2}$$

(S-IF)
$$\frac{\Gamma \vdash sp \sqsubseteq_s ep \qquad \Gamma \vdash se_1 \sqsubseteq_s e_1 \qquad \Gamma \vdash se_2 \sqsubseteq_s e_2}{\Gamma \vdash \textbf{if}(sp)\{se_1\} \textbf{ else}\{se_2\} \sqsubseteq_s \textbf{if}(ep)\{e_1\} \textbf{ else}\{e_2\}}$$

Fig. 9. Select rules for structural refinement $\sqsubseteq_s$ [8,46].

and *(b)* for each program expression in *se*, there is a corresponding textually match-ing program expression in *e*. The rule (S-REFINING) checks for structural refinement of a specification expression by a refining expression. (S-VAR) checks for textual match-ing of variable names using the auxiliary function *textualMatch*. For other program expressions, structural refinement boils down to structural refinement of their subex-pressions. The rule (S-EITHEROR) allows an observer to choose between behaviors in its either-branch or its or-branch. Similar to the refining relation, structural refinement requires structural similarity between the implementation of a conforming observer and the assumes block of its contract.

In Fig. 10, the assumes block, on lines 3–7, is structurally refined by the imple-mentation of the conforming observer `evalAndExp`, on lines 22–31 (ignoring runtime assertion checks), because the program expression *next.invoke*() on line 4 is structurally refined by the program expression in the implementation on line 23 and the specification expression on lines 5–6 is refined by a refining expression with the same specification on lines 25–29. Structural refinement guarantees that the implementation of `evalAndExp` has a *next.invoke*() expression as its control effect, as specified by the program expres-sion *next.invoke*() in its contract.

A refining expression claims that its body satisfies its specification. *Ptolemy*$_S$ uses runtime assertions to check this claim. In Fig. 10, runtime checks on lines 24 and 30 check that the body of the refining expression satisfies its precondition and postcondi-tion on lines 26 and 27.

Though similar, in the structural refinement $\sqsubseteq_s$ the implementation of an observer refines the assumes block of the translucid contract of its event, whereas in the refining relation $\trianglelefteq$ the contract of an event refines the contract of its superevent. A specification expression in a contract is structurally refined by a refining expression in $\sqsubseteq_s$ whereas it is refined by another specification expression in $\trianglelefteq$.

```
1  void event AndEv extends BinEv { ..
2    requires left != null && right != null && node != null
3    assumes {
4      next.invoke();
5      requires next.node().left!=null&&next.node().right!=null
6      ensures next.node().parent==old(next.node().parent);
7    }
8    ensures node.equals(old(node))
9  }
10 class ASTVisitor {
11   void visit(AndExp e) {
12     announce AndEv(e, e.left, e.right) {
13       assert(e != null);
14       e.left.accept(this);
15       e.right.accept(this);
16       assert(node.equals(old(node)));
17     }
18   } ..
19 }
20 class Evaluator { ..
21   void evalAndExp (AndEv next) {
22     assert(next.node().left!=null&&next.node().right!=null
              &&next.node()!=null);
23     next.invoke();
24     assert(next.node().left!=null&&next.node().right!=null);
25     refining
26     requires next.node().left!=null&&next.node().right!=null
27     ensures next.node().parent==old(next.node().parent){
28       BoolVal b1 = (BoolVal) valStack.pop();
29     }
30     assert(next.node().parent==old(next.node().parent));
31     assert(next.node().equals(old(next.node())));
32   }
33   when AndEv do evalAndExp; ..
34 }
```

Fig. 10. Conforming Evaluator and ASTVisitor.

Conforming Subjects

Definition 3 *(Conforming subject).* *For an event type ev with a translucid contract $\mathcal{G} = ($**requires** p **assumes** $\{se\}$ **ensures** $q)$, its subject with an announce expression* **announce** $ev(e^*)\{e'\}$ *in its implementation, is conforming if and only if:* $\Gamma \models \{p'\} e' \{q'\}$ *where* **requires** p' **assumes** $\{se'\}$ **ensures** $q' = topContract(ev)$

The definition says that for a subject of *ev* to be conforming its event body e' must satisfy the precondition p' and postcondition q' of the translucid contract of the event on top of the subtyping hierarchy of *ev*, right before the root event *Event*. The auxiliary function *topContract* returns the translucid contract of this event. As shown in Fig. 5, this is necessary for the non-decreasing relation in which observers of the event and observers of its superevent run before the event body e' in the chain of observers. Figure 10 shows the conforming subject ASTVisitor, on lines 10–19. Runtime assertions on lines 13 and 16 check for satisfaction of the precondition and postcondition of the top contract of AndEv, i.e. the translucid contract of ExpEv, by the event body.

Soundness Theorem

Theorem 1 formalizes soundness of *Ptolemy$_S$*'s Hoare logic.

Theorem 1 *(Soundness of Ptolemy$_S$'s Hoare logic).*   *Ptolemy$_S$'s Hoare logic, in Fig. 8, is sound for conforming Ptolemy$_S$ programs. In other words, any Hoare triple provable using Ptolemy$_S$'s logic, i.e. $\Gamma \vdash \{p\}\, e\, \{q\}$, is a valid triple, i.e. $\Gamma \models \{p\}\, e\, \{q\}$.*

The proof is based on induction on the number of events in a subtyping hierarchy and the number of their observers and uses conformance, refining and non-decreasing relations. Full proof of the theorem can be found in Sect. A.

4.2   Revisiting Reasoning About Announce and Invoke

Ptolemy$_S$'s reasoning rules (V-ANNOUNCE) and (V-INVOKE) are sound because the conformance, refining and non-decreasing relations allow, in any chain of observers, the implementation of an invoked observer to be inlined in place of invoke expressions of its invoking observer *without violating* the precondition and postcondition of the invoking observer. This in turn allows the chain of observers of an event and observers of its superevents, starting from the event body at the end of the chain back to its beginning, to be recursively inlined in an announce expression without violating the precondition and postcondition of the contract of the event.

To illustrate, reconsider reasoning about the behavior of the announce expression *announce AndEv(e, e.left, e.right)*, in Fig. 1. Upon announcement of AndEv, if there are no observers of AndEv or observers of its superevents BinEv or ExpEv in the chain of observers, then the event body *e.left.accept(this);e.right.accept(this)* executes. The subject ASTVisitor of AndEv is conforming and thus the event body satisfies the behavior of the contract of ExpEv, which is the top event in the hierarchy of AndEv. That is, the event body satisfies the precondition *node ! = null* and the postcondition *node.equals(old (node))* of ExpEv after the context *node* is replaced with parameter *e* of the announce expression:

(H-BODY)
$$\Gamma \models \{e\,!=null\}$$
$$e.left.accept(\textbf{\textit{this}});\ e.right.accept(\textbf{\textit{this}});$$
$$\{e.equals(\textbf{\textit{old}}\,(e))\}$$

The refining relation guarantees that the behavior of AndEv refines the behavior of ExpEv. That is, the precondition of AndEv implies the precondition of ExpEv, i.e. *left! = null && right! = null && node! = null $\Rightarrow$ node ! = null*, and the opposite is true for their postconditions, i.e. *node.equals(old (node)) $\Rightarrow$ node.equals(old (node))*. Using these implications, the rule (V-CONSEQ) and after replacing the context *node* with *e*, one can conclude that the event body satisfies the behavior of AndEv:

$$\Gamma \models \{e.left!=null\ \&\&\ e.right!=null\ \&\&\ e!=null\}$$
$$e.left.accept(\textbf{\textit{this}});\ e.right.accept(\textbf{\textit{this}});$$
$$\{e.equals(\textbf{\textit{old}}\,(e))\}$$

Since the event body is the only observer that executes upon announcement of AndEv, the announce expression can be replaced with the event body:

(H-Announce-Body)
$$\Gamma \models \{e.left! = null \ \&\& \ e.right! = null \ \&\& \ e! = null\}$$
$$announce \ AndEv(e, e.left, e.right)$$
$$\{e.left.accept(this); \ e.right.accept(this); \}$$
$$\{e.equals(old \ (e))\}$$

The judgement (H-Announce-Body) says the announce expression of AndEv with event body as its only observer satisfies the behavior of the translucid contract of AndEv.

However, the event body may not be the only observer of AndEv. Consider observers evaluator and tracer of event AndEv and ExpEv and the event body of AndEv, shown as $\mathscr{B}(AndEv)$, run in a chain χ_1: evaluator $\rightharpoondown$ tracer $\rightharpoondown$ $\mathscr{B}(AndEv)$. Again, conformance of ASTVisitor means that the event body satisfies the behavior of the contract of ExpEv, i.e. (H-Body). Recall that an observer of an event and the invoke expressions in its implementation have the precondition and postcondition of the contract of the event. The precondition of the invoke expression in the implementation of tracer implies the precondition of the event body, i.e. $node! = null \Rightarrow node! = null$ and the postcondition of the event body implies the postcondition of the invoke expression, i.e. $node.equals(old \ (node)) \Rightarrow node.equals(old \ (node))$. This in turn allows the event body, in grey, to be inlined in the place of the invoke expression in the implementation of tracer, in Fig. 3, without violating the precondition and postcondition of tracer:

(H-Tracer)
$$\Gamma \models \{e \ ! = null\}$$
$$e.left.accept(this); \ e.right.accept(this);$$
$$refining \ requires \ true$$
$$ensures \ e.parent == old \ (e.parent)\{..\}$$
$$\{e.equals(old \ (e))\}$$

Using the refining relation, the precondition of AndEv implies the precondition of ExpEv and the opposite is true for their postconditions. This means the precondition of the invoke expression in the implementation of evaluator implies the precondition of tracer, i.e. $left! = null \ \&\& \ right! = null \ \&\& \ node! = null \Rightarrow node \ ! = null$, and the postcondition of tracer implies the postcondition of the invoke expression in evaluator, i.e. $node.equals(old \ (node)) \Rightarrow node.equals(old \ (node))$. This allows the implementation of tracer in (H-Tracer) to be inlined, in grey, in place of the invoke expression in evaluator without violating its precondition and postcondition of evaluator:

(H-Evaluator)
$$\Gamma \models \{e.left! = null \ \&\& \ e.right! = null \ \&\& \ e! = null\}$$
$$e.left.accept(this); \ e.right.accept(this);$$
$$refining \ requires \ true$$
$$ensures \ e.parent == old \ (e.parent)\{..\};$$
$$refining$$
$$requires \ e.left! = null \ \&\& \ e.right! = null$$
$$ensures \ e.parent == old \ (e.parent)\{..\};$$
$$\{e.equals(old \ (e))\}$$

Since the announcement of AndEv causes the chain χ_1 to run, the inlined chain of observers in (H-EVALUATOR) can be replaced with the announce expression:

(H-ANNOUNCE-χ_1)
$\Gamma \models \{e.left! = \textbf{\textit{null}} \ \&\& \ e.right! = \textbf{\textit{null}} \ \&\& \ e! = \textbf{\textit{null}}\}$
  $\textbf{\textit{announce}} \ AndEv(e, \ e.left, \ e.right)$
  $\{e.left.accept(\textbf{\textit{this}}); \ e.right.accept(\textbf{\textit{this}}); \}$
  $\{e.equals(\textbf{\textit{old}} \ (e))\}$

The judgement (H-ANNOUNCE-χ_1) says that the behavior of the announce expression of AndEv with the chain of observers χ_1 satisfies the behavior of the contract of AndEv. (H-ANNOUNCE-BODY) and (H-ANNOUNCE-χ_1) say that the behavior of a chain of observers of AndEv and observers of its superevents, can be approximated with the precondition and postcondition of the translucid contract of the AndEv which is what the rule (V-ANNOUNCE) in *Ptolemy$_S$*'s reasoning logic says. A similar justification holds for the rule (V-INVOKE).

5   Applicability

Our proposed modular reasoning technique is not exclusive to *Ptolemy$_S$* and could be adapted to similar AspectJ-like [2] event-based systems such as join point types (JPT) [20] and join point interfaces (JPI) [19].

5.1   Join Point Types

With join point types, a subject (base) exhibits a join point type (event) using an ***exhibits*** statement and aspects (observers) advise the event and handle it using ***advises*** statements. A join point type can extend another join point type, inherit its context variables and add to them through width subtyping. Exhibiting a join point type causes its aspects and aspects of its super join point types to run in a chain where aspects can invoke each other using ***proceed*** statements. The execution order of aspects is specified using precedence declarations. Join point types do not support depth subtyping, however, this does not affect the applicability of *Ptolemy$_S$*'s reasoning technique to them.

Figure 11 shows parts of the expression language example rewritten using join point types where the subject ASTVisitor exhibits a join point instance AndEv, on lines 12–15, and the observer Evaluator advises the join point, on lines 19–26. Evaluator invokes the next observer in the chain of observers using a proceed statement on line 20, which takes as argument a join point instance jp of join point type AndEv. The join point type AndEv is declared on lines 1–9 and extends the join point type BinEv.

Figure 11 shows the syntactic adaptation of the translucid contract of the join point type AndEv, on lines 2–8, using a JML-like syntax. JML syntax is specifically chosen to minimize required syntactic changes. In a contract of a join point type, a JML model program [46] is similar to an assumes block and a proceed statement is equivalent to an invoke expression [8]. A variable ***next*** in the contract of a join point type is a placeholder for join point instances of that type, which contains values of its contexts.

```
1  joinpointtype AndEv extends BinEv {
2  /*@ requires node!=null && left!=null &&right!=null;
3   @ model_program {
4   @   proceed(next);
5   @   requires node.left!=null && node.right!=null;
6   @   ensures node.parent == old(node.parent);
7   @ }
8   @ ensures node.equals(old(node)); */
9  }
10 class ASTVisitor exhibits AndEv,.. {
11   void visit(AndExp e) {
12     exhibits new AndEv(e, e.left, e.right) {
13       e.left.accept(this);
14       e.right.accept(this);
15     }; ..
16   } ..
17 }
18 aspect Evaluator advises AndEv,.. { ..
19   void around(AndEv jp) {
20     proceed(jp);
21     refining
22       requires node.left!=null && node.right!=null;
23       ensures node.parent == old(node.parent){
24       .. //same as before
25     }
26   } ..
27 }
```

Fig. 11. Join point type AndEv and its translucid contract.

Although, a translucid contract of a join point type uses JML's syntax, its verification is completely different from JML. This is because a JML contract specifies the behavior and structure of only a single method whereas a translucid contract of a join point type specifies all bases and aspects of the join point type. Consequently, for the conformance relation, for each join point type, all of its bases and aspects must conform to the translucid contract of their join point type, i.e. structurally refine the contract and satisfy its preconditions and postconditions. Type checking rules of join point types could be augmented to check for structural refinement and runtime assertions could be added to bases and aspects to check for their satisfaction of preconditions and postconditions of their contract and their specification expressions. In addition to syntactic adaptations of structural refinement, the rule (S-VAR) should be slightly modified to allow for structural refinement of placeholder variables *next* by join point instance variables. Unlike *Ptolemy*$_S$ in which a variable *next* is structurally refined by a textually matching variable *next*, in join point types a variable *next* in a contract of a join point type is structurally refined by a join point instance variable in the implementation of an observer if their types are the same. For example, in Fig. 11, the variable *next* in the translucid contract of AndEv, on line 4, is structurally refined by the join point instance variable jp in the observer Evaluator, on line 20, because they both are of the same type AndEv.

Another difference between translucid contracts and JML contracts is that JML requires model programs of a type and its supertype to be the same [46], whereas in translucid contracts the assumes block of an event refines the assumes block of its superevent. Consequently, for the refining relation, *Ptolemy$_S$*'s specification inheritance could be adapted to join point types, mostly through syntactic adaptations, to statically guarantee the refining relation between translucid contracts of a join point type and its super type.

For the non-decreasing relation, precedence declarations of aspects could be statically checked to ensure that an aspect of a join point type runs before aspects of its super join point type or execution of aspects can be reordered dynamically at runtime to guarantee the non-decreasing relation.

5.2   Join Point Interfaces

In join point interfaces [19, 49], similar to join point types, a subject exhibits a join point interface (event) and observers advise the event and handle it. Exhibiting a join point interface causes its observers and observers of its super join point interfaces to run in a chain. *Ptolemy$_S$*'s modular reasoning is applicable to join point interfaces in the *absence of global join point interfaces* [19].

Figure 12 shows parts of the boolean expression example rewritten using join point interfaces. The subject ASTVisitor exhibits a join point instance AndEv, on line 33, and the observer Evaluator advises the join point, on lines 40–50. Evaluator invokes the next observer using a proceed statement on line 43 passing node, left and right for corresponding context variables of its event AndEv. The join point interface is declared on line 29 and extends the join point interface BinEv. The join point interface AndEv is declared similar to method signatures and its context variables are explicitly named in its observer Evaluator and its proceed statement. Translucid contracts can be added to join point interfaces in a JML-like syntax, similar to join point types. Translucid contract of a join point interface appears right before its declaration. Figure 12 shows the translucid contract for the join point interface AndEv, on lines 21–28.

For the conformance relation, for each join point interface all of its bases and aspects must conform to the JML-like translucid contract of their join point interface. Structural refinement could be added to type checking rules for join point interfaces and runtime assertions could be added to bases and aspects to check for their satisfaction of preconditions and postconditions. The rule (S-VAR) should be slightly modified to allow for structural refinement between possibly different names of a context variable in the join point interface and observer. Unlike *Ptolemy$_S$* in which a name of a context variable in a translucid contract is structurally refined by a textually matching variable name in the observer, a context variable in a contract of a join point interface is refined by a context variable in the implementation of an observer with the same type and a possibly different name. For example, in Fig. 12, the context variable right in the contract of AndEv is structurally refined by the context variable right_ in the observer Evaluator because they both refer to the same context variable and are of the same type. Positions of context variables right and right_ in the list of context variables in join point interface declaration, on line 29, and advising of the join point interface, on line 42, specify if two names refer to the same context variable.

For the refining relation, in addition to syntactic adaptations of the refining rules, the rule (R-INVOKE) should be slightly modified to allow refinement of corresponding *proceed* statements with varying number of context variables in the translucid contracts

```
1  /* join point interfaces */
2  /*@ requires node != null;
3   @ model_program {
4   @  proceed(node);
5   @  requires true;
6   @  ensures node.parent == old(node.parent);
7   @ }
8   @ ensures node.equals(old(node));
9  @*/
10 jpi void ExpEv(Exp node);

11 /*@ requires left != null && right != null;
12  @ model_program {
13  @  proceed(node, left, right);
14  @  requires node.left!=null && node.right!=null;
15  @  ensures node.parent == old(node.parent);
16  @ }
17  @ ensures node.equals(old(node));
18 @*/
19 jpi void BinEv(Exp node, Exp left, Exp right) extends ExpEv(node);

21 /*@ requires left != null && right != null;
22  @ model_program {
23  @  proceed(node, left, right);
24  @  requires node.left!=null && node.right!=null;
25  @  ensures node.parent == old(node.parent);
26  @ }
27  @ ensures node.equals(old(node));
28 @*/
29 jpi void AndEv(Exp node, Exp left, Exp right) extends BinEv(node, left,
       right);
30 /* subject */
31 class ASTVisitor exhibits AndEv,.. {
32  void visit(AndExp e) {
33   exhibit AndEv(e, e.left, e.right) {
34    e.left.accept(this);
35    e.right.accept(this);
36   };
37  } ..
38 }
39 /* observers */
40 aspect Evaluator {
41  Stack<BoolVal> valStack = ..
42  void around AndEv(Exp node, Exp left, Exp right_){
43   proceed(node, left, right_);
44   refining
45    requires node.left != null && node.right_ != null
46    ensures node.parent == old(node.parent){
47    .. // same as before
48   }
49  } ..
50 }
```

Fig. 12. Join point interface AndEv and its translucid contract on lines 21–28.

of a join point interface and its supertype. A proceed statement in a translucid contract of a join point interface refines a corresponding proceed statement in the translucid contract of its supertype if the number of context variables of subtype's proceed is more than or equal to the number of context variables in supertype's proceed and types of context variables of the same names are the same. This is because join point interfaces do not support depth subtyping of context variables. For example, the proceed statement on line 13 of the translucid contract of BinEv refines its corresponding proceed statement on line 4 of the contract of ExpEv, i.e. *proceed(node)* $\unlhd$ *proceed(node, left, right)*. *Ptolemy*$_S$'s specification inheritance could be adapted to join point interfaces, mostly through syntactic adaptations to statically guarantee the refining between translucid contracts of a join point interface and its super join point interface.

For the non-decreasing relation, similar to join point types, precedence declarations of aspects could be statically checked to ensure that an aspect of a join point interface runs before aspects of its super join point interface or execution of aspects can be reordered dynamically at runtime to guarantee the non-decreasing relation.

Global join point interfaces *Ptolemy*$_S$'s modular reasoning is applicable to join point interfaces only in the absence of global join point interfaces [19]. A global join point interface with its implicit event announcement allows a subject to announce an event without knowing about it. In implicit event announcement an event is announce implicitly without any *exhibits* statement. Reasoning about a subject in the presence of global join point interfaces requires a global inspection of all global join point interfaces to determine whether the subject announces any of the events declared by those global join point interfaces, which is not modular.

```
global jpi Object AllExcEv(): execution (* * (..));
```

Fig. 13. Global join point interface AllExcEv.

Figure 13 shows a global join point interface AllExcEv added to the boolean expression example. This causes AllExcEv to be announced implicitly during the execution of every method of every module of the example, including methods of the subject ASTVisitor in Fig. 1. With the presence of AllExcEv, to reason about the assertion Φ in the subject not only the behavior of observers of its event AndEv and its superevents should be understood but also the behaviors of the observers of AllExcEv. However, neither the implementation of ASTVisitor nor the events AndEv and its superevents say anything about announcement of AllExcEv, which in turn hinders modular reasoning about the subject and modular verification of Φ [19]. Adding a translucid contract to AllExcEv does not restore modular reasoning.

6   Modular Reasoning About Control Effects

Ptolemy$_S$ not only enables modular reasoning about behaviors of observers of an event but also their control effects [8, 32] in the presence of event subtyping. In *Ptolemy*$_S$, similar to Aspect-like [2] languages, observers run in a chain and invoke each other using an *invoke* expression. This in turn means an observer of an event can skip the execution of other observers of the event or observers of its superevents, including the event body, by not executing its invoke expression. Understanding the invocations among observers of an event and its superevents in a chain of observers falls under the category of modular reasoning about control effects of observers.

As an example of modular reasoning about control effects consider static verification of the control effect assertion Ψ that says *upon announcement and handling of AndEv, its event body, on lines 5–6 of* Fig. 1 *will be executed and will not be skipped*[5]. This is important because if the execution of the event body of AndEv is skipped, the right and left children of an AndExp expression and subtrees recursively rooted in these children are not going to be visited. The execution of the body of AndEv, shown as $\mathscr{B}$(AndEv), could be skipped in a chain of observers if any of observers of AndEv or observers of its superevents BinEv or ExpEv, which run before the event body, skip the execution of their invoke expression and break the invocation chain. For example, in chain χ_2: evaluator $\rightharpoonup$ tracer $\rightharpoonup$ $\mathscr{B}$(AndEv), the execution of $\mathscr{B}$(AndEv) is skipped if any or both invoke expressions in the implementations of evaluator, on line 55 of Fig. 3, or tracer, on line 41, goes missing.

To reason about the control effects of an announcement of an event, the control effects of all of its observers and observers of its superevents for their various execution orders must be understood, especially regarding the execution of their invoke expressions. Such reasoning is dependent on control effects of individual observers of the event and observers of its superevents and any changes in these control effects can invalidate any previous reasoning, which threatens its modularity.

Ptolemy$_S$'s translucid contracts enable modular reasoning about control effects of observers of an event and observers of its superevents, independent of observers and their execution orders. This is sound because each conforming observer of an event has the same control effects as the translucid contract of the event and *Ptolemy*$_S$'s refining relation ensures that the contract of an event refines the control effects of the contract of its superevent. Control effects are specified by program expressions in translucid contracts of events.

In *Ptolemy*$_S$, the assertion Ψ could be verified using the translucid contract of AndEv and especially its assumes block, on lines 21–25 of Fig. 4. The program expression *next.invoke*(), on line 22, guarantees that each observer of AndEv includes the invoke expression in their implementations and the refining relation ensures that each observer of superevents of AndEv contains the invoke expression in their implementations as well. This means that the invoke expression in the implementation of evaluator or tracer in χ_2 must be present or otherwise these observers will not be conforming to their translucid contracts. This in turn means that all the observers in the chain χ_2, including the event body at the end of the chain, are invoked and executed.

6.1   Control Interference of Subjects and Observers

Rinard *et al.* [50] classify the control interactions of a subject and observer of an event into four categories: *(i)* augmentation, *(ii)* narrowing, *(iii)* replacement and *(iv)* combination. These categories are concerned about the number of invoke expressions and their executions in an implementation of an observer. An augmentation observer executes its invoke expression exactly once, a narrowing observer executes it at most once,

---

[5] *Ptolemy*$_S$' core does not support throwing or handling of exceptions [9].

a replacement observer does not execute any invoke expressions and a combination observer executes its invoke expression zero or more times in its implementation.

Ptolemy$_S$'s translucid contracts allow modular reasoning about the control interference category of interactions of subjects and observers of an event, independent of observers of the event and observers of its superevents. To reason about the control interference of subjects and observers of an event, one uses the translucid contract of the event to decide about the the number of times invoke expressions of the translucid contract may execute. An invoke expression surrounded by an if conditional executes at most once, whereas an invoke expression surrounded by a loop may execute zero times or more. Otherwise, an invoke expression executes exactly once. This is sound because the structural refinement of the conformance relation requires each observer of an event to have the same control effects as its translucid contracts, especially regarding the number of invoke expressions in its implementation. The refining relation ensures that the control effects of observers of an event refine the control effects of observers of its superevents.

Augmentation interactions and observers. To illustrate the augmentation interaction, consider the observer Evaluator and subject ASTVisitor of the event AndEv. Using only the translucid contract of AndEv, on lines 20–26 of Fig. 4, one can conclude that subjects and observers of AndEv have an augmentation interaction in which Evaluator augments the behavior of its subject, i.e. Evaluator is an augmentation observer. This is because the assumes block of the contract of AndEv contains an invoke expression, on line 22, which is not surrounded by any conditionals or loops. This in turn means that the conforming observer Evaluator has only one invoke expression in its implementation which executes exactly once. For observers Checker and Tracer of superevents BinEv and ExpEv of AndEv, the refining relation ensures that they also have only one invoke expressions in their implementations and thus they are augmentation observers as well.

For an event with augmentation interactions and observers, one can conclude that upon announcement of the event all observers of the event and observers of its superevent including the event body execute and their executions cannot be skipped.

Replacement interactions and observers. To illustrate the replacement interaction, consider the event AndEv with its translucid contract in Fig. 4, but without its invoke expression. Using this contract one can conclude that subjects and observers of AndEv have a replacement interaction in which Evaluator replaces the body of its announce expression in a subject, i.e. Evaluator is a replacement observer. To structurally refine its contract, Evaluator cannot have any invoke expression in its implementation. The refining relation ensures that superevents BinEv and ExpEv cannot have invoke expressions in their contracts either and therefore observers Checker and Tracer are replacement observers as well.

For an event with replacement observers, one can conclude that upon announcement of the event the first observer of the event or its superevents executes and executions of the rest of the observers including the event body are skipped. This is because none of the observers have an invoke expression in their implementations.

Narrowing and combination interactions and observers. One can modularly reason about narrowing and combination interactions and observers in a similar fashion.

7   Event Specification Inheritance

To *manually* guarantee the refining relation among translucid contracts of an event and its superevent could be error prone and cause (partial) repetition of the contract of the superevent in the subevent. Repetition of contracts in turn could make their understanding and maintenance difficult [37,45].

To illustrate specification repetition, consider translucid contracts of events in Fig. 4 in which the postcondition of BinEV, on line 17, is changed from *true* to *node.equals(old (node))* for the contracts to manually refine each other. The code in grey shows specification repetitions such as the repetition of the whole contract of BinEv in AndEv, lines 11–17 and 20–26. Specification inheritance for translucid contracts of subtyping events can statically guarantee the refining relation among the contracts of events and avoid the specification repetition. Definition 4 defines inheritance for translucid contracts of subtyping events.

Definition 4 *(Inheritance for translucid contracts).* *For event types ev and ev′, where ev is a subevent of ev′, i.e. ev ≪: ev′, and their respective structurally similar translucid contracts $\mathscr{G} =$ (requires p assumes {se} ensures q) and $\mathscr{G}′ =$ (requires p′ assumes {se′} ensures q′), the extended translucid contract $\mathscr{G}_x =$ requires p_x assumes {se_x} ensures q_x that replaces the contract $\mathscr{G}$ of the subevent ev is defined as follows:*

(i) $p_x = p \wedge p′$ and $q_x = q \vee q′$

and for its assumes block se_x:

(ii) ∀ (spec = requires p_s ensures q_s) ∈ se and its corresponding (spec′ = requires $p′_s$ ensures $q′_s$) ∈ se′ then (spec_x = requires p_x ensures q_x) ∈ se_x such that $p_x = p_s \wedge p′_s$ and $q_x = q_s \vee q′_s$.

(iii) ∀ prog ∈ se and its corresponding prog′ ∈ se′ where textualMatch(prog, prog′), then prog ∈ se_x.

Ptolemy$_S$'s specification inheritance, in Definition 4, combines the translucid contracts of an event and its superevent to produce an extended translucid contract that replaces the translucid contract of the event. In the extended contract, *(i)* original preconditions of contracts of the event and its superevent are conjoined and their postconditions are disjoined. To combine assumes blocks of the event and its superevent *(ii)* corresponding specification expressions *spec* and *spec′* of the contracts are combined by conjoining their preconditions and disjoining their postconditions and *(iii)* textually matching corresponding program expressions *prog* and *prog′* of contracts are copied over to the combined translucid contract.

The event specification inheritance in Definition 4 guarantees the *Ptolemy$_S$*'s refining relation defined in Definition 1. In other words the translucid contract $\mathscr{G}′$ of the superevent ev′ is refined by the extended translucid contract $\mathscr{G}_x$ of its subevent ev. Translucid contract $\mathscr{G}′$ is refined by $\mathscr{G}_x$ if the behavior *requires p′ ensures q′* of $\mathscr{G}′$ is refined by the behavior *requires p_x ensures q_x* of $\mathscr{G}_x$ and the assumes block *se′* of $\mathscr{G}′$ is refined by the assumes block se_x of $\mathscr{G}_x$. The requirement *(i)* in the definition of event specification inheritance guarantees that the behavior of $\mathscr{G}′$ is refined by the behavior of $\mathscr{G}_x$. This behavioral refinement is similar to refinement of blackbox contracts [45].

```
 1  void event ExpEv {
 2    Exp node;
 3    requires node != null
 4    assumes {
 5      establishes next.node().parent==old(next.node().parent);
 6      next.invoke();
 7      establishes next.node().parent==old(next.node().parent);
 8    }
 9    ensures node.equals(old(node))
10  }
11  void event BinEv extends ExpEv {
12    BinExp node;
13    Exp left;
14    Exp right;
15    requires left!=null && right!=null
16    ensures node.equals(old(node))
17  }
18  void event AndEv extends BinEv {
19    AndExp node;
20  }
```

Fig. 14. Translucid contracts of `ExpEv`, `BinEv` and `AndEv` using specification inheritance and without specification repetition of Fig. 4.

The assumes block se' of $\mathscr{G}'$ is refined by structurally similar assumes block se_x of $\mathscr{G}_x$ if *(1)* for each program expression in se' there is a corresponding textually match program expression in se_x and *(2)* for each specification expression in se' there is a corresponding refining specification expression in se_x [46]. The requirement *(iii)* in the definition of specification inheritance guarantees *(1)* and the requirement *(ii)* guarantees *(2)*.

Unlike specification inheritance for blackbox specifications that only combines preconditions and postconditions [45], event specification inheritance combines greybox specifications containing assumes blocks that specify control effects. Also, event specification inheritance only combines structurally similar translucid contracts. Structural similarity is essential to allow for a static and syntactic definition of specification inheritance for greybox specifications. Without structural similarity the definition of specification inheritance may require complex or runtime trace verification techniques [46].

To illustrate event specification inheritance, consider Fig. 14 that rewrites the translucid contracts of events in Fig. 4 using event specification inheritance. The contract of `ExpEv` remains the same. However, its subevent `BinEv` inherits the assumes block of its superevent `ExpEv` and does not repeat it. Precondition and postcondition of `BinEv`, on lines 15 and 16, are combined by the precondition and postcondition of its superevent `ExpEv`, on lines 3–9. The contract for `AndEv` is completely inherited from its superevent `BinEv` and therefore is not repeated in `AndEv`.

Measuring specification reuse. Event specification inheritance decreases specification repetition by 62 % in the full version of the simple expression example, discussed in Sect. 1. Figure 15 shows specification reuse for events in this example. Specification reuse is measured by counting lines of code for translucid contracts of event declarations in two implementations of the expression example with and without specification

Lines of Code	without event subtyping	with event subtyping	Change
event declarations	174	66	**-62.1%**
Tracer observer	96	30	**-68.7%**
Checker observer	126	60	**-52.3%**
Evaluator observer	160	139	**-13.1%**
ASTAnnouncer subject	57	57	**-0.0%**
all other code	179	179	**-0.0%**
Total	792	531	**-33.0%**

Fig. 15. Specification and code reuse in $Ptolemy_S$ for the simple expression example of Sect. 1.

inheritance[6]. Lines of code are measured using the *cloc* tool[7] ignoring comments and whitespace lines.

Specification inheritance and reuse avoids repetition in events and not their observers and subjects. However, an observer of an event still can benefit from code reuse enabled by event subtyping which allows the observer to run when a subevent of the event is announced. Figure 15 shows code reuse for observers in the expression example. The observer Tracer benefits the most, because the observer handler methods for all events are identical and thus with event subtyping only one handler method can be reused for all the events. More complicated observers Checker and Tracer show 13–52 % code reuse. Subjects of events do not benefit from specification or code reuse because of event subtyping. The same is true for the rest of the code.

8 Dynamic Semantics

In this section, we present a substitution-based small-step operational semantics for $Ptolemy_S$ with special focus on announcing and handling of events in an event inheritance hierarchy and the non-decreasing relation on execution order of their observers. Rest of $Ptolemy_S$'s operational semantics can be found in Sect. B.

8.1 Dynamic Semantic Objects

$Ptolemy_S$'s operational semantics relies on few additional expressions that are not part of its surface syntax, as shown in Fig. 16, including *loc* to represent the locations in the store and *evalpost e q* to check that the expression *e* satisfies the postcondition *q*. $Ptolemy_S$ also uses three exceptions to represent dereferencing null references, i.e. *NPE*, runtime cast exceptions, i.e. *CCE*, and violations of translucid contracts, i.e. *TCE*.

---

[6] These two implementations can be found at http://sf.net/p/ptolemyj/code/HEAD/tree/pyc/ branches/event-inheritance/examples/101-Polymorphic-Contracts/ and http://sf.net/p/ptole myj/code/HEAD/tree/pyc/branches/event-inheritance/examples/101-Polymorphic-Contracts-No-Reuse/, respectively.

[7] Retrieved from: http://cloc.sourceforge.net/.

Added syntax:
$$e ::= loc \mid \textbf{\textit{evalpost}}\ e\ q$$
$$\mid \textbf{\textit{NPE}} \mid \textbf{\textit{CCE}} \mid \textbf{\textit{TCE}}$$
$$loc \in \mathcal{L},\ \text{a set of locations}$$

Evaluation contexts:
$$\mathbb{E} ::= - \mid \mathbb{E}\,.m(e...) \mid v.m(v...\mathbb{E}e...) \mid \mathbb{E}.f \mid \mathbb{E}\,.f{=}e$$
$$\mid \textbf{if}\ (\mathbb{E})\ \{\,e\,\}\ \textbf{else}\ \{\,e\,\} \mid \textbf{cast}\ c\ \mathbb{E} \mid t\ var{=}\mathbb{E};\ e$$
$$\mid \textbf{announce}\ (v...\mathbb{E}e...)\ \{e\} \mid \textbf{invoke}\,(\mathbb{E})$$
$$\mid \textbf{register}\,(\mathbb{E}) \mid \textbf{unregister}\,(\mathbb{E})$$
$$\mid \textbf{refining requires}\ \mathbb{E}\ \textbf{ensures}\ q$$

Evaluation relation: $\hookrightarrow$: $\langle e,S,\Pi,A \rangle \to \langle e',S',\Pi',A' \rangle$

Domains:

$\Sigma ::= \langle e,S,\Pi,A \rangle$	configurations
$S ::= \{loc_k \mapsto sv_k\}$	stores
$v ::= \textbf{\textit{null}} \mid loc$	values
$sv ::= or \mid ec$	storable values
$or ::= [c\,.F]$	object records
$F ::= \{f_k \mapsto v_k\}$	field maps
$\rho ::= \{var \mapsto v_k\}$	environments
$ec ::= \textbf{\textit{eClosure}}(H,e,\rho)$	event closure
$H ::= h{+}H \mid \bullet$	handler records list
$h ::= \langle loc,m \rangle$	handler record
$A ::= \{ev_k \mapsto O_k\}$	active objects map
$O ::= loc{+}O \mid \bullet$	active objects list
$k \in \mathcal{K},\ \text{is finite}$	

Fig. 16. Added syntax, evaluation contexts and configuration.

In *Ptolemy*$_\text{S}$'s core semantics, exceptions are terminal states [16]. Figure 16 also shows the evaluation contexts used in *Ptolemy*$_\text{S}$'s dynamic semantics. An evaluation context $\mathbb{E}$ specifies the evaluation order and the position in an expression where the evaluation is happening. *Ptolemy*$_\text{S}$ uses a left-most inner-most call-by-value evaluation policy.

Ptolemy$_\text{S}$'s operational semantics transitions from one configuration to another. A configuration Σ, in Fig. 16, contains an expression e, store S, store typing Π and a mapping A from events ev to their ordered list of observers O. A store maps locations to storable values sv which themselves are either an object record or or an event closure ec. An object record has a class name c and a map F from fields to their values. An event closure $eClosure(H,e,\rho)$ contains an ordered list of observer handlers H, an expression e and an environment ρ for running e. An observer handler method h contains a location loc that points to its observer object and a handler method name m. A value v is either a location loc or $null$. A store typing maps a location to its type and is maintained and updated by the dynamic rules only to be used in the soundness proof.

8.2   Dynamic Semantic Rules

Figure 17 shows dynamic semantic of $Ptolemy_S$-specific expressions. In $Ptolemy_S$, a subject announces an event using an announce expression, observers (un)register for the event using (un)register expressions and invoke each other using invoke expressions.

The rule (ANNOUNCE) says that upon announcement of an event ev an event closure $eClosure(H, e, \rho)$ is constructed that contains the list (chain) of observer handler methods of the event and the observer handler methods of its superevent, in H, the event body e and an environment mapping context variables var^* of the event to their values v^*, in ρ. The list H is constructed using the auxiliary function $handlersOf$, in Fig. 18. The function $handlersOf$ first computes the list of observer handler methods of the event ev, using $hbind$, and concatenates it to the handlers of the superevents ev' until the event $Event$ is reached. This in turn ensures that the observer handler methods of the event ev appear before the observer handler methods of its superevent ev' in the list of observer handler methods H, according to the non-decreasing relation. The event $Event$ has no observers since is not part of $Ptolemy_S$'s surface syntax and observers can not register for or handle it. The concatenate operator $\oplus$ ignores empty $\bullet$ elements. The function $hbind$ binds the observer loc, in the beginning of the $A[ev]$, to observer handler method m, using the auxiliary function $match$ and concatenates it to the bindings for the rest of $A[ev]$. After construction, the event closure is mapped to a fresh location loc and the execution of the chain of observer handler methods starts using the invoke expression, i.e. $loc.invoke()$.

(ANNOUNCE) also updates the store typing environment Π with a new mapping from the location loc to the type **thunk** ev of the event closure it points to. Recall that thunk types mark event closure types. The operator $\uplus$ is an overriding union operator.

Rules (INVOKEDONE) and (INVOKE) handle the base case and recursive case of observer invocation. The auxiliary function $methodBody$ emulates dynamic dispatch at runtime. After the execution of the observer handler method at the beginning of the list H, the event closure is updated to reflect the execution of the observer and the updated event closure is stored at a fresh location loc_1. (INVOKE) also updates the store typing environment Π with a mapping between location loc_1 of new event closure and its type.

A refining expression claims that its body satisfies the precondition and postcondition of its specification, which is checked by rules (REFINING) and (EVALPOST). Exceptional cases in rules (X-REFINING) and (X-EVALPOST) represent violation of precondition and postcondition (Fig. 19).

$Ptolemy_S$ also supports standard object-oriented expressions for object creation, getting and setting the value of a field, if conditionals, etc. Their semantics can be found in Sect. B.

9   Type Checking

In this section, we discuss $Ptolemy_S$'s static semantics with the focus on event subtyping, refining relation among greybox event specifications and non-decreasing relation. Rest of $Ptolemy_S$'s static semantics can be found in Sect. B.

Evaluation relation: $\boxed{\hookrightarrow: \langle e, S, \Pi, A \rangle \rightarrow \langle e', S', \Pi', A' \rangle}$

(ANNOUNCE)

$$\frac{\begin{array}{c}(c \ \boldsymbol{event} \ ev \ \boldsymbol{extends} \ ev'\{(t \ var)^* \ contract_{ev}\}) \in CT \\ loc \notin dom(S) \qquad H = handlersOf(ev) \qquad \rho = \{var_i \mapsto v_i \mid var_i \in var^* \wedge v_i \in v^*\} \\ S' = S \uplus (loc \mapsto \boldsymbol{eClosure}(H, e, \rho)) \qquad \Pi' = \Pi \uplus (loc : \boldsymbol{thunk} \ ev)\end{array}}{\langle \mathbb{E}[\boldsymbol{announce} \ ev \ (v^*) \ \{e\}], S, \Pi, A \rangle \hookrightarrow \langle \mathbb{E}[loc.\boldsymbol{invoke}()], S', \Pi', A \rangle}$$

(INVOKEDONE)

$$\frac{\boldsymbol{eClosure}(\bullet, e, \rho) = S(loc)}{\langle \mathbb{E}[loc.\boldsymbol{invoke}()], S, \Pi, A \rangle \hookrightarrow \langle \mathbb{E}[e], S, A, \Pi \rangle}$$

(INVOKE)

$$\frac{\begin{array}{c}\boldsymbol{eClosure}(\langle loc', m \rangle + H, e, \rho) = S(loc) \qquad [c . F'] = S(loc') \\ (c_2, t \ m(t_1 \ var_1)\{e'\}) = methodBody(c, m) \qquad e'' = [loc_1/var_1, loc'/\boldsymbol{this}]e' \\ loc_1 \notin dom(S) \qquad S' = S \uplus (loc_1 \mapsto \boldsymbol{eClosure}(H, e, \rho)) \qquad \Pi' = \Pi \uplus (loc_1 : \Pi(loc))\end{array}}{\langle \mathbb{E}[loc.\boldsymbol{invoke}()], S, \Pi, A \rangle \hookrightarrow \langle \mathbb{E}[e''], S', \Pi', A \rangle}$$

(REGISTER)

$$\frac{\forall ev \in eventsOf(loc) \ . \ A'[ev] = A[ev] + loc}{\langle \mathbb{E}[\boldsymbol{register}(loc)], S, \Pi, A \rangle \hookrightarrow \langle \mathbb{E}[loc], S, \Pi, A' \rangle}$$

(UNREGISTER)

$$\frac{\forall ev \in eventsOf(loc) \ . \ A'[ev] = A[ev] - loc}{\langle \mathbb{E}[\boldsymbol{unregister}(loc)], S, \Pi, A \rangle \hookrightarrow \langle \mathbb{E}[loc], S, \Pi, A' \rangle}$$

(REFINING)

$$\frac{n \neq 0}{\langle \mathbb{E}[\boldsymbol{refining} \ \boldsymbol{requires} \ n \ \boldsymbol{ensures} \ q \ \{e\}], S, \Pi, A \rangle \hookrightarrow \langle \mathbb{E}[\boldsymbol{evalpost} \ e \ q], S, \Pi, A \rangle}$$

(EVALPOST)

$$\frac{n \neq 0}{\langle \mathbb{E}[\boldsymbol{evalpost} \ v \ n], S, \Pi, A \rangle \hookrightarrow \langle \mathbb{E}[v], S, \Pi, A \rangle}$$

(ECGET)

$$\frac{\boldsymbol{eClosure}(H, e, \rho) = S(loc) \qquad v = \rho(f)}{\langle \mathbb{E}[loc.f], S, \Pi, A \rangle \hookrightarrow \langle \mathbb{E}[v], S, \Pi, A \rangle}$$

Fig. 17. Select rules for $Ptolemy_S$'s dynamic semantics, based on [16].

9.1 Type Attributes

Figure 20 defines the type attributes used in $Ptolemy_S$'s typing rules. The type attribute OK shows that a higher level declaration type checks, whereas OK in c shows type checking in the context of a class c. Other type attributes *var t* and *exp t* show variables and expressions of type t, respectively. Variable and store typing environments Γ and Π, respectively, map variables and locations to their types. The typing judgment $\Gamma, \Pi \vdash e : \theta$ says that in the variable typing environment Γ and the store typing environment Π, the expression e has the type θ. $Ptolemy_S$'s type checking rules use a fixed class table CT, which is a set of program's class and event type declarations. Top-level names in a program are distinct and inheritance relations on classes and events types are acyclic.

$$handlersOf(\textbf{\textit{Event}}) = \bullet \qquad \frac{(c \textbf{ event } ev \textbf{ extends } ev'\{form^* \ contract_{ev}\}) \in CT}{handlersOf(ev) = hbind(ev,S,A[ev]) \oplus handlersOf(ev')}$$

$$hbind(ev,S,\bullet) = \bullet$$

$$\frac{[c.F] = S(loc) \qquad B = bindingsOf(c)}{hbind(ev,S,loc+A[ev]) = match(B,ev,S,loc) \oplus hbind(ev,S,A[ev])}$$

$$bindingsOf(\textbf{\textit{Object}}) = \bullet \qquad \frac{(\textbf{class } c \textbf{ extends } d \ \{form^* \ meth^* \ binding^*\}) \in CT}{bindingsOf(c) = binding^* \oplus bindingsOf(d)}$$

$$match(\bullet,ev,S,loc) = \bullet$$

$$match((\textbf{when } ev \textbf{ do } m)+B,ev,S,loc) = (\langle loc,m \rangle + match(B,ev,S,loc))$$

$$\frac{[c.F] = S(loc) \qquad B = bindingsOf(c)}{eventsOf(loc) = registeredFor(loc,B)} \qquad registeredFor(loc,\bullet) = \bullet$$

$$registeredFor(loc,(\textbf{when } ev \textbf{ do } m)+B) = ev \oplus registeredFor(loc,B)$$

Fig. 18. Select auxiliary functions for $Ptolemy_{\mathbb{S}}$'s dynamic semantics, based on [9, 16].

(X-REFINING)
$$\frac{n == 0}{\langle \mathbb{E}[\textbf{refining requires } n \textbf{ ensures } q \ \{e\}],S,\Pi,A \rangle \hookrightarrow \langle \textbf{\textit{TCE}},S,\Pi,A \rangle}$$

(X-REGISTER)
$$\langle \mathbb{E}[\textbf{register(null)}],S,\Pi,A \rangle \hookrightarrow \langle \textbf{\textit{NPE}},S,\Pi,A \rangle$$

(X-UNREGISTER)
$$\langle \mathbb{E}[\textbf{unregister(null)}],S,\Pi,A \rangle \hookrightarrow \langle \textbf{\textit{NPE}},S,\Pi,A \rangle$$

(X-EVALPOST)
$$\frac{n == 0}{\langle \mathbb{E}[\textbf{evalpost } v \ n],S,\Pi,A \rangle \hookrightarrow \langle \textbf{\textit{TCE}},S,\Pi,A \rangle}$$

(X-CAST)
$$\frac{[c.F] = S(loc) \qquad c \not\leq t}{\langle \mathbb{E}[\textbf{cast } t \ loc],S,\Pi,A \rangle \hookrightarrow \langle \textbf{\textit{CCE}},S,\Pi,A \rangle}$$

Fig. 19. $Ptolemy_{\mathbb{S}}$'s exceptional dynamic semantics.

9.2 Static Semantics Rules

Figure 21 shows select typing rules for $Ptolemy_{\mathbb{S}}$. The rest of $Ptolemy_{\mathbb{S}}$'s typing rules, which are mostly standard object-oriented rules can be found in Sect. B.

The rule (T-EVENT) type checks the declaration of an event ev. Since ev extends another event ev', the rule ensures that ev is a valid subevent of ev', i.e. $ev \ll: ev'$, and its translucid contract refines the translucid contract of ev', i.e. $contract_{ev'} \trianglelefteq contract_{ev}$. The refinement of the translucid contract of ev' by the contract of ev is statically guaranteed by $Ptolemy_{\mathbb{S}}$'s specification inheritance. (T-EVENT) also checks, using the auxiliary function $isClass$, that the return type and types of context variables of ev are valid class

$$\theta ::=$$ type attributes

	OK	program/top-level decl.
	| OK in c	method, binding
	| *var t*	var/formal/field
	| *exp t*	expression

$t ::= c \mid$ int $\mid$ bool   types

$\Gamma ::= \{var : t\}$ variable typing environment
$\Pi ::= \{loc : t\}$ store typing environment
$\Gamma, \Pi \vdash e : \theta$ typing judgement

Fig. 20. Type attributes, based on [16].

types. Figure 22 shows the auxiliary functions used in *Ptolemy$_\mathbb{S}$*'s typing rules. The auxiliary function *isClass* simply ensures that its parameter is a class declared in the class table *CT*.

(T-SUBEVENT) checks that an event *ev* is a valid subtype of event *ev'*, regarding both width and depth subtyping. Width subtyping allows *ev* to declare context variables in addition to the context it inherits from its superevent *ev'*, i.e. *contextsOf(ev')* $\subseteq$ *contextsOf(ev)*. The auxiliary function *contextsOf* returns all the context variables of an event along with their types, including context inherited from all of its superevents. Depth subtyping allows *ev* to redeclare a context variable of its superevent *ev'*. To redeclare a context variable var_i of type t'_i, the redeclaring context variable must have the same name var_i and its type t_i must be a subtype of t'_i, i.e. $t_i \preccurlyeq t'_i$. Similar to class subtyping, event subtyping is a reflexive, transitive relation on event types, with a root event type **Event**.

(T-SUBEVENT) also ensures that the return type of an event *ev* is a *supertype* of the return type of its superevent *ev'*. This is necessary for the non-decreasing relation on observers of an event and its superevent, which ensures that an observer of an event runs before an observer of its superevents. The auxiliary function *returnType* returns the return type of an event.

(T-ANNOUNCE) type checks an announce expression. It ensures that the type of a parameter expression e_i is a subtype of its corresponding context variable var_i, i.e. $t'_i \preccurlyeq t_i$. Recall that an event can inherit context variables from its superevents and the announce expression must provide values for all context variables of the event.

(T-ANNOUNCE) also ensures that the type of the event body e' is the same as the return type of the top event in the event inheritance hierarchy. The top event of an event in an inheritance hierarchy is the superevent of the event right before the root event **Event**. For example, in Fig. 2, the event ExpEv is the top event for AndEv. The auxiliary function *topEvent* returns the top event of an event. The relation between the return type of the event body and the the return type of its top event is necessary for the non-decreasing relation in which the event body runs as the last observer.

(T-BINDING) type checks a binding declaration. It ensures that the body e of the observer handler method m refines the assumes block se of the translucid contract of its

(T-EVENT)
$$\frac{(c' \textbf{ event } ev' \textbf{ extends } ev'' \ \{(t' \ var')^* \ contract_{ev'}\}) \in CT}{\Gamma, \Pi \ \vdash contract_{ev'} \trianglelefteq contract_{ev} \quad \vdash ev \lll: ev' \quad isClass(c) \quad \forall t_i \in t^* \ . \ isClass(t_i)}{\vdash c \textbf{ event } ev \textbf{ extends } ev' \ \{(t \ var)^* \ contract_{ev}\} : \text{OK}}$$

(T-SUBEVENT)
$$\frac{contextsOf(ev') \subseteq contextsOf(ev)}{(t \ var)^* = contextsOf(ev) \quad (t' \ var')^* = contextsOf(ev')}{\forall \ (t_i \ var_i) \in (t \ var)^*, \ (t'_i \ var_i) \in (t' \ var')^* \ . \ t_i \preccurlyeq t'_i \quad returnType(ev') \preccurlyeq returnType(ev)}{\vdash ev \lll: ev'}$$

(T-ANNOUNCE)
$$\frac{(t \ var)^* = contextsOf(ev) \quad \forall e_i \in e^*, \ (t_i \ var_i) \in (t \ var)^* \ . \ \Gamma, \Pi \ \vdash e_i : exp \ t'_i \wedge t'_i \preccurlyeq t_i}{c'' \textbf{ event } ev' \textbf{ extends Event}\{\} = topEvent(ev)}{c = returnType(ev) \quad \Gamma, \Pi \ \vdash e' : exp \ c''}{\Gamma, \Pi \ \vdash \textbf{announce } ev \ (e^*) \ \{e'\} : exp \ c}$$

(T-BINDING)
$$\frac{(c \textbf{ event } ev \textbf{ extends } ev' \ \{form^* \ contract_{ev}\}) \in CT}{contract_{ev} = \textbf{requires } p \textbf{ assumes } \{se\} \textbf{ ensures } q}{(c \ m \ (\textbf{thunk } ev \ var) \ \{e\}) = methodBody(c', m) \quad se \trianglelefteq e}{\vdash \textbf{when } ev \textbf{ do } m : \text{OK in } c'}$$

(T-INVOKE)
$$\frac{c \textbf{ event } ev \textbf{ extends } ev' \ \{form^* \ contract_{ev}\} \in CT \quad \Gamma, \Pi \ \vdash e : exp \ thunk \ ev}{\Gamma, \Pi \ \vdash e.\textbf{invoke}() : exp \ c}$$

(T-REGISTER)
$$\frac{\Gamma, \Pi \ \vdash e : exp \ t}{\Gamma, \Pi \ \vdash \textbf{register}(e) : exp \ t}$$

(T-UNEGISTER)
$$\frac{\Gamma, \Pi \ \vdash e : exp \ t}{\Gamma, \Pi \ \vdash \textbf{unregister}(e) : exp \ t}$$

(T-EVALPOST)
$$\frac{\Gamma, \Pi \ \vdash e : exp \ t \quad \Gamma, \Pi \ \vdash q : exp \ t_2}{\Gamma, \Pi \ \vdash \textbf{evalpost } e \ q : exp \ t}$$

(T-SPEC)
$$\frac{\Gamma, \Pi \ \vdash p : exp \ t_1 \quad \Gamma, \Pi \ \vdash q : exp \ t_2}{\Gamma, \Pi \ \vdash \textbf{requires } p \textbf{ ensures } q \ : exp \ \bot}$$

(T-REFINING)
$$\frac{spec = \textbf{requires } p \textbf{ ensures } q \quad \Gamma, \Pi \ \vdash spec : exp \bot \quad \Gamma, \Pi \ \vdash e : exp \ t}{\Gamma, \Pi \ \vdash \textbf{refining } spec \ \{e\} : exp \ t}$$

(T-PROGRAM)
$$\frac{\forall decl \in decl^* \ . \quad \vdash decl : \text{OK} \quad \vdash e : exp \ t}{\vdash decl^* \ e : exp \ t}$$

(T-CLASS)
$$\frac{\forall meth \in meth^* \ . \quad \vdash meth : \text{OK in } c \quad \forall binding \in binding^* \ . \quad \vdash binding : \text{OK in } c}{isClass(d) \quad \forall (t \ f) \in form^* \ . \ isClass(t) \wedge f \notin dom(fieldsOf(d))}{\vdash \textbf{class } c \textbf{ extends } d \ \{form^* \ meth^* \ binding^*\} : \text{OK}}$$

Fig. 21. Select typing rules for $Ptolemy_S$ [9, 27].

$$\frac{(c\ \textbf{event}\ ev\ \textbf{extends}\ ev'\ \{(t\ var)^*\ contract_{ev}\}) \in CT \qquad (t'\ var')^* = contextsOf(ev')}{contextsOf(ev) = (t'\ var')^* \oplus (t\ var)^*}$$

$$contextsOf(\textbf{Event}) = \bullet \qquad \frac{(c\ \textbf{event}\ ev\ \textbf{extends}\ ev'\ \{form^*\ contract_{ev}\}) \in CT}{returnType(ev) = c}$$

$$\frac{(c\ \textbf{event}\ ev\ \textbf{extends}\ ev'\ \{form^*\ contract_{ev}\}) \in CT}{isEvent(ev)}$$

$$\frac{\textbf{class}\ c\ \textbf{extends}\ d\{form^*\ meth^*\ binding^*\} \in CT}{isClass(c)} \qquad \frac{t = \textbf{thunk}\ ev}{isThunkType(t)}$$

$$\frac{isClass(t) \lor isThunkType(t)}{isType(t)} \qquad \frac{\textbf{class}\ c\ \textbf{extends}\ d\{(t\ var)^*\ meth^*\ binding^*\} \in CT}{fieldsOf(c) = (var : t)^*}$$

$$\frac{\textbf{class}\ c\ \textbf{extends}\ d\{form^*\ meth^*\ binding^*\} \in CT \qquad (c''\ m\ (t\ var)^*\ \{e\}) \in meth^*}{methodBody(c,m) = (c''\ m\ (t\ var)^*\ \{e\})}$$

$$\frac{\textbf{class}\ c\ \textbf{extends}\ d\{form^*\ meth^*\ binding^*\} \in CT \qquad (c''\ m\ (t\ var)^*\ \{e\}) \notin meth^*}{methodBody(c,m) = methodBody(d,m)}$$

Fig. 22. Select auxiliary functions for $Ptolemy_S$'s typing rules, based on [9, 16].

event ev, i.e. $se \unlhd e$, as defined in Fig. 9. The auxiliary function *methodBody* returns the body of a method of a class defined in the class table CT. The rule also ensures that the return type of the observer handler method m is *the same* as the the return type of the event.

(T-INVOKE) type checks an invoke expression. The invoke expression invokes the next observer in the chain of observers. The chain of observers is included in the event closure receiver object e. The rule ensures that the event closure of an event ev is of type **thunk** ev. A thunk type marks the type of an event closure. The type of an invoke expression is the same as the return type c of its event ev. This is sound because the non-decreasing relation ensures that observers of an event run before observers of its super-event. Typing rules for register, unregister, specification, refining and evalpost expressions are intuitive.

(T-PROGRAM) type checks a program. A program type checks if declarations of each of event types and classes type check. (T-CLASS) type checks a class declaration. It ensures that each binding declaration of the class type checks.

9.3 Soundness of Type System

Theorem 2 (Soundness of Ptolemy$_S$'s semantics). *Ptolemy$_S$'s semantics is sound regarding its progress and preservation* [51].

The proof follows standard progress and preservation arguments. Full proof of the theorem can be found in Sect. B.

10   Binary Compatibility

A language such as Java defines a set of binary compatibility rules to enable reuse of binaries of the already compiled classes and prevent their unnecessary recompilation. A change to a class type is binary compatible if types that linked without error before the change to the type's binary continue to link without error after the change [52–54]. For example in Java adding a field to a subtype with the same name as a supertype's field or changes to the body of a method are binary compatible changes. To promote binary reuse, *Ptolemy*$_S$ and its compiler extend Java's binary compatibility rules to its event types using the following rules *(1)–(6)*.

1. Adding context variables. Adding a context variable declaration in an event type is not binary compatible. This is because a subject that announces the event now fails to link and a subevent of the event may violate its depth subtyping. After addition of a context variable to an event, an announce expression in a subject of the event or a subject of its superevent must be changed to pass in a value for the newly added context. Also, a subevent of the event with a context of the same name as the newly added context must be verified to ensure that the types of the two contexts are in a subtyping relationship to satisfy the depth subtyping. This is different from Java in which adding a field to a class is considered binary compatible.

2. Removing context variables. Similar to adding a context variable declaration, removing a context from an event is not binary compatible. This is because a subject of the event that announced the event and its observers that access the removed context now fail to link. An announce expression in a subject of the event or a subject of its subevent must be changed to pass in one less value for the newly removed context variable. An observer of the event or an observer of its subevent that access the removed context must be changed to not access the context. This is similar to Java where removing a public field of a class is binary incompatible.

3. Changing superevent. Changing the superevent of an event is binary compatible if it does not change the set of inherited context variables of the event and does not violate the subtyping and refining relations between return types and contracts of the event and its new superevent, respectively. Changes in the inherited context variables of the event could cause recompilations or verifications similar to adding or removing context variables, discussed above. The event must be verified to ensure that its return type is a supertype of the return type of its new superevent to satisfy the subtyping relation between return types of events. Finally, the event must be verified to ensure that its translucid contract refines the translucid contract of its new superevent to satisfy the refining relation. The verifier ensures there are no cyclic event inheritance relations. This is somewhat similar to Java in which changing a superclass of a class is binary compatible if it does not change the inherited fields and methods of the class.

4. Changing behavior. changing the behavior of an event by changing precondition and postcondition of its translucid contract is binary compatible. This is because of runtime assertion checking of contracts and event specification inheritance. In *Ptolemy*$_S$'s compiler, assertions that check for precondition and postcondition of the event invoke methods of a static class `Contract` in the event. To implement specification inheritance in a subevent of the event the assertions for the precondition and postcondition of the subevent invoke the methods of superevent's `Contract` class that check for precondition and postcondition of the event. Therefore, changing the behavior of the event does not require any changes in its subevent and is binary compatible. Without specification inheritance changing the behavior of an event is not binary compatible. This is because the behavior of a subevent must be changed to guarantee the refining relation between the subevent and its superevent.

5. Changing control effects. Changing control effects of an event by changing its assumes block and especially its program expressions is not binary compatible. This is because a translucid contract of a subevent of the event now fails to refine the translucid contract of the event and an observer of the event fails to conform to the contract of the event. The assumes block of a subevent must change to guarantee the refining relation between translucid contracts of the subevent and its superevent. The implementation of an observer of the event must change to conform to the assume block of the contract of the event.

6. Changing subjects and observers. Changing the implementation of a subject or an observer of an event is binary compatible if the subject or observer type check. For a changed observer of an event, type checking ensures that the conformance relation between the implementation of the observer and translucid contract of the event is not violated. For a changed subject of the event, type checking ensures that types of arguments of its announce expression are subtypes of the types of the context variables of its event.

Changed event	Change Description	Declaration		Subjects		Observers	
		ExpEv	BinEv	ExpEv	BinEv	ExpEv	BinEv
superevent ExpEv	1. add context int pos	R	V	R	V	✓	V
	2. remove context node	R	V	R	V	V	V
	3. change superevent to BinEv	R	V	V	V	V	V
	4. change *requires* to true	R	✓	✓	✓	✓	✓
	5. change *assumes*	R	R	✓	✓	R	R
subevent BinEv	1. add new context int pos	✓	R	✓	R	✓	✓
	2. remove context node	✓	R	✓	✓	✓	V
	3. change superevent to *Event*	✓	R	✓	V	✓	V
	4. add *requires* pos >= 0	✓	R	✓	✓	✓	✓
	5. change *assumes*	✓	R	✓	✓	R	R

Fig. 23. Binary compatibility change scenarios.

To illustrate, Fig. 23 shows different change scenarios and their binary compatibility for the event ExpEv and its subevent BinEv declared in Fig. 14 and their subjects and observers. In this figure, ✓ means binary compatible (no recompilation is required), *R* means binary incompatible (recompilation is required) and *V* means conditional binary compatibility under a set of conditions that should be verified; if the conditions are met, it is binary compatible and otherwise it is not. For example, adding an integer context variable pos to the declaration of the event ExpEv is not binary compatible and forces the event declaration to be recompiled. This requires the subevent BinEv to verify that it does not violate event depth subtyping after the addition of the context pos to ExpEv especially that BinEv may have a context variable with the same name pos and different type. Subjects of ExpEv should be recompiled to pass an extra argument for the newly added context and subjects of the subevent BinEv should verify that considering event subtyping they pass correct numbers and types of arguments for its context variables. Finally observers of ExpEv do not need any recompilation or verification because they are not accessing the newly added context pos. Observers of BinEv should be verified to ensure they assume correct types of context variables when accessing them especially if BinEv has a context variable with the same name as the added context pos to its superevent ExpEv.

11 Discussion

Implementation. To prove the feasibility of our proposed language, we implemented *Ptolemy$_S$*'s compiler on top of Ptolemy's compiler [27], which itself is an extension of the OpenJDK Java compiler. To the previous compiler, we added translucid contracts, static structural refinement, static event specification inheritance, runtime assertion checking of preconditions and postconditions of contracts and their specification expressions and a non-decreasing execution order of observers of an event and its superevents. Compared to Ptolemy's compiler, maintaining separate lists for observers of separate events, rather than a single global list, simplified the implementation of event announcement and handling especially with dynamic (un)registration of observers.

Limitation. A non-decreasing relation among observers of an event and its superevent(s) limits execution order of observers and could require a programmer to co-design the event subtyping hierarchy of a program and execution order of their observers. Without such a co-design there could be some execution orders of observers that may not be allowed by a specific event subtyping hierarchy. For example, with the event hierarchy in our expression language example, observer evaluator always runs before checker. Placement of invoke expressions in observers plays an important role in the functionality of a system. For example, although evaluator runs before checker, an expression is not evaluated unless it is first type checked. This is enforced because evaluator invokes the handler chain before evaluating an expression. An alternative to non-decreasing relation is an observer chain in which the precondition of an observer ob_1 implies the precondition of the next observer ob_2 in the chain and the postcondition of ob_2 implies the postcondition of ob_1.

Static conformance checking. In addition to static enforcing of the refining relation, *Ptolemy$_S$*'s event specification inheritance enables static checking of conformance between the implementations of subjects and observers of an event and its translucid contract. This is because, the event specification inheritance combines the translucid contracts of an event and its superevent in an inheritance hierarchy *without* requiring any dynamic information. This is in contrast to previous work on refinement of black-box contracts [55] where dynamically resolved pseudo-variables such as ***original*** are used to refer to the specification of previous observer in a chain of observers. Use of such dynamic features hinders static conformance checking because the value of the pseudo-variable *original* is determined at runtime depending on dynamic registration order of observers in the chain. For static conformance checking, following [56], subjects and observers of an event are combined with the extended translucid contract of the event into OpenJML [57] code for static verification of precondition, postcondition and specification expressions of the contract. Extended translucid contract of an event is constructed using event specification inheritance. Currently refinement of precondition, postcondition and specification expressions by the implementation of subjects and observers is checked using runtime assertions, as discussed in Sect. 4.1.

12 Related Work

Modular type checking. Previous work on join point types (JPT) [20], join point interfaces (JPI) [19] and Ptolemy's typed events [27] enables modular type checking of subjects and observers of subtyping event types. EventJava [12] extends Java with events and event correlation in distributed settings and Escala [7] extends Scala with explicitly declared events as members of classes. However, previous work is not concerned with modular reasoning about behaviors and control effects of subjects and observers of events using specification of subtyping event types.

Modular reasoning. Previous work on MAO [33], EffectiveAdvice [58], Effective Aspect [59], MRI [60] and the work of Khatchadourian *et al.* [31] enables modular reasoning, however, it does not use explicit interfaces among subjects and observers and therefore is not concerned about their subtyping. Previous work on crosscutting programming interfaces (XPI) [6], crosscutting programming interfaces with design rules (XPIDR) [32] and open modules [3] enables modular reasoning using explicit interfaces, however, it is not concerned about subtyping of these interfaces. Translucid contracts [8–10,35,61] proposes event type specifications to enable modular reasoning, however, they are not concerned with event subtyping. Other previous work [62] enable compositional global reasoning and not modular reasoning.

Modular reasoning about dynamic dispatch. Supertype abstraction [63] enables modular reasoning about invocation of a dynamically dispatched method in the presence of class subtyping [63], relying on a refinement relation among blackbox contracts of a supertype and its subtypes [37,64]. $Ptolemy_S$'s refining of event contracts is the inverse of the refinement in supertype abstraction and extends it to greybox contracts with control effects. Refinement in supertype abstraction relies on known links among method invocations and method names, whereas in $Ptolemy_S$ there is no link among subjects and observers of an event [9,29]. Subjects and observers do not know about each other and only know their event. Unlike a method invocation which invokes exactly one method, announcement of an event in $Ptolemy_S$ by a subject could invoke zero or more observers of the event and observers of its superevents where all these observers and the subject must conform to their event specifications. The challenge in supertype abstraction is modular reasoning about a method invocation independent of the dynamic types of its receiver, whereas in $Ptolemy_S$ the challenge is tractable reasoning about announcement and handling of an event, independent of its observers, observers of its superevents and their execution orders, while allowing reuse of events.

13   Conclusion and Future Work

In this work we identified combinatorial reasoning and behavior invariance as two problems of modular reasoning about subjects and observers in the presence of event subtyping. We proposed a refining relation among greybox event specifications of events in an inheritance hierarchy, a non-decreasing relation on execution orders of their observers and a conformance relation among subjects and observers of an event and their translucid contract to solve these problems in the context of a new language design called *Ptolemy*$_S$. We formalized *Ptolemy*$_S$'s sound static and dynamic semantics and Hoare logic for modular reasoning. We showed the applicability of *Ptolemy*$_S$'s modular reasoning to other event-based systems including join point types [20] and join point interfaces [19,49] and its use in modular reasoning about control interference. We proposed event specification inheritance to statically enforce the refining relation and enable specification reuse and defined the binary compatibility rules for *Ptolemy*$_S$'s event types and their specifications to enable binary reuse.

Future work includes a large experimental study similar to [24–26] to further investigate benefits of *Ptolemy*$_S$'s event model and its modular reasoning. It would also be interesting to examine the interplay between semantics of invoke and execution order of observers. Recent work has explored asynchronous execution of observers [65]. Examining the interplay of concurrency and event inheritance will also be interesting.

Acknowledgements. The authors would like to thank the anonymous TOMC and MODULARITY 2015 reviewers for valuable comments. Bagherzadeh, Dyer and Rajan were partly supported by the NSF grant CCF-10-17334. Fernando and Rajan were partly supported by the NSF grant CCF-08-46059. Rajan was also partly supported by the NSF grant CCF-11-17937. Sanchez was partly supported by NSF grant CCF-1017334.

A   Soundness of Reasoning

Theorem 1. *(Soundness of Ptolemy*$_S$'s *Hoare logic) Ptolemy*$_S$'s Hoare logic, in Fig. 8, is sound for conforming *Ptolemy*$_S$ programs. In other words, any Hoare triple provable using *Ptolemy*$_S$'s logic, i.e. $\Gamma \vdash \{p\}\, e\, \{q\}$, is a valid triple, i.e. $\Gamma \models \{p\}\, e\, \{q\}$.

Proof: To prove the soundness of *Ptolemy*$_S$'s Hoare logic, it is sufficient to prove the soundness of *Ptolemy*$_S$'s specific expressions [10], i.e. announce, invoke, refining and specification expressions in the rules (V-ANNOUNCE), (V-INVOKE), (V-REFINING) and (V-SPEC) in *Ptolemy*$_S$'s Hoare logic. This is because, previous work [38,47,48] proves the soundness of Hoare logic for object-oriented programs including *Ptolemy*$_S$'s standard object-oriented expressions.

The proof is based on induction on the number of events, i.e. number of superevents of an event, in a subtyping hierarchy and the number of their observers and uses conformance, refining and non-decreasing relations. The induction goes over the number of superevents first and then number of observers.

A.1   Invoke Expression

To prove soundness of (V-INVOKE) for an invoke expression, we should prove that in an observer *ob* of an event *ev* if the Hoare triple $\{p\}\, next.invoke()\, \{q\}$ is provable for its invoke expression, i.e. $\Gamma \vdash \{p\}$ *next.invoke*$() \{q\}$, then it is a valid Hoare triple, i.e. $\Gamma \models \{p\}$ *next.invoke*$() \{q\}$. We assume an arbitrary chain of observers $\chi_0 \rightharpoonup ob \rightharpoonup \chi$ in which χ_0 contains observers in the chain before ob and χ is the remainder of the chain after ob. The event body is at the end of the chain in χ. The invoke expression in ob invokes the next observer in χ.

There are two inductions. The first induction goes over the number of superevents of ev with base cases of zero and one superevent for ev. The second induction goes over the number of its observers in χ.

No superevent for ev For the induction over the number of observers in χ, we assume a base case with zero and one observer in χ.

For the base case with zero observers, the invoke expression in ob causes the execution of the event body, say e', in χ. The subject conformance relation, in Definition 3, guarantees that the event body e' respects the precondition p' and postcondition q' of the top contract of ev, i.e. $\Gamma \models \{p'\} e' \{q'\}$. The top contract of ev is the same as the contract for ev, i.e. $p = p'$ and $q = q'$, because ev does not have any superevents. This in turn means that (a) $\Gamma \models \{p\} e' \{q\}$. Because the execution of **next.invoke**$()$ in ob results in the execution of the event body, then in the judgement (a) the event body e' could be replaced with the invoke expression **next.invoke**$()$ to arrive at the goal judgement $\Gamma \models \{p\}$ *next.invoke*$() \{q\}$ which we wanted to prove.

For the base case with one observer ob_1 in χ, the invoke expression in ob causes the execution of the body e_1 of ob_1. The observer conformance relation, in Definition 2, guarantees that the body e_1 of the observer ob_1 respects the precondition p and postcondition q of the contract of ev, i.e. (b) $\Gamma \models \{p\} e_1 \{q\}$. And because the execution of **next.invoke**$()$ in ob results in the execution of e_1, then in the judgement (b) the body e_1 of ob_1 could be replaced with the invoke expression to arrive at the goal judgement $\Gamma \models \{p\}$ *next.invoke*$() \{q\}$ which we wanted to prove.

For the inductive case over the number of observers, we assume the induction hypothesis that the judgement $\Gamma \models \{p\}$ *next.invoke*$() \{q\}$ holds for the invoke expression in the observer ob with n observers in χ, and prove the judgement still holds for $n+1$ observers in χ. If the newly added observer is added right after ob and to the beginning of χ, then the observer conformance relation guarantees that its body respects the precondition and postcondition p and q of ev and the rest of the proof continues as in the base case with one observer. If the newly added observer is not added to the beginning of χ and is added somewhere down the chain χ, then using the induction hypothesis the judgement $\Gamma \models \{p\}$ *next.invoke*$() \{q\}$ holds mainly because the hypothesis ensures the invoke expression causes the invocation of an observer which respects p and q.

The inductive proof of the invoke expression for the case in which there is no superevent for ev is similar to the proof of soundness of reasoning using translucid contracts in previous work [8], in the absence of event subtyping.

One superevent. ev' **for** ev For the induction over the number of observers in χ, we assume base cases with *(1)* zero observer for ev and ev', *(2)* one observer for ev and zero observer for ev', *(3)* zero observer for ev and one observer for ev' and *(4)* one observer for ev and one observer for ev'.

The proof for the base case *(1)* is similar to the previous case with no superevent for ev and zero observers for ev. The subject conformance relation guarantees that the body

e' of the event ev respects the precondition p' and postcondition q' of the top contract for ev, which is the contract of ev', i.e. (a) $\Gamma \models \{p'\}\ e'\ \{q'\}$. The refining relation guarantees that the contract of ev refines the contract of ev', i.e. $p \Rightarrow p'$ and $q \Rightarrow q'$. Using these implications among preconditions and postconditions, the judgement (a) and the standard rule (V-CONSEQ) one can arrive at the conclusion $\Gamma \models \{p\}\ e'\ \{q\}$ and replace e' with the invoke expression.

The proof for case *(2)* is similar to the previous case with no superevent for ev and one observer for ev.

For the case *(3)* the conformance relation guarantees that the body e'_1 of the only observer ob'_1 of ev' respects the contract of its event, i.e. (b) $\Gamma \models \{p'\}\ e'_1\ \{q'\}$. The refining relation guarantees that the contract of ev refines the contract of ev', i.e. $p \Rightarrow p'$ and $q \Rightarrow q'$. Using these implications, the judgement (b) and (V-CONSEQ) one can arrive at the goal conclusion $\Gamma \models \{p\}\ e'_1\ \{q\}$ and then replace e'_1 with the invoke expression.

For the base case *(4)*, the ordering relation guarantees that the only observer ob_1 of ev is before the only observer ob'_1 of ev' in the chain χ. The observer conformance relation guarantees that the body e_1 of ob_1 respects the precondition p and postcondition q of ev. The rest of the proof is similar to the base case with no superevent and one observer.

For the inductive case over the number of observers, we assume the induction hypothesis that the judgement $\Gamma \models \{p\}\ \textit{next.invoke}()\ \{q\}$ holds for the invoke expression in the observer ob of event ev with n observers of ev and its superevent ev' in χ, and prove the judgement holds for $n+1$ observers in χ. The newly added observer can be an observer of ev or ev'. If the newly added observer is an observer of ev and it is added to the beginning of χ, the proof continues similar to the inductive case for no superevent case in which a new observer is added to the beginning of χ. If the newly added observer of ev is not added to the beginning of χ, then the ordering relation guarantees that it is added before any observer of ev', then the judgement $\Gamma \models \{p\}\ \textit{next.invoke}()\ \{q\}$ holds mainly because the induction hypothesis ensures the invoke expression causes the invocation of an observer which respects p and q. If the newly added observer is an observer of ev', then the ordering relation guarantees that it is added after any observer of ev, then the judgement $\Gamma \models \{p\}\ \textit{next.invoke}()\ \{q\}$ holds mainly because the induction hypothesis ensures the invoke expression causes the invocation of an observer which respects p and q.

k superevents for ev. For induction over the number of superevents, we proved the base case with zero and one superevent for ev. For the inductive case we assume the induction hypothesis that the judgement $\Gamma \models \{p\}\ \textit{next.invoke}()\ \{q\}$ holds for the invoke expression in the observer ob of event ev with n observers of ev and its k superevents in χ, and prove the judgement holds for $k+1$ superevents with arbitrary number of observers for the newly added superevent.

If there are no observers in χ, i.e. $n = 0$, and the newly added superevent $ev^{(k)}$ has no observers too, then the proof is the same as the case with no superevent and no observers. n is the number of observers in χ. If $ev^{(k)}$ has observers with $n = 0$ then the observer conformance relation guarantees that its first observers respect its precondition p^k and postcondition q^k and the refining relation guarantees that $p \Rightarrow p^k$ and $q \Rightarrow q^k$. Using these implications and the induction hypothesis we can arrive at the goal judgement $\Gamma \models \{p\}$ *next.invoke*() $\{q\}$, similar to the case for one superevent with no observer for the event and one observer for its superevent. If there are observers in χ, i.e. $n \neq 0$, then the ordering relation guarantees that observers of the newly added superevent ev^k are added to the end of χ, and then the judgement $\Gamma \models \{p\}$ *next.invoke*() $\{q\}$ holds mainly because the induction hypothesis ensures the invoke expression causes the invocation of an observer which respects p and q.

A.2   Announce, Refining and Specification Expressions

Announce expressions. The proof for an announce expression is similar to the proof for the invoke expression, especially that the semantics of an announce expression is given in terms of invoke expression in (ANNOUNCE) rule in Fig. 17. Both announce and invoke expression cause execution of a chain of observers of an event and its superevents.

Refining and specification expressions. For the refining expression in the rule (V-REFINING), the assumption of the rule that the body e of the refining expression satisfies its specification, i.e. $\Gamma \vdash \{p\} e \{q\}$ makes the conclusion valid. The validity of the rule (V-SPEC) is straightforward [46]. The rule (V-CONSEQ) is standard [38].   ∎

B   Soundness of Type System

Theorem 2. (Soundness of *Ptolemy$_S$*'s semantics) *Ptolemy$_S$*'s semantics is sound regarding its progress and preservation [51].

Proof: Soundness proof of *Ptolemy$_S$*'s type system follows standard progress and preservation arguments [51] using the refining and non-decreasing relations. Some details and definitions are adapted from previous work [8,9,15,16]. Figures 17, 18, 21, 22, 24 and 25 together show a complete list of *Ptolemy$_S$*'s static and dynamic semantics rules used in the proof.

B.1   Background Definitions and Lemmas

The following definitions are used in the progress and preservation arguments of *Ptolemy$_S$*'s soundness proof.

Definition 5 *(Location loc **has type** t **in store** S [16]). Location loc has type t in store S, written as $S(loc) : t$ where $t = \Pi(loc)$, if one of the following conditions hold:*

(I) type t is a class, i.e. isClass(t), and for some class name c with a set of fields F all the following holds:
   (a) $S(loc) = [c.F]$ and $\Pi(loc) = t$ and $c \preceq t$
   (b) $dom(F) = dom(fieldsOf(c))$ and $rng(F) \subseteq (dom(S) \cup \{null\})$
   (c) $\forall f \in dom(F)$ if $F(f) = loc'$ and $fieldsOf(c)(f) = u$ and $S(loc') = [u'.F']$ then $u' \preceq u$.
*(II) type t is an event closure type, i.e. isThunkType(t), where $t = $ **thunk** ev for some event type ev with return type c, list of handlers H, environment ρ, expression e and class name c' all the following holds:*

(T-METHODDECL)

$$\dfrac{(var:t)^*, \textbf{\textit{this}}:c \vdash e:\textbf{\textit{exp}}\ t''}{\vdash t'\ m((t\ var)^*)\ \{e\}:\text{OK in }c}$$

$$t'' \preccurlyeq t' \quad \textbf{class }c\textbf{ extends }d\{..\} \quad override(m,d,t^* \to t')$$

(T-CALL)

$$\dfrac{\Pi \vdash e:\textbf{\textit{exp}}\ t}{\Gamma,\Pi\ \vdash e.m(e^*):\textbf{\textit{exp}}\ t''}$$

$$t''\ m((t\ var)^*)\ \{e'\}=CT(t,m) \quad \forall\, e_i \in e^*\,.\ \Gamma,\Pi\ \vdash e_i:\textbf{\textit{exp}}\ t_i' \quad \forall\, t_i \in t^*,t_i'\,.\ t_i' \preccurlyeq t_i$$

(T-NEW)

$$\dfrac{isClass(c)}{\Gamma,\Pi\ \vdash \textbf{new }c():\textbf{\textit{exp}}\ c}$$

(T-CAST)

$$\dfrac{isClass(c) \quad \Gamma,\Pi\ \vdash e:\textbf{\textit{exp}}\ t}{\Gamma,\Pi\ \vdash \textbf{cast }c\ e:\textbf{\textit{exp}}\ c}$$

(T-GET)

$$\dfrac{\Gamma,\Pi\ \vdash e:\textbf{\textit{exp}}\ c \quad fieldsOf(c)(f)=t}{\Gamma,\Pi\ \vdash e.f:\textbf{\textit{exp}}\ t}$$

(T-SET)

$$\dfrac{\Gamma,\Pi\ \vdash e:\textbf{\textit{exp}}\ c \quad fieldsOf(c)(f)=t \quad \Gamma,\Pi\ \vdash e':\textbf{\textit{exp}}\ t' \quad t' \preccurlyeq t}{\Gamma,\Pi\ \vdash e.f=e':\textbf{\textit{exp}}\ t'}$$

(T-DEFINE)

$$\dfrac{\Gamma,\Pi\ \vdash e_1:\textbf{\textit{exp}}\ t_1 \quad \Gamma,\Pi,var:t \vdash e_2:\textbf{\textit{exp}}\ t_2 \quad isType(t) \quad t_1 \preccurlyeq t}{\Gamma,\Pi\ \vdash t\ var=e_1;e_2:\textbf{\textit{exp}}\ t_2}$$

(T-IF)

$$\dfrac{\Gamma,\Pi\ \vdash e_1:\textbf{\textit{exp}}\ t \quad \Gamma,\Pi\ \vdash e_2:\textbf{\textit{exp}}\ t \quad \Gamma,\Pi\ \vdash ep:\textbf{\textit{exp}}\ t}{\Gamma,\Pi\ \vdash \textbf{\textit{if}}(ep)\{e_1\}\ \textbf{\textit{else}}\ \{e_2\}:\textbf{\textit{exp}}\ t}$$

(T-NULL)

$$\dfrac{isClass(c)}{\Gamma,\Pi\ \vdash \textbf{null}:\textbf{\textit{exp}}\ c}$$

(T-VAR)

$$\dfrac{(var:t)\in \Gamma}{\Gamma,\Pi\ \vdash var:\textbf{\textit{var}}\ t}$$

(T-LOC)

$$\dfrac{\Pi(loc)=t}{\Gamma,\Pi\ \vdash loc:\textbf{\textit{exp}}\ t}$$

Fig. 24. Standard $Ptolemy_S$'s type checking rules [16].

(a) $S(loc)=eClosure(H,e,\rho)$

(b) $\Gamma,\Pi\ \vdash e:c'$ and $c' \preccurlyeq c$

(c) $\forall f \in dom(contextsOf(ev))$, either $\rho(f)=\textbf{null}$ or $\rho(f)=loc''$ where $S(loc'')=[c''.F']$ and $c'' \preccurlyeq contextsOf(ev)(f)$

(d) $\forall h = \langle loc',m \rangle \in H.\ \Pi(loc')=c'''$ and $(c_2,c\ m(t_1\ var_1))=methodBody(c''',m)$ then $t_1=t$

Definition 6 (Store S is consistent with store typing Π). *Store S is consistent with store typing Π and typing context Γ, written as $\Gamma,\Pi \cong S$, if and only if all the following conditions hold:*

$$\frac{loc \notin dom(S)}{S' = S \uplus (loc \mapsto [c . \{f \mapsto \textbf{\textit{null}} \mid f \in dom(\textit{fieldsOf}(c))\}]) \qquad \Pi' = \Pi \uplus (loc : c)}{\langle \mathbb{E}[\textbf{\textit{new }} c()], S, \Pi, A \rangle \hookrightarrow \langle \mathbb{E}[loc], S', \Pi', A \rangle}$$

(GET)

$$\frac{[c . F] = S(loc) \qquad v = F(f)}{\langle \mathbb{E}[loc.f], S, \Pi, A \rangle \hookrightarrow \langle \mathbb{E}[v], S, \Pi, A \rangle}$$

(SET)

$$\frac{[c . F] = S(loc) \qquad S' = S \uplus (loc \mapsto [c . F \uplus (f \mapsto v)])}{\langle \mathbb{E}[loc.f = v], S, \Pi, A \rangle \hookrightarrow \langle \mathbb{E}[v], S', \Pi, A \rangle}$$

(DEF)

$$\frac{e' = e[v/var]}{\langle \mathbb{E}[t \; var = v; \; e], S, \Pi, A \rangle \hookrightarrow \langle \mathbb{E}[e'], S, \Pi, A \rangle}$$

(CALL)

$$\frac{[c.F] = S(loc)}{(c_2, t \; m((t \; var)*)\{e\} = \textit{methodBody}(c, m) \qquad e' = e[v*/var*, loc/\textbf{\textit{this}}]}{\langle \mathbb{E}[loc.m(v*)], S, \Pi, A \rangle \hookrightarrow \langle \mathbb{E}[e'], S, \Pi, A \rangle}$$

(CAST)

$$\frac{[c' . F] = S(loc) \qquad c' \preccurlyeq t}{\langle \mathbb{E}[\textbf{\textit{cast }} t \; loc], S, \Pi, A \rangle \hookrightarrow \langle \mathbb{E}[loc], S, \Pi, A \rangle}$$

(NCAST)

$$\langle \mathbb{E}[\textbf{\textit{cast }} c \; \textbf{\textit{null}}], S, \Pi, A \rangle \hookrightarrow \langle \mathbb{E}[\textbf{\textit{null}}], S, \Pi, A \rangle$$

(IFTRUE)

$$\frac{v \neq 0}{\langle \mathbb{E}[\textbf{\textit{if}}(v)\{e_1\} \; \textbf{\textit{else}}\{e_2\}], S, \Pi, A \rangle \hookrightarrow \langle \mathbb{E}[e_1], S, \Pi, A \rangle}$$

(X-GET)

$$\langle \mathbb{E}[\textbf{\textit{null}}.f], S, \Pi, A \rangle \hookrightarrow \langle NPE, S, \Pi, A \rangle$$

(IFFALSE)

$$\frac{v == 0}{\langle \mathbb{E}[\textbf{\textit{if}}(v)\{e_1\} \; \textbf{\textit{else}}\{e_2\}], S, \Pi, A \rangle \hookrightarrow \langle \mathbb{E}[e_2], S, \Pi, A \rangle}$$

(X-SET)

$$\langle \mathbb{E}[\textbf{\textit{null}}.f = v], S, \Pi, A \rangle \hookrightarrow \langle NPE, S, \Pi, A \rangle$$

Fig. 25. $Ptolemy_\mathbb{S}$'s operational semantics for standard OO expressions, based on [16].

(a) $dom(S) = dom(\Pi)$
(b) $\forall loc \in dom(S), S(loc) : \Pi(loc)$, i.e. $S(loc)$ has type $\Pi(loc)$.

The following lemmas are used in progress and preservation arguments of $Ptolemy_\mathbb{S}$'s soundness proof. Proofs of these lemmas could be easily adapted from previous work on $MiniMAO_0$ [15] and therefore are skipped.

Lemma 1 (Substitution). *If* $\Gamma, var_1 : t_1, .., var_n : t_n, \Pi \vdash e : t$ *and* $\forall i \in [1, n]. \Gamma, \Pi \vdash e_i : t_i'$ *where* $t_i' \preccurlyeq t_i$ *then* $\Gamma, \Pi \vdash e[var_1/e_1, .., var_n/e_n] : t'$ *for some* $t' \preccurlyeq t$.

Lemma 2 (Environment contraction). *If* $\Gamma, a : t', \Pi \vdash e : t$ *and* a *is not free in* e, *then* $\Gamma, \Pi \vdash e : t$

Lemma 3 (Environment extension). *If* $\Gamma, \Pi \vdash e : t$ *and* $a \in dom(\Gamma)$ *then* $\Gamma, a : t', \Pi \vdash e : t$

Lemma 4 (Replacement). *If* $\Gamma, \Pi \vdash \mathbb{E}[e] : t$ *and* $\Gamma, \Pi \vdash e : t'$ *and* $\Gamma, \Pi \vdash e' : t'$ *then* $\Gamma, \Pi \vdash \mathbb{E}[e'] : t$.

Lemma 5 (Replacement with subtyping). *If* $\Gamma, \Pi \vdash \mathbb{E}[e] : t$ *and* $\Gamma, \Pi \vdash e : u$ *and* $\Gamma, \Pi \vdash e' : u'$ *such that* $u' \preccurlyeq u$ *then* $\Gamma, \Pi \vdash \mathbb{E}[e'] : t'$ *where* $t' \preccurlyeq t$.

B.2   Progress

Theorem 3 (Progress). *Let* $\langle e, S, \Pi, A \rangle$ *be a configuration with a well typed expression* *e, store S, store typing* Π *and active object map A, such that store S is consistent with store type* Π, *i.e.* $\Gamma, \Pi \cong S$. *If e has type t, i.e.* $\Gamma, \Pi \vdash e : t$, *then either*

– $e = loc$ *and* $loc \in dom(S)$
– $e = $ **null**, *or*
– *one of the following holds:*
  - $\langle e, S, \Pi, A \rangle \hookrightarrow \langle e', S', \Pi', A' \rangle$.
  - $\langle e, S, \Pi, A \rangle \hookrightarrow \langle x, S', \Pi', A' \rangle$ *and* $x \in \{NPE, CCE, TCE\}$

Proof: The proof is by cases on the evaluation of expression e:

1. $e = loc$. Since e is well-typed and using (T-LOC), $loc \in dom(\Pi)$. Using store consistency $\Gamma, \Pi \cong S$, $loc \in dom(S)$.
2. $e = $ **null**. The case is trivial.

Proof of cases for *Ptolemy$_S$*'s announcement and handling of events, and registration and unregistration of observers are adapted from Ptolemy [16].

3. $e = \mathbb{E}[$**announce** $ev(v^*)]$. Using well-typedness of e and (T-ANNOUNCE), event type ev is a declared event type in class table CT. (T-ANNOUNCE) ensures that all the context variables of ev are passed to the announce expression with appropriate types which in turn allows (ANNOUNCE) to construct the event closure and take a step.
4. $e = \mathbb{E}[loc.\textbf{invoke}()]$. Using (T-INVOKE) and store consistency, $loc \in dom(S)$ and $\Pi(loc) = $ **thunk** ev which ensures that loc is pointing to an event closure in the store for event ev. If the list of observer handlers H is not empty, then based on part (d) of Definition 5 the location loc' that is pointing to the first observer handler in the event closure is well-typed and therefore $loc' \in dom(S)$ which in turn allows (INVOKE) to take an step. Otherwise, if H is empty (INVOKEDONE) takes an step.
5. $e = \mathbb{E}[\textbf{register}(loc)]$. Using (T-REGISTER) and store consistency, (REGISTER) can take a step by adding a well-type location loc to the list of active objects $A[ev]$. (T-BINDING) ensures that the event ev that observer instance loc is bound to, in the auxiliary function *eventsOf*, is a valid event type declared in the class table CT.
6. $e = \mathbb{E}[\textbf{unregister}(loc)]$. Similar to previous case, using (T-UNREGISTER) and store consistency, (UNREGISTER) can take a step by removing a well-typed location loc from the list of active objects $A[ev]$.

Proof of cases for *Ptolemy$_S$*'s checking of translucid contracts are:

7. $e = \mathbb{E}[\textbf{refining requires} \ n \ \textbf{ensures} \ q]$. (T-REFINING) ensures that precondition is well-typed which in turn allows (REFINING) to take an step and reduce to an *evalpost* expression, if the precondition holds, i.e. $n \neq 0$. Otherwise, (X-REFINING) takes a step.

8. $e = \mathbb{E}[\textit{evalpost } n \; q]$. (T-REFINING) ensures well-typedness of its postcondition q and body e, which in turn allows (EVALPOST) to take an evaluation step, if its postcondition holds, i.e. $n \neq 0$. In case the postcondition is violated, the rule (X-EVALPOST) takes a step.

The following cases takes a step into exceptional terminal states and thus are trivial.

9. $e = \mathbb{E}[\textit{register}(\textit{null})]$, $e = \mathbb{E}[\textit{unregister}(\textit{null})]$, $e = \mathbb{E}[\textit{null}.m(e^*)]$, $e = \mathbb{E}[\textit{null}.f]$, $e = \mathbb{E}[\textit{null}.f = v]$, $e = \mathbb{E}[\textit{cast } c \; \textit{null}]$.

The following cases for standard object-oriented expressions either are trivial or could be easily adapted from MiniMAO$_0$ [15].

10. $e = \mathbb{E}[\textit{loc}.f]$, $e = \mathbb{E}[\textit{loc}.f = v]$, $e = \mathbb{E}[\textit{cast } t \; \textit{loc}]$, $e = \mathbb{E}[\textit{loc}.m(v^*)]$.
11. $e = \mathbb{E}[t \; \textit{var} = v; e]$, $e = \mathbb{E}[\textit{if}(v)\{e_1\} \; \textit{else}\{e_2\}]$, $e = \mathbb{E}[\textit{new } c()]$ are trivial. ∎

B.3   Preservation

Theorem 4 (Preservation). *Let e be an expression, S a store, Π a store typing and A a map of active objects where store S is consistent with store typing Π, i.e. $\Gamma, \Pi \cong S$. If $\Gamma, \Pi \vdash e : t$ and $\langle e, S, \Pi, A \rangle \hookrightarrow \langle e', S', \Pi', A' \rangle$ then $\Gamma \Pi' \cong S'$ and there exists a type t' such that $t' \preccurlyeq t$ and $\Gamma \Pi' \vdash e' : t'$.*

In the above definition Π' is the store typing built and maintained in *Ptolemy$_S$*'s dynamic semantic rules.

Proof: The proof is by cases on the evaluation relation $\hookrightarrow$:

Proofs for expressions which announce and handle events and (un)register observers are adapted from Ptolemy [9, 16].

1. (ANNOUNCE). $e = \mathbb{E}[\textit{announce } ev \; (v^*) \; \{e\}]$ and $e' = \mathbb{E}[\textit{loc}.\textit{invoke}()]$, where $(c \; \textit{event } ev \; \textit{extends } ev'\{(t \; \textit{var})^* \; \textit{contract}_{ev}\}) \in CT$, $\textit{loc} \notin \textit{dom}(S)$, $H = \textit{handlersOf}(ev)$, $\rho = \{\textit{var}_i \mapsto v_i \mid \textit{var}_i \in \textit{var}^* \wedge v_i \in v^*\}$, $S' = S \uplus (\textit{loc} \mapsto \textit{eClosure}(H, e, \rho))$, and $\Pi' = \Pi \uplus (\textit{loc} : \textit{thunk } ev)$.

To show the store consistency $\Gamma | \Pi' \cong S'$, part (a) of Definition 6 holds since (ANNOUNCE) adds a fresh location $\textit{loc}$ to domains of both store S and store typing Π. Part (b) of store consistency definition holds for all locations $\textit{loc}' \neq \textit{loc}$, according to $\Gamma, \Pi \cong S$. To show that part (b) holds for $\textit{loc}$, we have to show that part (II) of Definition 5 holds for $\textit{loc}$.

Part (a) of part (II) of Definition 5 holds, since $S'(\textit{loc}) = \textit{eClosure}(H, e, \rho)$ and $\Pi'(\textit{loc}) = \textit{thunk } ev$. Part (b) holds since using (T-ANNOUNCE), the fact that because of the refining relation the return type of the event body e is the same as the top event of ev and considering that the return type c of ev is the supertype of the return type of its top event, if $\Gamma, \Pi \vdash e : c'$ then $c' \preccurlyeq c$. For part (c) for all $f \in \textit{dom}(\textit{contextsOf}(ev))$, $\rho(f) = \textit{null}$ or $\rho(f) = \textit{loc}''$. Part (c) holds trivially if $\rho(f) = \textit{null}$. Otherwise if $\rho(f) = \textit{loc}''$ then according to store consistency $\Gamma, \Pi \cong S$, $\textit{loc}'' \in \textit{dom}(S)$. If $[c''.F] = S(\textit{loc}'')$ then $\Gamma, \Pi \vdash \textit{loc}'' : c''$ and (T-ANNOUNCE) ensures $c'' \preccurlyeq \textit{contextsOf}(ev)(f)$. Then sing Lemma 3 we have

$\Gamma|\Pi' \vdash loc'' : c''$ where $c'' \preccurlyeq contextsOf(ev)(f)$.

Now we show $\mathbb{E}[loc.\textit{invoke}()] : t'$ for some $t' \preccurlyeq t$. Let $\Gamma, \Pi \vdash \textbf{\textit{announce}}\ ev(v^*)\{e\} : t$. Using (T-ANNOUNCE), t $\textbf{\textit{event}}$ ev $\textbf{\textit{extends}}$ $ev'\{..\} \in CT$ and using the relation between return types of the event body and the return type of events in its hierarchy for the refining relation, if $\Gamma, \Pi \vdash e : u$ then $u \preccurlyeq t$. Let $\Gamma, \Pi \vdash loc.\textit{invoke}() : t'$. Using (T-INVOKE), $\Pi(loc) = \textbf{\textit{thunk}}\ ev$ where $S(loc) = eClosure(H, e, \rho)$ such that $u \preccurlyeq t'$. Thus we have $u \preccurlyeq t$ and $u \preccurlyeq t'$ which means $t = t'$. Since subtyping relation $\preccurlyeq$ is reflexive then $t' \preccurlyeq t$.

2. (INVOKEDONE). $e = [loc.\textit{invoke}()]$ and $e' = \mathbb{E}[e'']$, where $eClosure(\bullet, e'', \rho) = S(loc)$. Store consistency is trivial since neither store nor store typing changes.

   Now we show $\Gamma, \Pi \vdash \mathbb{E}[e''] : t'$ for some $t' \preccurlyeq t$. Let $\Gamma, \Pi \vdash e'' : u'$ and $\Gamma, \Pi \vdash loc.\textit{invoke}() : u$. Using (T-INVOKE), $\Gamma, \Pi \vdash loc : \textbf{\textit{thunk}}\ ev$ for some ev with return type u. Using store consistency and Definition 5 part (II) item (b) and assumption $eClosure(\bullet, e'', \rho) = S(loc)$, we have $u' \preccurlyeq u$. Finally using Lemma 4 we have $t' \preccurlyeq t$.

3. (INVOKE). $e = \mathbb{E}[loc.\textit{invoke}()]$ and $e' = \mathbb{E}[e_1[loc_1/var_1, loc'/\textbf{\textit{this}}]]$, where $eClosure(\langle loc', m\rangle + H, e'', \rho) = S(loc)$, $[c.F'] = S(loc')$, $(c_2, t\ m(t_1\ var_1)\{e_1\}) = methodBody(c, m)$, $loc_1 \notin dom(S)$, $S' = S \uplus (loc_1 \mapsto eClosure(H, e'', \rho))$, and $\Pi' = \Pi \uplus (loc_1 : \Pi(loc))$.

   To show store consistency, $\Gamma|\Pi' \cong S'$, part (a) of Definition 6 holds since (INVOKE) adds a fresh location loc_1 to the domain of both store S and store typing Π. Part (b) of store consistency definition holds for all locations $loc \neq loc_1$, using $\Gamma, \Pi \cong S$. To show that part (b) holds for loc_1 as well, we have to show that part (II) of Definition 5 holds for loc_1. Part (a) of part (II) of Definition 5 holds since $S'(loc_1) = eClosure(H, e'', \rho)$ and $\Pi'(loc_1) = \Pi(loc)$. Using (T-INVOKE) then $\Pi(loc_1)$ is an event closure thunk type $\textbf{\textit{thunk}}\ ev$ for some event ev with return type c. Part (b) holds since using (T-ANNOUNCE), if $\Gamma, \Pi \vdash e'' : c'$ then $c' \preccurlyeq c$. For part (c) for all $f \in dom(contextsOf(ev))$, $\rho(f) = \textbf{\textit{null}}$ of $\rho(f) = loc''$. Part (c) holds trivially if $\rho(f) = \textbf{\textit{null}}$. Otherwise if $\rho(f) = loc''$ according to store consistency $\Gamma, \Pi \cong S$, $loc'' \in S$. If $[c''.F] = S(loc'')$ then $\Gamma, \Pi \vdash loc'' : c''$ and (T-ANNOUNCE) ensures $c'' \preccurlyeq contextsOf(ev)(f)$. Using Lemma 3 we have $\Gamma|\Pi' \vdash loc'' : c''$ where $c'' \preccurlyeq contextsOf(ev)(f)$.

   Now we show that $\mathbb{E}[e_1[loc_1/var_1, loc'/\textbf{\textit{this}}]] : t'$ for some $t' \preccurlyeq t$. Let $\Gamma, \Pi \vdash loc.\textit{invoke}() : u$ and $e_1 : u'$, which also hold in $\Gamma|\Pi'$, using Lemma 3. Using (T-INVOKE) then $\Gamma\Pi' \vdash loc : \textbf{\textit{thunk}}\ ev$ for some ev with return type u. Location loc' in the event closure $eClosure(\langle loc', m\rangle + H, e'', \rho) = S'(loc)$ points to the class which contains the next handler method m to be run by the invoke expression. Expression e_1 is the body of m where using (T-BINDING) and (T-SUBEVENT), $u' \preccurlyeq u$. Using Lemma 1 then $\Gamma\Pi' \vdash e_1[loc_1/var_1, loc'/\textbf{\textit{this}}] : u''$ such that $u'' \preccurlyeq u'$. Since $u' \preccurlyeq u$ and $u'' \preccurlyeq u'$ then $u'' \preccurlyeq u$. Using Lemma 4, $t' \preccurlyeq t$.

4. (ECGET). $e = \mathbb{E}[loc.f]$, $e' = \mathbb{E}[v]$ where $eClosure(H, e'', \rho) = S(loc)$ and $v = \rho(f)$. Showing store consistency is trivial.

Now we show $\Gamma, \Pi \vdash \mathbb{E}[v] : t'$ for some $t' \preccurlyeq t$. Let $\Gamma, \Pi \vdash loc.f : u$ and $\Gamma, \Pi \vdash v :$ u'. Using store consistency and part(c) of Definition 5 part (II), $u' \preccurlyeq u$. And using Lemma 5, $t' \preccurlyeq t$.

5. (REGISTER). $e = \mathbb{E}[register(loc)]$, and $e' = \mathbb{E}[loc]$.
   Store consistency is trivial.
   Now we show $\Gamma, \Pi \vdash \mathbb{E}[loc] : t'$ for some $t' \preccurlyeq t$. Let $\Gamma, \Pi \vdash register(loc) : u$ and $\Gamma, \Pi \vdash loc : u'$. Using (T-REGISTER), $u' = u$. Using Lemma 5 we have $\Gamma, \Pi \vdash$ $\mathbb{E}[loc] : t'$ for some $t' \preccurlyeq t$. Note that subtyping relation $\preccurlyeq$ is reflexive and transitive.
6. (UNREGISTER). $e = \mathbb{E}[unregister(loc)]$, and $e' = \mathbb{E}[loc]$. Similar to the case for (REGISTER).

Proofs for expressions that check translucid contracts are:

7. (REFINING). $e = \mathbb{E}[\textit{refining requires } n \textit{ ensures } q \; \{e\}]$, $e' = \mathbb{E}[\textit{evalpost } e \; q]$ where $n \neq 0$.

   Store consistency is trivial.

   Now we show $\Gamma, \Pi \vdash \mathbb{E}[\textit{evalpost } e \; q] : t'$ for some $t' \preccurlyeq t$. Let $\Gamma, \Pi \vdash$ $[\textit{refining requires } n \textit{ ensures } q \; \{e\}] : u$. Using (T-REFINNING) then $\Gamma, \Pi \vdash e : u$. Using (T-EVALPOST) then $\Gamma, \Pi \vdash \textit{evalpost } e \; q : u$. Using Lemma 4 and reflexivity of subtyping relation we have $t' \preccurlyeq t$.
8. (EVALPOST). $e = \mathbb{E}[\textit{evalpost } v \; n]$, $e' = \mathbb{E}[v]$ where $n \neq 0$.

   Store consistency is trivial since neither store nor store typing changes.

   Now we show $\Gamma, \Pi \vdash \mathbb{E}[v] : t'$ for some $t' \preccurlyeq t$. Let $\Gamma, \Pi \vdash v : u$. Using (T-EVALPOST) then $\Gamma, \Pi \vdash \textit{evalpost } v \; n : u$. Using Lemma 1 and reflexivity of subtyping relation we have $t' \preccurlyeq t$.

Proof for expressions that throw exceptions are the following:

9. (X-REFINING). $e = \mathbb{E}[\textit{refining requires } n \textit{ ensures } q \; \{e\}]$, $e' = \textbf{\textit{TCE}}$ where $n == 0$.
   Here e is reduced to a terminal condition **TCE** which is not applicable to subject reduction theorem [15].
10. (X-SET), (X-GET), (X-CALL), (X-CAST), (X-(UN)REGISTER), (X-EVALPOST). The same argument used for (X-REFINING) applies to these rules as well.

Proofs for standard object-oriented (OO) expressions are as the following:

11. Proofs for standard OO expressions in (NEW), (SET), (GET), (CAST), (NCAST) and (CALL) could be easily constructed by adapting MiniMAO$_0$ [15] proofs for the same rules.   ∎

References

1. Bagherzadeh, M., Dyer, R., Fernando, R.D., Sánchez, J., Rajan, H.: Modular reasoning in the presence of event subtyping. In: Proceedings of the 14th International Conference on Modularity, MODULARITY 2015, pp. 117–132. ACM, New York (2015)
2. Kiczales, G., Hilsdale, E., Hugunin, J., Kersten, M., Palm, J., Griswold, W.G.: An overview of AspectJ. In: Knudsen, J.L. (ed.) ECOOP 2001. LNCS, vol. 2072, pp. 327–354. Springer, Heidelberg (2001). doi:10.1007/3-540-45337-7_18
3. Aldrich, J.: Open modules: modular reasoning about advice. In: Black, A.P. (ed.) ECOOP 2005. LNCS, vol. 3586, pp. 144–168. Springer, Heidelberg (2005). doi:10.1007/11531142_7
4. Sullivan, K., Griswold, W.G., Song, Y., Cai, Y., Shonle, M., Tewari, N., Rajan, H.: Information hiding interfaces for aspect-oriented design. In: Proceedings of the 10th European Software Engineering Conference Held Jointly with 13th ACM SIGSOFT International Symposium on Foundations of Software Engineering, ESEC/FSE-13, pp. 166–175. ACM, New York (2005)
5. Griswold, W.G., Sullivan, K., Song, Y., Shonle, M., Tewari, N., Cai, Y., Rajan, H.: Modular software design with crosscutting interfaces. IEEE Softw. 23(1), 51–60 (2006)
6. Sullivan, K., Griswold, W.G., Rajan, H., Song, Y., Cai, Y., Shonle, M., Tewari, N.: Modular aspect-oriented design with XPIs. ACM Trans. Softw. Eng. Methodol. 20(2), 5:1–5:42 (2010)
7. Gasiunas, V., Satabin, L., Mezini, M., Núñez, A., Noyé, J.: Escala: modular event-driven object interactions in Scala. In: Proceedings of the Tenth International Conference on Aspect-oriented Software Development, AOSD 2011, pp. 227–240. ACM, New York (2011)
8. Bagherzadeh, M., Rajan, H., Leavens, G.T., Mooney, S.: Translucid contracts: Expressive specification and modular verification for aspect-oriented interfaces. In: Proceedings of the Tenth International Conference on Aspect-oriented Software Development, AOSD 2011, pp. 141–152. ACM, New York (2011)
9. Bagherzadeh, M., Rajan, H., Darvish, A.: On exceptions, events and observer chains. In: Proceedings of the 12th Annual International Conference on Aspect-oriented Software Development, AOSD 2013, pp. 185–196. ACM, New York (2013)
10. Sánchez, J., Leavens, G.T.: Separating obligations of subjects and handlers for more flexible event type verification. In: Binder, W., Bodden, E., Löwe, W. (eds.) SC 2013. LNCS, vol. 8088, pp. 65–80. Springer, Heidelberg (2013). doi:10.1007/978-3-642-39614-4_5
11. Hoffman, K., Eugster, P.: Bridging Java and AspectJ through explicit join points. In: Proceedings of the 5th International Symposium on Principles and Practice of Programming in Java, PPPJ 2007, pp. 63–72. ACM, New York (2007)
12. Eugster, P., Jayaram, K.R.: EventJava: an extension of Java for event correlation. In: Drossopoulou, S. (ed.) ECOOP 2009. LNCS, vol. 5653, pp. 570–594. Springer, Heidelberg (2009). doi:10.1007/978-3-642-03013-0_26
13. Clifton, C., Leavens, G.T.: Obliviousness, modular reasoning, and the behavioral subtyping analogy. In: Software-engineering Properties of Languages for Aspect Technologies, SPLAT 2003 (2003)
14. Kiczales, G., Mezini, M.: Aspect-oriented programming and modular reasoning. In: Proceedings of the 27th International Conference on Software Engineering, ICSE 2005, pp. 49–58. ACM, New York (2005)
15. Clifton, C., Leavens, G.T.: A design discipline and language features for modular reasoning in aspect-oriented programs. Technical report 05–23, Iowa State University (2005)
16. Rajan, H., Leavens, G.T.: Ptolemy: a language with quantified, typed events. In: Vitek, J. (ed.) ECOOP 2008. LNCS, vol. 5142, pp. 155–179. Springer, Heidelberg (2008). doi:10.1007/978-3-540-70592-5_8

17. Rajan, H., Sullivan, K.J.: Unifying aspect- and object-oriented design. ACM Trans. Softw. Eng. Methodol. **19**(1), 3:1–3:41 (2009)
18. Rajan, H., Leavens, G.T.: Quantified, typed events for improved separation of concerns. Technical report 07–14, Iowa State University (2007)
19. Bodden, E., Tanter, E., Inostroza, M.: Join point interfaces for safe and flexible decoupling of aspects. ACM Trans. Softw. Eng. Methodol. **23**(1), 7:1–7:41 (2014)
20. Steimann, F., Pawlitzki, T., Apel, S., Kästner, C.: Types and modularity for implicit invocation with implicit announcement. ACM Trans. Softw. Eng. Methodol. **20**(1), 1:1–1:43 (2010)
21. Rebêlo, H., Leavens, G.T., Bagherzadeh, M., Rajan, H., Lima, R., Zimmerman, D.M., Cornélio, M., Thüm, T.: Modularizing crosscutting contracts with AspectJML. In: Proceedings of the Companion Publication of the 13th International Conference on Modularity, MODULARITY 2014, pp. 21–24. ACM, New York (2014)
22. Sánchez, J., Leavens, G.T.: Reasoning tradeoffs in languages with enhanced modularity features. In: Proceedings of the 15th International Conference on Modularity, MODULARITY 2016, pp. 13–24. ACM, New York (2016)
23. Rajan, H., Dyer, R., Hanna, Y.W., Narayanappa, H.: Preserving separation of concerns through compilation. In: Software-engineering Properties of Languages for Aspect Technologies, SPLAT 2006 (2006)
24. Dyer, R., Rajan, H., Cai, Y.: An exploratory study of the design impact of language features for aspect-oriented interfaces. In: Proceedings of the 11th Annual International Conference on Aspect-oriented Software Development, AOSD 2012, pp. 143–154. ACM, New York (2012)
25. Dyer, R., Rajan, H., Cai, Y.: Language features for software evolution and aspect-oriented interfaces: an exploratory study. In: Leavens, G.T., Chiba, S., Tanter, É. (eds.) Transactions on Aspect-Oriented Software Development X. LNCS, vol. 7800, pp. 148–183. Springer, Heidelberg (2013). doi:10.1007/978-3-642-36964-3_5
26. Dyer, R., Bagherzadeh, M., Rajan, H., Cai, Y.: A preliminary study of quantified, typed events. In: Workshop on Empirical Evaluation of Software Composition Techniques, ESCOT 2010 (2010)
27. Fernando, R.D., Dyer, R., Rajan, H.: Event type polymorphism. In: Proceedings of the Eleventh Workshop on Foundations of Aspect-Oriented Languages, FOAL 2012, pp. 33–38. ACM, New York (2012)
28. Xu, J., Rajan, H., Sullivan, K.: Understanding aspects via implicit invocation. In: Proceedings of the 19th IEEE International Conference on Automated Software Engineering, ASE 2004, Computer Society, pp. 332–335. IEEE, Washington (2004)
29. Dingel, J., Garlan, D., Jha, S., Notkin, D.: Towards a formal treatment of implicit invocation using rely/guarantee reasoning. Formal Aspects Comput. **10**(3), 193–213 (1998)
30. Gamma, E., Helm, R., Johnson, R., Vlissides, J.: Design Patterns: Elements of Reusable Object-oriented Software. Addison-Wesley Longman Publishing Co. Inc, Boston (1995)
31. Khatchadourian, R., Dovland, J., Soundarajan, N.: Enforcing behavioral constraints in evolving aspect-oriented programs. In: Proceedings of the 7th Workshop on Foundations of Aspect-oriented Languages, FOAL 2008, pp. 19–28. ACM, New York (2008)
32. Rebelo, H., Leavens, G.T., Lima, R.M.F., Borba, P., Ribeiro, M.: Modular aspect-oriented design rule enforcement with XPIDRs. In: Proceedings of the 12th Workshop on Foundations of Aspect-oriented Languages, FOAL 2013, pp. 13–18. ACM, New York (2013)
33. Clifton, C., Leavens, G.T., Noble, J.: MAO: ownership and effects for more effective reasoning about aspects. In: Ernst, E. (ed.) ECOOP 2007. LNCS, vol. 4609, pp. 451–475. Springer, Heidelberg (2007). doi:10.1007/978-3-540-73589-2_22
34. Parnas, D.L.: On the criteria to be used in decomposing systems into modules. Commun. ACM **15**(12), 1053–1058 (1972)

35. Bagherzadeh, M.: Enabling expressive aspect oriented modular reasoning by translucid contracts. In: Proceedings of the ACM International Conference Companion on Object Oriented Programming Systems Languages and Applications Companion, OOPSLA 2010, pp. 227–228. ACM, New York (2010)

36. Büchi, M., Weck, W.: The greybox approach: when blackbox specifications hide too much. Technical report 297, Turku Center for Computer Science (1999)

37. Leavens, G.T., Naumann, D.A.: Behavioral subtyping, specification inheritance, and modular reasoning. ACM Trans. Program. Lang. Syst. **37**(4), 13:1–13:88 (2015)

38. Hoare, C.A.R.: An axiomatic basis for computer programming. Commun. ACM **12**(10), 576–580 (1969)

39. Leavens, G.T., Baker, A.L., Ruby, C.: Preliminary design of JML: a behavioral interface specification language for Java. SIGSOFT Softw. Eng. Notes **31**(3), 1–38 (2006)

40. Rajan, H.: Unifying aspect- and object-oriented program design. Ph.D. thesis, Charlottesville, VA, USA AAI3189305 (2005)

41. Rajan, H.: Design pattern implementations in Eos. In: Proceedings of the 14th Conference on Pattern Languages of Programs, PLOP 2007, 9:1–9:11. ACM, New York (2007)

42. Rajan, H., Sullivan, K.J.: Classpects: unifying aspect- and object-oriented language design. In: ICSE 2005

43. Rajan, H., Sullivan, K.: Eos: Instance-level aspects for integrated system design. In: Proceedings of the 9th European Software Engineering Conference Held Jointly with 11th ACM SIGSOFT International Symposium on Foundations of Software Engineering, ESEC/FSE-11, pp. 297–306. ACM, New York (2003)

44. Morgan, C.: Procedures, parameters, and abstraction: separate concerns. Sci. Comput. Programm. **11**(1), 17–27 (1988)

45. Dhara, K.K., Leavens, G.T.: Forcing behavioral subtyping through specification inheritance. In: Proceedings of the 18th International Conference on Software Engineering, ICSE 1996, Computer Society, pp. 258–267. IEEE, Washington (1996)

46. Shaner, S.M., Leavens, G.T., Naumann, D.A.: Modular verification of higher-order methods with mandatory calls specified by model programs. In: Proceedings of the 22Nd Annual ACM SIGPLAN Conference on Object-oriented Programming Systems and Applications, OOPSLA 2007, pp. 351–368. ACM, New York (2007)

47. Abadi, M., Leino, K.R.M.: A logic of object-oriented programs. In: Dershowitz, N. (ed.) Verification: Theory and Practice. LNCS, vol. 2772, pp. 11–41. Springer, Heidelberg (2003). doi:10.1007/978-3-540-39910-0_2

48. Boer, F.S.: A WP-calculus for OO. In: Thomas, W. (ed.) FoSSaCS 1999. LNCS, vol. 1578, pp. 135–140. Springer, Heidelberg (1999). doi:10.1007/3-540-49019-1_10

49. Inostroza, M., Tanter, E., Bodden, E.: Join point interfaces for modular reasoning in aspect-oriented programs. In: Proceedings of the 19th ACM SIGSOFT Symposium and the 13th European Conference on Foundations of Software Engineering, ESEC/FSE 2011, pp. 508–511. ACM, New York (2011)

50. Rinard, M., Salcianu, A., Bugrara, S.: A classification system and analysis for aspect-oriented programs. In: Proceedings of the 12th ACM SIGSOFT Twelfth International Symposium on Foundations of Software Engineering, SIGSOFT 2004/FSE-12, pp. 147–158. ACM, New York (2004)

51. Wright, A., Felleisen, M.: A syntactic approach to type soundness. Inf. Comput. **115**(1), 38–94 (1994)

52. Forman, I.R., Conner, M.H., Danforth, S.H., Raper, L.K.: Release-to-release binary compatibility in SOM. In: Proceedings of the Tenth Annual Conference on Object-oriented Programming Systems, Languages, and Applications, OOPSLA 1995, pp. 426–438. ACM, New York (1995)

53. Gosling, J., Joy, B., Steele Jr., G.L., Bracha, G., Buckley, A.: The Java Language Specification, Java SE 7th edn, 1st edn. Addison-Wesley Professional, Boston (2013)
54. Drossopoulou, S., Wragg, D., Eisenbach, S.: What is Java binary compatibility? In: Proceedings of the 13th ACM SIGPLAN Conference on Object-oriented Programming, Systems, Languages, and Applications, OOPSLA 1998, pp. 341–361. ACM, New York (1998)
55. Thüm, T., Schaefer, I., Kuhlemann, M., Apel, S., Saake, G.: Applying design by contract to feature-oriented programming. In: Lara, J., Zisman, A. (eds.) FASE 2012. LNCS, vol. 7212, pp. 255–269. Springer, Heidelberg (2012). doi:10.1007/978-3-642-28872-2_18
56. Sánchez, J., Leavens, G.T.: Static verification of PtolemyRely programs using OpenJML. In: Proceedings of the 13th Workshop on Foundations of Aspect-oriented Languages, FOAL 2014, pp. 13–18. ACM, New York (2014)
57. Cok, D.R.: OpenJML: JML for Java 7 by extending OpenJDK. In: Bobaru, M., Havelund, K., Holzmann, G.J., Joshi, R. (eds.) NFM 2011. LNCS, vol. 6617, pp. 472–479. Springer, Heidelberg (2011). doi:10.1007/978-3-642-20398-5_35
58. Oliveira, B.C.D.S., Schrijvers, T., Cook, W.R.: EffectiveAdvice: disciplined advice with explicit effects. In: Proceedings of the 9th International Conference on Aspect-Oriented Software Development, AOSD 2010, pp. 109–120. ACM, New York (2010)
59. Figueroa, I., Tabareau, N., Tanter, É.: Effective aspects: a typed monadic embedding of pointcuts and advice. In: Chiba, S., Tanter, É., Bodden, E., Maoz, S., Kienzle, J. (eds.) Transactions on Aspect-Oriented Software Development XI. LNCS, vol. 8400, pp. 145–192. Springer, Heidelberg (2014). doi:10.1007/978-3-642-55099-7_5
60. Oliveira, B.C.D.S., Schrijvers, T.: Cook, W.r.: MRI: modular reasoning about interference in incremental programming. J. Funct. Program. 22(6), 797–852 (2012)
61. Bagherzadeh, M., Rajan, H., Leavens, G.T., Mooney, S.: Translucid contracts for aspect-oriented interfaces. In: Proceedings of the 9th Workshop on Foundations of Aspect-oriented Languages, FOAL 2010 (2010)
62. Figueroa, I., Schrijvers, T., Tabareau, N., Tanter, E.: Compositional reasoning about aspect interference. In: Proceedings of the 13th International Conference on Modularity, MODULARITY 2014, pp. 133–144. ACM, New York (2014)
63. Leavens, G.T., Weihl, W.E.: Specification and verification of object-oriented programs using supertype abstraction. Acta Inf. 32(8), 705–778 (1995)
64. Liskov, B.H., Wing, J.M.: A behavioral notion of subtyping. ACM Trans. Program. Lang. Syst. 16(6), 1811–1841 (1994)
65. Long, Y., Mooney, S.L., Sondag, T., Rajan, H.: Implicit invocation meets safe, implicit concurrency. In: Proceedings of the Ninth International Conference on Generative Programming and Component Engineering, GPCE 2010, pp. 63–72. ACM, New York (2010)

Software Unbundling: Challenges and Perspectives

João Bosco Ferreira Filho[1](✉), Mathieu Acher[2], and Olivier Barais[2]

[1] School of Computer Science, University of Birmingham, Birmingham, UK
`j.ferreirafilho@cs.bham.ac.uk`
[2] Inria and Irisa, Université Rennes 1, Rennes, France
`{mathieu.acher,olivier.barais}@irisa.fr`

Abstract. Unbundling is a phenomenon that consists of dividing an existing software artifact into smaller ones. It can happen for different reasons, one of them is the fact that applications tend to grow in functionalities and sometimes this can negatively influence the user experience. For example, mobile applications from well-known companies are being divided into simpler and more focused new ones. Despite its current importance, little is known or studied about unbundling or about how it relates to existing software engineering approaches, such as modularization. Consequently, recent cases point out that it has been performed unsystematically and arbitrarily. In this article, our main goal is to present this novel and relevant concept and its underlying challenges in the light of software engineering, also exemplifying it with recent cases. We relate unbundling to standard software modularization, presenting the new motivations behind it, the resulting problems, and drawing perspectives for future support in the area.

Categories and Subject Descriptors: D.2.9 Software Engineering: Distribution, Maintenance, Enhancement

Keywords: Unbundling · Modularization · Features · Aspects · Reengineering · Refactoring · Evolution

1 Introduction

Software is designed to meet user needs and requirements, which are constantly changing and evolving [35]. Meeting these requirements allows software companies to acquire new users and to stay competitive. For example, mobile applications compete with each other to gain market share in different domains; they constantly provide new features and services for the end user, growing in size and complexity. In some cases, the software artifact absorbs several distinct features, overloading the application and overwhelming the user and his/her acceptance of the software product [21] – he/she has to carry dozens of Swiss Army knives in his smart phone.

© Springer International Publishing Switzerland 2016
S. Chiba et al. (Eds.): ToMC I, LNCS 9800, pp. 224–237, 2016.
DOI: 10.1007/978-3-319-46969-0_6

A recent phenomenon is to unbundle these dense pieces of software into smaller ones, trying to provide simpler and more focused applications. *Unbundling consists of dividing an existing software artifact into smaller ones, each one serving to different end use purposes.* It requires an unplanned coarse-grained modularization of mature software: unplanned because it is very hard to foresee that an application will, in some point of the future, need to be split into smaller ones; while regarding the granularity, the unbundled applications can be seen as coarse modules composed by dozens of classes and packages.

The main claim and goal of modularization techniques when applied to mature code is to improve software properties like maintainability and understandability [30]. When unbundling, this is not the case; these desired good properties become means, instead of ends of the process. The goal is the division itself, in order to attend to market issues imposed by trends of usage and competition to gain market share. Meanwhile, the good properties of modularity may work as enablers to accomplish unbundling.

Despite the importance of unbundling in today's software industry, no studies have been conducted to conceptualize or analyse these challenges. This article is a first step to fill this void. Our main contributions are: to define and analyse the unbundling phenomenon (Sect. 2); to present the main challenges of unbundling, showing examples of this current phenomenon and explaining how it relates to existing software engineering approaches for software modularization (Sect. 3); and to draw perspectives on how to facilitate and better exploit unbundling (Sect. 4).

This article builds upon our original paper [15] and the feedbacks we gathered at MODULARITY'15 [17]. We extend the work [15] as follows: (1) we further discuss challenges related to the user acceptance of unbundled software, discussing the risks for a company's user base; (2) we describe the reasoning over the consequences in the application's infrastructure and surrounding services; (3) we include a concrete case of a mobile client when explaining the granularity challenges; and (4) we extend the literature review.

2   The Unbundling Phenomenon

Recently, many well-known software companies started to divide their mobile applications into smaller ones. This is the case of Foursquare, Dropbox, LinkedIn, Evernote, Facebook and Google. Some of them, like Foursquare, have split into two, continuing with the original one and separating part of its features into a second brand new application (in this case, Swarm); some others unbundled into several applications, for example, LinkedIn originated Pulse, Connected, Job Search, Recruiter, Sales Navigator and Slide Share. IBM also adopted the strategy of dividing their software and services to better adequate to market and regulatory needs [20].

In all these cases, unbundling was essentially about identifying parts of the original software that could be isolated in separated applications. For doing this, these parts must be reengineered in a new software, according to a high-level end user *purpose*. A purpose is a high-level and often subjective end user goal when using the software product, it can be the reason why the user acquired the product (e.g., sharing photos, making todo lists, searching places, etc.), and it can gather a set of requirements or features of it. Ideally, one application should serve one primary purpose, however secondary purposes often start as small features of the application, and then they grow until they are a considerable part of the software, which can now be separated as a self-contained purpose.

Reengineering these parts that serve different purposes comprehends: (1) decoupling them from other parts that will not be in the same application, so they can exist separately; (2) developing missing parts that were removed during refactoring or that are necessary to make the part usable (e.g., changing a user interface code to show only a group of functionalities). In the case of mobile applications, software companies are trying to follow the principle of having one major purpose per application, so the user knows why and how to use it, avoiding numerous, cluttering and confusing features. In this way, application vendors create a strong identity for their products and link them well-defined purposes.

Figure 1 gives an overview of the unbundling process. Let us consider that an original software artifact Θ is a candidate to be unbundled. Θ contains different parts $\Theta = \{a_1, a_2, a_3, \ b_1, b_2, b_3, \ c_1, c_2, c_3\}$ expressed in any unit (e.g., class, method, block, statement). These parts can be associated or intersect each other. Let us also consider that there exists subsets of parts in Θ that implement different high-level purposes, which is a motivation for unbundling Θ into different applications containing these different parts. In the example of Fig. 1, the subsets of parts $\{a_1, a_2, a_3\}$ and $\{b_1, b_2, b_3\}$ are isolated into two new applications Δ_1, Δ_2 because they serve two distinct end user purpose. This isolation implies changing the structure of the part to make it decoupled or even adjusting its behaviour to work in a different context (a_1 is reengineered into a_1' in Fig. 1).

As also illustrated in Fig. 1, it is possible that the new software artifacts share common parts among them and with the original one (c_1, c_2, c_3). This is the case, for example, of parts responsible for the implementation of crosscutting concerns or of essential functionalities of any application derived from the original one, such as authentication, storage, cryptography modules, etc. It is also possible that the new software artifacts demand new parts ($n_1, n_2, n_3, n_4, n_5, n_6$) to implement new functionalities or to adapt the existing ones to the new context.

In Fig. 1, Δ_1 can be the original software without the secondary purpose parts, as it is of the company's interest to continue their original software product in order to keep its associated market share. However, if the result of the Unbundling δ was only Δ_1 without any other new applications, we would call it **Reductive Unbundling**. From this perspective, unbundling can help reducing the original application, removing nearly-unused/dead code without the need to make it usable in another application. The difference between actual dead code elimination [24, 45] and reductive unbundling is that, before the unbundling, the eliminated code could still be executed at run-time in the original application, which does not fit the definition of dead code.

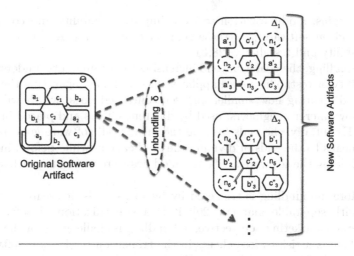

Fig. 1. Unbundling.

In summary, if we think of *unbundling as a process*, we can enumerate the following key activities that it encompasses:

- Identifying distinct end user purposes when using a software candidate to unbundling;
- Identifying the parts of the original software that relates to each identified purpose;
- Extracting and reengineering the parts to be placed in the different new software artifacts;
- Identifying and extracting common parts so they can be reused;
- Occasionally implementing new parts that will complement the existing ones in the new software artifact.

3 Challenges

In this section, we present seven key challenges of unbundling. In order to efficiently handle unbundling, it is essential to: (1) understand its new causes and objectives, which are different from standard modularization; (2) handle an unplanned need for correcting the software structure, so it can better evolve and grow; (3) manage the software parts from a high-level perspective related to an end user purpose, which is a coarser-grained abstraction when compared to existing software engineering abstractions; (4) handle the division itself and the isolation of existing parts of software to work on different applications; and (5) unbundling efficiently by avoiding code replication.

3.1 New Causes and Objectives

The *causes and objectives* of unbundling differentiates from the ones of modularizing, or simply componentizing [42], or aspectualizing [4,29,36] software.

Since its origins, modularization seeks to improve flexibility and comprehensibility of a given software [34]; these goals have been enlarged to also consider maintainability and testability [28, 31].

In unbundling, the goal is beyond increasing maintainability, understandability, flexibility or testability of an application; it aims at separating the software artifact and creating new smaller and self-contained ones, which will then be managed by different engineers, used by different clients and placed in different domains. Essentially, the ends become the means: all software good properties are now means to the ends of dividing the application, while before, modularizing and dividing the software artifact in modules were means to reach such good properties.

Therefore, unbundling is triggered by business goals, it creates new opportunities with separable markets [20]; it is a specialization of software businesses. From a marketing perspective, unbundling is challenging for the company because there is a risk to lose clients in the transition to the new software. On the other hand, if the transition succeeds, it can open a new market and attract more clients.

From a software engineering perspective, modularization is an established good practice and it is driven by developers or stakeholders that are related to the development process. Market competition is often what drives unbundling – maintainability or any other software engineering concepts are less important when faced to the needs of competing to a market share or simply aligning the software to a new trend of use. The way that developers thought about the software modularization can be very different from the division imposed by these high-level purposes. However, this does not prevent that software engineering best practices also become a trigger for unbundling, probably if the way the application is structured starts to interfere with the company's business.

3.2   Unplanned Corrective Evolution

Two essential characteristics present in software to be unbundled are: it is already mature, and the possibility of splitting it into several other software artifacts was not conceived in earlier stages of its development. Therefore, unlike, for example, Software Product Lines (SPL) [9], unbundling is not a long-term strategy that is planned in advance by the company. The fact that the software artifact is already mature and no longer in a conceptual phase implies that unbundling is a corrective action that has to handle code with all its existing good or bad design and implementation choices. Another challenge is that the software is up and running, having numerous clients relying on it, therefore the evolution must not interfere with this relationship; this interference is very likely to happen if a bad release of the unbundled software is launched.

3.3   Coarse-grained Modules

The criteria used when decomposing systems into modules have been studied for decades [34]; from sub-routines to features [22], the unity of modularity is a primary concern in software design and implementation. These units are conceived by stakeholders directly involved with the code (e.g., developers, architects). As the motivation of unbundling is to separate distinct end user purposes residing in one single software artifact, it is necessary to group the set of software parts in the original software product that meets these purposes.

This coarser-grained modularization raises the challenge of having to categorize the existing fine units and associate them to greater goals, which may or may not be explicitly modeled in the software. These purposes are rather high level abstractions that are used to sell the software to a client. In the example of Foursquare and Swarm, the purpose of *checking in places* (i.e., the act of confirming your current location within a place, possibly sharing it with friends) was extracted from the original application (Foursquare) and placed in a new one (Swarm); checking in places gathers functional and non-functional finer features of the software like: geographic location, map visualization, social network sharing, etc.

In Fig. 2, we illustrate, using the case of www.wordpress.com mobile client, that sometimes these different end-user purposes are evidently identifiable and are even reflected in the application's GUI. On the left-hand side of Fig. 2, we see activated the tab of the mobile app that allows the user to manage her website, while on the right-hand side, there is the tab for reading news from other users' websites. From the end-user point of view, these are dissociated functionalities that could therefore be in two different applications. Wordpress has chosen to keep the news feed in the same application, in the opposite way of LinkedIn, which has launched an application (Pulse) that isolates this functionality. A look into the Wordpress mobile application code https://github.com/wordpress-mobile/WordPress-Android reveals that there are 73 classes associated with the Reader tab, scattered through 8 different packages, evidencing the coarser nature of the end-user purpose.

3.4 Dividing and Isolating

Dividing software has always proved challenging; many different software engineering approaches have been proposed to decompose [3,33] code or slicing programs [43].

As explained in the last subsection, unbundling has to handle coarser abstractions, but still actually managing finer ones. The problem is that this is not always intuitive, as classes, components, aspects or features are not perfect modular units, they share dependencies and interactions [5]. Therefore, parts of the original software product may end up present in different purposes, or the functioning of a feature can be affected by the presence or absence of another, which makes the task of dividing and isolating purposes hard.

A great challenge is to make current componentization, aspectualization, feature extraction techniques [1,40] to work seamlessly with an additional level of abstraction: the purpose. These techniques work by analysing the software and evaluating its parts, clustering them in categories according to their structure and semantics as criteria. In unbundling, this division must be enriched with the

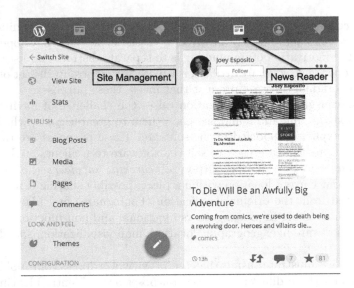

Fig. 2. Wordpress mobile client.

end user purpose—we cannot assume that end user purposes correspond directly to aspects/concerns of software development—driving the division itself.

Considering the steps of the unbundling process, we can state that the essential challenges of it are comprehended in dividing and isolating parts of software: (1) identifying, (2) extracting and (3) reengineering existing features. Identifying is challenging because of the complicated matching between one single high-level and often subjective purpose to concrete fine-grained implementations. Extracting the features imposes the difficulty of not breaking the semantics of the code after removing parts of it, thoroughly analysing the dependencies from statement to component levels. And finally, reengineering the parts is challenging because it depends on the two past activities and because it demands knowledge on the new application environment in which the new parts are now placed.

Besides their own challenging nature, these activities can become more difficult according to how strong is the relationship between modules of the original software artifact that belong to different purposes (i.e., the coupling degree). On the other hand, unbundling may be facilitated if the modularity units belonging to a purpose present a high cohesion (i.e., their functions relate only to the given purpose).

3.5 Code Replication

As dividing and isolating legacy software parts is a hard task, one can be tempted to simply clone and own the original application, but only hiding the secondary purpose features from the end user. However, this leads to lots of replicated and useless code, decreasing the comprehensibility and maintainability of the software artifact, also demanding additional memory space in limited devices.

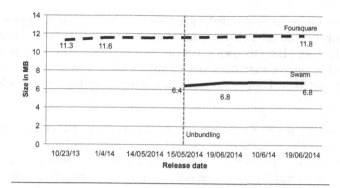

Fig. 3. Foursquare and Swarm size evolution.

Figure 3 shows the evolution over time of Foursquare and Swarm mobile applications with respect to their sizes in MB. After the unbundling, the Foursquare user started to need two applications for doing what he/she used to do with only one application, and about 7 MB more of storage, not considering the additional RAM that Swarm consumes. Although these numbers do not clearly prove that there is code replication, it gives us initial insight that unbundling in an efficient way is challenging. This is also true in other unbundling cases and the problem can get more important as the number of unbundled applications increases.

3.6 Services and Infrastructure

Software is becoming increasingly pervasive; it spreads over different devices and can use several remote services running in the cloud. It is very likely that the end-user purpose to be unbundled is also scattered through these different locations. Therefore, unbundling an application may also require refactoring of currently consumed/provided services and infrastructures. One example is an application's related API. API's must reflect the functionalities provided by an application and therefore, if these functionalities change, the API should be adapted to reflect it. Whether engineers should also split the API into the same number of sub-API's than of sub-apps will depend on several aspects: how interesting (economically) is dividing also the API, if it was designed generically enough to be intuitive to use even after the apps division, if it is also becoming a monolith that needs unbundling, how difficult is it to migrate to a new version and if the old version must be deprecated.

Although unbundling is relatively recent, we can already notice these challenges in current cases. For instance, Dropbox is deprecating its old API to give room to a simpler new one:

"As part of this effort to simplify our platform, we've decided to deprecate the Sync and Datastore APIs over the next 12 months." Dropbox team.

The Foursquare team decided to move forward smoother, deprecating only features from the old API that are not used anymore within the new apps. On another note, they chose to keep the same User Model for both apps, so services like authentication are shared by both applications, even though that a user of Swarm may not be a Foursquare user too, which can have implications to the API's users:

> *"We expect the majority of Swarm users to also have Foursquare installed, but implementing a fallback to the web view-based implementation of auth has always been recommended as well, especially to account now for Swarm users that may not have Foursquare installed."* Foursquare team.

3.7 User Acceptance

Evolving software is challenging for many engineering reasons [26], and it can also be risky if we consider the end-user adoption [37]. Many studies [8,11,18,41] have investigated how software is perceived by users (or even how user's personality influences this perception [46]); essentially, these studies try to model and relate the user's intention to use an application, which goes beyond the applications' easiness of use, it also encompasses expectations about applications' privacy, social influence, cost, performance, etc.

Unbundling must take into account these issues, specially the ones related to user's resistance to changes. An unbundling candidate application has a user base that is already acquainted to the way that the app works, which functionalities it has, and how to use them or where to find them on the GUI. On the one hand, moving these features from one application to another can cause unsatisfied users, who can give negative feedback in the application's reviews/comments page in their different mobile application stores. Critics such as *"I hear the argument why you split the features between this and Swarm, but you're bleeding a fan base"* or *"It used to be better when check-ins were all in a single app"* are numerous at the Foursquare reviews; it happens similarly with the Messenger application that was unbundled from Facebook: *"I never liked the fact that we are forced to download this 2nd app just to chat"*.

On the other hand, an unbundled app can also please more flexible users if it clearly brings new features or eases user experience. In recent interview to a global media company, Stan Chudnovsky—Messenger's head of product—claimed the importance of having unbundled Messenger from Facebook: *"If Messenger were still buried within the main app, video calling would be buried within that, and it just wouldn't ever find the light of day"*. Indeed, many users have written positive feedback in Messenger's reviews page, complimenting the new features brought by the unbundled app, such as *"I just love it it's now updated and added video calls, hd video calls, voice call, voice chat and much more things available in it"*.

Hence, companies need to comprehend and assess the risks involved in splitting their applications from the point of view of the user. Scientifically identifying and studying the correlations between unbundling and the user adoption can be very challenging, as it involves many dependent variables that are hard to be isolated in an empirical study.

4 Perspectives

In the following, we present the perspectives for analysing and leveraging unbundling, describing key topics that can be the starting point for a research roadmap.

Unbundling can take advantage from existing modularization approaches. Although we still need experiences on whether these techniques actually facilitate or not unbundling, our intuition is that code with cohesive and decoupled coarse-grained modularity units is easier to be unbundled. Therefore, a first perspective is that refactoring approaches for modularization of legacy code should be adapted to cope with the new challenges of unbundling, such as maximizing cohesion, minimizing coupling and mapping modularity units to usage purposes in order to facilitate the concrete division of the software.

Ideally, unbundling should be as much automated as possible. As a perspective, we envision automated techniques to analyse and execute unbundling. For example, detecting patterns of application usage (as in [7,14]) in order to classify features that are frequently used or not, features that are always used by a profile of user and others by other profiles and so on. These patterns would serve to make explicit the different purposes that the user has when manipulating the software product, better motivating and justifying a division. As for the automation of the division itself, we envision future research on techniques to extract and isolating features in separated applications [19,23,32], going beyond the simple synthesis of feature models [6,12,39,44]. Similarly there is a large amount of approaches to locate concerns, to mine aspects or to automate the refactoring of applications in a more modular way [2,13,16,25,38].

Another perspective is to systematize the unbundling process. Even though unbundling is not a desired or planned event in software lifetime, it can be exploited as a first step to move towards a product line paradigm or a software ecosystem [10,27]. For this, the original application can be seen as a source of reusable assets that, if efficiently extracted and isolated, could be the basis to construct several different new applications. This systematization is justified when the company desires, as long-term vision, to carry on building a family of applications for a specific domain, sharing commonalities and managing variabilities.

Unbundling can happen in other kinds of software. Particularly, there is the case of big and complex APIs and frameworks, which provide several features for programmers in a specific domain; they sometimes provide much more than the programmer needs or their use can vary according to different purposes. Therefore we can envision unbundling these artifacts to better suit the needs of different end user purposes, reducing the overload of using a given framework or API. Besides numerous artefacts of a project can be considered as part of the unbundling process. Source code, but not only: documentation, bug reports, or mailing lists can also be used for identifying an unbundling criterion. The unbundling can also be applied over multiple artefacts (e.g., source code together with the documentation).

5   Conclusion

We presented in this article the novel phenomenon of software unbundling, showing evidences in the domain of mobile applications. In order to better understand it, we explained the process of unbundling, introducing how an original software artifact is transformed into two or more new ones. We then discussed the problems and challenges of unbundling, also relating it to standard planned modularization. Finally, we discussed perspectives on the support of this new phenomenon. Our main conclusion is that unbundling needs special support and the existing modularization techniques can help in this task; because of its unpredictability, its high-level abstractions and its need for concrete isolation of software parts, unbundling raises new challenges that merit to be further investigated, understood and supported.

As long-term future work, we consider the points explained in the perspectives section: (1) using separation of concerns techniques for unbundling and analysing quantitatively and qualitatively how they perform, (2) explore automated techniques for unbundling, (3) develop systematic methods and processes, (4) leverage unbundling in different kinds of software-intensive systems. In short-term, we want to proceed on analysing unbundling cases deeper, studying the division and distribution of features from the original software products into the new ones.

Acknowledgement. We would like to thank the participants of MODULARITY'15 for the feedbacks, suggestions, and discussions. The research leading to these results has received funding from the European Commission under the Seventh (FP7 - 2007-2013) Framework Programme for Research and Technological Development (HEADS project).

References

1. Acher, M., Cleve, A., Collet, P., Merle, P., Duchien, L., Lahire, P.: Extraction and evolution of architectural variability models in plugin-based systems. Softw. Syst. Model. **13**, 1367–1394 (2013)
2. Adams, B., De Meuter, W., Tromp, H., Hassan, A.E.: Can we refactor conditional compilation into aspects? In: Proceedings of the 8th ACM International Conference on Aspect-Oriented Software Development, AOSD 2009, pp. 243–254. ACM, New York (2009). http://doi.acm.org/10.1145/1509239.1509274. ISBN: 978-1-60558-442-3

3. Agesen, O., Ungar, D.: Sifting out the gold: delivering compact applications from an exploratory object-oriented programming environment. ACM SIGPLAN Not. **29**, 355–370 (1994). ACM

4. Ajila, S.A., Gakhar, A.S., Lung, C.-H.: Aspectualization of code clones - an algorithmic approach. Inf. Syst. Front. **16**, 835–851 (2013)

5. Apel, S., Von Rhein, A., Thüm, T., Kästner, C.: Feature-interaction detection based on feature-based specifications. Comput. Netw. **57**(12), 2399–2409 (2013)

6. Bcan, G., Acher, M., Baudry, B., Nasr, S.: Breathing ontological knowledge into feature model synthesis: an empirical study. Empirical Softw. Eng. **21**, 1794–1841 (2016). http://dx.doi.org/10.1007/s10664-014-9357-1. ISSN: 1382–3256

7. Böhmer, M., Hecht, B., Schöning, J., Krüger, A., Bauer, G.: Falling asleep with angry birds, facebook and kindle: a large scale study on mobile application usage. In: Proceedings of the 13th International Conference on Human Computer Interaction with Mobile Devices and Services, pp. 47–56. ACM (2011)

8. Chen, B., Sivo, S., Seilhamer, R., Sugar, A., Mao, J.: User acceptance of mobile technology: a campus-wide implementation of blackboard's mobilel learn application. J. Educ. Comput. Res. **49**(3), 327–343 (2013)

9. Clements, P., Northrop, L.M.: Software Product Lines: Practices and Patterns. Addison-Wesley Professional, Upper Saddle River (2001). ISBN: 0201703327

10. Costa, G., Silva, F., Santos, R., Werner, C., Oliveira, T.: From applications to a software ecosystem platform: an exploratory study. In: Proceedings of the Fifth International Conference on Management of Emergent Digital EcoSystems, pp. 9–16. ACM (2013)

11. Davis, F.D.: Perceived usefulness, perceived ease of use, and user acceptance of information technology. MIS Q. **13**, 319–340 (1989)

12. Davril, J.-M., Delfosse, E., Hariri, N., Acher, M., Cleland-Huang, J., Heymans, P.: Feature model extraction from large collections of informal product descriptions. In: ESEC/FSE (2013)

13. Eaddy, M., Aho, A.V., Antoniol, G., Guéhéneuc, Y.-G.: Cerberus: Tracing requirements to source code using information retrieval, dynamic analysis, and program analysis. In: Proceedings of the 2008 The 16th IEEE International Conference on Program Comprehension, ICPC 2008, Washington, DC, USA, pp. 53–62. IEEE Computer Society (2008). http://dx.doi.org/10.1109/ICPC.2008.39. ISBN: 978-0-7695-3176-2

14. Falaki, H., Mahajan, R., Kandula, S., Lymberopoulos, D., Govindan, R., Estrin, D.: Diversity in smartphone usage. In: Proceedings of the 8th International Conference on Mobile Systems, Applications, and Services, pp. 179–194. ACM (2010)

15. Ferreira Filho, J.B., Acher, M., Barais, O.: Challenges on software unbundling: growing and letting go. In: 14th International Conference on Modularity 2015, Fort Collins, CO, United States (2015). https://hal.inria.fr/hal-01116694

16. Figueiredo, E., Cacho, N., Sant'Anna, C., Monteiro, M., Kulesza, U., Garcia, A., Soares, S., Ferrari, F., Khan, S., Castor Filho, F., Dantas, F.: Evolving software product lines with aspects: an empirical study on design stability. In: Proceedings of the 30th International Conference on Software Engineering, ICSE 2008, pp. 261–270. ACM, New York (2008). http://doi.acm.org/10.1145/1368088.1368124. ISBN: 978-1-60558-079-1

17. France, R.B., Ghosh, S., Leavens, G.T., (eds.): Proceedings of the 14th International Conference on Modularity, MODULARITY 2015, Fort Collins, CO, USA, ACM, 16–19 March 2015

18. Gallego, M.D., Luna, P., Bueno, S.: User acceptance model of open source software. Comput. Hum. Behav. **24**(5), 2199–2216 (2008)

19. Hariri, N., Castro-Herrera, C., Miràkhorli, M., Cleland-Huang, J., Mobasher, B.: Supporting domain analysis through mining and recommending features from online product listings. IEEE Trans. Softw. Eng. **99**, 1 (2013). ISSN: 0098–5589

20. Humphrey, W.S.: Software unbundling: a personal perspective. IEEE Ann. Hist. Comput. **24**(1), 59–63 (2002)

21. Ickin, S., Wac, K., Fiedler, M., Janowski, L., Hong, J.-H., Dey, A.K.: Factors influencing quality of experience of commonly used mobile applications. IEEE Commun. Mag. **50**(4), 48–56 (2012)

22. Kästner, C., Apel, S., Kuhlemann, M.: Granularity in software product lines. In: Proceedings of the 30th International Conference on Software Engineering, pp. 311–320. ACM (2008)

23. Kästner, C., Dreiling, A., Ostermann, K.: Variability mining: consistent semiautomatic detection of product-line features. IEEE Trans. Softw. Eng. **40**, 67–82 (2014)

24. Knoop, J., Rüthing, O., Steffen, B.: Partial dead code elimination, vol. 29. ACM (1994)

25. Marcus, A., Sergeyev, A., Rajlich, V., Maletic, J.I.: An information retrieval approach to concept location in source code. In: Proceedings of the 11th Working Conference on Reverse Engineering, WCRE 2004, Washington, DC, USA, pp. 214–223. IEEE Computer Society (2004). http://dl.acm.org/citation.cfm?id=1038267. 1039053. ISBN: 0-7695-2243-2

26. Mens, T., Wermelinger, M., Ducasse, S., Demeyer, S., Hirschfeld, R., Jazayeri, M.: Challenges in software evolution. In: Eighth International Workshop on Principles of Software Evolution, pp. 13–22. IEEE (2005)

27. Messerschmitt, D.G., Szyperski, C.: Software Ecosystem: Understanding an Indispensable Technology and Industry, 1st edn. MIT Press Books, Cambridge (2005)

28. Mortensen, M.: Improving software maintainability through aspectualization (2009)

29. Mortensen, M., Ghosh, S., Bieman, J.M.: A test driven approach for aspectualizing legacy software using mock systems. Inf. Softw. Technol. **50**(7), 621–640 (2008)

30. Mortensen, M., Ghosh, S., Bieman, J.M.: Aspect-oriented refactoring of legacy applications: an evaluation. IEEE Trans. Softw. Eng. **38**(1), 118–140 (2012)

31. Munoz, F., Baudry, B., Delamare, R., Le Traon, Y.: Usage and testability of AOP: an empirical study of AspectJ. Inf. Softw. Technol. **55**(2), 252–266 (2013)

32. Nadi, S., Berger, T., Kästner, C., Czarnecki, K.: Where do configuration constraints stem from? an extraction approach and an empirical study. IEEE Trans. Softw. Eng. **41**, 820–841 (2015)

33. Ossher, H., Tarr, P.: Using multidimensional separation of concerns to (re) shape evolving software. Commun. ACM **44**(10), 43–50 (2001)

34. Parnas, D.L.: On the criteria to be used in decomposing systems into modules. Commun. ACM **15**(12), 1053–1058 (1972)

35. Pohl, K.: Requirements Engineering: Fundamentals, Principles, and Techniques. Springer, Heidelberg (2010)

36. Rebêlo, H., Leavens, G.T., Bagherzadeh, M., Rajan, H., Lima, R., Zimmerman, D.M., Cornélio, M., Thüm, T.: Modularizing crosscutting contracts with AspectJML. In: Proceedings of the of the 13th International Conference on Modularity, pp. 21–24. ACM (2014)

37. Sanakulov, N., Karjaluoto, H.: Consumer adoption of mobile technologies: a literature review. Int. J. Mob. Commun. **13**(3), 244–275 (2015)

38. Savage, T., Revelle, M., Poshyvanyk, D.: Flat3: feature location and textual tracing tool. In: Proceedings of the 32nd ACM/IEEE International Conference on Software Engineering - ICSE 2010, vol. 2, pp. 255–258. ACM, New York (2010). http://doi. acm.org/10.1145/1810295.1810345. ISBN: 978-1-60558-719-6
39. She, S., Ryssel, U., Andersen, N., Wasowski, A., Czarnecki, K.: Efficient synthesis of feature models. Inf. Softw. Technol. **56**(9), 1122–1143 (2014). http://dx.doi.org/10.1016/j.infsof.2014.01.012
40. Tip, F., Sweeney, P.F., Laffra, C., Eisma, A., Streeter, D.: Practical extraction techniques for Java. ACM Trans. Program. Lang. Syst. (TOPLAS) **24**(6), 625–666 (2002)
41. Venkatesh, V., Morris, M.G., Davis, G.B., Davis, F.D.: User acceptance of information technology: toward a unified view. MIS Q. **27**, 425–478 (2003)
42. Washizaki, H., Fukazawa, Y.: A technique for automatic component extraction from object-oriented programs by refactoring. Sci. Comput. Program. **56**(1), 99–116 (2005)
43. Weiser, M.: Program slicing. In: Proceedings of the 5th International Conference on Software Engineering, pp. 439–449. IEEE Press (1981)
44. Weston, N., Chitchyan, R., Rashid, A.: A framework for constructing semantically composable feature models from natural language requirements. In: SPLC (2009)
45. Xi, H.: Dead code elimination through dependent types. In: Gupta, G. (ed.) PADL 1999. LNCS, vol. 1551, pp. 228–242. Springer, Heidelberg (1998)
46. Zhou, T., Lu, Y.: The effects of personality traits on user acceptance of mobile commerce. Intl. J. Hum. Comput. Interact. **27**(6), 545–561 (2011)

Dynamic Dispatch for Method Contracts
Through Abstract Predicates

Wojciech Mostowski[1]([⊠]) and Mattias Ulbrich[2]

[1] Centre for Research on Embedded System, Halmstad University, Halmstad, Sweden
wojciech.mostowski@hh.se
[2] Karlsruhe Institute of Technology, Karlsruhe, Germany
ulbrich@kit.edu

Abstract. Dynamic method dispatch is a core feature of object-oriented programming by which the executed implementation for a polymorphic method is only chosen at runtime. In this paper, we present a specification and verification methodology which extends the concept of dynamic dispatch to design-by-contract specifications.

The formal specification language JML has only rudimentary means for polymorphic abstraction in expressions. We promote these to fully flexible specification-only query methods called *model methods* that can, like ordinary methods, be overridden to give specifications a new semantics in subclasses in a transparent and modular fashion. Moreover, we allow them to refer to more than one program state which give us the possibility to fully abstract and encapsulate two-state specification contexts, i.e., history constraints and method postconditions. Finally, we provide an elegant and flexible mechanism to specify restrictions on specifications in subtypes. Thus behavioural subtyping can be enforced, yet it still allows for other specification paradigms.

We provide the semantics for model methods by giving a translation into a first order logic and according proof obligations. We fully implemented this framework in the KeY program verifier and successfully verified relevant examples. We have also implemented an extension to KeY to support permission-based verification of concurrent Java programs. In this context model methods provide a modular specification method to treat code synchronisation through API methods.

1 Introduction

The possibility to override the implementation of a method defined in a supertype is the essential polymorphism feature of the object orientation paradigm. The mechanism which chooses at runtime the implementation to be taken for a method invocation is called *dynamic dispatch*. Also in the context of *design-by-contract* (DbC) [34] and behavioural subtyping [16], different implementations for the same operation can coexist – if they adhere to a common specification. It is most natural that not only the *implementations* but also the *specifications* vary from subtype to subtype, for instance by adding implementation-dependent

© The Author(s) 2016
S. Chiba et al. (Eds.): ToMC I, LNCS 9800, pp. 238–267, 2016.
DOI: 10.1007/978-3-319-46969-0_7

aspects. The dynamic dispatch mechanism should, hence, also be available for the formulation of *formal* specifications in an equally flexible way.

For instance, the precondition of a method may be weakened in a subclass according to the principle of behavioural subtyping. When at some place in the program this method is invoked, the precondition to be established at that point depends, like the chosen implementing code, on the dynamic type of the receiver object. Instead of spelling out the definition of this specification element, it should be possible to refer to it *symbolically*. Only when the dynamic type of the object is known, one also knows the actual contract definition.

Having an explicit symbol to represent a component of a method contract also increases the modularity of the DbC methodology. A method may thus require in its contract that the precondition for a method call on one of its parameters holds. The corresponding method call on the parameter is then valid without the caller needing to know what the condition actually says. This makes specifications more modular and local since the contracts need not concern themselves with implementation details from external classes.

In this paper, we propose a universal solution to make dynamic dispatch for specifications possible by employing multi-state abstract functions/predicates through Java Modelling Language (JML) model methods. Model methods are like usual Java methods subject to dynamic dispatch. Since they resemble normal methods in syntax and semantics, this is a most natural extension to the DbC paradigm and, hence, should be easily adoptable by programmers.

Although (one-state) model methods are already part of the JML syntax definition [11, 28], they lack a clear semantics and are not fully and soundly implemented in any JML-based tool. We provide a precise semantics by giving an explicit logical encoding of overridable model methods in a first-order verification logic. This encoding is used in the implementation of our approach within the KeY program verifier [2, 4]. In KeY Java programs and their JML specifications are translated to proof obligations and then proved correct by the KeY verification engine that provides a high degree of automation, and allows for user guided proof interactions where necessary. The work we present here builds on top of previous work done with KeY to support abstract specifications [45, 47].

Other verification systems have similar support for specification abstraction (see, e.g., [24, 29]), but none of them allow the specifier to refer to two or more program states in one function, i.e., functions refer to one state of the program only. In turn it is, e.g., impossible to define functions that would fully encapsulate a non-trivial relation between the pre and post state of the method. We enrich the concept of abstract predicates by allowing them to refer to more than one program state. This allows us, in particular, to use model methods to abstract and encapsulate specification contexts in which more than one program state is referred to. This is the case for postconditions or history constraints which may refer to the state before and after a method invocation.

In this context our work provides the following contributions. We define overridable model methods with strict semantics that integrate with the JML specification methodology. We provide the ability to relate several program states within one model method. In particular, *two-state* methods for pre and post program states, and *no-state* methods for defining program independent axioms and lemmas to further improve modularisation of specifications. The resulting mechanism is universal enough to be used in any specification artefact (pre- and postconditions, but also, e.g., framing clauses), and, because of the preserved dynamic dispatch principle, provides true data encapsulation on specification level relieving the specifier from enforcing exposure of private data to specifications. Furthermore, our model methods themselves are equipped with contract specifications, this in effect provides a modular lemma mechanism for the underlying abstract predicates. Finally, within the scope of such lemma annotations, we provide a flexible mechanism to specify the relationship between supertype and subtype predicate implementations. Thus one can enforce specification paradigms like behavioural subtyping [32] and others, and gains liberty to integrate such schemes within one program. In the paper we discuss how model methods are integrated into the KeY Dynamic Logic and how the new specifications are translated into proof obligations. The new framework has been fully implemented in KeY and we verified relevant examples with the new implementation. All these examples were either not specifiable and verifiable at all, or extremely difficult to verify in the previously existing framework.

We have also applied model methods to support modular verification of concurrent Java programs specified with permission annotations [22,38]. In particular, we have used model methods to provide fully modular and reusable specifications for Java API synchronisation methods. In this paper we show an example of how we achieve this.

This paper is an extended and revised version of our paper presented at the Modularity conference held in Fort Collins, U.S. in March 2015 [39]. In particular, Sects. 5 and 7 are new in this version, the former discusses how we can specify behavioural subtyping (or other schemes) in our specification approach, the latter discusses two use cases for model methods using substantial examples. Furthermore, at its end, Sect. 4 now discusses in more detail how termination clauses for recursive model methods are checked. Finally, in Sect. 6 we now also briefly discuss the verification performance gains that can be achieved with abstract specifications. The complete paper is organised as follows. Section 2 briefly introduces the Java Modelling Language as implemented in KeY. In Sect. 3 we give a motivating example to demonstrate the use of model methods. The integration of model methods into dynamic logic is described in Sect. 4, while Sect. 5 discusses our mechanism to enforce behavioural subtyping in specifications. Sect. 6 shortly discusses some implementation practicalities and mentions one more small example. Section 7 presents two more uses cases of providing generic API specifications with model methods, Sect. 8 reports on related work, and finally Sect. 9 concludes the paper.

2   The Java Modeling Language and an Extension

2.1   Basic JML

JML is a behavioural interface specification language realising the DbC principle [34] for the Java programming language [11,28]. JML annotations reside in special Java comments starting with the @ sign. The specifications define constraints for the implementation of the declarations. A program is called correct with respect to its formal specification if no run of the program can ever lead to a state which does not fulfil all specification elements.

JML can be used in different verification scenarios: (1) for runtime verification when actually running the code, (2) for static deductive functional verification in which the implementation is formally proved correct with respect to its specification. In this paper we concentrate on the latter application case, although the presented specification concepts can also be integrated into runtime verification methods.

In the concept of DbC, there are essentially two constructions: *object invariants* (annotated to class declarations) and *method contracts* (annotated to method declarations). An object invariant is a predicate which defines when its object is in a valid state. Method contracts formally define the observable behaviour of methods, and are composed of one or more of the following. A **requires** clause (a.k.a. *precondition*) defines a condition under which the method may be invoked and then has the effects of the contract. An **ensures** clause (a.k.a. *postcondition)* defines a condition which holds after the execution of the method. *History constraints* are like postconditions that apply to all methods of a class. An **assignable** clause (a.k.a. *frame*) defines which part of the heap may be written to during the execution of the method. Finally, an **accessible** clause defines the part of the heap the method may read from at most. In our nomenclature we refer to it as a *dependency frame*, we explain the details in Sect. 4.

The expression language of JML is an extension of side-effect-free Java expressions. It adds a handful of specification-only constructs, most notably the first-order-logic quantifiers (**\forall**, **\exists**). Methods may be invoked in JML expressions if the method does not change existing locations on the heap; such methods are called **pure**. In history constraints and postconditions it is possible to refer to two states of program execution: the state *before* the method was invoked and the state *after* the execution. The before-state is accessed with the **\old** operator applied to an expression. Postconditions can also refer to the result of the method call with the **\result** keyword.

JML offers several other specification elements (e.g., to handle exceptions) that are not essential here, hence we omit them.

2.2   JML* – Location Sets and Observer Symbols

JML* is a recent extension of JML to work with location sets and abstract predicates. JML supports the concept of so-called *store-ref expressions* which are syntactic entities corresponding to sets of locations on the heap. Benjamin Weiß proposes in [45, 47] to make sets of location first class citizens in JML, to follow the specification style and verification method of dynamic frames [25]. A new primitive data type **\locset** is introduced to represent sets of locations on the heap. A location is a pair of an object reference together with a non-static field name, a pair of an array reference together with an integer index, or the name of a static field. The following set theoretic constructors are introduced: **\nothing**, $\{\!\{\cdot\}\!\}$, $\cdot\cup\cdot$ to resp. construct the empty set, singletons and set union. The predicate $\cdot\subseteq\cdot$ can be used to express a subset relationship. The expression $\{\!\{\texttt{o.f}\}\!\}\cup\{\!\{\texttt{o.g}\}\!\}$, for instance, denotes the two element set $\{(o,f),(o,g)\}$. Expressions of type **\locset** are typically used in **assignable** or **accessible** clauses.

JML* employs location sets to model relevant segments of the heap. However, if other approaches that model heap structures differently by means of other abstract datatypes (like, e.g., in the flexible framework presented in [26]) are at the base of a specification language, model methods could also be used to abstract from them.

To model abstractions of the program state, it is useful to add declarations to the program which exist only for the sake of specification and verification and which are not visible to the compiler. JML provides two means for this purpose: (1) **ghost** field declarations, which introduce new, specification-only heap locations. Their values can and must be updated explicitly by specification-only statements within the code of the methods, (2) **model** field declarations which do not denote locations, but provide *abbreviations* or *abstractions* of the state. Their value is updated implicitly by changing the value of locations that the model elements *depend* on. Such state abstractions can be in particular used to abstract **assignable** and **accessible** frames mentioned above. In JML* both ghost and model fields can be used for this purpose. While abstracting location sets through ghost variables tends to make reasoning easier than with model fields, the latter provide a cleaner specification style. With model elements, the specifier needs not explicitly update the specification state of the verified programs (which on the other hand helps the verification engine to find proofs). In our examples and explanations to follow we also show how abstractions of locations sets are achieved with model methods and what are the corresponding issues for behavioural subtyping. Finally, despite that they can be used for similar purpose, ghost and model fields are in principle independent concepts as far as the reasoning logic is concerned. Ghost fields have successfully been used for the specification and verification of dynamic frames within the Dafny verifier [29].

Model fields [12] are used in other verification approaches (e.g., [11, 30, 47]) to abstract from implementation details. Apart from being debated about [8], model fields have obvious shortcomings. First, model fields cannot depend on any arguments, like methods do, so they are truly only state *observing* functions rather than state *querying* functions. Second, as realised in JML*, any additional properties (i.e., lemmas) of model fields are specified globally with class invariants. This destroys modularity, in that (a) the properties are not explicitly attached to a particular model field, i.e., properties of all model fields

```
class Cell {                            class Recell extends Cell {
  int val;                                int oval;

  /*@ ensures \result == val; @*/         /*@ ensures val == oval; @*/
  int/*@ pure @*/get(){                   void undo(){val = oval;}
    return val;
  }                                       /*@ ensures oval == \old(val); @*/
                                          void set(int v){
  /*@ ensures val == v; @*/                 oval = val;
  void set(int v){val = v;}                 super.set(v);
}                                         }
                                        }
class Client{
  /*@ ensures c.val == v; @*/
  static void callSet(Cell c, int v){
    c.set(v);
  }
}
```

Fig. 1. `Cell/Recell` example.

are thrown into one invariant "bag", (b) consequently, the properties of each model field often need to be re-proved several times. Because of these reasons, proper specification inheritance is very limited. In this paper we show how the notion of a model field is naturally extended to a model method to remedy all of the mentioned problems. In turn, we provide a fully functional multi-state abstract predicate mechanism for modular specifications that maintain full data encapsulation of the specified program, mitigating any need to expose private data to specifications.

We continue with a motivating example, which should also explain the workings of JML* in a more accurate way. More examples are briefly discussed towards the end of the paper.

3   Motivating Example

We motivate and explain our specification approach by means of a small Java example. Though small, it captures a typical and intricate situation which occurs symptomatically when object-oriented programs are extended by classes overriding methods with additional unforeseen features. Traditionally, such situations would require that the specification of the original code be re-adjusted to accommodate the new behaviour. Using model methods with dynamic dispatch, such re-adjustment is not needed.

The challenge, shown in Fig. 1, has originally been proposed in [43] and has been dealt with in [5] using a higher order separation logic. This first figure shows the program annotated with traditional specification means. Cell objects encapsulate integer values which can be set using a method set and be retrieved using get. The class Recell, which extends Cell, allows an additional one level undo operation which restores the cell value to the state before the most recent call to set. The class Client provides a method callSet which indirectly calls the set method of the Cell argument it receives. This particular indirection may seem artificial, but indirection is a very natural phenomenon in object orientation, e.g., in a situation where this operation is done only conditionally or after some locks have been acquired or in combination with other operations.

The contract of callSet copies the postcondition of Cell.set literally. It does not guarantee the stronger postcondition of Recell.set if the argument is of type Recell. The present contract does not suffice to verify the following test case:

```
Recell rc = new Recell();
rc.set(4);
Client.callSet(rc, 5);
rc.undo();
assert rc.get() == 4;
```

While this program would not fail its assertion, the proof for that would not succeed as the abstraction of callSet by its contract neglects the additional postcondition oval == \old(val) introduced in Recell and only ensures the weaker postcondition of Cell.

This could be amended by introducing case distinctions on the type of the argument in the postcondition of Cell.set. An additional clause c **instanceof** Recell ==> ((Recell)c).oval == \old(c.val) would achieve this. However, it has significant limitations regarding the modularity of the specification: (1) Details on the implementation of Recell are revealed where it is not necessary and should be kept under the hood and, more severely, (2) the implementation of Recell might not yet be known at the time that Cell is implemented or specified. Assume Cell and Client are part of a library and Recell is a user-written extension. How can the library account for all potential extensions?

This is precisely where abstract predicates in the form of model methods can be used to solve the issue. In Fig. 2, the example has been reformulated using a model method setPost (lines 4–6) formalising the postcondition of the method set (used in line 15). The model method has a body which defines its value. In this case, it returns true if and only if its argument x is equal to the value stored in field val. Looking at class Cell alone, no semantic change has been done.

Things change when the class Recell is again added to the scenario. In Recell, the model method setPost is overridden and adds a condition to the result obtained by Cell.setPost. By redefining the predicate locally for all instances of class Recell, the semantics of the contract Cell.set has now also changed, although syntactically it is the same. As the contract refers to the post-condition only *symbolically*, its semantics is left open and can be redefined by an implementing class. Furthermore, setPost makes use of its **two-state** declaration in class Recell as the definition relates values from two execution

```
    class Cell {                              class Recell extends Cell {
2     int val;                                  int oval;

4     /*@ ensures \result ==> get()==x;        /*@ model two_state
      @ model two_state                        boolean setPost(int x) {
6     boolean setPost(int x) {                   return super.setPost(x) &&
        return val == x;                          ↪ oval == \old(get());
8     } @*/                                    } @*/

10    /*@ ensures \result == val; @*/          /*@ ensures get() == \old(oval); @*/
      int /*@ pure @*/ get() {                 void undo() { val = oval; }
12      return val;
      }                                        void set(int x) {
14                                               oval = get();
      /*@ ensures setPost(v); @*/              super.set(x);
16    void set(int v) { val = v; }             }

    }                                        }
```

Fig. 2. Cell/Recell example annotated with model methods.

states, namely `\old(get())` and `oval`. The two states that this definition refers to are the pre- and post-state of the method `set`.

The redefinition of `setPost` in `Recell` cannot be arbitrary, however. The model method has got a contract (line 4) saying that whenever its result is true, the condition `val == x` needs to hold. All overriding implementations need to obey that contract, but may add to it. This ensures behavioural subtyping.

The above example test case can be proved correct if the model method invocation `c.setPost(v)` is used as postcondition for `Client.callSet` abstracting away from the actual definition of the postcondition.

Figure 3 shows the scenario including the frame conditions where the frame has also been abstracted by a single state model method `footprint()`. Furthermore, the extended version has another model method `setPre` used to abstract the concrete precondition of `set`. In the classes `Cell` and `Recell` this method always returns true. In a new subclass `IncreaseCell`, it returns true only if the argument `v` is greater than the cell's value `val`. The precondition is only satisfied if the value to be set is strictly increased. According to Liskov's behavioural subtyping paradigm [16,21,32], this strengthening of the precondition in a subclass would not be admitted. Using model methods, however, one can specify such strengthened preconditions without violating the principle since both methods describe the situation locally for their respective enclosing class. The method contract in Line 4 in Fig. 2 says what the postcondition `setPost` must at least imply, it can thus not be weakened arbitrarily. No contract has been set up for `setPre` such that no restriction exists for the implementation of `setPre` in subclasses. Model method specifications allow the specifier to choose flexibly how the implementations of different classes relate to each other – depending on the need of the verification scenario.

Method frames are also subject to behavioural subtyping. The `footprint()` model method is declared and defined once in the superclass `Cell` to contain all

```
class Cell {                          class Recell extends Cell {
  int val;                              int oval;

  /*@ accessible \nothing;              /*@ model two_state
    @ ensures \result ⊆ this.*;         boolean setPost(int x) {
    model \locset footprint() {           return super.setPost(x) &&
      return this.*; } @*/                      ↪oval==\old(get());
                                        } @*/
  /*@ accessible footprint();
    @ ensures \result ==> get()==x;     /*@ ensures get()==\old(oval);
    @ model two_state                     @ ensures oval == \old(oval);
    boolean setPost(int x) {             @ assignable footprint(); @*/
      return get()==x; } @*/           void undo() { val = oval; }


  /*@ accessible footprint();          void set(int x) {
    @ model                              oval = get();
    boolean setPre(int x) {              super.set(x);
      return true; } @*/               }
                                      }
  /*@ accessible footprint();
    @ ensures \result == val; @*/
  int /*@ pure @*/ get() { return val;}  class IncreaseCell extends Cell{
                                         /*@ model
  /*@ requires setPre(v);                boolean setPre(int v) {
    @ ensures setPost(v);                  return v > val; } @*/
    @ assignable footprint(); @*/      }
  void set(int v) { val = v; }
}
```

Fig. 3. Extended Cell/Recell example annotated with footprint specifications.

locations of the Cell object. In the context of the Cell class alone the postcondition we have specified for footprint() may seem obvious and redundant. However, it limits the shape of the footprint for the sub-classes with an upper bound, and this particular postcondition enforces frame related behavioural subtyping on the methods that refer to this model method in their assignable clauses. Namely, the footprint of the sub-classing objects can only shrink or stay the same, but it cannot grow beyond the extension of the super class. In this example, the (syntactical) upper bound of **this.*** covers the footprints of all classes in Fig. 3, however, as with other specifications, the subtyping requirement for frames can be limiting. We elaborate on this in Sect. 5, where we discuss how the user can specify the relationship between of supertype and subtype implementations of model methods with certain flexibility. If strict behavioural subtyping is required (according to [32]), it can be achieved, but it is not mandatory in our framework.

4   Translation into Java Dynamic Logic

To verify a Java program, we translate the program and its specification into proof obligations in Java Dynamic Logic (JavaDL from now on), the logic of the KeY theorem prover [2]. JavaDL is a hierarchically typed first order logic in which the type system contains the reference types of the Java language (java.lang.Object and its subtypes) together with the types Int^1, *Bool*, *Heap*, *LocSet* and *Field*. Every type is subtype of the top type *Any*.

We write $f : T_1 \times \ldots \times T_n \rightarrow T$ to denote a function symbol mapping n elements of types $T_1, \ldots, T_n$ to an element of type T. We write $s : T$ if s is constant symbol or a logical variable symbol. For an n-ary predicate symbol p, we write $p : T_1 \times \ldots \times T_n$ to denote that it represents a relation on these types. JavaDL uses the standard first-order operators $\neg, \rightarrow, \wedge, \vee, \forall, \exists$, and $\leftrightarrow$ for, respectively, negation, implication, conjunction, disjunction, universal and existential quantification, and equivalence.

Besides the standard first-order operators, JavaDL provides, for every type T, the membership predicate symbols $\cdot \sqsubseteq T : Any \rightarrow Bool$ and $\cdot \sqsubseteq_! T : Any \rightarrow Bool$. The formula $t \sqsubseteq T$ is true if the value of the expression t is of type T or of one of its subtypes; the formula $t \sqsubseteq_! T$ is true if the value of t is of type T but not of any strict subtype of T. Thus, $t \sqsubseteq T$ in JavaDL is closely related to the expression t **instanceof** T in Java and $t \sqsubseteq_! T$ to t.getClass() == T.**class**.

JavaDL is a dynamic logic [20] in which Java program code can be used to construct formulas. For a Java code fragment π and a formula φ, the composition $[\pi]\varphi$ is again a formula which holds in a state iff φ holds in the corresponding end state after the execution of π (if it exists)[2]. The substitution of a term s for a (program) variable x in a term t is denoted by $\{x := s\}t$ in which the type of expression s must be a subtype of the type of x.

In JavaDL, the Java heap memory is modelled using the type *Heap* implementing the *theory of arrays* [33]. The elements of *Heap* are the possible memory states of the program. Two heap objects are relevant for the evaluation of JML expressions: The symbol $h : Heap$ holds the current heap state, i.e., the memory at the current execution point, and variable $h_0 : Heap$ refers to the *base heap* of the current method frame, i.e., to the memory in the pre-state of the method call. We assume heaps to be two-dimensional arrays with one index of type *Object* and the other of type *Field* capturing all fields appearing in the program. Every declaration of a member (field, (model) method) m in class C gives rise to a function symbol named C::m; in case of a field f this is C::f : *Field*. In case of a (model) method m, a function symbol C::m is introduced which takes the heap as explicit argument. We call such a symbol *observer function symbol* since it gives a value which depends on the heap context, but without itself residing in a location on the heap.

Reading from a location on the heap is done using a family of function symbols $select_T : Heap \times Object \times Field \rightarrow T$ for every type T. Two additional variables *self* and *result* exist for the translation of the **this** reference and the result value of the method. Their types depend on the proof obligation context.

---

[1] All numeric primitive Java types **int**, **long**, ... are mapped to *Int*. We do not support floating point types.

[2] $[\pi]\varphi$ is thus semantically equivalent to $wlp(\pi, \varphi)$ of the weakest precondition calculus [17].

JML E	JavaDL $\widehat{E}$
`this`, `\result`	*self*, *result*
`\old`(E)	$\{h := h_0\}\widehat{E}$
E.field$_{C,T}$	$select_T(h, \widehat{E}, \text{C::field})$
E.query$_{C,T}(F_1, \ldots, F_n)$	$\text{C::query}(h, \widehat{E}, \widehat{F_1}, \ldots, \widehat{F_n})$
E.twostate$_{C,T}(F_1, \ldots, F_n)$	$\text{C::twostate}(h, h_0, \widehat{E}, \widehat{F_1}, \ldots, \widehat{F_n})$

Fig. 4. Translation of JML expressions into JavaDL, name$_{C,T}$ refers to the entity of type T introduced in class C, query$_{C,T}$ is a one-state, twostate$_{C,T}$ a two-state model method.

Figure 4 shows a synopsis of the translation of the most important JML expressions E to their respective counterpart $\widehat{E}$ in JavaDL.

4.1 Model Methods

In JML, expressions can also refer to regular or model methods as long as they are declared pure. Unlike fields that declare locations on the heap, methods do not reside in locations on the heap but compute a value which *depends* on the values of locations on the heap. Model methods are always automatically considered *strictly* pure since they are meant to observe the heap without changing it. "Strictly" means that not even object creation is allowed that is normally considered pure behaviour. The reason for also excluding object creation is the non-determinism it would introduce. If a JML model method and its contract are defined according to the following general schema (all clauses in [...] are optional)

```
class C {
 /*@ [private] behavior
 @    [requires pre;]
 @    [ensures post;]
 @    [accessible acc, [acc'];]
 @    [measured_by mby;]
 @ [two_state] model R m(T₁ p₁, ..., Tₙ pₙ) { return exp; }
 @*/
}
```

then the function symbol C::m : $Heap \times Heap \times C \times T_1 \times \ldots \times T_n \to R$ is introduced to represent the model method in JavaDL. The symbol takes the current heap, the base heap, the receiver object and the method parameters as arguments. The second heap argument is used only if the method is annotated with the modifier **two_state**. The second argument to the **accessible** clause is also only relevant if **two_state** is specified; we come back to the declaration of the clause shortly in Sect. 4.2. For model methods declared without the **two_state** modifier, the second quantification over h_0 and the second heap argument to

C::m must be dropped in the formulas in this section. The semantics of the symbol is coupled to the expression in the **return** statement by the following definition axiom.

$$\forall h, h_0 : Heap, self : C, p_1 : T_1, \ldots, p_n : T_n;$$

$$(self \sqsubseteq_! C \wedge \widehat{pre} \rightarrow \mathsf{C::m}(h, h_0, self, p_1, \ldots, p_n) = \widehat{exp}). \quad (1)$$

The function symbol C::m is determined by the class (or interface) C in which the method m has been first declared. All method definitions overriding that initial declaration refer to the same function symbol (and not to a new symbol). By constraining the same function, they realise the dynamic dispatch of model methods. That is, the function symbol is always the same, while its meaning implied by the exact type of *self* changes. For any subclass C' of C, another axiom for C::m is added. If C' chooses not to override m, an axiom is added as if the definition with the body of the superclass-method had been copied. The guard $self \sqsubseteq_! C$ (respectively, $self \sqsubseteq_! C'$ in the axiom for C') ensures that the definition only applies if the receiver object *self* is *exactly* of the defining type. These typing guards make sure that (possibly contradicting) definitions of the function C::m constrain different parts of its domain. Finally, even though the axiom is constrained to *exact* instances of a class C, for all subclasses of C the axiom is repeated, either by looking up the model method definition freshly introduced in a subclass, or by copying the definition from the superclass when the model method is not overridden.

The axiom is also guarded by the precondition $\widehat{pre}$ of the contract. It is not strictly necessary to restrict the domain in which C::m can be applied but we decided that it is better to allow a specifier to say under which conditions a model method is defined. Also to deal with welldefinedness and wellfoundedness (see Sect. 4.3), it is important to be able to restrict the definitions to arguments for which they make sense.

Our model method body (see above) consists only of a single side-effect-free **return** statement and definition (1) can make use of its expression directly. To extend the framework to methods with non-trivial method bodies, the above axiom would need to involve a dynamic logic operator and read (for a one-state model method)

$$\forall h : Heap, self : C, p_1 : T_1, \ldots, p_n : T_n; (self \sqsubseteq_! C \wedge \widehat{pre} \rightarrow$$

$$\big[\mathtt{result} = \mathtt{self.m}(p_1, ..., p_n);\big] (\mathsf{C::m}(h, self, p_1, \ldots, p_n) = result)),$$

ensuring that the value of the function symbol is the same as the result value of the method call. This formula points out a crucial advantage of dynamic logic in comparison to other program logics like Hoare logic: dynamic logic is closed under all its operators which allows us to state the quantified program formula directly in JavaDL. That is, the program modality is not required to be a top level operator, it appears as a sub-formula under the quantifier. In Hoare calculus this would require using meta-constructs over the program correctness triplet.

Besides its method body, a model method may also have a functional contract (in particular a postcondition). Unlike the body which *defines* the value of the function symbol, the contract *describes a property* of the symbol and is not an axiom, but a theorem. To establish the correctness of the contract theorem, it suffices to prove that the definition makes the postcondition true, i.e., that

$$\forall h, h_0 : Heap, self : C, p_1 : T_1, \ldots, p_n : T_n;$$
$$(self \sqsubseteq_! C \wedge \widehat{pre} \rightarrow \{result := \mathsf{C}::\mathsf{m}(h, h_0, c, p_1, \ldots, p_n)\}\widehat{post}). \quad (2)$$

follows from axiom (1).[3]

If (2) is shown for every class C' extending C (with a corresponding type guard), the statement is shown for all conceivable instances of C. Therefore, when using the proved contract as additional assumption, it is safe to omit the type guard $self \sqsubseteq_! C$ from (2). This approach is still modular, however, the verification of C happens independently of that of its subclasses. At the time of verification, one can even be oblivious to the existence of subtypes. If the contract is annotated with the Java modifier **private**,[4] it applies to class C only and is not to be inherited to subclasses. Hence, the proof obligation and theorem are concerned only with exact instances of the class.

The two-state model method `setPost` from the motivating example in Fig. 2 is translated into a function symbol Cell::setPost : $Heap \times Heap \times Cell \times Int \rightarrow Bool$ which is constrained as follows:

$$\forall h, h_0 : Heap, c : Cell, v : Int;$$
$$(c \sqsubseteq_! Cell \rightarrow \qquad\qquad\qquad\qquad\qquad\qquad (3)$$
$$(\mathsf{Cell}::\mathsf{setPost}(h, h_0, c, v) \leftrightarrow \mathsf{Cell}::\mathsf{get}(h, c) = v))$$
$$\wedge\ (c \sqsubseteq_! Recell \rightarrow$$
$$(\mathsf{Cell}::\mathsf{setPost}(h, h_0, c, v) \leftrightarrow (\mathsf{Cell}::\mathsf{get}(h, c) = v\ \wedge \qquad (4)$$
$$select_{Int}(h, c, \mathsf{Recell}::\mathsf{oval}) = \mathsf{Cell}::\mathsf{get}(h_0, c))))$$
$$\wedge\ (\mathsf{Cell}::\mathsf{setPost}(h, h_0, c, v) \rightarrow \mathsf{Cell}::\mathsf{get}(h, c) = v) \qquad (5)$$

True is taken as precondition for `setPost` as none has been explicitly specified. Constraints (3) and (4) are model method definitions according to (1); (5) is the contract theorem after (2). It is obvious that both implementations in `Cell` and `Recell` imply this contract.

---

[3] One also has to show that the method's framing condition specified with the **assignable** clause holds. Recall that model methods are assumed to be strictly pure, so it would be required to additionally prove that no locations on either of the two heaps h and h_0 are changed or created. This is trivial to show when we only allow single side-effect-free **return** statements for model method bodies, so we omit this here for clarity. However, our implementation does include this check in the anticipation of also accepting model methods with non-trivial bodies. In Sect. 5 we explain more about **assignable** frame conditions for regular Java methods in the context of behavioural subtyping.

[4] The modifier is applied to the *contract*, not the model method declaration itself.

4.2   Framing

For the sake of a modular proof, the user of an observer symbol should not have access to its definition (i.e., method body). It may be wise to hide it from the user (for encapsulation) or its full definition may even not be known in a modular context in which additional classes may be added later. In order to reason about observers without access to their definitions, it is crucial that one is able to deduce that an observer does not change if only heap locations that it does not depend on have been modified.

An observer function modelling a model method takes heap argument(s). However, its valuation depends not on the entire heap(s) but only on a set of locations on that heap(s). If it can be established that this location set is interpreted equally in two heaps, the model method must result in the same value in both states.

To this end, we make use of the **accessible** clause[5] that a model method may declare. In it, a set of locations acc can be specified describing the locations upon which the evaluation of a method can depend at $most$: if all memory locations in $\widehat{acc}$ have the same value in both heaps, then the values returned by the model method must be the same. In JavaDL, every location is a pair of an object and a field. This subsumes array references and static field references: in case of arrays the field part is obtained from the Int value representing the index into the array, for static field references a fixed dummy object reference is used.

Such knowledge is essential for modular verification and data encapsulation: at verification time, the implementation of a (model) method may not be known (a situation very common in programming against interfaces), but restrictions of the set of accessible locations may be part of the contract. Knowing that an evaluation does not depend on recent changes on the heap lifts both specifications and proofs to a higher level of abstraction, i.e., the equality of expressions can be established without knowing their exact definitions.

The fact that two heaps h_1, h_2 evaluate the locations in $\widehat{acc}$ equally is formally expressed by the formula $same(h_1, h_2, \widehat{acc})$ defined by

$$same(h_1, h_2, \widehat{acc}) := \forall o : Object, f : Field;$$
$$(\{(o, f)\} \subseteq \{h := h_1\}\widehat{acc}) \rightarrow select_{Any}(h_1, o, f) = select_{Any}(h_2, o, f).$$

This yields the following conditional equality for model methods (in which $\widehat{pre}_i$ and $\widehat{acc}_i$ abbreviate $\{h := h_i\}\widehat{pre}$ and $\{h := h_i\}\widehat{acc}$, respectively):

$$\forall h_1, h_2, h_1', h_2' : Heap, self : C, p_1 : T_1, \ldots, p_n : T_n;$$
$$(self \sqsubseteq_! C \wedge \widehat{pre}_1 \wedge \widehat{pre}_2 \wedge$$
$$same(h_1, h_2, \widehat{acc}_1) \wedge same(h_1', h_2', \widehat{acc}_1') \rightarrow$$
$$\mathsf{C::m}(h_1, h_1', self, p_1, \ldots, p_n) = \mathsf{C::m}(h_2, h_2', self, p_1, \ldots, p_n)). \quad (6)$$

---

[5] We also call it the *dependability* location set, while other approaches may have still different name for it, e.g., *influence* set in [31] that essentially serves the same purpose of providing the read frame of a method.

The evaluations of the query symbol must be shown equal under the conditions that the (1) two pre-state heaps h_1 and h_2 satisfy $\widehat{pre}$, (2) they evaluate equivalently on the set $\widehat{acc}$, and (3) two post-state heaps h_1' and h_2' also evaluate equivalently on $\widehat{acc}'$. [6] Like in the case of the functional method contract in (2), an additional type guard $self \sqsubseteq_! C$ may be used when proving the *dependency contract* for class C. The stronger version without the type guard may be used when adding (6) as an assumption in other proofs.

The one-state method `get` in Fig. 3 has **accessible** clause **this** `.footprint()`, its concrete one-state instance of (6) therefore has only one pair of heap variables and reads (after simplification):

$$\forall h_1, h_2 : Heap, c : Cell;\, (same(h_1, h_2, \mathsf{Cell::footprint(heap, c)}) \rightarrow$$
$$\mathsf{Cell::get}(h_1, c) = \mathsf{Cell::get}(h_2, c)). \quad (7)$$

For *exact* instances of *Cell*, the footprint is defined as the set containing all object fields (**this.***), with `val` being the only field the *same* predicate in (7) is thus equivalent to $select_{Any}(h_1, c, \mathsf{Cell::val}) = select_{Any}(h_2, c, \mathsf{Cell::val})$ in that case.

4.3 Termination

Showing termination for programs is optional, considering the partial correctness problem alone can be challenging enough. For the definition of model methods, however, it is a central point that must not be omitted. A model method definition gives rise to a universally quantified axiom claiming that the function has certain properties even if it may be unsatisfiable. Consider for instance the problematic declaration

```
class X { /*@ model int bad() { return this.bad() + 1; } @*/ }
```

for which the model method would be translated into the axiom

$$\forall h : Heap, self : X;\, (self \sqsubseteq_! X \rightarrow \mathsf{X::bad}(h, self) = \mathsf{X::bad}(h, self) + 1),$$

which is obviously inconsistent. Consistency can be guaranteed if termination (or *wellfoundedness*) of all recursive method references is checked. Here, the **measured_by** clauses are employed to avoid such unsatisfiable recursive definitions. We require that all definitions are primitive recursive. The variant *mby* specifies for each method a termination measurement which must be decreased in all referenced (model) method invocations in *exp*. To this end, an additional proof obligation per model method is generated to ensure this. Assuming that the variant of a model method referenced in *exp* is *mby'*, it has to be shown that *mby'* is a strict non-negative predecessor of *mby*, i.e., $0 \le mby' < mby$.

---

[6] Note that there are two separate accessible sets, $\widehat{acc}$ for the pre-state heap and $\widehat{acc}'$ for the post-state heap, as these can be specified separately according to the schema in Sect. 4.1. If only the post-state heap is referenced in the model method definition, then only one accessible clause *acc* is specified with the other one assumed empty (like for model method `setPost` in Fig. 3).

In practice, one may also encounter mutually recursive definitions of model methods. In this case simple integer expressions as termination clauses are in general not sufficient. For that reason, we additionally allow tuples of integer expressions with a standard lexicographic order to serve as termination clauses and the above mechanism is modified accordingly to check the lexicographic ordering of the expressions instead. Furthermore, to weaken the resulting proof obligations, we use the welldefinedness checking technique described in [14] exploiting the logical structure of the expression.

5 Support for Behavioural Subtyping

Behavioural subtyping is a built-in feature of JML: Reasoning modularly in the face of extensible class hierarchies is impossible if the substitution principle does not apply. In terms of contracts, this principle means that every (non-private) method contract introduced in a class must be obeyed by all extending subclasses as well.

Additional contracts may be specified in subclasses giving new use cases for a method in this subclass. Hence, by adding new contracts, one can weaken the overall precondition or strengthen the postcondition. It is, however, not possible to make the precondition stronger or the postcondition weaker. Frame conditions specified through the **assignable** clauses are technically part of the postcondition, as they are checked with the following formula attached to a postcondition:

$$\forall o : Object, f : Field; (\{(o, f)\} \subseteq \widehat{frame} \lor select_{Any}(h, o, f) = select_{Any}(h', o, f)),$$

where $\widehat{frame}$ is translation of the clause **assignable** frame; of the method under inspection and h with h' are the method's pre-state and post-state heaps, respectively. As a postcondition, the frame condition cannot be weakened either meaning that the frame cannot *grow* in subclasses.

Programmers employ inheritance not only to implement behavioural subtyping [35], but also for purposes like, e.g., code reuse or specialisation. Hence, a more flexible way to deal with the inheritance of specification clauses is desired which allows more liberal notions of inheritance. In particular, in the context of framing subclasses are likely to extend the footprint of the superclass to provide additional functionality, rather than shrinking it. For example, in our `Recell` class in Fig. 3 (page 9) a new field `oval` is added.

By using model methods one is not bound to behavioural subtyping in the same rigorous fashion as with pure JML. In addition to the possibility to name specification artefacts (possibly without knowing their meaning), nothing is a priori said about the relationship of an abstract predicate definition in one class and its redefinition in a subclass. These may, in general, be unrelated, i.e., without logical consequence relationship in either way.

In this unrestricted fashion, model methods would be too arbitrary, and in most practical cases one wants to establish a formal relationship between different realisations of the same predicate. To this end, we introduced new keywords with which consequences can be expressed concisely.

The special postcondition **\covariant** can be used to specify that any reimplementation a model method must at least guarantee what is guaranteed in this implementation. For example, the method postCondition specified as

```
/*@ model_behaviour
      ensures \covariant;
      model boolean postCondition() { return R; } @*/
```

requires all redefinitions to imply R, for instance by returning R in conjunction with more information. The identifier **\covariant** is an abbreviation for the expression **\result ==>** R. Correspondingly, a method can be specified to be **\contravariant** by which the condition R **==> \result** is abbreviated. For location sets model methods expressing frames the two keywords express subset relation instead of implication, so, e.g., **\covariant** is an abbreviation for **\result** $\subseteq R$.

With these new annotations, it is possible to stipulate behavioural subtyping. A generic abstract method specification using model methods and behavioural subtyping would hence read:

```
/*@ ensures \contravariant;
  @ model abstract boolean preCondition();
  @
  @ ensures \covariant;
  @ model abstract two_state boolean postCondition();
  @
  @ ensures \covariant;
  @ model abstract \locset footprint(); @*/

/*@ normal_behaviour
  @ requires preCondition();
  @ ensures postCondition();
  @ assignable footprint(); @*/
  void method() { ... }
```

Programming languages other than Java have different notions of behavioural subtyping. In the Eiffel [36] programming language, for instance, preconditions are – like postconditions – *co*variant. Using the model method framework, it is perfectly possible to argue and reason about such constructions also within Java and JML. With treating variance by annotations, one is more flexible and can easily choose between different paradigms within the same program. Finally, in [21] several other notions of behavioural subtyping are surveyed with different *grading* in the context of object orientation and class invariants are discussed.

6   Model Methods in Practice

The model methods have been fully implemented in the current official KeY release 2.4. The translation in the actual implementation is more sophisticated

```
/*@ requires \disjoint(footprintUntilLeft(t),t.footprint());
  @ ensures \result ==> t.left==null || leftSubTree(t.left);
  @ ensures \result ==> footprint()==footprintUntilLeft(t) ∪ t.footprint();...
  @ accessible footprintUntilLeft(t);
  @ measured_by height;
  @ model boolean leftSubTree(Treet){
    return t==this || (left!=null && left.leftSubTree(t));
    }@*/
```

Fig. 5. An excerpt of the solution to the Tree challenge from [9].

than in our presentation. In particular, the implementation also accounts for the
wellformedness of heap expressions, possible **null** references, exceptions, object
creation, etc. A lot of the effort has gone into extending the JML* parser to
accept the new syntax. On the level of the prover engine, the previously existing
support for model fields and parameter-less observer symbols was extended to
support model methods. In particular, the KeY data structures were changed
to allow for the observer symbols to take additional heap arguments as well as
formal parameter arguments. Consequently, the generation of the corresponding
proof rules and proof obligations changed accordingly. The only really new thing
in terms of the implementation are the contract rules that allow the use of model
method specifications as lemmas. That is, we had to implement generation of
proof rules representing formula (2) for every model method specified with a
contract rule. The implementation of all the other formulas was an extension
and adoption of existing rules for model fields.

The Cell example that we have used in this paper is part of the KeY distribution, along with other small examples. All of these examples are proven correct
fully automatically by KeY. One particular example that we used as a test bed
when implementing model methods is a binary tree deletion of minimal element
challenge from the VerifyThis 2012 verification competition. Although this challenge does not, e.g., require the use of two-state model methods or in fact even
inheritance, the solution that uses model methods is far more elegant than all
the other solutions we have (unsuccessfully) tried previously. The challenge and
our solution are described in full in [9], here we only present the essence of our
solution.

The competition challenge is about verifying an iterative procedure for
removing the minimal element from a binary search tree with an obvious recursive linked data structure representation. That is, the class Tree declares field
val for the node value, and two fields, left and right, linking the left and
the right subtrees, with **null** denoting the leaves of the tree. The essence of our
solution to the challenge is the leftSubTree(Tree t) model method, which
by recursion checks whether the given tree t is one of the sub-tree nodes reachable through following the left links from the current node. Through specifying
an appropriate method contract for leftSubTree, this method is delegated to
maintain a set of crucial facts about the binary tree structure. For example,
if the tree t is in fact a node somewhere in the path of left links, then we
know that so is t.left (if not null) or that we can partition the current tree

footprint between all the tree nodes before t is reached and the footprint of t itself. These footprints are again defined with model methods. Figure 5 shows an excerpt of the specification for leftSubTree. The reminder of the solution is to maintain the validity of the leftSubTree predicate while the tree is being iterated by the algorithm to find the node to be removed. By the specification of leftSubTree this removal is guaranteed to only change a small part of the tree and keep the overall binary search tree structure intact. Because of the use of several model methods that are recursive and mutually dependent, this challenge is only provable interactively by the current version of KeY, nevertheless, model methods were the enabling factor to solve the challenge at all.

Apart from increased expressiveness, model methods also allow one to optimise the verification effort in terms of the size of the underlying proof, especially in the context of an evolving specification when earlier proof attempts can be reused to prove subsequent versions of the program correct. This is because model methods allow us to reason without looking into definitions, at least up to a certain point. In other words, some part the proof is independent of the specification and consequently can be reused. The actual effort in a repeated proof attempt starts only when the model method definitions are expanded and the proof has to be guided according to these (possibly updated) definitions. Earlier studies [10] showed that the corresponding gains can be as large as halving the proof effort when one compares a situation of applying proof reuse enabled by using abstract specifications (in our case model methods) to a situation when no proof reuse is possible due to fully concrete specifications that require a complete new proof with each new version of the specification.

7 Example Use Cases

In this section we describe two somewhat more elaborate use cases for model methods. The first one is the well known visitor design pattern, the second one sits in the context of permission-based reasoning about concurrent programs, a capability recently added to KeY. In both examples model methods are crucial to provide generic, client independent specifications of library methods that can be later instantiated for a particular case.

7.1 Specifying the Visitor Design Pattern

The visitor design pattern [19] is particularly well suited to be specified and verified using abstract predicates as devised in this paper.

The situation is thus: A library defines a class hierarchy in which a number of classes implement a common interface Component. This interface requires a method accept(Visitor v). The respective subclasses that implement the interface realise this acceptance method by delegating the call to a method specially crafted for this particular subclass within the visitor. By this extra indirection, the visitor pattern thus allows dynamic method dispatch by the type of its argument (and not of the receiver).

```
interface Component {                class CompA extends Component {
/*@ public normal_behaviour           int val;
    requires \invariant_for(v);        void accept(Visitor v) { v.visitA(this);}
    requires v.preVisit(this);        }
    ensures \invariant_for(v);
    ensures v.postVisit(this);        class CompB extends Component {
    assignable v.modVisit(this); @*/   String val;
  void accept(Visitor v);              void accept(Visitor v) { v.visitB(this);}
}                                     }
```

```
interface Visitor {                          /*@ public normal_behaviour
/*@ ensures \contravariant;                   @ requires preVisit(a);
    ensures \result ==> \invariant_for(c);    @ ensures postVisit(a);
    model boolean preVisit(Component c)        @ assignable modVisit(a);
      ↪{return false;}                         @*/
                                             void visitA(CompA a);
    ensures \covariant;
    ensures \result ==> \invariant_for(c);   /*@ public normal_behaviour
    model two_state boolean postVisit         @ requires preVisit(b);
      ↪(Component c) {return true;}           @ ensures postVisit(b);
                                              @ assignable modVisit(b);
    ensures \covariant;                       @*/
    model \locset modVisit(Component c)      void visitB(CompB b);
      ↪{return \everything;}@*/          }
```

Fig. 6. Generic library specifications for the visitor pattern.

```
class LenVisitor implements Visitor {
  int len;

  /*@ model boolean preVisit(Component c) {
        return (len >= 0 && \invariant_for(c)); }
      model boolean postVisit(Component c) {
        return (len >= \old(len) && \invariant_for(c)); }
      model \locset modVisit(Component c) {return this.*;}@*/

  void visitA(CompA a){len += Math.abs(a.val);}
  void visitB(CompB b){len += b.val.length();}
}

//@ requires \invariant_for(a) && \invariant_for(b);
static void test(CompA a, CompB b) {
  LenVisitor lv = new LenVisitor();
  a.accept(lv); b.accept(lv);
  assert lv.len >= 0;
}
```

Fig. 7. Using the visitor pattern.

The use case (the actual visitor implementation) of the pattern is usually not known at the time the library is defined. Moreover, often there is not only one visitor, but an application requires multiple different visitor implementations to perform different (not a-priori known) tasks on the data structure.

It is evident that the component hierarchy and the visitor interface cannot be specified concretely with all use cases in mind. Even if they were known a priori, incorporating all possible visitation purposes into one specification would make that clumsy, unnecessarily large, and non-scalable. That is where model methods can be used to an advantage: The visitor interface and the component type hierarchy can be specified with model methods in contracts to leave the details of the specification open and to be refined in the implementations while the library specification stays agnostic to these implementations.

Figure 6 shows the general specification setup. The interface `Component` is the base type for all components open for visitation. The JML contract of method `accept` uses the model methods `preVisit` and `postVisit` in the pre- and postcondition. Two classes `CompA` and `CompB` implement the interface and inherit the contract for their delegating implementations of the `accept` method. `CompA` wraps an integer value while `CompB` contains a `String` value.

The visitor interface defines model methods `preVisit`, `postVisit` and `modVisit` to abstract away from the precondition, postcondition, and the frame clause of the `visit` methods. The concrete visitation methods use these model methods in their abstract contracts and thus remain ignorant of the purpose of later introduced visitors without loss of precision. To enforce the behavioural subtyping principle for the possible implementations of the visitor interface, the three model methods are equipped with subtyping enforcing contracts as stipulated in Sect. 5. Furthermore, the definitions of these three model methods are made most general in each case to allow for arbitrary subclass modification as far as behavioural subtyping is concerned. That is, the **false** precondition can always be made weaker, while the **true** postcondition and **\everything** frame can always be made stronger.

However, the framework of components and visitor must fit together. There are proof obligations to be discharged showing that the `accept` methods fulfil the interface's contracts. Since they just replicate the visitor's contract as their own, these conditions are easily proved.

As a concrete example use case of the visitor pattern, Fig. 7 shows a visitor which accumulates the lengths of `Components`. The implementation named `LenVisitor` stores the accumulated length in a field named `len`. For `CompA` the absolute value of the integer field is added to `len` and for `CompB` the length of the string is added. In the test case, it is to be proved that the length field of the concrete visitor is always positive.

Note that the specification for the visitor interface and the component types did not have to be changed for the specification of the use case. This is the essence of using abstract predicates to enable modular design and to reduce the specification effort. However, it does not necessarily imply a substantial reduction of the proof effort. As noted at the end of Sect. 6, the use of abstract predicates can support proof reuse, but does not in general mean that proofs can be skipped. In particular, if we were to subclass the `LenVisitor` class in some simple way without modifying either of the model methods or the visit methods, we would still have to reverify the visit methods in the new subclass. The reason is that these methods, remaining syntactically the same, may still call other methods declared in the `LenVisitor` class that can get new implementations in the subclass of `LenVisitor`. This reproving can be avoided by proving contracts not for exact instances a concrete class but for instances of all subclasses as well. Such stronger proof obligations are more difficult to prove, however, since they must not depend on overridable definitions from the declared class. The bottom line is though, that after introducing a new subclass, no superclass has to be ever re-specified or re-proved to be correct.

7.2   Permission-Based Reasoning with Model Methods

Permission-based reasoning is an established method for verifying concurrent programs with the design-by-contract style specifications enriched with *fractional* permission annotations [7]. In the context of concurrent execution, permission annotations protect access to heap locations for each thread, adherence to these annotations is verified locally for each thread and primarily establishes non-interference of threads; programs are guaranteed to be free of data races. Additionally, programs are also verified to satisfy classical DbC functional properties, however, the scope of such properties is limited; heap locations potentially modified by other threads can never be relied upon in the context of the local thread [6].

The main complication in permission-based reasoning are program synchronisation points, e.g., mutual exclusion locks or spawned threads. Permissions are then transferred between one thread and the lock, or between multiple threads. In most approaches synchronisation is generally considered to be a primitive operation of the programming language and the verification logic is equipped to handle the corresponding program constructs. In particular, in Separation Logic like approaches [44] the notion of a resource invariant (or monitor) serves as a primary means to specify the behaviour of (primitive) locks [41]. Using a *would-be* Separation Logic-like JML notation, Fig. 8 shows a simple example of a Java program with **synchronized** block protecting a single variable counter for multiple thread use. The **monitor** keyword specifies the necessary resource invariant $Perm(\mathbf{this}.c, 1)$ – on synchronisation the currently running thread temporarily receives a full (read and write) permission on the counter variable granting the thread the right to change the associated memory location. As stated above, no functional specification can be given for **this**.c outside of the **synchronized** block, in particular in the contract of `increase`, due to the lack of a suitable permission.

The **synchronized** block is a very basic synchronisation method and by itself provides only a mutual exclusion locking. Supporting more synchronisers, e.g., a semaphore for shared read access, requires combining **synchronized** with additional Java code. To this end, the Java API offers a synchronisation

```
public class Counter {
  private int c; //@ monitor Perm(this.c, 1);

  public void increase() { synchronized(this) { this.c++; } }
}
```

Fig. 8. An example resource invariant with a permission annotation.

framework, the java.util.concurrent library [27], that provides a collection of synchronisation mechanisms implemented with more primitive operations, like compare-and-swap or volatile variables. For most of those API methods, resource invariants do not scale directly and need extensions. For example, for a read-write lock the invariant differs depending on the actual lock mode (read or write). Ultimately, the library methods should have generic specifications that the clients can instantiate to achieve a particular data protection for multiple thread access, and model methods provide just the right mechanism to achieve this.

Supporting permission-based reasoning in the KeY system is achieved by operating on two heaps simultaneously in JavaDL [37] – the regular memory heap like before, and an additional permission heap that tracks permissions to the corresponding heap locations. These two heaps are integrated into the logic, but they are also made explicit in JML* specifications to allow the separation of functional properties (actual values on the heap) and non-interference properties (permissions to heap locations). Our definitions from Sect. 4 extend naturally to account for the additional permission heap, it is handled in a similar fashion as the pre- and post-heap to support the **two_state** predicates.

In this context, Fig. 9 shows a modular, reusable specification of a lock, which is then instantiated to protect a shared counter. Interfaces LockSpec and Lock are our library-level specifications, the Counter class is the client. LockSpec is simply a specification template for the lock, and in fact it could have been in its entirety a *model interface*, but technically it could not yet be supported by KeY. In LockSpec four methods are declared that clients should instantiate and the consistent method is defined that ensures the consistency of client provided specifications. The framing of regular and permission heaps is encapsulated with further model methods, however, for clarity the figure shows only one of them (fpPerm).

The state predicate of the lock defines the state of the permissions on the heap for when the lock is engaged and when it is released. The client defines the lock state over just one permission to the val field of the Counter class. The lock state is expressed using a symbolic permission data type [22] denoted in [[...]]. When not engaged, the lock holds the full permission to the val field, when locked the permission is temporarily transferred from the lock object to the currently running thread **\ct**. The status predicate provides an abstraction of the lock state – directly stated read and/or write permissions that the lock grants, here a write permission to the val field. The predicate also serves

```
public interface LockSpec {
  //@ accessible<permissions> fpPerm(); ...; model \locset fpPerm();
  //@ accessible...; model boolean state(boolean locked);
  //@ accessible...; model boolean status(boolean locked);
  //@ accessible...; model two_state boolean lockTr();
  //@ accessible...; model two_state boolean unlockTr();
  /*@ ensures \result;
    accessible...;
    model final two_state boolean consistent() { return
        (\old(state(false)) && \old(status(false)) && lockTr() ==>
          (state(true) && status(true))) &&
        (\old(state(true)) && \old(status(true)) && unlockTr() ==>
          (state(false) && status(false))); } @*/ }

public interface Lock {
  //@ public instance ghost LockSpec spec;

  //@ requires spec.status(false);
  //@ ensures spec.status(true) && spec.lockTr();
  //@ assignable<permissions> spec.fpPerm(); ...
  public void lock();

  //@ requires spec.status(true);
  //@ ensures spec.status(false) && spec.unlockTr();
  //@ assignable<permissions> spec.fpPerm(); ...
  public void unlock();
}

public class Counter implements LockSpec {
  private int val;
  private Lock lock; //@ invariant lock.spec == this && ...;

  /*@ model boolean state(boolean locked) { return \perm(val) ==
        locked ? [[ \ct, lock ]] : [[ lock ]]; } @*/
  /*@ model boolean status(boolean locked) { return locked ?
        \writePerm(\perm(val)) : !\readPerm(\perm(val)); } @*/
  /*@ model two_state boolean lockTr() { return \perm(val) ==
        \transferPermAll(lock, \ct, \old(\perm(val))); } @*/
  /*@ model two_state boolean unlockTr() { return \perm(val) ==
        \returnPerm(\ct, lock, \old(\perm(val))); } @*/

  //@ requires status(false); ensures status(false);
  //@ assignable<permissions> fpPerm(); ...
  public void increase() { lock.lock(); val++; lock.unlock(); }
}
```

Fig. 9. An example of a generic specification of a mutual exclusion lock and the corresponding client instantiation (strongly abbreviated for clarity, full version of the example is available with the development version of the KeY system).

as a *token* that indicates whether the lock is engaged or not. The transfer predicates lockTr and unlockTr define the permission transfers that occur on lock engaging and releasing. They are **two_state** because they describe the relation between the permissions before and after the call to the lock and unlock methods of the lock. The client defines the transfer functions to fully transfer the permission to val between the lock and the current thread. Through its simple postcondition, the consistent predicate ensures that there is consistency between the above methods. Namely, the application of the transfer function lockTr to an unlocked state and status of the lock should result in a locked one, and vice versa. Then, the fpPerm predicate defines the frame of the permission heap that the specification works with – only the permissions to the val field are changed. The specifications of the lock itself merely points to the predicates defined in the LockSpec interface. The binding between the client instantiated lock specification and the lock is provided by the spec ghost field of Lock – the client refers itself as holding the specification. Finally, the top-level specification for the increase method simply states that it should be used only when the lock is not already engaged. The verification of increase establishes that all concurrent accesses to the val field are non-interfering.

Our specification does not enforce the lock to be a mutual exclusion or a shared one, this distinction is only made by the client. Particular API instances of the Lock interface would have such distinction embedded in the implementation, like the ReentrantReadWriteLock that provides two sub-locks for the shared and exclusive access. A fully configurable specification that can be related to particular implementations of the lock, like presented in [3], would require further extensions of our specification shown here. Still, the example we presented here is a typical use case for model methods to provide generic, client independent specifications for the purpose of reasoning about data non-interference.

8   Related Work

Parkinson and Bierman have presented in [43] a separation logic framework for programs with inheritance improving on their earlier paper [42]. One of the declared goals and actual achievements of the paper was to avoid repetition of proofs of a method unless it has been overridden. Our motivating example presented in Sect. 3 has been taken from this publication. The approach put forward in [43] rests on the differentiation of *static* versus *dynamic* specifications. Dynamic specifications correspond in our solution to contracts for model methods, while static specifications are reflected in the definitions of model methods. Another contribution of [43] is the extension of the concept of an abstract predicate to abstract predicate families in their (higher order) specification logic. The publication [5] also uses the example from [43]. The authors present an approach in higher-order logic separation logic, formalised in Coq, that allows even more powerful quantifications than can be achieved with abstract predicate families. Their proofs are interactive. The specification and verification framework for Eiffel function delegates presented by Nordio et al. [40] allows reasoning about programs using function objects by means of fixed abstract specification predicates for pre-/post- and frame-conditions. In comparison, in our approach there are no predefined predicates or place holders for particular specification elements, we simply provide a flexible mechanism to define, overload, and use abstract predicates anywhere in the specification and allow for arbitrary composition of these predicates, and additionally we provide a flexible mechanism to optionally enforce behavioural subtyping. Both approaches, however, allow for the use of two-state predicates.

Cok presents in [13] a survey on using model fields and methods in JML specifications. Overriding of model fields is covered, but they are not used as a means to abstract away from method contracts. The Dafny language and verification system [29] uses functions to define abstraction predicates which correspond to our model methods. Until recently the Dafny language did not support subtyping [1], and it does not support two-state predicates. In [10], the authors abstract from contract components by predicates to decouple deductive reasoning about programs from the applicability check of contracts. This increases the reuse potential of proofs in case of changing specifications and, thus, makes the program verification process more modular. However, subtyping between predicates is not considered. Darvas [14, 15] covers the issue of queries in specifications in a logical setting similar to ours. In particular, welldefinedness and wellfoundedness are treated in depth. We employ techniques from his thesis to conduct termination proofs in our approach. The approach does not distinguish between contracts (postconditions) and definitions (method bodies) and needs a satisfiability check for the specifications. An advantage of our approach is that *satisfiability* of the model method description does not need to be shown as the return statement always gives an explicit witness to the value of the method. Inheritance and two-state predicates are not considered by Darvas.

The first occurrence of calculus rules for dynamic dispatch of regular method invocations in program verification is by Soundarajan [46], the concept has since been introduced into many verification tools for languages with polymorphism.

In the context of concurrent reasoning using permissions we mentioned the mechanism of resource invariants commonly used in Separation Logic based approaches [43]. This encapsulation idea has been later developed towards the notion of concurrent abstract predicates, now used in at least two Separation Logic formalisms [18, 23]. Concurrent abstract predicates provide essentially the same functionality for Separation Logic as model methods in our work, namely they enable data and specification encapsulation and generic library specifications that can be instantiated by clients.

9   Conclusion

We have presented a specification style which uses overridable model methods to abstract away from concrete method specifications and, hence, allows us to refer to them symbolically. Our specifications give rise to proof obligations with dynamic frames as presented in [45, 47]. We go a step further than [45, 47] by enabling fully flexible state queries with parameters and by providing means for two-state specifications and a fully modular lemma mechanism for model methods via contracts. The main contribution of this work is that model methods make the concept of modular method specification more flexible and in some cases the verification performance can be improved. Dynamic method dispatch gives model methods a semantics that depends on the typing context. Behavioural subtyping [16] can canonically be preserved using method contracts, but the approach is more flexible and also allows for contract relationships that do not adhere to behavioural subtyping. In cases where behavioural subtyping or another scheme of specification inheritance should be preserved we provided a flexible mechanism that can enforce that.

Acknowledgements. We are very grateful to Peter H. Schmitt for his constructive suggestions and valuable comments which helped improve this paper and to Jesper Bengtson for pointing out this problem to us and ensuing discussions. The work of Wojciech Mostowski is supported by ERC grant 258405 for the VerCors project and by the Swedish Knowledge Foundation grant for the project AUTO-CAAS. The work of Mattias Ulbrich is supported by the DFG (German Research Foundation) under the Priority Programme SPP1593: Design For Future – Managed Software Evolution.

References

1. Ahmadi, R., Leino, K.R.M., Nummenmaa, J.: Automatic verification of Dafny programs with traits. In: Proceedings of the 17th Workshop on Formal Techniques for Java-Like Programs (FTfJP), pp. 4:1–4:5. ACM (2015)
2. Ahrendt, W., Beckert, B., Bruns, D., Bubel, R., Gladisch, C., Grebing, S., Hähnle, R., Hentschel, M., Herda, M., Klebanov, V., Mostowski, W., Scheben, C., Schmitt, P.H., Ulbrich, M.: The KeY platform for verification and analysis of Java programs. In: Giannakopoulou, D., Kroening, D. (eds.) VSTTE 2014. LNCS, vol. 8471, pp. 55–71. Springer, Heidelberg (2014). doi:10.1007/978-3-319-12154-3_4
3. Amighi, A., Blom, S., Huisman, M., Mostowski, W., Zaharieva-Stojanovski, M.: Formal specifications for Java's synchronisation classes. In: Lafuente, A.L., Tuosto, E. (eds.) 22nd Euromicro International Conference on Parallel, Distributed, and Network-Based Processing, pp. 725–733. IEEE Computer Society (2014)
4. Beckert, B., Hähnle, R., Schmitt, P.H. (eds.): Verification of Object-Oriented Software: The KeY Approach. LNCS, vol. 4334. Springer, Heidelberg (2007). doi:10. 1007/978-3-540-69061-0

5. Bengtson, J., Jensen, J.B., Sieczkowski, F., Birkedal, L.: Verifying object-oriented programs with higher-order separation logic in Coq. In: Eekelen, M., Geuvers, H., Schmaltz, J., Wiedijk, F. (eds.) ITP 2011. LNCS, vol. 6898, pp. 22–38. Springer, Heidelberg (2011). doi:10.1007/978-3-642-22863-6_5
6. Blom, S., Huisman, M., Zaharieva-Stojanovski, M.: History-based verification of functional behaviour of concurrent programs. In: Calinescu, R., Rumpe, B. (eds.) SEFM 2015. LNCS, vol. 9276, pp. 84–98. Springer, Heidelberg (2015). doi:10.1007/978-3-319-22969-0_6
7. Boyland, J.: Checking interference with fractional permissions. In: Cousot, R. (ed.) SAS 2003. LNCS, vol. 2694, pp. 55–72. Springer, Heidelberg (2003). doi:10.1007/3-540-44898-5_4
8. Eisenbach, S., Leavens, G.T., Müller, P., Poetzsch-Heffter, A., Poll, E.: Formal techniques for Java-like programs. In: Buschmann, F., Buchmann, A.P., Cilia, M.A. (eds.) ECOOP 2003. LNCS, vol. 3013, pp. 62–71. Springer, Heidelberg (2004). doi:10.1007/978-3-540-25934-3_7
9. Bruns, D., Mostowski, W., Ulbrich, M.: Implementation-level verification of algorithms with KeY. Int. J. Softw. Tools Technol. Transfer 17, 729–744 (2015)
10. Bubel, R., Hähnle, R., Pelevina, M.: Fully abstract operation contracts. In: Margaria, T., Steffen, B. (eds.) ISoLA 2014. LNCS, vol. 8803, pp. 120–134. Springer, Heidelberg (2014). doi:10.1007/978-3-662-45231-8_9
11. Chalin, P., Kiniry, J.R., Leavens, G.T., Poll, E.: Beyond assertions: advanced specification and verification with JML and ESC/Java2. In: Boer, F.S., Bonsangue, M.M., Graf, S., Roever, W.-P. (eds.) FMCO 2005. LNCS, vol. 4111, pp. 342–363. Springer, Heidelberg (2006). doi:10.1007/11804192_16
12. Cheon, Y., Leavens, G., Sitaraman, M., Edwards, S.: Model variables: cleanly supporting abstraction in design by contract. Softw. Pract. Exp. 35(6), 583–599 (2005)
13. Cok, D.R.: Reasoning with specifications containing method calls and model fields. J. Object Technol. 4, 77–103 (2005)
14. Darvas, Á.: Reasoning About Data Abstraction in Contract Languages. Ph.D. thesis, ETH Zurich (2008)
15. Darvas, Á., Leino, K.R.M.: Practical reasoning about invocations and implementations of pure methods. In: Dwyer, M.B., Lopes, A. (eds.) FASE 2007. LNCS, vol. 4422, pp. 336–351. Springer, Heidelberg (2007). doi:10.1007/978-3-540-71289-3_26
16. Dhara, K.K., Leavens, G.T.: Forcing behavioral subtyping through specification inheritance. In: Proceedings of ICSE, pp. 258–267. IEEE Computer Society (1996)
17. Dijkstra, E.W.: A Discipline of Programming. Prentice Hall, Inc., Englewood Cliffs (1976)
18. Dinsdale-Young, T., Dodds, M., Gardner, P., Parkinson, M.J., Vafeiadis, V.: Concurrent Abstract Predicates. In: D'Hondt, T. (ed.) ECOOP 2010. LNCS, vol. 6183, pp. 504–528. Springer, Heidelberg (2010). doi:10.1007/978-3-642-14107-2_24
19. Gamma, E., Helm, R., Johnson, R.E., Vlissides, J.: Design Patterns, Elements of Reusable Object-Oriented Software. Addison-Wesley, Reading (1999)
20. Harel, D., Kozen, D., Tiuryn, J.: Dynamic Logic. MIT Press, Cambridge (2000)
21. Hatcliff, J., Leavens, G.T., Leino, K.R.M., Müller, P., Parkinson, M.: Behavioral interface specification languages. ACM Comput. Surv. 44(3), 16:1–16:58 (2012)
22. Huisman, M., Mostowski, W.: A symbolic approach to permission accounting for concurrent reasoning. In: 14th International Symposium on Parallel and Distributed Computing (ISPDC 2015), pp. 165–174. IEEE Computer Society (2015)
23. Jacobs, B., Piessens, F.: Expressive modular fine-grained concurrency specification. SIGPLAN Not. 46(1), 271–282 (2011)

24. Jacobs, B., Smans, J., Philippaerts, P., Vogels, F., Penninckx, W., Piessens, F.: VeriFast: a powerful, sound, predictable, fast verifier for C and Java. In: Bobaru, M., Havelund, K., Holzmann, G.J., Joshi, R. (eds.) NFM 2011. LNCS, vol. 6617, pp. 41–55. Springer, Heidelberg (2011). doi:10.1007/978-3-642-20398-5_4
25. Kassios, I.: The dynamic frames theory. Formal Aspects Comput. **23**, 267–288 (2011)
26. Kulczycki, G., Smith, H., Harton, H., Sitaraman, M., Ogden, W.F., Hollingsworth, J.E.: The location linking concept: a basis for verification of code using pointers. In: Joshi, R., Müller, P., Podelski, A. (eds.) VSTTE 2012. LNCS, vol. 7152, pp. 34–49. Springer, Heidelberg (2012). doi:10.1007/978-3-642-27705-4_4
27. Lea, D.: The java.util.concurrent synchronizer framework. Sci. Comput. Program. **58**(3), 293–309 (2005)
28. Leavens, G.T., Poll, E., Clifton, C., Cheon, Y., Ruby, C., Cok, D., Müller, P., Kiniry, J., Chalin, P., Zimmerman, D.M., Dietl, W.: JML Reference Manual (2008)
29. Leino, K.R.M.: Dafny: an automatic program verifier for functional correctness. In: Clarke, E.M., Voronkov, A. (eds.) LPAR 2010. LNCS (LNAI), vol. 6355, pp. 348–370. Springer, Heidelberg (2010). doi:10.1007/978-3-642-17511-4_20
30. Leino, K.R.M., Müller, P.: A verification methodology for model fields. In: Sestoft, P. (ed.) ESOP 2006. LNCS, vol. 3924, pp. 115–130. Springer, Heidelberg (2006). doi:10.1007/11693024_9
31. Leino, K.R.M., Müller, P.: Verification of equivalent-results methods. In: Drossopoulou, S. (ed.) ESOP 2008. LNCS, vol. 4960, pp. 307–321. Springer, Heidelberg (2008). doi:10.1007/978-3-540-78739-6_24
32. Liskov, B., Wing, J.M.: Specifications and their use in defining subtypes. In: Paepcke, A. (ed.) Proceedings of OOPSLA, Washington DC, USA, pp. 16–28. ACM Press (1993)
33. McCarthy, J.: Towards a mathematical science of computation. Inf. Process. **1962**, 21–28 (1963)
34. Meyer, B.: Applying "design by contract". Computer **25**(10), 40–51 (1992)
35. Meyer, B.: The many faces of inheritance: a taxonomy of taxonomy. IEEE Comput. **29**(5), 105–108 (1996)
36. Meyer, B.: Object-oriented Software Construction, 2nd edn. Prentice-Hall, Upper Saddle River (1997)
37. Mostowski, W.: A case study in formal verification using multiple explicit heaps. In: Beyer, D., Boreale, M. (eds.) FMOODS/FORTE -2013. LNCS, vol. 7892, pp. 20–34. Springer, Heidelberg (2013). doi:10.1007/978-3-642-38592-6_3
38. Mostowski, W.: Dynamic frames based verification method for concurrent Java programs. In: Gurfinkel, A., Seshia, S.A. (eds.) VSTTE 2015. LNCS, vol. 9593, pp. 124–141. Springer, Heidelberg (2016). doi:10.1007/978-3-319-29613-5_8
39. Mostowski, W., Ulbrich, M.: Dynamic dispatch for method contracts through abstract predicates. In: 15th International Conference on MODULARITY (MODULARITY 2015), pp. 109–116. ACM (2015)
40. Nordio, M., Calcagno, C., Meyer, B., Müller, P., Tschannen, J.: Reasoning about function objects. In: Vitek, J. (ed.) TOOLS 2010. LNCS, vol. 6141, pp. 79–96. Springer, Heidelberg (2010). doi:10.1007/978-3-642-13953-6_5
41. O'Hearn, P.W.: Resources, concurrency and local reasoning. Theor. Comput. Sci. **375**(1–3), 271–307 (2007)
42. Parkinson, M.J., Bierman, G.M.: Separation logic and abstraction. In: Proceedings of POPL (2005)
43. Parkinson, M.J., Bierman, G.M.: Separation logic, abstraction and inheritance. In: Proceedings of POPL (2008)

44. Parkinson, M.J., Summers, A.J.: The relationship between separation logic and implicit dynamic frames. In: Barthe, G. (ed.) ESOP 2011. LNCS, vol. 6602, pp. 439–458. Springer, Heidelberg (2011). doi:10.1007/978-3-642-19718-5_23
45. Schmitt, P.H., Ulbrich, M., Weiß, B.: Dynamic frames in Java dynamic logic. In: Beckert, B., Marché, C. (eds.) FoVeOOS 2010. LNCS, vol. 6528, pp. 138–152. Springer, Heidelberg (2011). doi:10.1007/978-3-642-18070-5_10
46. Soundarajan, N., Fridella, S.: Reasoning about polymorphic behavior. In: Proceedings of TOOLS, pp. 346–358. IEEE Computer Society (1998)
47. Weiß, B.: Predicate abstraction in a program logic calculus. Sci. Comput. Program. **76**(10), 861–876 (2011)

Author Index

Printed in the United States
By Bookmasters